FINDING YOUR FATHER'S WAR

FINDING YOUR FATHER'S WAR

A Practical Guide to Researching
and Understanding Service
in the World War II US Army

Jonathan Gawne

CASEMATE
Philadelphia

Published by
CASEMATE
1016 Warrior Road
Drexel Hill, PA 19026

Tel: (610) 853-9131
Fax (610) 853-9146
www.casematepublishing.com

ISBN 1-932033-14-9

Cataloging-in-Publication data is available
from the Library of Congress.

TABLE OF CONTENTS

To those who served,
but have no one to tell their stories.

INTRODUCTION

War is a nasty, gruesome business. It has far less glory than popularly supposed, and is, as a rule, a waste of good lives. It is one of the most brutal, repulsive, and yet undeniably fascinating activities known to mankind. We all know it is awful, yet we still fight, and every American generation has its own veterans of one sort or another.

The reason for wanting to trace someone's service in World War II comes from a desire to gain an understanding of what they went through, with an eye toward catching a glimpse of the horror, boredom, or endless frustration that is war. It should not be so much an attempt to find out how this medal was won, or how that bunch of prisoners was taken; rather, it should be to try to comprehend how the war changed a man (or woman's) life.

My father fought in World War II. It was not until after his death that I felt I had even a fraction of an understanding of what he had accomplished and experienced. Growing up during my generation, it was understood that everyone's dad had participated in the war. If not World War II, they had been in Korea. Vietnam was going on, but it was far too remote for a kid to understand: there were no movies or TV shows about that war yet. Old men, like my grandfather, had been in World War I. It was a given thing.

So I grew up knowing my dad had been in the war. I knew he had fought in France. I recall he did not like to watch war films or TV shows much, but when he did he balanced his involuntary blurting out of "They're bunching up!" with his almost gleeful exclamation of "He flinched!" when an actor would close his eyes and flinch when firing a gun. To this day I cannot watch any war film without keeping an eye out for both.

He never talked of the war without being prodded, and when he did it tended to be recollections of the hi-jinks the men played on new recruits in the pre war "Old Army." With Vietnam underway he publicly said that when my brother and I were of draft age, the family would move to Canada. Here was my father, who had a pile of medals in his dresser, military binoculars in his closet, and spoke of tough sergeants that could curse for hours at a time without ever repeating themselves, suggesting we should avoid being drafted at all costs. I was too young to connect his nightmares with the fact that his uniform hung unseen in the back of a basement closet.

When I asked about the war he tried to answer, but it tended to be the same few stories. I couldn't understand how he could have forgotten so much about it. He didn't know where he had fought; he couldn't recall the names of most of the men he had served with; and I know he wished I would let the war die.

I didn't. I read everything I could about it. I went to archives and visited battlefields. After his death I began contacting veterans from his unit. I started piecing things together. I began to write books and articles on the war. All to try and figure out the impact it had had on my father. It has helped me understand him somewhat better.

A week does not go by without someone contacting me for help in trying to find information on their own World War II veteran. Sometimes I can help—mostly just offer advice. That's what this book is: advice on how to go about your own quest. If it was an easy task, there would no need for such a book.

I have deliberately decided to limit the scope of this book to the US Army. The Navy and Marines have their own slant on record keeping. However the individual records of the Navy, Marines, and Coast Guard are easy to retrieve from the National Personnel Records Center. The majority of the Army and Army Air Force records were destroyed in the infamous fire of 1973. This means that anyone attempting to dig into an Army background will have a lot more work to do.

To have any luck at all in investigating military service, one has to know the basics: rank, unit size, and structure, why decorations were given, and so on. Then you need to know what information you might be able to locate and where to look for it. Almost as hard is to be able to put it all together into an understandable format.

It was a big war. Men served in just about every part of the world, from tiny islands in the Pacific, Caribbean outposts, the railways in the Iraqi desert to the snow-covered weather stations of Greenland and beyond. Not every soldier fought on the front line. Do not be discouraged if your father wasn't a paratrooper at Normandy or a tank commander at Bastogne. Truth is always more interesting than fiction, and every task in the Army was an important one in supporting the final victory over the Axis.

The internet is changing the way people do research. When I started this book there was no way to easily trace an APO number, or connect a serial number with a name. In the short span of time since then, the official APO listing has been made available online and the National Archives have put the World War II serial number database online. What is true today, such as the difficulty in obtaining morning reports, may be totally different in a few month's time. To help keep up with those changes. I have created a web page with the links mentioned in this book. As I find more that might be of help, I will add them to the list at: www.fatherswar.com.

So you may by now wonder what I found out about my own father's war. He joined the Army in 1941 to get his year of service out of the way. He was sent to help fill up a National Guard Division (the 43d), and on December 7, 1941 discovered he was stuck in the Army for the duration of the war.

His regiment was broken up when the 43d went to a three regiment structure, and he found his company sent to Christmas Island in the Pacific to defend it against the Japanese. With no invasion forthcoming and nothing else to do, he took the officer's candidate test and was sent to Infantry Officer's School at Ft. Benning. Georgia. Earning his 2d lieutenant's bars he was sent to the 26th Infantry Division as a regimental gas officer. On an exercise he accidentally tear-gassed the regimental commander eating lunch, and was promptly transferred to the 8th Infantry Division in Northern Ireland as a rifle platoon leader.

Landing in France on the 4th of July 1944, his unit had a rough fight when it went into combat. He was wounded but stayed on the line, as he was the last officer in the company. For this he received a Purple Heart and a Bronze Star for valor. Moving into Brittany, his new company CO was wounded and he was given command of the company. During an attack south of Brest he tried to break the German line by charging a machine gun, and was severely wounded. He earned a second Purple Heart and a second Bronze Star in doing so.

Evacuated by air to England, he spent a long time in the hospital before being shipped home. Finally able to return to duty, he was made officer in charge of troop trains until the war ended. He spent a long time regaining his strength as well as dealing with his experiences. He was recalled for active duty during the Korean War, but the fact that he had lost his ribs on one side and could hardly run 100 yards eventually spared him that conflict. He died in 1987 after a liver tumor was misdiagnosed as scar tissue from one of his wartime injuries.

Although with his kids my father was always reticent about his wartime experiences, and I only learned about most of them after he was gone, he did leave me with an astute suggestion. As a final piece of advice on how to try to learn more about World War II, my father once told me that all you have to do is read Ernie Pyle's stories and look at Bill Mauldin's cartoons.

It was good advice that remains true even today.

Framingham, Mass, June 2006.

BOOKS

Bill Mauldin:

Bill Maudlin's Army, Presidio Press, Novato, CA, 1983 (reissue), ISBN 0-89141-159-3.
Up Front, W. W. Norton, New York, 2000 (reissue), ISBN 0-393-05031-9.

Ernie Pyle:

Brave Men, University of Nebraska Press, Lincoln, NE, 2001 (paperback reissue), ISBN 0-8032-8768-2
Here is Your War, University of Nebraska Press, Lincoln, NE, 2004, (paperback reissue) ISBN 0-8032-8777-1

NOTE ON SOURCES

Where applicable I have listed sources that provide greater detail on various subjects. One of the main sources is the US Army's own series of official histories of World War II. These are commonly known as "the green books" due to their dark green covers and binding. Written over the years from 1945 to the current day, they provide some of the best detailed information on various aspects of the Army.

These books should be available in larger libraries, and continue to be sold by the US Government Printing Office (http://www.gpoaccess.gov) in both the traditional green hardcover and less expensive paperback versions. Do not pay extravagant prices demanded by book dealers claiming they are out of print.

The green books (see appendix I for a detailed list) have some minor errors and omissions (some having been written before the breaking of the Axis codes was declassified) but they remain a superb source of basic information. Some authors have made entire careers by taking sections of these books and reworking the material. The green books are the Army's official view of the war, and the information and the statistics provided in them should be taken as fact until proven otherwise.

The combat histories are sometimes faulted for providing information that differs from the veteran's recollections. Keep in mind, however, that the authors of the green books worked from official records and took as fact what was written down in those records. If no one was around to witness an event, or if it was written up incorrectly, one cannot place the blame on the official historians.

All photos and illustrations not otherwise credited are from the author's collection. Most of the illustrations are from period wartime army publications. For privacy reasons I have blocked out any serial numbers on original paperwork.

NOTE ON BOOKS AND WEBSITES

Throughout the book you will find blue boxes marked either "Books", "Websites" or "Films." These, it is hoped, will help you in finding more information on a given subject without having to plow through the bibliography.

All book titles are given with ISBN number information where possible, to make it easier for you to locate them. Both the book and website information was checked for accuracy just before publication, but information can change—new editions of books are published and websites, in particular, can be in flux.

THE WAR IN A NUTSHELL

The Roll-up to War

The war did not start on December 7, 1941. Some will argue with some force-fulness that it started the day the Treaty of Versailles, which formally ended World War I, was signed. In terms of a shooting war, World War II began in the early 1930s when Japan began its military expansion in China, and Italy invaded Ethiopia. When the world's major Western powers refused to stand up against such aggression on behalf of countries unable to defend themselves, Germany took advantage of this perceived weakness and occupied the Rhineland, Austria, and Czechoslovakia; Japan expanded in China; and Italy seized Albania.

Why America did not immediately spring into action in the late 1930s to counter this open aggression can perhaps best be understood by examining how the once-powerful American Army of World War I was allowed to dwindle away into a small, poorly equipped and funded force. The American Army of the 1920s and 1930s had experienced a steady stream of budget cuts. Its soldiers were often considered little better than lazy bums by growing segments of the country's population. Some hotels and restaurants refused to serve soldiers.

When World War I-era equipment wore out, it was rarely replaced. Many other countries funded continued research and development of military equipment and tactics, but America did not to any significant extent, and thus fell behind. America entered World War II with tanks and aircraft that had more in common with 1918 than 1941.

In 1932, the American Army was ranked 17th internationally in size. Six years later it had slipped to 18th. In 1934, the Army's entire combat strength could be comfortably seated in Chicago's Soldiers' Field stadium.[1] It was not only small in size, but far behind nearly every other major country in terms of training, technology, and morale.

Many of the Army's best officers were offered much better civilian-sector jobs, but elected to stay in the military because of their dedication to country and the belief that one day their skills would be desperately needed. It is sobering to think how World War II might have turned out if men like Marshall, Eisenhower, and Bradley (to say nothing of the many outstanding lower-ranking men) had put themselves first and left the Army for a higher paying job.

The size of Germany's army was limited by the Treaty of Versailles. In order to exceed this cap and prepare men for military service (as well as to help the national economy), Adolf Hitler created the Arbeitsdienst (work service), in which young men spent one year doing various public service work projects.

1

Coincidentally, this time also served as an extended period of basic training, where drill was performed with shovels instead of rifles.

America had a similar program called the Civilian Conservation Corps, or CCC. This program was instituted during the Great Depression to put men to work. In 1933, men from all across the country were offered jobs working outdoors in pseudo-military organizations. While military training was strictly prohibited, the CCC program was run by military officers and staff, who were the best qualified to organize and manage large groups of men. CCC workers received surplus dark green military uniforms.

For many American men, the CCC offered their first taste of life in a military-style organization.

Treaties obligated Britain and France to support Poland if she was attacked. When Germany invaded Poland on 1 September 1939, Britain and France mobilized against Germany but did not send troops to Poland's aid. Russia and Germany had signed a Non-Aggression Pact with a secret protocol that effectively divided Poland between them. This alignment of the major European powers, just as it had in World War I, forced other countries to take a stand, one way or another. Within a short time, most of Europe was again at war.

In 1939, a majority of Americans wanted nothing to do with another European war. Just as they had largely ignored Japanese aggression in China, Americans followed the fighting on the European continent with the interest of a neutral bystander. This new war, most Americans believed, had nothing to do with the USA. Many, however, believed that unless the aggressive Fascist countries of the world were stopped, they would continue to enlarge their empires around the globe until the war eventually directly threatened America. It was not a question of if we would eventually join the war, but when we would do so. The longer America waited, the stronger her enemies would become.

When France fell quickly to Germany in 1940, it appeared that nothing could stop Hitler's military machine. It was only a matter of time, or so it appeared to many observers the world over, before Britain was overrun and defeated. America would have to prepare for war whether she wanted one or not. On 16 September 1940, Congress instituted a draft by passing the Selective Training and Service Act. Although not officially at war, America had taken a major first step in preparing to fight one.

The Draft

The 1940 Selective Training and Service Act was passed in an effort to spread the burden of military service fairly across the country. It called for a draft of men ages 21 to 36. The first draftees would be called to flesh out the Regular and National Guard units to wartime strength. These units would be put through a period of instruction designed to make them combat ready. If

America was not yet at war by October 1941, the draftees would be allowed to go home. They could be easily recalled, if needed, as fully trained soldiers. No more than 900,000 men were to be in the service at any one time, and none could be sent outside the country except to our territories and to the Philippines. On the first day of the Act, 16 October 1940, 16,000,000 men registered for the draft.

In 1940, most men believed they would do their one year of service and get it out of the way. Once their year of service was completed, they believed they could then settle into a civilian job or married life. As many of them discovered, while they went in expecting to serve for one year, they remained in the service for five years.

The draft was handled at a local level. The Army believed that local boards better understood the needs of their area, and knew which men really did need hardship deferments. Local draft boards assigned draft numbers at random, a draft classification ranging from IA (available for general military service) to IV-F (physically, mentally, or morally unfit). Of those deemed unfit, 30%, (or almost 2,000,000 men), were rejected on psychiatric grounds.[2] Draft numbers were randomly picked on a national level to determine the order in which men were chosen. Numbers assigned at random locally and then chosen nationally prevented anyone from feeling the system was rigged. As the war went on, men were eventually called up for the draft in the order of their birthday as they became old enough to serve.

When the summer of 1941 arrived, the war in Europe was still ongoing. The Army knew that a wide-scale discharge of men at that time would wreak havoc in unit organization. Once the men were let go, it would be costly and difficult to bring them back and reintegrate them into existing units. The soldiers, however, wanted out. They began to use the term "OHIO," which stood for "Over the Hill in October" as a protest against being held in service for more than one year. To keep the Army intact Congress passed the Service Extension Act of 1941, but only by the narrow margin of a single vote. This extended the one year term of service to eighteen months. This piece of legislation was not popular with the troops. However, the Army made it easier for those with genuine hardships to be discharged from service.

After Pearl Harbor, Congress occasionally changed the draft standards to keep up with the needs of the war. At the lower end, men only 18 years old were called up. The upper age varied over the course of the war, with men as old as 45 eligible for service. The Navy took the oldest men (up to age 51), and allowed those with construction backgrounds to serve in its construction battalions.

The draft was often the butt of many jokes and the subject of frustration, but it played a critically important role in winning World War II. No one was exempt unless he could show a good reason. Unlike the Civil War, the rich could not pay to get out of service; and unlike during Viet Nam, attending college did not protect you from the draft.

One of the reasons for the draft, other than the primary purpose of filling the ranks of country's military services, was that the government believed it was best able to assign men to their optimum military use. Under strict volunteer service, potential recruits were lured by fancy uniforms or promises of special duty or education. Because of this, men flocked to join the Marines or the Navy. The Army had a greater number of volunteers for the Air Corps than places for them to serve. By standardizing the entry of manpower into the services, the military could determine whether a man had a special talent that was needed somewhere, or which branch of service needed troops at a particular time. The draft also let the military bring in the exact number of men it needed or could actually train at a specific time, instead of hoping to meet enlistment quotas or being flooded with more bodies than it could handle.

Early in the war, a man could defer himself from the draft by volunteering for one of the services. The Navy worked this to its advantage by allowing high school students to volunteer for the Navy, but not have to report for duty until after graduation. To eliminate these loopholes, men were no longer allowed to voluntarily enlist in the military after January 1943. If they wanted to join before they were drafted, they could request their draft board call them up next. This was sometimes known as "volunteering for the draft."

The War Department required that each soldier have at least a fourth grade education and know how to read and write the English language. A small number of individuals who did not meet these minimum standards were accepted into the military, and the Army published a training manual called "The Army Reader," which helped develop basic reading and writing skills for the less educated.

Many soldiers complained because they believed they had been treated unfairly by their draft boards. Some felt that others were given special treatment, and this may have been the case in some situations. The government kept a careful eye out for overt favoritism, but on the whole the selective service system worked with a remarkable degree of fairness.

The Development of the Wartime Army

The early stages of the war saw the Army repeatedly rip apart its units in order to form new ones. Every new unit was formed around a cadre: a core of trained men. One of the more frustrating things men had to endure was learning how to work together as a team, only to have some of the best officers and men abruptly transferred away, sent off to form the core of another newly-forming unit. There was, however, a powerful logic behind this invasive procedure.

The armed forces expanded at a tremendous pace. In September 1939, a presidential order raised the army from 17,000 to 227,000 men. The latter figure was continuously raised until some 4,000,000 men were in the service by 1942. It was vital that new units have some men with experience to help train new recruits—even if it meant disrupting an already trained unit.

So many new units were being organized that the Army developed strict timetables for how to start a unit from scratch. The core of men was selected a set number of days ahead of schedule and arrived at the appointed place to get things ready for the raw recruits, who arrived as planned to fill in the ranks. With so many new units forming in the early years of the war, soldiers had a good chance of putting any special knowledge to use. One old soldier told every recruit to tell the Army he could type (even if he could not) because it all but guaranteed he would be assigned as a clerk and given a desk job instead of a combat role.

The first step in becoming a soldier was the trip to a reception center for induction. Induction was the term used for actually becoming a member of the Army. A man was inducted into the Army whether he enlisted or was drafted. The recruit was sworn in, tested, and his paperwork started. He was also issued basic articles of clothing and began to learn the unique elements of Army life.

A soldier's formal record of his time in the Army began with his induction into the service. This was recorded on Service Record AGO, Form 24, also known as the "compiled military record of the individual serviceman.[3]

One of the first and most important things a soldier learned was read to him. Every man had to listen to a reading of the Articles of War—the Army's laws. According to regulations, these were read to each man again at regular intervals throughout their Army service so that no one could claim he did not know what they were. Another reason was because many soldiers could barely read themselves. The number of illiterate troops in World War II was low when compared to other wars, but it was easy to find men who could barely sign their own name.

Each soldier was tested and questioned to see if he had any special skill the Army could put to good use. If so, and if the Army actually had an opening for that skill, he was assigned accordingly. Most of the specialized positions were filled quickly, and as the war continued, even most highly skilled men were used as replacements for combat outfits. Recruits stayed at the reception center until the Army had an opening for them. For most men, this meant waiting until a batch of soldiers was collected for a specific unit. This explains why so many units were composed of men from one geographic area. It was not part of any Army plan, but if a train arrived at a reception center with a group of men who had been inducted in upstate New York, for example, there was a good chance most of them would be selected en masse to serve in one unit.

Some effort was made to break up the National Guard units and spread men from one region around the Army. This was to avoid the chance of particular hardship falling on a single community. The most celebrated case of this was Company A, 116th Infantry Regiment, from Bedford, Virginia. The original peacetime-strength company came from the local Bedford area. When the unit landed in the first wave on Omaha Beach on D-Day, the small town lost nineteen of its young men in one morning.[4]

Most recruits were assigned to a unit in what seemed a haphazard way. A new batch of men would come into the reception center, line up alphabetically, and be divided into two groups. One group would be sent off to be trained as truck drivers while the other would be assigned to an infantry unit. As far as the Army was concerned, the entire process was designed to get the right number of men to where they were needed the most.

Although many veterans disagree, the Army did indeed try to take into account a man's skill and civilian occupation when assigning him. This was hard to do, however, because the Army needed large numbers of combat troops, and most of the specialist positions were filled rapidly during the war's early months. When the author's father enlisted, he was told he could go into the infantry or the coastal artillery. When he told the sergeant to put him in the coastal artillery because he liked to fish, he was quickly assigned to the infantry.

The Army had a rationale for how it trained men. Marching and drill were effective ways of moving large groups of men without having to gather them up and watch out for stragglers. Inspections taught soldiers to take care of their uniforms, equipment, and weapons. New soldiers quickly learned it was easier to keep things clean and tidy all the time than to have to work to make them so at the last minute.

Recruits also learned quickly that a "fort" was an army base with a permanent contingent of men to run it, while a "camp" was a semi-permanent establishment where the staff would leave when it was not in use. A bivouac was nothing more than a campsite or place to stay. "To bivouac" meant "to camp." Soldiers would bivouac in the fields but be "billeted" when housed in a public or private building.

Time off from the Army came in two forms: leave and furlough. Leave (short for leave of absence), was three days or less in duration. A man had to have a pass he could show to any military authority to prove he had permission to be away from his unit. A furlough was of longer duration. Soldiers could request up to 30 days of furlough a year, but no more than 15 days at a time.

Furloughs were not a viewed as a privilege, but rather as a reward for good service. Men could be prohibited from taking a furlough if their officers believed they had not earned the right to enjoy one.

In today's Army, recruits pass through very specific basic and advanced training schools. World War II-era training was much simpler and can be broken down into three main types: divisional, non-divisional, and replacement.

Most divisions were trained all at once. In the early days, the first few divisions had so many troops pulled out of them to act as cadres for newly forming units that it must have seemed to many as if their division started from scratch.

The Army developed the curriculum and number of hours the soldiers should be trained in various topics. At the outset, this training was related to individual skills. Thereafter, it moved to skills used at the company level, battalion level, and finally to regimental-level exercises. Basic training, which included how to march, salute, and so forth, was included in the initial part of the procedure, and was not held separately.

Weapons training included a test at the firing range to determine whether a soldier had qualified with that weapon, and if so, at what level. The three levels of skill were marksman, sharpshooter, and expert. Before World War II, troops were actually paid extra if they qualified as an expert, but during the war, this qualification only meant a different badge on the uniform.

Non-divisional units went through a similar training program. The manpower core showed up to form the unit; the rest of the troops arrived to fill it; and the basic skills were taught first (normally a thirteen-week period) and built toward the more complicated skills.

Training never ended, for as soon as a unit was ready, a group of men was transferred off to form a new core of men for another unit. Others were promoted to fill their slots, new soldiers were brought in, and everyone kept training until the entire unit was up to speed again. Some men repeated the training program several times.

Once the bulk of the units were formed, the Army's goal was to produce qualified replacements for combat units. This was the job of the Replacement Training Center (RTC). An RTC specialized in training men for a specific branch, so you can find them referred to as IRTC (Infantry Replacement Training Camp), ARTC (Artillery Replacement Training Center), and so forth.

The average training period at an RTC was thirteen weeks. The first two weeks were spent in recruit training (wearing the uniform, drill, how to salute). The next eight weeks were spent training at the company level. This was where the men learned how to operate the equipment or weapons found in a company. The last three weeks were concerned with applying what had been learned to support battalion and regimental operations.

Once the Army had its divisional-sized units ready, it decided to hold large-scale training exercises to test out various tactical theories and put senior officers and support units to the test. The pre-World War II Army did not have the funding to bring enough units together for such large-scale maneuvers.

The first and most famous of these exercises was the Louisiana Maneuvers of 1941. It was the largest ever conducted by the US Army.[5] The operation used eighteen divisions and a number of groups and battalions divided up between five corps. These troops were split between the Second (red) and Third (blue) field armies in September 1941. Mock war was waged through the area with umpires identifying casualties. Most soldiers thought the maneuver was a waste of time. The senior officers, however, realized it was a valuable test to see how various units worked together, which officers could keep up the pace of a modern war, and whether the support systems would work in the field. A second major maneuver was held in the Carolinas two months later.

The soldiers found the maneuvers both exciting and frustrating. Operating under simulated combat conditions was exciting and a unique experience for most of the men, though being marked as casualties from an unseen artillery bombardment by an umpire who showed up out of nowhere was more than a little maddening. Men who had passed through the Louisiana Maneuvers had many stories to tell.

Some claimed the simulation was worse than any combat they experienced. They encountered poisonous snakes, chiggers, ticks, and other irritating and potentially dangerous pests. As bad as these were, some of the older officers were even worse. One colonel had his men stand in the pouring rain so they would get used to being in all types of weather. He didn't have them dig in, drill, or perform any tasks. Instead, he simply made them stand endlessly in the rain. There were other large-scale maneuvers in places like Tennessee and the Carolinas, but participants claimed Louisiana was the worst because of the swampy terrain, poor weather, and snakes.

The Army Specialized Training Program (ASTP) was developed to keep up the flow of technically trained men such as doctors, engineers, and chemists. This program allowed bright young men to attend a college program at government expense. They were commissioned upon graduation and almost always given a non-combat position. The ASTP was disbanded later in the war and the majority of its student soldiers were eventually used as infantry replacements.

When a unit was trained and the Army believed it was ready for combat, it was moved to the West Coast if it was going to the Pacific Theater or the East Coast if it was heading to Europe.

The destination was not always readily apparent to the men because trains often left in one direction before turning around and heading in another. Clues as to the ultimate destination could occasionally be gleaned from the equipment that was issued (sun helmets or cold weather clothing, for example), but this gear was often ordered turned in at the last moment. Most men chalked this up to Army stupidity, but in reality most of it was an attempt to keep enemy agents from figuring out where a particular unit was headed.

The last stop before leaving the USA was a camp next to a Port of Embarkation (POE). A POE was a specific port used to ship men overseas. At these camps the men experienced Preparation for Overseas Movement (POM). Everything was checked and double-checked. Inspections were held to make sure everyone had their uniforms and equipment (and that it was in good shape). Records were examined to make sure everything was up to date and properly recorded.

The shoulder sleeve insignia of the Army Specialized Training Program

Soldiers were encouraged to make out their wills, and specific attention was paid to the government-issued life insurance policy. This $10,000 policy was offered to every soldier. It was the only life insurance available to a man setting off for war. For a small monthly payment, a GI could make sure his family had some money in case he was killed. In the 1940s, $10,000 was a lot of money, so it was not taken lightly. Some had no family and assigned it to another soldier or a friend.

There are stories of women who took advantage of the situation and married one (or more) of these men just to become the beneficiary of their insurance payment. Airmen were often a primary target of these scams because the casualty rate for them was so high.

The shoulder sleeve insignia of the Port of Embarkation personnel. These men handled all Army facilities on both the East and West coasts for shipping men overseas.

Once everything was deemed in order, the average GI walked up a gangplank onto a ship and was assigned a bunk in a crowded compartment. After the voyage, during which most of the men became seasick, they landed on a foreign shore ready to do their part to fight the enemy.

The shortage of available shipping space to carry men and equipment across the ocean played a large role in how the war evolved. It took a long time to stockpile enough men and equipment overseas to directly confront the enemy in Europe. As a result, the first real attack on Germany and its allies was undertaken by the Army Air Force.

During the early months of the war in Europe, the AAF took more casualties than any other branch of service. Survival rates for aircrew were very low. Once the Army ground forces entered into combat, that statistic quickly changed.

BOOKS

The U.S. Army GHQ Maneuvers of 1941, by Christopher Gabel, Dept. of the Army, 1991, ISBN 0160612950

Europe or the Pacific?

The primary question on every soldier's mind was where he would be sent to fight. Both Europe and the Pacific had their good points and their drawbacks. The Pacific was made up of beautiful tropical islands which for many promised sun-soaked boredom surrounded by sandy beaches. There were no freezing temperatures and blizzards like those found in Europe. However, the warm weather was not unlike the Louisiana climate, and the thought of living with countless insects, fungi, snakes, and exotic diseases tempered the desire to fight in the South Pacific.

Europe, especially after June 1944, offered combat troops near-continuous combat with few opportunities for leave, while the Pacific allowed for some rest between operations once an island was captured. Some soldiers believed the Germans were a more deadly enemy, but the Japanese were more fanatical and did not follow the accepted rules of warfare. The Pacific offered great natural beauty, but Europe was the birthplace of much of our country's history and offered sightseeing opportunities few men would otherwise experience. Of course, most of the soldiers rarely got a chance to play tourist in Europe until after the Germans surrendered in 1945.

The reality was that both theaters hosted experienced and deadly enemies, and there were few if any advantages to serving in either location. Indeed, these regions were so strikingly different that the men in each essentially fought in two completely different wars. Relatively few soldiers fought in both theaters. After the war, many veterans enjoyed arguing why "their" war was actually the harder one to fight and win.

No matter what theater a man fought in, he almost certainly had memories of spending time on cramped troop-ships.

Shipping space was always in short supply, so every extra soldier that could be crammed into the limited space was important.

National Archives

Shoulder sleeve insignia of the Southeast Asia Command, Army Service Forces Western Pacific, US Army Pacific, GHQ Southwest Pacific, Kiska Task Force, and the China-Burma- India Theater.

BOOKS

Touched With Fire: The Land War in the South Pacific, by Eric Bergerud, Penguin, New York, 1997, ISBN: 0140246967

Eisenhower's Lieutenants: The Campaign of France and Germany, 1944–1945, by Russell Weigley, Indiana State University Press, 1990, ISBN 0253206081

Casualties

A wound did not always mean a trip back to a hospital. Many minor injuries were handled in the field and the soldier returned quickly to duty. For example, gunshots that punched through flesh without breaking any bones or damaging any organs or an artery were usually treated at an aid station so the men could quickly return to the front lines. Men were hurt in a wide variety of ways, and not only by enemy fire. Routine traffic accidents accounted for many injuries, as did twisted backs and ankles. Extreme weather often incapacitated men. The cold winter temperatures and constant exposure to snow and ice caused terrible frostbite and trench foot.

Soldiers knew there were only three ways to get out of combat: finish the war, get killed, or get wounded. They often talked about the lucky guys who suffered a "million dollar wound." This was an injury that was severe enough to take them out of combat, but one unlikely to result in any permanent injury. In other words, it was a wound a man would willingly "pay a million dollars for." On average, 3.4 men were wounded for every man killed in action.[6]

Every unit had its own section of attached medical personnel. They were assigned at roughly one medic per platoon. The aid man, as he was called, was the soldier who moved up with the unit in combat and had to venture out under enemy fire to help the wounded.

These medics wore a Red Cross armband and often a similar insignia on their helmets so the enemy would not fire at them. The bright red cross, however, acted as an enticing target for many enemy soldiers. Even if the enemy respected the Geneva Convention rule about not firing on medical personnel, a Red Cross did not offer any protection against stray bullets or shell fragments.

Medics were universally known by the nickname "Doc." When a man was injured, the medic would check the wound, sprinkle on some sulfa powder to help prevent infection, bandage it, and, if necessary, give him a shot of morphine. Morphine not only dulled the pain, but helped prevent a wounded man from going into shock.

When it was possible to evacuate wounded men, they were taken back to the battalion aid station, where a doctor would examine them. Walking wounded were men who could move under their own power without assistance. Otherwise, stretchers were brought up or men detailed to help them back to safety. As the war progressed, jeeps were used whenever possible to carry the wounded back from the front.

Once at the battalion aid station, casualties were tagged to denote whatever treatment they had received at the front or at the station. The battalion surgeon—usually a generic doctor, though every medical unit commander was known as a "surgeon"—might risk an emergency operation, but his primary task was to stabilize the men so they could be moved farther back to a better medical facility. Almost always, the greatest risk to wounded men was the loss of blood. The American use of whole blood and blood plasma to put the vital fluids back into a wounded man's body saved a large number of lives.

Each regiment had a medical collecting company whose job it was to transport casualties from the aid stations to the division clearing company. For this task they used three-quarter-ton trucks rigged as ambulances. From the clearing company, the casualties were sorted by type of injury. Those who required immediate surgery were sent to a surgical hospital. Those who did not need surgery were sent to an evacuation hospital. Casualties could be grouped and sent on by truck, train, aircraft, or ship. The final stop was a general hospital, which was a large permanent installation.

When a man no longer needed treatment but just time for recovery, he was sent to a convalescent hospital. Every facility except the general hospitals were mobile units usually housed under tents and moved forward as the war progressed.

At every level in the evacuation chain, soldiers were evaluated to determine who should be sent back. The goal was to keep as many combat soldiers as close to the front as possible. If a soldier could recover and be returned to duty, he was kept in the theater of operations and not returned to the States. The trip home was only for men who would never be able to go back into action.

As the war progressed, men were sent back from the front line with "battle fatigue" or "battle stress." Extensive research on this concluded that every man could only take so much stress (the amount varied from man to man) before he suffered "battle fatigue" and could no longer fight effectively. It was often difficult for a soldier to tell when he had suffered too much stress, but the lack of sleep, poor food, and exposure to the elements only added to the strain of knowing he might be suddenly killed or wounded.

Some officers believed the average time a man could spend in combat before reaching the breaking point was 140 to 180 days. The reason more men did not crack was that most infantry units had an almost complete turnover of man-power in 80–90 days, which meant few troops stayed long enough in combat to suffer true battle fatigue.[7]

The British handled combat fatigue by rotating their units in and out of the combat zone to give their soldiers a rest. The Americans, however, did not have enough units to allow for this.

A good number of men evacuated for battle fatigue were treated close to the front lines by administering drugs that let them sleep for twenty-four hours. For some men, this was all they needed to be able to return to the front. Men who had been sent into combat with little training often responded well to classes given by a veteran soldier, who taught them that they had some control over their fate in combat. Others suffered severe psychological damage that lasted for years and, in some cases, for the rest of their lives. At the very least, most combat veterans suffered from occasional nightmares for years after the war.

> **FILMS**
>
> Anyone interested in this subject should find a copy of the film *Let There be Light*. It is an amazing documentary on combat fatigue.
>
> This film was made after the war to educate the public about the issue, but was kept under wraps for many years.

If a man was killed or died of his wounds at a hospital, his body was collected by a graves registration detachment and taken to a central location. Once there, all the bodies were identified (if possible), personal belongings were collected and tagged for forwarding to next of kin, and the corpses buried in temporary graves.

A myth perpetuated by Hollywood is that dog tags were taken from the body when a man was killed. This was not the case. Both dog tags stayed with the body until it was buried. One was then used for the temporary grave marker, and the other was either placed on the casket or kept with the body itself.

Beginning in May 1946, the next of kin was able to decide if they wanted the body returned to the States or moved to one of the large permanent cemeteries scattered around the world. At the end of the war there were 396 temporary cemeteries containing approximately 150,000 American remains.[8] The first remains arrived back in the United States in 1947. Approximately 19,650 soldiers who fought in World War II were unaccounted for, but each year additional remains are discovered.

Many are now being identified through DNA testing. If you are related to a man who is still listed as Missing In Action (MIA) from any war, you should contact The Joint POW/MIA Accounting Command to see if your DNA should be placed on file for any future discoveries.

Soldiers were also captured and held as prisoners of war (POWs). The men captured by the Germans were treated reasonably well until the final months of the war when conditions rapidly deteriorated. Nearly 94,000 Americans were captured by the Germans in Europe. Of those, only 1,121 died in captivity.[9] Soldiers captured by the Japanese, however, usually suffered terribly. The Japanese believed that anyone who surrendered was beneath contempt, and so they treated their prisoners little better than animals.

A much greater proportion of POWs in the Pacific Theater died while in captivity. Many were murdered outright, though most were starved to death while performing slave labor or died of disease.

The Manpower Shortage of 1944

The overall strategy of the war was to send only as many men to the Pacific Theater as needed to defend against the Japanese. The bulk of the Army was fed into Europe to fight and defeat Germany and Italy, a threat deemed a higher priority than Imperial Japan. The first ground combat in Europe was the invasion of North Africa, which quickly demonstrated what concepts the Army had gotten right, and which it had gotten wrong. Although the Americans fighting in North Africa encountered many problems and did not always perform as their officers hoped, the battle at Kasserine Pass was not the debacle some claim it to be. The Americans learned quickly, and with the help of their British allies, trapped and eliminated a German army comparable to the one lost at Stalingrad on the Eastern Front in early 1943.

The lessons learned in combat in North Africa prompted the Army to institute a number of changes. The infantry had borne the brunt of the fighting and needed something to boost its morale. Replacements were renamed "reinforcements." The term "replacements" indicated someone had to be "replaced" for some reason, and that reason was almost certainly injury or death. According to the Army policymakers, the term "reinforcements" did not sound as ominous. As a result, Replacement Training Centers became Reinforcement Training Centers.

In 1943, the infantry composed only 6% of the army but had suffered 53% of the casualties. Two things that infantrymen responded well to were promotions (the number of PFC ratings was increased, assistant squad leaders were made sergeants, and squad leaders were made staff sergeants) and the receipt of a Combat Infantryman's Badge (CIB). The CIB was a badge that could only be worn by infantrymen who had seen combat. It also brought with it a $10/month increase in pay. For the men who slept in mud, froze, baked, and rarely got out of the front line, it was small compensation indeed.

There was also an Expert Infantryman's Badge, which could be earned by taking a rigorous series of tests on everything an infantryman needed to know. This award resulted in another $5/month bump in pay.

Before the real shooting began, the Army had its theories and formulas to determine types of replacements and how many of each would be needed. Once the ground forces began engaging the enemy, however, these calculations had to be totally revised because the infantry (riflemen in particular) comprised the vast majority of casualties. The shortage of infantrymen became acute in late 1944, when there were just were not enough riflemen to fill the ranks.

Entire units were disbanded and the troops given a quick retraining course in being an infantryman. Hospitals and service units were combed for men who could be put on the line. Previously the replacements, or rather reinforcements, could fill up the infantry companies fairly quickly after a few days. The shortage meant many were staying under strength for long periods of time. It was not uncommon for rifle units to be at half their normal strength, or worse.

In desperation to find more infantrymen, the Army sacrificed one of its sacred cows: the segregation of units by race. Black service troops in the ETO were allowed to volunteer for retraining as infantry and put into special fourth platoons in some infantry companies. The extra manpower was welcome in the front lines, and although never given much publicity, the Negro Volunteer Infantry Program was a great success.

The Army Service Training Program (ASTP) was canceled and those student-soldiers were used as infantry replacements. One positive aspect of this decision was that combat units got a number of very intelligent men as replacements. The German Luftwaffe (air force) was all but eliminated by late 1944, so many anti-aircraft artillery (AAA) units were disbanded and their troops sent to infantry units.

Once the Army landed in France in June 1944 and began driving inland later that summer, the supply problems for the troops rose considerably. Nearly everything was in short supply, including ammunition, food, fuel, and clothing. To help get supplies up to the front line, every available truck and driver were put to work hauling material from the stockpiles in Normandy.

This massive supply effort was known as the Red Ball Express, and men from many different units played a key role in keeping the combat troops supplied.

Points, Redeployment, and Discharge

As the Army pushed deeper into Germany, the men were forbidden from having private dealings with German civilians. Fines were set for anyone caught having unapproved contact with the enemy, which was known as fraternization. One soldier, Roscoe Blunt of the 84th Infantry Division, was fined in April 1945 for talking to a German woman about having some of his clothes washed. He always believed he had been unjustly punished, and apparently others agreed, for in 2000 he was officially pardoned for his wartime misdeed by President Clinton.[10]

Long before the war ended in Europe there were plans underway to shift men from the ETO to the Pacific to defeat the Japanese. In World War I, the men who had entered the Army last were the first to be discharged. That rather unusual policy was not well received by either the men in the ranks or the general public, and the last thing the Army was going to do was repeat the mistake. The concept adopted for ending World War II was more logical: the first in uniform would be the first discharged.

In an effort to be fair to everyone, a system known as the Adjusted Service Rating was developed (known universally as the "points" system). This was set up so that men could be sorted according to how long they had been in uniform or overseas the longest. Men were awarded points as follows:

> 1 point for every month in service since 16 Sept 1940
> 1 point for every month overseas since 16 Sept 1940
> 5 points for every award of the Purple Heart (for a wound)
> 5 points for every decoration
> 12 points for every child under 18 (maximum of three)

The magic number at the end of the war that would allow a man to be discharged was 85 points (44 for WACs). After men with 85 points or more had been discharged, the Army would slowly lower the point total needed to go home. This meant that men who had served overseas would be discharged first, and men who had been in combat would be the first of those to leave. When the war in Europe ended, men with the most points (known as "high-point men") were shifted to units where everyone had a similar point total. These high-point units were sent home and the men discharged.

Men with fewer points would have to wait until the discharge point level dropped. The low-point men were shifted to low-point units and prepared for redeployment to the Pacific Theater. Those with the fewest points, and hence had probably done the least fighting, were slated to be sent home in a unit, given a furlough, a period of refresher training, and then sent off to fight Japan. Luckily for them, the war ended before they were needed.

The transfer of men in an effort to sort them into low- and high-point units adds to the confusion of tracking a man's service. The last unit a man served in is not always the one he fought with. Soldiers did not want to take off the shoulder insignia of the unit they had been with in combat, and in many cases they refused to put on a different shoulder patch. To allow for this, the Army decided to let men who had served overseas wear the shoulder patch of their unit on their right sleeve. (The left sleeve was always for the unit to which they were currently assigned.) This is why the patch worn on the right sleeve is known as the "combat patch."

Once back in the States, a returning soldier was sent to a separation center. Assuming his point score was enough for discharge, and he was not one of a handful of men who had skills listed as being scarce or in high demand (such as an Asian language translator or radio intelligence control chief), he was processed out and on his way home within 48 hours.

Once at a separation center, men eligible for discharge had to be checked and all physical problems that he might later try and claim as a service-related disability recorded. His records were brought up to date, and someone would try and convince him to stay in the Army (or at least join the Reserves). Thereafter, he received his discharge, a piece of paper that said he had done his duty and was no longer subject to military laws or regulations. Each soldier was given a small gold badge to wear on his civilian clothing to indicate he had been discharged. The badge had the design of an eagle, but was universally known as "the ruptured duck" (the eagle's head is turned right as if he was being checked for a hernia). A similar cloth insignia was sewn onto the right breast of his uniform so he could wear it on his way home and in future parades, with everyone knowing he had served his time and been discharged. A discharge meant he was a free man and no longer had to do guard duty or salute every officer he saw.

America wanted to assist its returning servicemen, so programs were put into place to help them get back into civilian life. Discharged men who had not found a job were paid $20 a week for up to 50 weeks. This allowed many to relax at home for a while and slowly readjust to being a civilian. They could also get a loan to start a business or buy a farm. The most popular and far-reaching program was the GI Bill, which paid for discharged men to go to technical school or college. This bill allowed men who would never have been able to get an advanced education to attend some of the best colleges in the country.

FOOTNOTES

1   Edward Coffman, The Regulars, p. 234.

2   Albert Cowdry, Fighting for Life, p. 27.

3   TM 12-250 Administration, 1942, p. 132.

4   Curiously, one of those killed on 6 June 1944 came from right around the corner from the author's house in Massachusetts.

5   Christopher Gabel, U.S. *Army Maneuvers of* 1941, p. iii.

6   Gilbert Beebe, *Battle Casualties*, p. 35

7   Albert Cowdry, *Fighting for Life*, p.151

8   Logistics in World War II: Final report of the Army Service Forces, p. 238

9   John Nichol, *The Last Escape*, p. 447.

10   Roscoe Blunt's memoir of the war is *Foot Soldier*.

Men of the 10th Mountain Division prepare to return home at the end of the war.

They are wearing the khaki cotton uniform used in warm climates.

Some of the men wear decorations, including the Combat Infantry Man's Badge on their left pocket indicating they have already been in combat.

FINDING YOUR FATHER'S WAR

Section 1

INTRODUCTION TO ARMY UNITS

This section contains background information on the composition of the World War II US Army.

It is important, before attempting to locate information on your relative's service, that you understand concepts such as rank, branches of service, and unit size.

The sergeant, with his three stripes, was considered the backbone of the Army.

This is the very standard of a World War II sergeant, wearing the typical wool uniform with M1 Garand rifle.

National Archives

The Pre-War US Army
The ABC's of Army Units
Rank: Enlisted Men, Officers, Warrant Officers
Branches of Service: Combat Branches, Service Branches, Medical Department,
Other Non-Branch Groups
Training Organization – Race – Campaign Participation

THE PRE-WAR US ARMY

The units on active duty during the 1920s and 1930s were known to many as the "Old Army" or the "Real Army." Regulars consisted of the permanent professional component of the Army. The men lived in barracks and wore the uniform every day. Many were longtime career soldiers who had served their country for 30 years. Many people involved with these units during the pre-World War II days boasted of their tough-as-nails sergeants who could lick any man in the unit, swear for hours without repeating themselves, and drink everyone under the table. "Regulars," as they were known, were admired as tough soldiers—even though many had never fired a shot in anger.

During these pre-war days, everything revolved around the regiment. Each soldier belonged to one specific regiment and remained there for the duration of his service, unless he transferred to another unit. Enlisted men and NCOs often spent their entire careers in one regiment—and even the same company within the regiment.

Most who changed regiments were officers shifting around to gain experience. Before World War I, officers rarely if ever left their regiments, and were only promoted when a vacancy occurred within their regiment. Traditions ran deep, and training was paramount. Life in the military was considered "easy" during the 1930s. Sayings such as "a day in the army is like a Sunday on the farm" were commonplace. The men performed their basic functions and in return received clothing, food, and a place to sleep.

Having a guaranteed bed and warm food was not easy to come by during the Great Depression, which made life in the service look better than the more uncertain civilian existence. However, discipline was harsh. Many sergeants preferred taking a troublemaker out behind the latrine to teach him a lesson with his fists rather than bothering officers about an infraction of the rules.

Officers lived in another world and often their men did not see them for days. Orders were given by the officers to the NCOs, who in turn passed them on to the men.

BOOK NOTES

For a good examination of the pre World War II Army, see *Something About a Soldier*, by Charles Willeford, Random House, New York, 1986, ISBN 0-394-55022-6

For an overview of the Regular Army from 1898-1941, see *The Regulars*, by Edward Coffman, Belknap Press, Harvard, 2004, ISBN 0-674-01299-2

It was not unusual for long-serving sergeants to know more about their units and the men than the officers, many of whom were new and thus inexperienced. The sergeants were the backbone of the Army and taught valuable lessons to the newly-minted lieutenants.

And then the war came.

The Reserves

The Army Reserves during World War II consisted of undermanned units staffed by officers (and a handful of NCOs) on the reserve lists. The development of the Reserves came about after problems we experienced in World War I finding enough officers to run the Army. The theory was that units with a backbone of officers could, as needed, be easily fleshed out by simply adding recruits. These paper Reserve units were not activated. The men assigned to them were called to active duty and sent to whatever unit needed them. The so-called Reserve Divisions were later activated and filled with new men.

There was an attempt to form a reserve of enlisted men before the war, but the effort failed. Few men wished to hold an NCO position in the Reserves, although an officer's reserve commission was considered desirable and a bonus on one's resume. With the declaration of war in December 1941, the Reserves were called to active duty and sent wherever they were needed. Many Reserve officers were not called up for active duty because of their age or mental and/or physical condition. Many of those unfit for active duty had remained on the reserve roster after World War I without anyone thinking about whether they were suitable for service.

National Guard

The National Guard was composed of troops who reported in peacetime directly to their state governor instead of the President. These men were the descendants of the local state militias, and were brought to some level of standardization during World War I.

Before World War II, many National Guard units had become something akin to a men's club, with ranks and positions offered on a political basis. In one Connecticut rifle company, for example, orders were given in Italian because most of the men hailed from the same Italian neighborhood. Guardsmen reported for drill or a meeting once a month, and attended a training camp for two weeks every summer. Membership was highly desirable in most low income areas because the pay for these drills and camps supplemented family income during the Depression years.

BOOK NOTES

For an excellent discussion on the transition of a National Guard unit to active service, see: *Beyond the Beachhead*, by Joe Balkowski, Stackpole Books, Mechanicsburg, PA, 1999 & 2005, ISBN 0-81173-237-1

Many senior officers and enlisted men in the National Guard saw some level of action during the Great War. Between the wars, however, they played their summer war games, marched in local parades, and turned out to assist their states in times of emergency. In order to be called up for active duty, the National Guard had to be "Federalized," or called into federal service. When this was authorized by Congress, the National Guard was officially moved from state to federal control.

The National Guard played an important role during World War II. The eighteen National Guard divisions (along with other smaller units) were federalized during the limited emergency in 1940 and 1941. These Guard units, along with the Regular Army units, were fleshed out from a low peacetime strength to full wartime capacity with volunteers and draftees. During peacetime, a Guard infantry squad was composed of eight men. By adding four new recruits, it was brought up to the wartime strength of an even dozen.

Federalizing also allowed the government to remove older, less efficient officers. Many men were eliminated from the roster because of their age or a lack of physical ability. Keeping a well known older Guardsman on duty in a local company was one thing, but when the time came for active duty, many could no longer handle the rigors of field life.

There were also political cliques to break up. As a result, few Guard units went off to war with the same officer structure they had enjoyed during peacetime. It was the Army's policy to mix up the units to eliminate favoritism in an effort to help organizations perform as well as possible.

A lesser known segment of the Army was the State Guard. These were the men who took over defense and emergency situations in their home states once the National Guard units left for active duty. Similar in function to the British Home Guard, the State Guard was composed of men who, for one reason or another, were not able to serve on active duty. Generally equipped with whatever uniforms and equipment was left in the armories when the National Guard left, State Guard troops continued to report directly to their governor and played a minor, though important, home front role during the war. These units still exist today as State Defense Forces.

The Army of the United States

Although separate groups in peacetime, the three components of the Army were brought together in wartime under the name of the Army of the United States (AUS).

Promotions in the AUS were considered temporary for the duration of the war. Many officers held two ranks: their permanent rank from their army component and their wartime temporary rank in the AUS.

This arrangement prevented the smaller postwar Army from being overrun with colonels and generals.

THE ABC'S OF ARMY UNITS

In order to fully understand the Army, it is important to be able to tell one unit from another. While this can be and often is initially bewildering, it is a fairly simple task if you divide a unit designation into three component parts: its specific number, type or specialty, and size.

With few exceptions, that is all there is to it.

UNIT SIZE	NUMBER OF MEN	COMMANDED BY
Squad	12 men	Sergeant
Platoon	50 men	Lieutenant
Company	184 men	Captain
Battalion	900 men	Major
Regiment	3,200 men	Colonel
Division	15,000 men	Major General
Corps	75,000 men	Lieutenant General
Field Army	300,000 men	General
Army Group	600,000+ men	General

(Note: based on standard Infantry units—sizes varied over time and by branch)

There are a few rules you should keep in mind regarding the numbering of units.

Battalions and companies, for example, have unique designation numbers only if they are not an organic part of another unit. For example, every infantry regiment has three battalions, each numbered 1, 2, and 3. As a result, there were dozens of "3d Infantry Battalions" in the Army. However, there was only one "3d Battalion, 3d Infantry Regiment, 3d Infantry Division, 3d Corps, 3d Army" in World War II. None of these many "3d" numbered units were related in any way to one another. Similarly, there were more than 23,300 squads in the 288 infantry regiments that served in World War II. That number alone makes it obvious why it is important to be able to determine the exact (and distinctive) unit designation.

What a soldier often called "his outfit" was also known as a unit or organization. A smaller section or "piece" of a unit was known as an element or component of that unit. The initial forming of a unit was referred to as its activation, and the date of activation became its birthday. The date a unit was dismantled and deactivated can also be determined.

Over time, it was not unusual for the Army to activate and deactivate the same unit many times. Sometimes when this happened units were renamed or given a new number, which is known as being re-designated or re-flagged.

Unit Definitions[1]

Army: The largest administrative and tactical unit of a land force, made up of a number of corps and divisions; also known as a field army.

Battalion: A tactical unit made up of a headquarters and two or more companies, batteries, or similar organizations. It may be part of a regiment, but separate battalions existed that were administrative as well as tactical units. Abbreviated as "bn."

Battery: A tactical and administrative artillery unit corresponding to a company or similar unit in other branches of the army. Abbreviated as "btry."

Brigade: A tactical unit smaller than a division and larger than a regiment. Normally commanded by a brigadier general and usually consisting of troops of a single branch, such as infantry, artillery, or cavalry. Abbreviated as "brig."

Company: The basic administrative and tactical unit of most branches of the military service, larger than a platoon but smaller than a battalion. Equivalent to a battery of artillery, troop of cavalry, or an aviation squadron. Usually commanded by a captain. Abbreviated as "co."

Corps: A tactical unit larger than a division and smaller than an army. A corps usually consists of two or more divisions, together with auxiliary arms and services. Also used to refer to a subdivision of one of the arms of service (i.e., Coast Artillery Corps, Corps of Engineers, Quartermaster Corps, etc.).

Division: A major administrative and tactical unit. Larger than a regiment or brigade, and smaller than a corps. Usually commanded by a major general. It was the smallest Army organization that contained every element under a unified command (combat, engineer, medical, signal, etc.). Abbreviated as "div."

Platoon: The basic tactical unit of the army and a subdivision of a company, battery, or troop. Composed of two or more squads or sections and usually commanded by a lieutenant. Abbreviated as "plat."

Regiment: An administrative and tactical unit of the army. A regiment was larger than a battalion, smaller than a brigade or division, and is usually commanded by a colonel. A "separate regiment" was one not assigned to a division or a brigade. Abbreviated as "regt."

Section: A tactical unit smaller than a platoon but larger than a squad. In some organizations a section, rather than a squad, was the basic tactical unit. Abbreviated as "sec" or "sect."

Squad: A group of enlisted men organized as a team. The smallest tactical unit consisting of only as many men as a leader could easily direct in the field. Squads varied in size in different branches of the Army. Abbreviated as "sqd."

Squadron: Administrative and tactical unit of the Army in the Cavalry. It was composed of two or more troops of cavalry. A squadron is equivalent to a battalion in other branches of the Army. Abbreviated as "sq."

Troop: Administrative and tactical unit in the Army. In the Cavalry, a subdivision of a squadron. A troop corresponds to a company in other branches of the Army, to a battery in artillery, or a squadron in aviation. Abbreviated as "tr."

COMMAND AND STAFF

Every unit had a commanding officer or "CO." This left no doubt in anyone's mind exactly who was in charge. A CO was ultimately responsible for everything that happened in his unit. He was the final arbiter of all decisions. His second in command was called the executive officer. The "Exec" or "XO" helped the commander while serving as an understudy in case he was killed, wounded, or otherwise incapacitated. Thus, if the CO was absent or hurt, command fell to the executive officer. The Exec's place was at the unit command post, which left the commander free to move about the battlefield as needed.

The "staff" consisted of a group of soldiers, primarily officers, who assisted the commander. It is helpful to think of them as advisors or assistants. Every unit of battalion size and larger had a staff of varying size. Staff officers were divided into two main types: "regular" and "special."

There were four types of "regular" staff officer, numbered one through four, and each had a specific function. Those who operated in units smaller than a division were labeled S1, S2, S3, and S4. In divisions and organizations larger than that, regular staff officers were designated G1, G2, G3, and G4. The "G" stood for "general staff," and these officers were directed by another officer known as the Chief of Staff. In the smaller units, the executive officer was considered to be the Chief of Staff.

The S1 (or G1) was the personnel officer. He was in charge of everything that had to do with assignments, decorations, transfers, and the request for replacements. An officer designated by the Army as an "adjutant" played a similar role to an S1 or G1. The adjutant was the officer in charge of all non-combat related correspondence, personnel matters, and other administrative duties. The S1 was considered the adjutant of units up to and including the size of brigades.

The S2 (or G2) was the intelligence officer. He oversaw information concerning the enemy, and any information that was useful in a battle, such as the terrain features, weather, and so forth.

The S3 (or G3) was the Operations Officer. He was responsible for training and developing the plans for combat. He could propose a course of action to the commander, who made the ultimate decision on whether or not to adopt the plan. The S3 worked at the elbow of the commander, and so almost always knew what was going on at all times. Because of this, he was often considered as the third man in command. If the commander and executive officer were hurt, the S3 would step in to lead until a new commander could be appointed.

The S4 (or G4) was the supply officer. He was in charge of making sure the unit had everything it needed to function properly, including food and ammunition. He made sure the troops had a place to stay, and that trucks arrived on time to move them to a new location.

Each staff officer had his own section of men to help him out. The sections were known either by name or number. Intelligence soldiers, for example, were referred to as the Intelligence Section or simply the S2 section. The four staff numbers were often used as abbreviations, and it is not uncommon to find records stating, "The 2 was called for," or "the 4 took care of it." After World War II, a fifth staff position for civil affairs was developed.

"Special" staff officers were those who possessed a very specific area of expertise, such as engineering, medical, or communications. In many cases the special staff officer was a commander for the type of troops within his area of knowledge. Thus, the senior military police officer (known as the Provost Marshal) was considered the special staff officer for police-related matters.

Officers in any unit could be assigned on an as-needed basis to many different jobs. These included, but were not limited to, public relations officer, mess officer, gas officer, prison officer, athletic officer, post exchange officer, or trial officer. These were not official positions, but simply responsibilities in addition to the officer's other regular duties.

If a commander wanted someone to be in charge of anything, he would just make up the job title and assign someone to it.

Generally, the lowest ranking officers or new arrivals in the unit were given the more tiresome and unimportant jobs.

ORGANIC AND ATTACHED

Two important Army concepts involve "organic" and "attached" units.

An organic unit was a permanent sub-section of a larger unit. An artillery battalion, for example, was permanently assigned to an infantry division, and that division's organization was based upon that artillery battalion being available at all times. It was rare for organic units to be transferred, but if need be they could be temporarily assigned elsewhere as needed. This might include being sent to assist a neighboring unit for a specific assignment, for example.

Units not permanently assigned to a larger unit were considered "attached." A common attachment in the war was the addition of one tank battalion, one tank destroyer battalion, and one AAA battalion assigned to each infantry division. Attached units were permanently assigned to the theater, field army, or corps, and parceled out on an as-needed basis. A corps commander could assign his extra artillery units to a specific division to help it with an attack, but he could also withdraw them and reassign them at any time.

DIVISIONAL AND NON-DIVISIONAL UNITS

Another important concept to understand is the difference between divisional and "non-divisional" units.

The division was the standard unit used in World War II combat. Divisions were organized by type: infantry, armored, cavalry, airborne, or mountain divisions and had all troop-types necessary for combat (both front-line and support) organically assigned to them. The organic sub-units of divisions rarely changed. Everyone in a division wore the same shoulder patch.

Non-divisional units were those that were not an organic part of a division. Often known as independent units, these included tank battalions, artillery brigades, engineer battalions, and signal companies.

For the most part, non-divisional units were organizations the size of battalions or companies. Before World War II, units were part of a specific regiment (the traditionally sized unit of the Army). This proved cumbersome, however, and most of the non-infantry regiments were broken up early in the war into their component battalions. Thus it was possible for someone to have been in the 28th Field Artillery Regiment when the war broke out, and in the 28th Field Artillery Battalion at a later date.[2]

Most non-division units in a combat zone were assigned to field army and corps headquarters. Various types of non-divisional units were attached to these headquarters as needed and it was quite common for these non-divisional units to be shifted from one unit to another.

Tracking a unit attached to a division is relatively easy, but tracking non-divisional units can be rather more difficult because they were often transferred between higher headquarters and attached to different units. Non-divisional units wore the shoulder patch of the unit they were assigned to, and not those to which they were temporarily attached. This could be the theater, army group, army, or corps.

Slightly more than 50% of the men in the Army served in non-divisional units.

TABLES OF ORGANIZATION (T/O)

Every unit in the Army had a master document setting forth the number of men it was authorized to have, together with their rank and specialty. This document was known as the Table of Organization (T/O).

After the middle of 1943, a listing of authorized equipment was also included, and the name was changed to Table of Organization and Equipment (T/O&E). Tables of Organization were issued from division down to company level. Units larger than a division (corps and armies) had Tables of Organization both for their headquarters elements and for their sub-units.

The T/O helped the Army place equipment and manpower where it could be best utilized. Trucks were pooled so they did not sit idle. Weapons were assigned by range. An 81mm mortar, for example, was able to cover an area wider and deeper than one company could man, so the mortars were organized one level higher (at battalion), where they could be used to support more than one company at a time. Artillery larger than 155mm was assigned to corps level commands and above because its range could cover the area of several divisions simultaneously.

The less a particular unit was needed at a certain level, the higher the level it was assigned to. For example, a rifle company would have limited use for a mapmaking unit. A division would have some use for it, but an Army covered so much territory it could keep a mapmaking company constantly at work. The point of the T/O was to put men and equipment where they would be utilized most efficiently.

T/Os rarely remained the same for very long because of changes to a unit's manpower and equipment. Generally speaking, the trend was to eliminate excess manpower and increase combat strength.

> BOOK NOTES
>
> *The Organization of Ground Combat Troops*, by Kent Greenfield, Center of Military History, United States Army , Carlisle, PA, 1987

For example, one soldier might have a job as a jeep driver at the beginning of the war, and this would be reflected as such on the T/O.

In its ceaseless effort to increase combat strength, the War Department would try to have the soldier assume the duties of another man when he was not driving. This, in turn, allowed a second soldier to transfer to a combat slot.

At the beginning of World War II, many T/Os were little more than theoretical wish lists of what officers believed they might need in their respective units. Experiences altered these expectations. From October 1942 to October 1943, for example, T/Os changed considerably as the Army tried to centralize services and streamline units to eliminate waste.

During this time period, most transfers were the result of men shipping off for a new unit, or trimmed from the T/O as it was changed.

FIELD ARMIES AND ARMY GROUPS

The largest combat unit was an army group. These were formed when there were two or more field armies in a theater. An army group was no more than headquarters elements, a collection of non-divisional units, and two or more field armies. There were only three army groups in World War II: the 12th under General Omar N. Bradley, the 6th under General Jacob L. Devers, and the 15th under Mark W. Clark.

The second largest Army unit was the field army, which was normally referred to as simply an "army." This dual usage of the term "army" often causes a great deal of confusion. There is "the Army," which covers the entire land military force of the country, and "an army," which is a unit composed of two or more corps. To prevent confusion, field armies are referred to by their designation number spelled out, such as Third Army or Seventh Army.

At the start of World War II, four field armies were assigned specific sections of the USA to protect in case of enemy attack. When it became clear the United States homeland was not in any real danger and that the war would be fought overseas, some of the field armies (actually just a headquarters element) were sent off to combat. Two field armies, the Second and Fourth, remained in the USA to control the units training in the States. By January 1945, these Armies were devoid of units because almost all of the troops had been sent overseas.

Eleven field armies were activated during World War II: the First through the Tenth, and the Fifteenth. The only soldiers who wore the shoulder patch of an Army were the men assigned to the headquarters element, and those in the pool of non-divisional units assigned directly to the field army or army group.

Logistical support for the fighting men was handled through the field army. It was at that level that most of the support and supply units were assigned. Field armies did, however, have some combat units, such as independent tank battalions, artillery battalions or engineer battalions that they could send to where they were most needed.

An attempt was made to standardize the composition of these Army units, and the result was called the "type" Army. This was a list of what, in theory, each field army should have. The "type" Army was a tool to help figure out how many, and what type, non-divisional units to organize.

In practice, the "type" Army system was not followed in the field. However, the list of "type" Army units provides a good example of what an Army might have at its disposal.

The main elements consisted of three corps, one AAA brigade, three General Service Engineer regiments, six engineer battalions, two heavy pontoon battalions, and topographic, water purification, and camouflage battalions.

A large variety of specialized support units were found in each Army. These included ambulance battalions, engineer camouflage companies, bakery companies, laundry companies, signal construction companies, and even signal pigeon companies.

"Armies and corps (also groups)," writes one historian, "were simply so many containers, between which the actual contents of the army—T/O divisions, battalions and companies—were passed back and forth. Units were taken out of containers in the United States, shipped overseas, and put into new containers on arriving in the theater."[3]

CORPS

A corps is a headquarters unit designed to command two or more divisions. Like a field army, a corps had a number of attached units in a pool it could assign wherever they were needed. However, a corps was strictly a combat headquarters and had little in terms of logistical or support units, which were managed at field army level. The rationale behind this arrangement was simple: it allowed the corps commander to fight without having to deal with administrative or supply issues.

Like the field army, there was an attempt to standardize the corps into a "type" corps for planning purposes. The main elements of a corps included three divisions, one AAA regiment, one cavalry regiment, two engineer combat regiments, one field artillery brigade, one tank destroyer group, and one signal bat-

"TYPE" CORPS 1942	XVIII CORPS NOVEMBER 1943 [4]
3 Infantry Divisions	2 Infantry Divisions
1 Antiaircraft Regiment	1 Armored Division
1 Cavalry Regiment, Mechanized	5 Tank Battalions
1 Field Artillery Brigade	1 Cavalry Regiment, Mechanized
2 Engineer Combat Regiments	2 Chemical Battalions
1 Topography Company	*2 Engineer Combat Group Headquarters*
1 Medical Battalion	4 Engineer Combat Battalions
1 MP Company	2 Light Pontoon Companies
1 Maintenance Battalion	1 Treadway Bridge Company
2 Truck Companies	*1 Corps Artillery Headquarters*
1 Medium Maintenance Company	2 Artillery Group Headquarters
1 Gas Supply Company	1 Observation Battalion
1 Service Company	2 155mm Gun Battalions
1 Signal Battalion	2 155mm Howitzer Battalions
5 Tank Destroyer Battalions	4 4.5" Gun Battalions
4 Aviation Observation Battalions	2 MP Companies
	2 Signal Battalions
	1 Radio Intercept Company
	1 Tank Destroyer Group Headquarters
	5 Tank Destroyer Battalions

The original corps organization had a large number of support units in its structure. To free it so the corps commander only had to be concerned about fighting, these units were moved to Army level. In this table, the sample corps from late 1943 consists only of the units needed to wage effective combat. Notice that there were no supply or maintenance units. Also note the group headquarters (in italics) to coordinate artillery, engineer, and tank destroyer units.

talion. Twenty-four corps were activated during World War II. In practice, the only organic elements in a corps were the small command group, a headquarters company, a signal battalion, and an artillery headquarters company (to command any attached artillery units).

Early in the war, the Army experimented with a few armored corps composed of only tank and mechanized units. The idea was to allow the infantry divisions to man the front lines while the armored corps broke through enemy defenses.

Men serving in these armored corps wore the armored triangle shoulder patch with a Roman numeral (instead of the Arabic number worn by armored divisions). The concept was discarded in favor of a generic corps headquarters able to command any type of troops.

BRIGADES, GROUPS, AND TASK FORCES

Brigades and groups were headquarters elements designed to command one or more regiments or battalions. Beginning in December 1942, the Army broke down the non-infantry regiments into component battalions, but kept some of the regimental headquarters to use as brigade or group headquarters. They were used to provide a means to organize a flexible unit on an as-needed basis. The Army tried to have one group headquarters to command every four independent battalions. The group headquarters did not have an administrative function because all battalions were self-contained. Instead, the group headquarters directed the efforts of the battalions under its command. Brigade headquarters were used to command more than one group. All supply and administrative functions went directly from the battalion to the field army.

As a general rule, non-divisional combat troops were broken down into battalions, while non-divisional service troops were broken down into companies. This allowed for self-contained companies to handle small tasks without having to assign a large unit which might end up spread over a big area.

Even though the Tank Destroyer battalions (TDs) were considered independent units, there was occasionally a need to operate a number of them together. Similarly, it was useful to have a number of AAA battalions coordinated under one headquarters from time to time. Thus, the independent TD or AAA battalions could be sent off on separate duties, or assigned together under the direction of a group or brigade headquarters. The only men actually assigned to a group or brigade would be the men in that headquarters element.

Brigade headquarters were formed for only tank destroyer, anti-aircraft, and field artillery. One airborne infantry brigade headquarters was also formed. Only one TD brigade was sent overseas, but it was used to good effect as the headquarters for Task Force A in the Brittany breakout.

Task forces, on the other hand, were temporary collections of units put together under one command for a specific assignment. They varied considerably in size and configuration. A group of companies could just as easily be called a "task force" as a division-sized collection of men. Traditionally, a task force was named after the man commanding it. Most task forces were ad hoc formations in effect for a short period of time. No records were kept for task forces, per se, though records were kept on the various components of each task force.

DIVISIONS

The division is the unit that most (divisional) soldiers think of as "their" unit or outfit. The division was the largest unit that had a set organization, and the smallest to have a mix of sub-units from various branches. A division was organized to be self-sufficient and able to fight on its own without additional support. The Army considered the division as the "smallest composite unit which is capable of operating independently."[5]

There were ninety-two divisions activated during World War II. Only two did not see the end of the war: the Philippine Division was destroyed in combat, and the 2d Cavalry Division was deactivated in 1944. Each division had a specific shoulder patch, and the sight of this insignia often brings a lump to an old soldier's throat. (For details of all the divisional patches, see appendices A & B.)

There were seven types of divisions in the US Army during World War II: Infantry, Motorized, Armored, Cavalry, Airborne, Light, and Mountain.

On average, each division was authorized to have 13,400 men. These were directly supported (generally speaking) by 11,300 men in combat arms (assigned to corps Artillery units, Tank battalions, Engineer battalions, etc). Each division was also supported by 5,200 service troops in the combat zone, and another 13,500 men in the rear areas.[6]

Infantry Divisions

The Army had sixty-six infantry divisions in World War II. Four of these (the Americal, the Philippine, and the 24th and 25th divisions) were formed overseas. More divisions were planned, but when the Army discovered it could not keep up with the casualties it was suffering, plans for additional divisions were scrapped. Nearly all other countries pulled combat-exhausted divisions out of line to rest and refit, and replaced them with fresh divisions. The American Army, however, limited the number of divisions in action and pumped replacements into each division as needed.

Before the war, the Army used what was referred to as the "square" division, a unit composed of two brigades, each of two regiments (roughly 22,000 men). This was a World War I-era organization designed to allow two regiments to fight at the front, with one behind each in reserve. The Army entered World War II with a "triangular" division—one with two regiments on line, but only a third to back up whichever front regiment needed assistance. This organization was often referred to as "two up and one back." Brigade headquarters were done away with, and the entire unit streamlined down to roughly 15,000 men.

This change from a square to a triangular division (referred to as triangularization) rendered one entire regiment and a number of other divisional troops

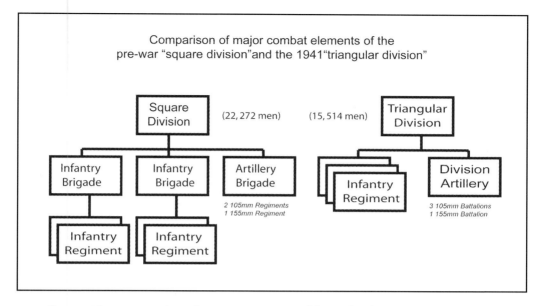

Comparison of major combat elements of the
pre-war "square division" and the 1941 "triangular division"

superfluous. The spare unit and men were removed from the division and used to form other units. This was one of the few times when units organic to a division were moved around. Knowing where the spare components of the old square divisions went can be important in tracking a man's service.

Triangularization hit National Guard units the hardest because they had kept the same organization since World War I and hoped to stay that way. The change to a triangular formation meant each National Guard division had to get rid of one-quarter of its manpower. The new organization allowed the Army to shrink old divisions, and use the excess manpower as the core for new formations.

For example, the 26th "Yankee" Infantry Division started with the 51st Brigade (composed of the 101st and 181st Infantry Regiments), and the 52d Brigade (composed of the 104th and 182d Infantry Regiments). Triangularization resulted in the two brigade headquarters being disbanded and the extra troops sent elsewhere. The 182d Regiment was removed from the division and assigned to the Americal Division in the Pacific. The 181st Regiment was broken up, but some of its troops were used to help build a new third regiment for the 26th Division, the newly formed 328th Infantry Regiment. Other excess smaller units were sent wherever the Army could use them.

Triangularization resulted in smaller divisions that were better able to respond to fluctuating battlefield conditions. According to the theorists, one regiment would fix the enemy in place by laying down a field of fire, while the second regiment maneuvered into position to attack the enemy in flank (the side). The third regiment, meanwhile, remained in reserve, ready to exploit any opportunities that arose.

This triangular technique of engaging the enemy is still used by many armies today.

The triangular organization was utilized throughout the Army. Platoons had three squads, rifle companies had three rifle platoons, rifle battalions had three rifle companies, and infantry regiments had three rifle battalions. Heavier weapons with longer range were sometimes placed in a heavy weapons unit that could cover the frontage of the two infantry units.

As the months and years passed during World War II, divisions became smaller as non-essential men and equipment were eliminated from the organization. When the war broke out, there were officially 15,245 men in an infantry division. This number fell in 1941 to 14,253, was revised again in 1943, and in January 1945, the size of an infantry division was reduced to only 14,037 men. The positions eliminated were from headquarters and support troops. Nothing was done to cut back the actual combat strength of the unit.

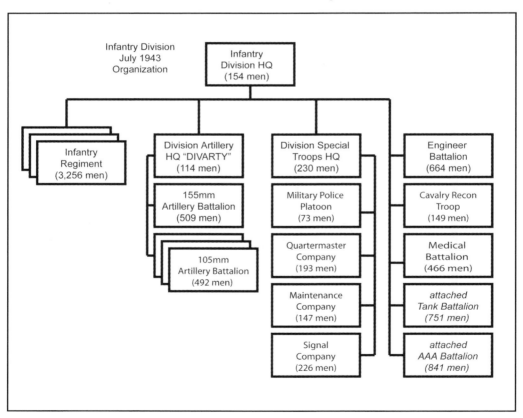

The standard organization of an infantry division was fixed at three infantry regiments, three 105mm artillery battalions (one generally assigned to support each infantry regiment), and a fourth 155mm artillery battalion. Other than a division headquarters, the other components of a division included a medical battalion, engineer battalion, signal company, cavalry reconnaissance troop, maintenance company, military police platoon, and a quartermaster company.

Although the elements of a division could support one another as needed, most divisions established a standard for how things were set up. A Regimental Combat Team (RCT) was based around one infantry regiment and one 105mm artillery battalion. Other smaller elements, such as engineer and medical support, were attached as needed. Some units developed standard attachments that worked together for long periods of time. For the 399th Infantry Regiment, the standard RCT was the infantry regiment, the 925th Field Artillery Battalion, Company C of the 325th Engineer Combat Battalion, Company C of the 325th Medical Battalion, and a Wire Team from the 100th Signal Company.

Noticeably absent from the division organization was a tank, tank destroyer, and anti-aircraft unit. The Army believed these could be attached and shifted from division to division as needed. In practice, the troops found it was much more effective to have a specific tank, TD, and AAA battalion assigned to every division on a near-permanent basis. This allowed men to get acquainted with one another and to work better together.

An infantry division was also known as a "leg" unit because it moved from place to place almost exclusively on foot. Unlike other divisions that drove or flew into combat, the infantry marched. The American Army was by far the most mechanized military force in the world, but the average soldier continued to make his way to battle on foot. As the traditional song said, "What do you do in the Infantry? You march, you march, you march!"

Motorized Divisions

America's industrial capacity made it possible for the Army to experiment with motorized divisions. This meant that every man in what had been a standard infantry division had a place to ride on a vehicle. A motorized division could be moved in one long convoy if needed.

This concept was thought by many to be the future of the Army. Before the end of 1942, the 4th, 6th, 7th, 8th, 9th, and 90th infantry divisions were being transformed into motorized divisions. After extensive testing of this concept, however, the Army determined it was a waste of resources, and by June 1943 the trucks were removed and the units returned to standard infantry divisions.

Infantry divisions did not need to move everyone at one time. It was far more effective to group all the trucks in independent truck units that could then, in turn, be directed to carry the soldiers where they were most needed. When organized this way, the trucks could be used to haul supplies one day, soldiers the next, prisoners on the third day, and so on. This maximized the use of available trucks that would otherwise sit empty waiting until the companies they were slated to carry needed them.

Light Divisions

The Army also experimented with the concept of light divisions. These were units equipped with far fewer vehicles and heavy equipment so they could function in areas that had few roads, like jungles and mountains. For transport, light divisions used handcarts, mules, sleds, and jeeps. Three light divisions were formed in 1943: the 71st Light Division (pack, jungle), the 10th Light Division (pack, alpine), and the 89th Light Division (truck). Tests showed that the light division concept would not work because of the extra support these units needed in order to remain adequately supplied. The 71st and 89th Light Divisions were transformed back to standard infantry divisions. The 10th Light Division, however, was converted into a specialized mountain division.

The Mountain Division

There was only one mountain division in the US Army. The 10th Light Division was converted to the 10th Mountain Division in late 1944. It was formed of men who had some knowledge of skiing and outdoor life. Skiing at the time was a sport for the upper class, so this division had more than its share of men from good families with some college education. Their training in mountain climbing was put to good use in the rocky terrain of Italy.

Airborne Divisions

Also known as parachute infantry divisions, these units jumped from aircraft or rode gliders into battle. By the end of the war, five divisions had airborne status: the 11th, 13th, 17th, 82d, and the 101st.

The airborne (A/B) forces started out with one "test platoon" experimenting with parachutes at Fort Benning, Georgia. Airborne divisions were initially small, roughly 8,500 men instead of the 14,500 men most infantry divisions carried on their rosters. They had slightly more than 400 vehicles instead of an infantry division's 2,000. The airborne division was composed of one parachute regiment and two glider regiments. Artillery support consisted of light 75mm pack howitzers, and the division had limited support troops.

After December 1944, the airborne T/O was revised to include two parachute regiments and one glider regiment. Heavier 105mm artillery and support elements were added to bring divisional strength up to almost 13,000 men. The four A/B divisions in the ETO were revised to the new standard, but the 11th A/B in the Pacific remained at the old T/O.[7]

Cavalry Divisions

The horse cavalry was once a key part of the Army. At the start of World War II, the Army realized it needed to finally do away with the horse and move to mechanized warfare. One experiment resulted in horse-mechanized units in which the horses were transported in trucks until they reached the battlefield. Motorcycles were also examined as a possible replacement for horses. Attempts to shift the cavalryman from horse to motorized vehicle took place within the 1st and 2d Cavalry Divisions. The 1st Cavalry was sent to the Pacific, however, where it fought as traditional infantry. The 2d Cavalry was sent to North Africa, where it was eventually deactivated, broken up, and used for service units.

Armored Divisions

The American Army had sixteen tank divisions in World War II. There were two types of armored division organizations after 1942: "heavy" and "light." These terms had nothing to do with the type of tanks, but the quantity of them.

Initially, an armored division was composed of an armored brigade of two light tank regiments and one medium tank regiment, supported by an artillery regiment with two battalions, an armored infantry regiment with an artillery battalion, and various support elements. This traditional "fixed" regimental organization was revised in March 1942.

The 1942 reorganization developed what was known as the "heavy" armored division. This reorganization did away with the brigade structure and replaced it with two flexible headquarters known as the Combat Command (CC). The two tank regiments maintained their three battalions, but the regiment now included two medium and one light tank battalions. The artillery was reorganized into three battalions without the regimental headquarters.

In September 1943, the Army decided to reorganize the armored divisions again, this time into new "light" divisions. Every armored division except two (the 2d and 3d) were ordered to make the switch. The new "light" organization reduced the number of tank battalions from six to three, but each battalion was enlarged so the division only had roughly one-third fewer tanks. Regiments and their headquarters were eliminated. No unit in the division was larger than a battalion.

The various elements in an armored division could be swapped between any of three flexible headquarters elements. These HQs were called Combat Command A (CCA), Combat Command B (CCB), and Combat Command Reserve (CCR). These combat command headquarters were nothing more than a handful of men. The division commander could assign any part of his division, breaking down battalions into the smaller elements of companies and platoons as needed, to any of the combat commands.

A soldier could spend the entire war assigned to one combat command, or he could find the unit he was in bounced back and forth, as needed, between all of them. This arrangement allowed for maximum flexibility and, although rather confusing at times, worked well in practice.

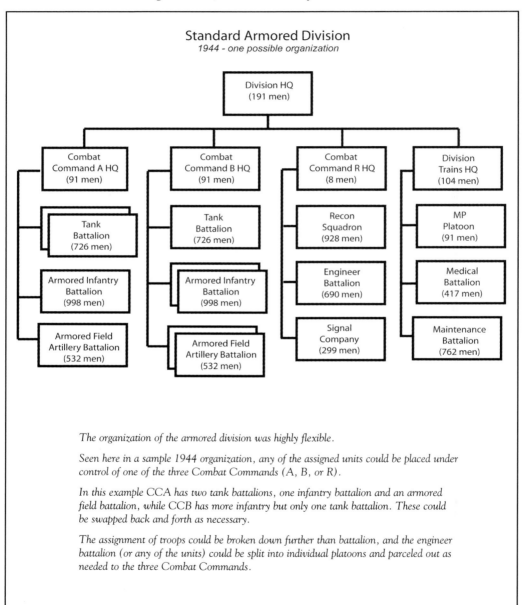

The organization of the armored division was highly flexible.

Seen here in a sample 1944 organization, any of the assigned units could be placed under control of one of the three Combat Commands (A, B, or R).

In this example CCA has two tank battalions, one infantry battalion and an armored field battalion, while CCB has more infantry but only one tank battalion. These could be swapped back and forth as necessary.

The assignment of troops could be broken down further than battalion, and the engineer battalion (or any of the units) could be split into individual platoons and parceled out as needed to the three Combat Commands.

In theory, CCA and CCB were assigned the bulk of the combat troops, and CCR was allocated the support units. In practice, however, the combat troops in most armored divisions were balanced relatively equally between the three combat commands. An average combat command consisted of one tank battalion, one armored infantry battalion, and one artillery battalion.

On average, combat commands were the size of a brigade. They could be further broken down into task forces (roughly the size of a reinforced battalion) or Battle Groups (roughly the size of a reinforced company). Given the flexible nature of an armored division, temporary groupings of units smaller than a combat command were generally named after their commander. Thus, a task force led by Lt. Col. William Lovelady (of the 3d Armored Division) was called "Task Force Lovelady." Many combat commands and task forces had a standard grouping of units, but the only way to know for certain the exact component units of, for example, Task Force Lovelady, is to check the records for the 3d Armored Division at a specific date.

Tanks themselves were divided into two classes: light and medium. Light tank companies used the M5 Stuart, a light but fast vehicle. All other American tank companies were in the medium class. These were mainly a version of the tried and true M4 Sherman tank. The Americans did not build and use "heavy" tanks in World War II because every vehicle had to be transported across the ocean to a combat theater. Although many American tanks had lighter armor and firepower than their German counterparts, they were more reliable.

One oddity of armored units was that jeeps, the famous quarter-ton vehicle, were known as "peeps." This term seems only to have been used in armored units, and disappeared soon after the war. The somewhat rare amphibious jeep developed its own nickname: the "seep."

Ghost and Phantom Divisions

Reference is sometimes made to "ghost" or "phantom" divisions. These units never existed, but names and insignia were created and used to try to fool the Germans into thinking there were more troops in an area than there really were. Some were units that had been scheduled for activation, but never actually organized. Others were total fabrications.

Shoulder sleeve insignia of FUSAG, the First U.S. Army Group. A unit that did not exist except on paper. There is no evidence that ghost patches such as these were ever actually worn.

There were also ghost or phantom corps, and even a ghost army (the 14th). No men were ever assigned to these units. They existed only on paper, and it is debatable if more than a handful of their patches were ever made.

BOOK NOTES

Operation Fortitude, by Roger Hesketh, Overlook Press, New York, 2000 ISBN 1-58567-075-8

Ghosts of the ETO, by Jonathan Gawne, Casemate, Havertown, PA, 2002, ISBN 0-9711709-5-9

BRIGADES

At the start of the war, brigades were composed of two regiments. To streamline the Army, the brigade was essentially eliminated as a unit, per se. Brigades were maintained as a headquarters available for attaching various units on an as-needed basis. Only artillery, anti-aircraft artillery, and tank destroyer brigades were organized during the war.

REGIMENTS

The regiment is the traditional unit of the Army. Most history and heritage is passed down on a regimental level. Just as divisions have shoulder patches, regiments have enameled metal crests worn on the dress uniform. Every regiment had a specific number to identify it. There was, however, a 3d Infantry Regiment, and also a 3d Armored Regiment, so when using unit numbers in your research, the branch is always as important as the number.

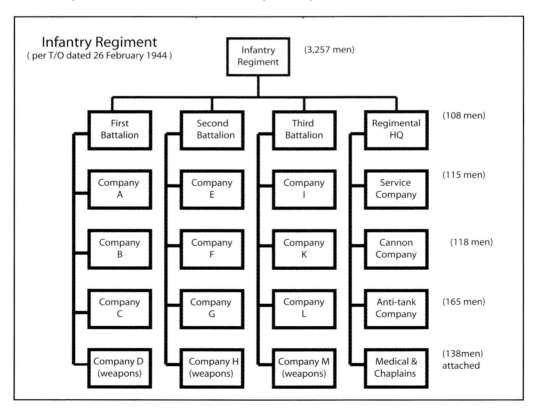

Except for infantry, engineer, and a few armored organizations, most regiments were broken up into their component battalions during World War II. Regiments and every unit smaller than a regiment were, for the most part, composed only of men from their specific branch. For example, every man in an infantry regiment belonged to the infantry. The only exception to this rule was the few attached medical personnel. Even these men, however, were considered "attached," and thus not officially part of the regiment.

Infantry regiments had a headquarters element and three rifle battalions. Each infantry regiment had six short-barreled 105mm howitzers in a unit known as a "Cannon Company." In keeping with the policy that every man in an infantry regiment was an infantryman, these artillery pieces were manned by men from the infantry. Each regiment also had an antitank company with 37mm (57mm after 1943) anti-tank guns, as well as a mine laying platoon.

BATTALIONS AND SQUADRONS

The battalion was a common unit size in World War II. There were two types of battalions: those that were organically part of a larger unit (rifle battalions were part of infantry regiments, for example) and those that were independent. In cavalry and mechanized units, a battalion-sized unit was known as a squadron.

Each infantry regiment had three rifle battalions numbered the 1st, 2d, and 3d battalions. This is one of the few times where the unit number means little. Every regiment had a 1st battalion. Independent battalions had their own unique identification number. If a battalion number is other than 1–4, it is very important to identify if it is an independent unit rather than an organic part of a larger unit.

The rifle battalion was the smallest infantry unit in which the commander was normally within small arms range of the front line. Rifle battalions were composed of a small headquarters element, three rifle companies, and a fourth, heavy weapons, company. The companies in an infantry regiment were lettered A–M (except for J, which was not used). Companies A, B, C, and D were always in the 1st Battalion; E, F, G, and H were always in the 2d Battalion, and companies I, K, L, and M were always in the 3d Battalion. Of these 12 companies, D, H, and M were always the heavy weapons companies. If you know the letter designation of a company, you automatically know the number of the battalion in which it served.

This unit mascot is pictured with his unit's Command Post (CP) sign.

The shape of the sign is the same as the 28th Infantry Division shoulder patch, indicating the division.

"Easy" stands for Company E, although there are a few different Company E's in the 28th.

The number is no help as no unit is designated. "2" in the 28th Division probably indicates Second Battalion, of which Company E is always a part.

From this image there is actually no way to tell which of the three infantry regiments of the 28th Division the photo is from.

Author's Collection

COMPANY, BATTERY AND TROOP

The company was and still is the standard administrative unit in the Army. In the cavalry, a company is called a troop; in the artillery, it is called a battery. A company is the smallest element that keeps records of its service. Once a man is assigned to a company, he could be moved around to the various smaller elements in it, as needed. The various small elements assigned to a headquarters were always lumped into a unit called the headquarters company. Soldiers rarely knew anyone outside their own company. This was his home in the Army.

Companies may have been commanded by a captain, with a lieutenant as his executive officer (the assistant commander), but it has always been said that a company is run by the 1st sergeant (the senior NCO). In combat, the high turnover of officers meant that it was common to find lieutenants serving as company commanders.

A rifle company was composed of three rifle platoons and a weapons platoon. A heavy weapons company (companies D, H, and M), were composed of 81mm mortars and heavy water-cooled machine guns. Unlike the rifle companies, which were rarely separated, the weapons companies were often broken up to support whichever rifle company needed an added punch.

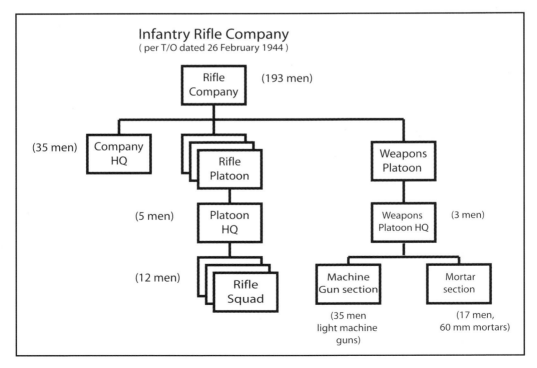

Infantry Rifle Company
(per T/O dated 26 February 1944)

Rifle Company (193 men)

(35 men) Company HQ

Rifle Platoon

(5 men) Platoon HQ

(12 men) Rifle Squad

Weapons Platoon

(3 men) Weapons Platoon HQ

Machine Gun section (35 men light machine guns)

Mortar section (17 men, 60 mm mortars)

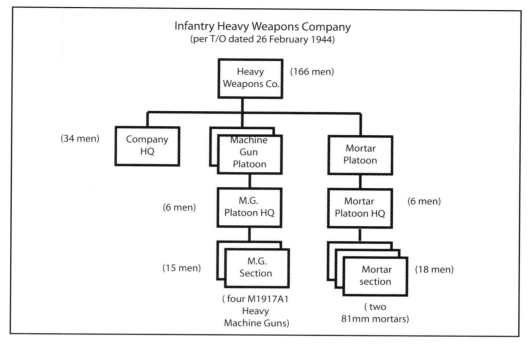

Infantry Heavy Weapons Company
(per T/O dated 26 February 1944)

Heavy Weapons Co. — (166 men)

(34 men) — Company HQ

Machine Gun Platoon

Mortar Platoon

(6 men) — M.G. Platoon HQ

Mortar Platoon HQ — (6 men)

(15 men) — M.G. Section

Mortar section — (18 men)

(four M1917A1 Heavy Machine Guns)

(two 81mm mortars)

In every company there were a few key NCOs. The 1st sergeant was the senior NCO. He saw that all guard and fatigue details were assigned and finished. He received the reports of the platoon sergeants and passed them on to the company commander. Because of his knowledge of the men in the company, he served as the primary assistant to the commander on personnel matters. If the company commander was the father of the outfit, the 1st sergeant was the mother. As top NCO in the unit, 1st sergeants were traditionally known as "Top" or the "Top Kick" of the company. A good example of how a 1st sergeant ran a company is shown in the fictional but generally accurate film "*From Here to Eternity.*" This film is also instructive in what the Army unofficially could do to motivate recalcitrant soldiers.

The mess sergeant ran the company mess (kitchen) and made sure the men were properly fed. The supply sergeant requisitioned needed supplies and equipment and maintained the

Each battalion had three rifle companies, and one weapons company. The weapons company was composed of 81mm mortar crews and soldiers with the M17A1 machine gun. The large cylinder around the barrel contained water, which cooled the weapon down as it fired. As long as water was fed into it, the machine gun could fire continuously without overheating. National Archives

inventory and records of everything issued. The company clerk (there could be more than one) was typically a corporal and did all the clerical work, typing up the reports and rosters. In combat, clerks were typically pulled back to regimental HQ, where they worked under the regimental personnel officer.

Platoons

The smallest unit normally commanded by a commissioned officer (a lieutenant) was the platoon. Rifle platoons were composed of 41 men and were equipped with Garand rifles and Browning Automatic Rifles (BARs). The weapons platoon in a rifle company was armed with small 60mm mortars and light air-cooled machine guns.

Squads

The squad is the smallest standard-sized unit in the Army. It was considered to be the largest group that one man could effectively control by voice or hand signals.

A squad was commanded by an NCO. In peacetime, squads consisted of eight men (the maximum number of men the Army believed could be directly controlled). This number was raised to twelve during the war, which made it easier to keep the squad at a minimum strength of eight men). The squad could be broken down, as needed, into smaller sections.

Rifle Squad

Staff Sergeant — Sergeant — Privates and PFCs

Squad Leader — Assistant Squad Leader — Scouts — BAR Team — Riflemen

Detachments, Sections

A detachment was simply a group of soldiers put together for a specific purpose. It could be a detachment of men being sent off to paint a building, or a standard grouping of men used as a headquarters detachment. Detachment is a catch-all term used to cover any non-standard size unit.

Sections were small groups that also did not fit into any category. Generally they were smaller than a squad, but some branches of service used the term in place of squad to indicate their smallest grouping of men.

RANK

One of the most important concepts to understand about the Army is its use of rank. Every soldier is given a rank so everyone knows who can give orders to whom. Army rank is a two-tiered class system consisting of officers and enlisted men. Historically, officers came to the Army from society's upper class; an intelligent, well trained, and educated group of men. Enlisted men, on the other hand, were drawn from the working class, and generally were not as well educated or trained.

World War II continued the democratization of the military that had begun as early as the Civil War, and which accelerated during World War I. An intelligent person from a poor background, with little or no education, could be selected by his battlefield performance or through testing for officer training.

ENLISTED MEN

The bulk of the Army during World War II was composed of enlisted men. Their ranks ranged from private through master sergeant. The term "enlisted men" is a generic description that includes not just soldiers who voluntarily enlisted, but also those who were drafted or federalized from the National Guard. In most cases, when someone uses the term "enlisted man," he is referring to a soldier serving in one of the two lowest ranks: private or private first class (abbreviated as Pvt. and Pfc.). Enlisted men who achieved higher rank with supervisory responsibilities were usually referred to by their rank rather than the catch-all phrase, "enlisted man."

The majority of soldiers who served in World War II were privates or privates first class. There was little real difference between these two ranks, although a Pfc. was paid slightly more each month. Each company was limited to a specific number of Pfc. ranks (or "ratings"). Theoretically, the "best" privates in each company were supposed to be designated Pfcs. During World War II, promotion to that rank was not automatic and thus not dependent upon the amount of time served. Promotion to Pfc. was performed at the company level and was announced in company general orders.

The men who oversaw or "supervised" the enlisted men during World War II were known as Non-Commissioned Officers (NCOs, or non-coms). This is also true today. These corporals and sergeants controlled the day-to-day activities of the men. Generally, NCOs were the most experienced enlisted men. When World War II began, most of the sergeants had already served many years in the Army. One of the benefits of being an NCO was the ability to avoid guard duty or fatigue details, such as working in the kitchen (KP, or Kitchen Police) or

ENLISTED MEN—RANK, INSIGNIA, PAY				
[NO INSIGNIA]				
RANK	PRIVATE	PRIVATE FIRST CLASS	CORPORAL	SERGEANT
PRE-WAR MONTHLY BASE PAY	$30	$36	$54	$60
POST JUNE 1942 MONTHLY BASE PAY	$50	$54	$66	$78
RANK	STAFF SERGEANT	TECHNICAL SERGEANT	FIRST SERGEANT	MASTER SERGEANT
PRE-WAR MONTHLY BASE PAY	$72	$84	$84	$126
POST JUNE 1942 MONTHLY BASE PAY	$96	$114	$138	$138

policing the area (cleaning up the grounds and picking up trash). According to a time-honored tradition, promotion to an NCO rank was officially performed at the regimental level after the recommendation of a company commander. These promotions were announced in regimental general orders as described in Army Regulation (AR) 615-5.

BOOK NOTES

For a thorough and interesting history of non-commissioned ranks, see:

Guardians of the Republic: A History of the Non-Commissioned Officer Corps of the US Army, by Ernest Fisher, Stackpole Books, Mechanicsburg PA, 2001, ISBN 0-81172-784-X

Sergeant ranks were sometimes referred to by the number of chevrons (the upper angle) and rockers (the lower arc) on their stripes. The number of chevrons reflected the specific rank. For example, if a soldier was described as having "three up, two down," he was a technical sergeant. The lowest rank of sergeant was a "three striper," commonly called a "buck" sergeant.

Before World War II, NCOs could not transfer between regiments unless they started in the new unit as a private. While officers lived and ate in separate facilities, the NCOs did so with the enlisted men. Most senior NCOs had their own private or semi-private rooms in the barracks. It has long been said that officers command the Army, but sergeants actually run it. Officers issue the orders, and the sergeants tell the men what to do and see to it that it is done properly. An unspoken Army rule was that NCOs overseeing enlisted men at work were not to perform any of the same work themselves.

There are two main types of World War II stripes. On the left is a cotton light colored version, designed to be worn on the summer weight (washable) clothing.

Two major wartime changes in the Army affected enlisted men. In June 1942, an Army-wide pay raise provided more money for the troops, although pay for higher ranking officers remained the same. In December 1943, in an effort to boost the morale of the infantry, NCO ranks in infantry units were raised. Assistant squad leaders became sergeants, squad leaders became staff sergeants, and platoon sergeants became technical sergeants. The number of authorized slots for Pfc's in infantry units was increased to one-half of all privates. It was hoped that the additional pay and rank would offset the rigors and dangers of being in an infantry unit and thus help morale.

In the center is a darker olive drab variety designed for winter (wool) uniforms. Both have very dark blue backing. In practice, both were used fairly interchangeably.

At the right is the post-war Korea era coloration with the backing lightened so the blue color is more apparent.

Author's Collection

The entry of the United States into World War II dramatically increased the Army's need for more men with technical skills. As a result, a new category of NCO was authorized in January 1942: technicians. These soldiers were paid more for their specific skills, but did not require the command authorization of a higher rank. In September 1942, the rank stripes included a letter "T" to indicate the soldier wearing it was a technician. Long after the end of the war, the Army changed the term to "specialist," which is still in use today.

Technician ratings are not to be confused with the more traditional rank of technical sergeant. For command purposes, technicians ranked just below the equivalent of their stripes. A technician 3d grade (Tech/3) ranked just below a staff sergeant when it came to giving orders.

TECHNICIANS—RANK, INSIGNIA, PAY			
	![5th grade insignia]	![4th grade insignia]	![3d grade insignia]
RANK	5TH GRADE	4TH GRADE	3D GRADE
EQUIVALENT TO	CORPORAL	SERGEANT	STAFF SERGEANT
POST JUNE 1942 BASE PAY	$66	$78	$98

OFFICERS—RANK, INSIGNIA, PAY, POSITIONS, EQUIVALENTS

	Insignia Color	Rank	Base Pay	Normal Position	Navy Equivalent
	GOLD	2d LIEUTENANT	$125.00	PLATOON LEADER	ENSIGN
	SILVER	1st LIEUTENANT	$166.77	PLATOON LEADER	LIEUTENANT
	SILVER	CAPTAIN	$200.00	COMPANY COMMANDER	LIEUTENANT J.G.
	GOLD	MAJOR	$250.00	BATTALION COMMANDER	LIEUTENANT COMMANDER
	SILVER	LIEUTENANT COLONEL	$291.67	STAFF OFFICER	COMMANDER
	SILVER	COLONEL	$333.33	REGIMENTAL COMMANDER	CAPTAIN
	SILVER	BRIGADIER	$500.00	BRIGADE	COMMODORE
	SILVER	MAJOR GENERAL	$666.66	DIVISION	REAR ADMIRAL
	SILVER	LIEUTENANT GENERAL	$708.33	CORPS	VICE ADMIRAL
	SILVER	GENERAL	$850.00	ARMY OR ARMY GROUP	ADMIRAL
	SILVER	GENERAL OF THE ARMIES		SPECIAL	ADMIRAL

OFFICERS

An officer is defined as "a person lawfully invested with military rank and authority by virtue of a commission issued him by or in the name of the sovereign or chief magistrate of a country."[8]

Officers are more formally known as "commissioned officers" because they hold a commission for their rank. A commission is the formal written authority providing them with their rank and status. They are officers and gentlemen by act of Congress. The US Constitution gives the Congress "the power . . . to provide for the common defense . . . to raise and support Armies." Included within this authorization is the ability of Congress to offer commissions for officer rank. Senior officers require Congressional approval to be promoted. The rest of the Army's officers are put on promotion lists, which Congress generally approves en masse.

The lowest ranking commissioned officer is a 2d lieutenant. He is always considered higher in rank that the most senior enlisted man. Thus, it was not uncommon to find a young "wet-behind-the-ears" lieutenant giving orders to a sergeant, even though the NCO had decades of service experience. Officers, generally speaking, had either attended college or earned a degree; while enlisted men had little or no college experience.

Perhaps it is helpful to consider officers as the managers of the Army. They plan ahead for future events and take responsibility for the men under their command. Day-to-day and routine activities in the Army were run by the NCOs. Traditionally, officers slept and ate separately from the enlisted men in order to avoid undue familiarity that might affect their decision-making in time of battle. An officer's uniform was (and is) different from an enlisted man's, and officers also enjoyed special privileges, such as a monthly ration of two bottles of liquor. There is an old Army saying that "rank hath its privileges" (RHIP). Ask any enlisted man and he will quickly confirm that statement.

The division between the officer and enlisted class was an important one in the Army. Officers had their own clubs, messes, and living quarters. Bill Mauldin, one of the greatest Army cartoonists of World War II, drew a classic cartoon with two officers admiring a sunset. "Beautiful sunset," remarks one of the officers. "Is there one for the enlisted men?"

The theory behind this separation was simple: officers might have to order men to their deaths, and it would be easier for both if the officer was not a friend, but a little-known person of absolute authority to be obeyed at all times.

World War II was the breaking point for many of the Army's older, formalized policies. Afterward, the sharp line between the worlds of the enlisted man and officer was blurred. Today, no one gives a second thought to officers and enlisted men eating together in the same mess hall or the fact that they wear essentially the same uniform, albeit with different insignia. In the early years of the war, this would have been considered heresy by the old Army officer class.

There were many ways to become an officer in the US Army. One of the few requirements to attend Officer's School was to score 110 or better on an intelligence test known as the Army General Classification Test (AGCT). All men took this test and were grouped into five sections by score: Class V, under 69 (very inferior); Class IV, 70–89 (inferior); Class III, 90–109 (average); Class II, 110–130 (superior); and Class I, 130 or higher (very superior). The higher the score, the better the chance a man had of becoming an officer.

If an aspiring officer wanted to carve out a career in uniform, the best way to do so was to graduate from the United States Military Academy at West Point. The academy provided four years of free (though grueling) college education and, upon graduation, commission as a 2d lieutenant. West Point was an established "Old Boys' Club." Graduates often protected and advanced one another's careers. Because of the heavy demand for officers during the war, the Army modified its policy at West Point. After October 1942, only three years of instruction were needed to graduate with a commission. In 1943, there were two different graduating classes, in January and June.

The shoulder sleeve insignia of men assigned to The United States Military Academy at West Point.

Author's Collection

Men attending a regular college could participate in the Reserve Officer's Training Program (ROTC). This was a program that commissioned college students as reserve officers after four years of part-time training while in school. They could be called up in time of an emergency. The ROTC program was established after problems were experienced during World War I in finding enough trained officers. Generally speaking, reserve officers were (and still are) called up for a few weeks of duty every year to keep their skills sharpened and up to date.

Some colleges during World War II, such as Clemson University, Virginia Military Institute, Norwich University, and the Citadel, were military colleges. Graduates were eligible to receive an Army commission.

Other land grant schools required all able-bodied men to take the basic ROTC course during their first two years of college. After that time, the student could complete the advanced ROTC program in his last two years and receive a commission. During these final years, participants were eligible for a government stipend to help offset tuition costs. When war broke out in December 1941, more than 125 colleges and universities in America offered ROTC programs.

A little-known method of commissioning officers was the Citizen's Military Training Camp (CMTC). Like ROTC, these training camps also developed out of the need for more officers. CMTC offered men who could not afford to go to college the ability to receive military training and thus be eligible for an Army commission. Participants in the four-year CMTC program attended a month-long camp each summer for four consecutive summers.

This insignia was worn by men attending one of the Officer Candidate Schools.

Although effective, the CMTC program was suspended shortly after World War II broke out because of a shortage of instructors and training areas.

The most common method of commissioning in World War II was Officer's Candidate School, or OCS. These were branch-specific army training schools that took in a civilian or enlisted man and, after approximately 90 days, turned out a fresh 2d lieutenant.

The design incorporates the three letters O, C, and S.

Author's Collection

The short turnaround time for such a newly-minted lieutenant gave rise to the derogatory term "ninety-day wonder." Every branch had its own officer's school. Artillery officers were trained at Fort Sill, Oklahoma; officers destined for armored units at Fort Knox, Kentucky; quartermaster officers at Fort Lee, Virginia, or Fort Warren, Wyoming, and so on. Only about one-third of the men who graduated from OCS were high school graduates, and another slim handful (6.5%) did not even reach that level of education. Thus, a remarkable percentage of men without any college experience were made officers solely upon their ability as demonstrated in OCS.[9]

Enlisted men selected for OCS were automatically promoted to the rank of corporal. Once they were ready to graduate, they were officially discharged from the US Army in order to receive their commission. This was done because a soldier could not be both an enlisted man and a commissioned officer at the same time. This procedure caused some to joke that they should walk away after they had received their discharge, but before they had accepted their commission!

Some men were given direct commissions into the Army as officers because of their specific experience or some particular specialist skill they possessed. Examples included men with legal, dental, or medical degrees. Some industry experts in areas such as railroad management or chemistry were also put straight into uniform. Direct commissions in the Army were rare, however. Most such experienced men were required to go through some form of OCS before being commissioned. The Navy, on the other hand, was far more lenient in handing out commissions to capable men it believed did not require any additional military training.

Despite all these programs, experienced officers were in short supply for most of the war. In 1943, only one out of 50 officers had any previous experience in the military.[10] The loss of men to combat-related injuries seriously depleted the officer ranks.

Battlefield commissions were one way to maintain the supply of officers at the front. There were two types of battlefield commissions. Until late 1944, a battlefield commission entailed promoting a man to 2d lieutenant because of his demonstrated leadership abilities in the field. This was not without its problems, however, because it was often difficult for these new officers to return to their units where they had previously served as enlisted men. This was solved by sending the former enlisted man to a different unit once he was commissioned. Many soldiers turned down battlefield commissions because they did not want to be sent off to serve with strangers.

Another problem faced by battlefield-commissioned officers was that they did not possess any more training than a regular enlisted man. They had little or no knowledge of the specific tasks officers needed to perform on a daily basis. They did not know how to handle the paperwork, and had little or no experience coordinating different units. In the European Theater of Operations (ETO), a school was set up at Fontainebleau, France, to offer a crash course for new officers. Men selected from the ranks and sent back to participate in a stateside service school for officer training were not considered battlefield commissioned officers, while men who were sent to Fontainebleau for this special course were considered battlefield commissioned officers.[11]

There was a provision for 2d lieutenants in a combat unit to be eligible for promotion to 1st lieutenant once they demonstrated their ability on the battlefield. Many lieutenants were promoted in this manner after their first or second time in combat. As long as they demonstrated to their superiors they could operate on the battlefield, they were promoted.

Officer ranks were divided into three groups. Lieutenants and captains were known as company grade officers. Captains generally commanded companies, and lieutenants led the platoons that made up a company. Majors, lieutenant colonels, and colonels were known as field grade officers. These higher ranks operated above company levels in larger units. Colonels (also known as full colonels or "bird colonels" because of the eagles on their rank insignia) commanded regiments.

The highest ranking officer was a general. These were and are the senior men in command, with stars on their shoulders. The elite of the Army, they carried important responsibilities. Generals commanded divisions, corps, and field armies, and were the equivalent of admirals in the Navy. Generals had men assigned to them as personal assistants (aides).

In business terms, generals can be thought of as vice presidents and CEO's. Field grade officers were promoted by a system of seniority, but generals were specifically selected by the President of the United States (or his designates) to make sure only the best men reached that important rank.

Before World War I, promotions were based upon seniority within an officer's regiment. Casualties suffered by a regiment in combat, for example, were often replaced by junior officers from within the same unit. Officers serving in regiments that did not see combat would not achieve promotion, sometimes for years on end. This stagnation was hard on morale. Regulations to address this inequity were instituted before World War II, and a single master list for promotions was created.

When one officer in the Army moved up, another was promoted to take the first officer's previous rank, regardless of which unit he served in. This was a peacetime policy. Although it was maintained during the war for permanent ranks, it did not affect temporary ranks. The major exception to the promotion list was for chaplains and medical officers, who were promoted based upon their time in service.

Officers were required to follow certain customs in the pre-war Army. For example, they had to call upon their commanding officer within 24 hours of arrival at a new post. Similarly, all officers were expected to call upon a newcomer. At some posts, regular weekly courtesy calls were expected. These were short formal visits of no more than 15 minutes, and everyone was supposed to leave calling cards. Every officer was expected to call on his commanding officer on New Year's Day. There was an Army taboo against an officer in uniform carrying an umbrella or a bundle, or pushing a baby carriage.

Pre-war officers often referred to "The Hump" when discussing promotions. "The Hump" was the large number of officers on the promotion list, a bottleneck created by the increase in the number of officers commissioned in 1920. Because there were far more field grade officers than needed, promotions for lieutenants and captains in the 1930s were few and far between. Getting over "The Hump" meant waiting until the large number of World War I-era officers died or left the service for one's turn at promotion.

Waiting through "The Hump" demoralized many junior officers, who left the Army for the civilian world. In 1940, a revitalization act was passed to address this serious problem. It decreed that every 2d lieutenant was to be promoted to 1st lieutenant after three years of service; a 1st lieutenant to captain after 10 years; a captain to major after 17 years; a major to lieutenant colonel after 23 years, and to full colonel after 28 years. Thus, any officer who maintained a good service record would automatically reach colonel in 28 years. All officers were retired at age 60, though generals could serve until age 62.

The best field grade officers were sent for additional training to the Command and General Staff College at Ft. Leavenworth, Kansas. This course taught them how to handle larger units, as well as how to perform various staff functions. Additional Army education was conducted at the Army War College at Carlisle Barracks, Pennsylvania, where only the top officers were trained in the political and economic factors of war. The Army War College, along with another major military institute, the Army Industrial College in Washington, DC (which dealt with economic and industrial factors in gearing up for war), were closed at the beginning of World War II because of a shortage of officers to run them. The regular courses at the Command and General Staff school were shortened for the duration of the war.

There were also upper age limits for officers serving with troops in the field. For example, 2d lieutenants could not serve with combat units after the age of 30, colonels after age 55, and so forth. When officers reached the age limit and could not be promoted, they were shifted to administrative duties. No age limits were placed on generals above the rank of major general.

The top rank was a five-star general (General of the Army). Only four men reached this rank during World War II: George C. Marshall, Douglas MacArthur, Dwight D. Eisenhower, and Henry H. Arnold. Fleet Admiral, the equivalent Navy rank, was awarded to only three men: William D. Leahy, Earnest J. King, and Chester W. Nimitz. After the war, William F. Halsey (Navy) and Omar N. Bradley (Army) were promoted to five stars. Before World War II, there had only been four Generals of the Army: Ulysses S. Grant, William T. Sherman, Philip Sheridan, and John J. Pershing. In 1976, Congress posthumously awarded George Washington the same rank.

The rank of field marshal was used by many nations for commanders in charge of units larger than a field army. This rank has never been used in the United States. However, the government of the Philippines gave Douglas MacArthur this esteemed rank before American involvement in World War II. MacArthur is the only American to ever have held the rank of field marshal.

The Army realized in the late 1930s that it would need to expand substantially its small pre-war group of officers in order to fight a major war. It also appreciated that once a major war ended, it would be left with a large number of senior officers and few slots available for junior officers. For this reason, the majority of promotions during World War II were of a temporary status. When hostilities ended, temporary ranks were withdrawn and the officers who held them reduced to their permanent rank.

It was not uncommon for someone to have served as a full colonel during the war, only to be reduced to a lowly captain or major. This reduction had nothing to do with performance, but was instead a method to ensure the right types and numbers of officers were on hand for the transition to a peacetime Army.

Unlike enlisted men, officers could be "reclassified." This meant they could be examined to determine whether they should be transferred to a different specialty, reduced in rank with fewer responsibilities, or dismissed from the service altogether. Reclassification was used to shift officers to specialties and branches where they were genuinely needed, or to rid the service of incompetent men. Reclassification was routinely misused. For example, officers who were afraid of combat were sometimes "reclassified" to administrative duties or to assignments in the rear. Enlisted men who avoided combat, by contrast, were threatened with courts-martial and a firing squad. This provides yet another good reason to respect combat officers who remained at the front and did their jobs.

One of the big differences between officers and NCOs was how they could legally punish soldiers. By regulation, NCOs were not allowed to issue any punishment to enlisted men. They could recommend punishment to the company commander if they felt it necessary. According to Army Regulation (AR) 104, company grade officers could issue punishment without the need for courts-martial as long as the punishment was no longer than one week. Typical "company punishments" included the loss of privileges, being restricted to barracks or camp, or the addition of extra duties, such as KP.

NCOs, however, could get around this regulation by assigning special "duties" to the men. In place of punishment, an NCO might order an enlisted man to dig a deep hole and, once it was dug, flick his cigarette into it and order him to fill it back up. Judicious use of this authority caused enlisted men to fear their NCOs more than the officers. Enlisted men, though, could try and "out sergeant" the sergeant by interpreting their orders literally.

For example, one sergeant ordered an enlisted man to paint a room.

"Everything, sergeant?" asked the soldier.

"Yes, everything," came the reply.

The soldier complied and painted the walls, ceiling, floor, light bulbs, desk, and even the papers on the desk.

When the NCO exploded with rage, the soldier responded, "But sergeant, you specifically told me to paint everything, and I was just following your orders."

These soldiers learned what a Sergeant can do instead of "punishing" them. They were assigned to dig this hole under the hot sun at the desert training center. When completed, the Sergeant, traditionally, would toss either a used match or cigarette butt into the hole and order them to fill it back up.

Author's Collection

57

Officers were expected to know the exact date upon which they were commissioned or promoted to a new rank. This was known as their "date of rank." It was the best way to know who, in a group of officers of the same rank, was in charge. The man whose date of rank was the earliest, even by a single day, was the senior officer. If a number of men were commissioned on the same day (like a graduation at West Point), seniority was decided by their academic standing at the academy, or by age.

WARRANT OFFICERS

Between NCO and officer is the relatively rare rank of warrant officer (WO). These men held positions that needed great experience or skill, but they did not have enough command responsibility to require an officer's commission. Generally speaking, WOs worked with bands, personnel, or food preparation matters. In World War II, there were three classes of WOs. Most were long serving NCOs with a vast wealth of knowledge and experience with the Army. Initially a position used to reward veteran sergeants, WO status became something that exceptional NCOs aspired to as the pinnacle of their career.

In November 1942, a flight officer rank was established with the same insignia as a warrant officer, junior grade, except the enamel was blue. The position of flight officer was abolished in 1945. A number of flight officers were used as glider pilots in airborne landings. All told, roughly 2,500 men served as flight officers during World War II. Of that number, 17 shot down five or more enemy aircraft and were recognized as "aces."

Soldiers and officers were referred to by their rank. Warrant officers, however, were traditionally called "Mr." or "Chief." In January 1944, women were authorized to hold warrant ranks. Although the branch color was brown (taken from the brown enamel on their rank insignia), all warrant officers wore silver and black piping in place of a branch color.

WARRANT OFFICERS—RANK, INSIGNIA, PAY			
Insignia	Insignia Color	Rank	Monthly Base Pay
	GOLD AND BROWN	WARRANT OFFICER	$150.00
	GOLD AND BROWN	CHIEF WARRANT OFFICER	$175.00
	GOLD AND BLUE	FLIGHT OFFICER	$150.00

BRANCHES OF SERVICE

The Army can be divided into two major groupings: the unit with which each man identifies with, and the separate branches of the service. As discussed earlier, every man belonged to some type of unit (regiment, battalion, etc.) that was his home.

The Army was subdivided by specialty into different branches of service. The combat arms (referred to as simply "Arms") included the infantry, cavalry and artillery, and the "Services," which included supporting Arms such as quartermasters and signalmen.

Before World War II, each of these branches was a domain unto itself. The Chief of Infantry commanded all infantry units, while the Chief of Artillery decided whether his men would follow slightly different regulations than those serving in other branches.

This posed a problem. It was hard for an Army to properly coordinate its component pieces when the Chief of Signals was insisting on developing a type of telephone that the infantry, for example, believed was the wrong type. While the branches generally cooperated well when it really mattered, time was often wasted squabbling while everyone pushed for their own policies. The Army put a stop to this in July 1940 by centralizing the power of the various branch chiefs under a General Headquarters in Washington, DC. In March 1942, the situation was changed again so that the Army had three major subdivisions: the Army Ground Forces for combat units; the Army Service Forces (known for a while as the Service of Supply) for support functions; and the Army Air Force (AAF). Before this time, the aviation arm had been just one more branch in the Army, and was known as the Army Air Corps.[12]

Many believed the AAF's unique status demanded it be separated from the ground troops. However, during World War II, the AAF served as a part of the Army. Some aspects of the actual flying organizations, however, were specific to them. The various numbered Air Forces (such as 8th Air Force, for example) are best considered as similar to field armies. (See Appendix E for more info on the Army Air Force.)

Each branch of the Army had its own insignia that was worn on the collar of a dress uniform. Officers wore the insignia without a backing, while enlisted men wore theirs with a solid circular backing. This allowed other soldiers to instantly know a man's specialty. Each branch also had its own color or color combination, which was worn on the hat cord of the campaign hat (Boy Scout type). In World War II, this was generally seen on the piping of enlisted men's caps.

Each branch of service had one or more special schools, within which men were trained in their military specialty. They were also involved in developing equipment, doctrine, and organizations related to their specific areas.

Unlike the pre-war days, the War Department headquarters could overrule branch chiefs, but the manner in which the men were trained and the doctrines developed were generally quite effective.

For the most part, men in a branch-specific unit (such as an infantry regiment or signal company) were all from the same branch. For example, the radiomen in an infantry regiment and the artillerymen in the infantry regiment cannon company were all from the same branch of service. They were all infantrymen—not Signal Corps men and artillerists brought in for their special talents. Thus, the Signal Corps might oversee the development and procurement of communications equipment, and coordinate training for men from other branches.

Medics proved the primary exception to this rule. They were attached to almost every unit, but remained part of the Medical Corps.

THE MAJOR BRANCH SCHOOLS IN WORLD WAR II	
Infantry School	Fort Benning, GA
Artillery School	Fort Sill, OK
Armored School	Fort Knox, KY
Engineer School	Fort Belvoir, VA
Adjutant General School	Camp Lee, VA
Chaplain School	Harvard University / Fort. Devens, MA
Chemical Warfare School	Edgewater Arsenal, MD
Medical Field Service School	Carlisle Barracks, PA
Provost Marshall General School (MP)	Fort Oglethorpe, GA / Fort Custer, MI
Ordnance School	Aberdeen, MD
Signal School	Fort Monmouth, NJ
Transportation School	Fort Eustis, VA

THE COMBAT BRANCHES

The Infantry

The infantryman (the Army's "common soldier"), carried a rifle or machine gun and slogged his way across the battlefields on foot. The infantry is often called the "Queen of Battle," an apt comparison to the most powerful piece on a chess board. These were the men who lived on the ground in every sort of weather imaginable. They did the bulk of the fighting and dying. Their mission was to find and kill or capture the enemy. The infantry included specialized troop types like paratroops (airborne infantry), glider troops, rangers, mountain troops, and so forth.

The main administrative unit of the infantry was the company. Each company numbered around 184 men and was commanded by a captain. The Infantry's branch color was light blue.

The branch insignia worn by all infantrymen was a set of crossed muskets. During World War I, an attempt was made to update the muskets to reflect more modern weapons, but it was finally decided to keep the traditional insignia. The Army did not want to establish a precedent for changing the insignia every time a new rifle was developed.

The standard infantry unit is the regiment. The regiment was the repository of the unit history and honors. A numbered infantry unit, such as 28th Infantry, for example, referred to an infantry regiment. Infantrymen were called "Doughboys" during World War I. During World War II, an infantryman was commonly referred to as a G.I. (short for Government Issue). Another popular (though today not as well known) nickname was "the PBI," for "the poor bloody infantry." The infantry shouldered the brunt of the fighting throughout the war and suffered far more casualties than any other branch.

BOOK NOTES

An excellent overview of the infantry in World War II is the three-book series: *US Infantryman in World War II*, by Robert Rush, Osprey Publishing, Oxford, UK, 2002, ISBNs 1-84176-330-6, 1-84176-331-4 and 1-84176-332-2

Infantry memoirs: *Company Commander*, by Charles McDonald, Burford Books, 1989, ISBN 1-58080-038-6, and *Roll Me Over*, by Raymond Gantter, Presidio Press, Novato, CA, 1997, 0-8041-1605-9

For glider troops: *Silent Wings*, by Gerald Devlin, St Martin's Press, New York, 1987, ISBN 0-312-72460-8

For paratroops: *Vanguard of the Crusade*, by Mark Bando, The Aberjona Press, Bedford, PA, 2003, ISBN 0-9717650-0-6

For infantry weapons: *US Infantry Weapons of World War II*, by Bruce Canfield, Andrew Mowbray, Lincoln, RI, 1996, ISBN 0-917218-67-1

For rangers: *Rangers in World War II*, by Robert Black, Presidio Press, Novato, CA, 2001, ISBN 0-8041-0565-0

There were only six official Ranger battalions (numbered one through six) in World War II. They were highly trained infantry units. The 1st, 3d, and 4th battalions served in the Mediterranean Theater; the 2d and 5th in the Northern ETO; and the 6th in the Pacific Theater.

A number of soldiers passed through what they called "Ranger training." This was a form of advanced infantry training, but the men were not considered true Rangers. The Second Army Ranger School at Camp Forrest, Tennessee awarded a small embroidered tab with the word "Ranger" in white letters on a red background to everyone who graduated from the "unofficial" Ranger program. This was worn beneath the standard division shoulder sleeve insignia as a mark of advanced training.

The Artillery

In 1907, the Artillery was subdivided into two elements: Field Artillery, which was responsible for manning guns in land battles, and the Coastal Artillery, whose artillerists manned the large guns protecting the American coastline.

The Artillery's main administrative unit was the battery, which was the equivalent of the infantry company. A battery was composed of roughly 100 men and commanded by a captain. The headquarters company was known as the headquarters battery. The standard artillery unit was the regiment. In 1940, the regiments were broken up, and during World War II a numbered artillery unit (such as the 26th Artillery) was referred to as an artillery battalion. Artillery battalions averaged 500 men each.

There were three primary types of artillery used during the war: guns, howitzers, and mortars. Guns fired at a relatively flat trajectory and were normally sighted directly on the target (i.e., using direct fire techniques). Mortars fired in a high arc and were used to shoot over buildings, trees, or other obstructions. Howitzers composed the bulk of the artillery used during World War II. Like mortars, they fired in an arc, though their range was much farther than any mortar. More often than not, howitzers and mortars utilized "indirect fire," which meant the targets were not in the direct line of sight of the gun crew.

The power of an artillery unit varied significantly depending upon the type of weapon used. As a result, after the official unit

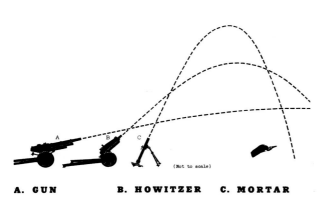

(Not to scale)

A. GUN   B. HOWITZER   C. MORTAR

designation, artillery units were generally referred to by the type of weapon and method of transportation. Two examples include the 250th Field Artillery Battalion (105mm How-Trk-D), or the 265th Field Artillery Battalion (240mm How Trac-D). The 105mm howitzer was a truck-drawn unit, while the 240mm howitzer was a tractor-drawn unit. The abbreviations used to describe the method of transport are as follows:

Horse-D	Horse Drawn
Pack	Packed on mules
Trk-D	Truck Drawn
Trac-D	Track Drawn
SP	Self Propelled

Forward Observers (FOs) were men sent from a battery to the front lines to direct artillery fire. They served alongside the infantry but were never considered part of the infantry unit. The FO observed the target and sent back information across phone lines or via radio to the Fire Direction Center (FDC). This unit used complicated mathematical formulas to instruct the firing batteries on the proper elevation of the guns and the precise direction of the target. FOs had the most hazardous assignment in the Artillery. Because they were up front with the infantry, they had to expose themselves to find enemy targets and were often killed as a result.

Artillery weapons ranged in size from 75mm to 240mm. The two most common sizes of artillery used in World War II were 105mm and 155mm howitzers. Most guns were towed by trucks or tractors, but some were mounted on tracked vehicles and known as self-propelled guns (SPs, or SPGs). The Army put fewer heavy weapons into service because it believed aerial bombardment could handle that job more efficiently than artillery.

The 75mm pack howitzer could be taken apart, and each part carried by an individual or by mule or horse. Although few initially believed these guns would find profitable employment in modern warfare, the pack howitzer proved extremely valuable in the mountains of Italy and in the jungles of the Pacific. The 60mm and 81mm mortars were used in the infantry units, and the larger 4.2-inch chemical mortar was used by chemical warfare units. There were few artillery units armed with mortars, but those that were carried the Army's largest mortar: the 914mm "Little David," which was never used in combat.

An unusual unit was the 771st Field Artillery. This ETO battalion was equipped with captured German and French guns ranging in size from 88mm to 155mm.Using captured weapons and ammunition meant that less material had to be shipped overseas to Europe. By the end of the war, there were even a few artillery units using 4.5-inch rockets.

There were also observation battalions. These did not have any firepower, but were instead units equipped to coordinate and direct the fire of multiple artillery battalions. Aside from visual observation, they used flash and sound ranging, which plotted the direction of enemy gun flashes and used the time delay in sound to provide distance.

Of all the Army ground units, the Artillery was the only one that had its own aircraft. Many Artillery units had two light planes known as spotter, or liaison, aircraft. These small planes (similar to today's Piper Cubs) were used to observe enemy activities and to direct the fire of friendly guns. These aircraft explain why pilots and air medals are found amongst ground unit troops.

The branch insignia for the Field Artillery is a set of crossed cannons. The nickname for artillerists was "redlegs," which alluded to the red stripes (the branch color) that used to be worn on their trousers.

Coast Artillery (Antiaircraft Artillery)

Until World War II, the Coast Artillery was considered one of the most important branches of service because it was the first line of defense against an invasion of the American homeland. With the realization that air power could defend the country far better than fort-mounted cannon, the Coast artillery rapidly declined in status.

In World War I, anti-aircraft fire was assigned to the Coast Artillery because its gunners had the most experience firing at moving targets. These units were called anti-aircraft artillery (AAA) and used heavy guns and machine guns, supported by searchlights, to shoot down enemy aircraft.

Shoulder Sleeve Insignia of the 1st–4th Coast Artillery, the 9th Coast Artillery, the Hawaiian Coast Artillery Brigade, and Hawaiian Coastal Defense Command.

Shoulder Sleeve Insignia of the Eastern, Central, Southern and Western Antiaircraft Commands.

By 1944, the German Luftwaffe was nearly destroyed and viewed as much less of a threat than at the beginning of the war. Therefore, many anti-aircraft units were retrained as infantry replacements. More than 250 AAA units were disbanded during the war to provide replacements for other units.

It is interesting to note that the Coast Artillery had its own small naval force called the Mine Planter Service. This group was responsible for deploying mines in defense of American harbors.

The Coast Artillery was rolled into the Field Artillery in 1950. Seven years later, a new branch, the Air Defense Artillery, was formed. This new branch took charge of developments in missiles because its main purpose was to shoot down enemy aircraft.

The Coast Artillery wore crossed cannons with an artillery shell in the center. The branch color was also red.

The Cavalry

The Cavalry was the third major combat branch in the Army (the other two being Infantry and Artillery). By the late 1930s, the era of horse cavalry had essentially reached its end. The branch insignia of crossed sabers denoted a time when cavalrymen charged the enemy and fought from the saddle. Their yellow branch color echoed the old cavalry scarves worn on the American frontier. The majority of World War II cavalrymen served on lightly armored fast vehicles, such as armored cars. The cavalry company was traditionally known as a "troop," and used mainly for reconnaissance purposes.

Cavalry squadrons were known as either horse or mecz (mechanized) units. There were two cavalry divisions in World War II: the 1st Division, which saw action in the Pacific Theater, and the 2d Division, which was sent to North Africa. Neither used horses in combat.

The job of mechanized cavalry units was primarily to scout for information. They were also used to patrol areas manned by few troops to make sure the enemy had not entered the area. "Screening an area" meant forming motorized patrols to keep enemy units from entering a region undiscovered.

The mainstay of the cavalry during World War II was the M-8 armored car armed with a 37mm gun.

This six-wheeled vehicle was lightly armored, but its fast speed made it perfect for reconnaissance roles.

National Archives

The Armored Command

The history of tanks in the Army is a long and complicated one. Initially created as a separate arm (the Tank Corps) in World War I, not a single American-built tank saw combat service during the conflict. The early tankers rode into battle in both British and French-made tanks. After the war, tanks were assigned as support weapons to the infantry and their separate branch status was rescinded.

When the Germans invaded Poland, the Low Countries, and France in 1939–1940, the world suddenly sat up and took notice that massed tanks were the future of land warfare. In a scramble to prepare for the inevitable, the Americans began developing an armored force organized along the lines of the Air Force. Armored divisions were placed under Armored Corps (with a similar shoulder insignia, but with Roman numerals to designate the number of the Armored Corps). The theory was that infantry would hold the front, while tanks were massed at specific locations to break through the enemy line. Experiments in field maneuvers, however, demonstrated that combined forces of infantry and armor were more effective. The result was that the use of Armored Corps was discarded in August 1943 in favor of a more flexible integrated system.

When the armored force concept was done away with, the tank branch headquarters was renamed the Armored Command, and later to the Armored Center. Armor was not considered a full branch of its own until 1950, though it was more or less treated as a separate branch during World War II. Men trained in a different branch of service adopted the Armor insignia as if it was a regular combat arm.

The Army also used amphibian tank battalions during World War II. The amphibian tractor units used amphibious tracked vehicles to carry troops over coral reefs and onto land. Amphibious tank units used tanks equipped with a flotation device (such as the Duplex Drive "DD" tanks used in Normandy) and an amphibious tracked vehicle with a tank turret attached.

Light tank units were normally composed of the M3 or M5 Stuart. The majority of tank units were considered "medium" and equipped with the M4 Sherman. Note that there were two M3 tanks: one was an M3 Stuart light tank, the other an M3 Grant medium tank. There were dozens of items used in the Army designated "M3." All this meant was that the item in question was the third official version (third model=M3). There were even more items officially designated "M1," but this term is primarily applied today to the M1 Garand Rifle.

The major armor unit was an Armored division, although there were a number of independent tank battalions that could be shuttled around as needed. The administrative unit was a company. Tank crews were similar to an infantry squad (four or five men commanded by an NCO). Four or five tanks made up a tank platoon under the command of a lieutenant. Armored units used infantry-style unit terminology instead of cavalry terms like "troop" because of their previous close association with the Infantry. Tankers wore an insignia of a side view of a World War I trapezoidal tank and used the colors green and white.

One of the major criticisms of American tanks in World War II was that they were not as powerful as their German counterparts. One reason is that, unlike the Germans, every single American vehicle had to be light enough to be transported by sea to get into combat. Here an American Sherman drives off the bow ramp of an LST (Landing Ship Tank). American tanks, however, were far more reliable and mechanically sound than German models.   National Archives

---

BOOK NOTES:

Forward Observers: *FO: Enemy North, South, East, West*, by Robert Weiss, Strawberry Hill Press, 1989, ISBN 0-8940712-3-8

Liaison Aircraft: *Janey: A little Plane in a Big War*, by Alfred W. Schultz, Southfarm Press, 1988, ISBN 0-9133373-1-5

For the story of armored field artillery: *Honor Untarnished: A West Point Graduate's Memoir of World War II*, by Donald V. Bennett, St Martin's Press, New York, 2003, ISBN 0-7653-0657-3

British and American Artillery of World War II, by Ian Hogg, Greenhill Books, London, 2002, ISBN1-85367-478-8

Mortar units: *You Can't Get Much Closer Than This: Combat With Company H, 317th Infantry Regiment, 80th Division*, by A.Z. Adkins, Jr. and Andrew Z. Adkins, III, Casemate, Havertown, PA, 2005, ISBN 1-932033-28-9

Books on the early days of the cavalry in World War II: *First to Warn*, by George Koch, 2001, and *The Twilight of the U.S. Cavalry* by Lucian Truscott III, University Press of Kansas, 1989, ISBN 0-7006-0403-0

For more information on the sometimes confusing organization of Armored units: *US Armored Divisions*, by Steven Zaloga, Osprey Publishing, Oxford, UK, 2004, ISBN 1-84176-564-3

For info on tank maintenance units: *Death Traps* by Belton Cooper, Presidio Press, New York, 2003, ISBN 0-89141-814-8

SERVICE BRANCHES

Adjutant General's Department

The Adjutant General's (AG's) office was the Army's administrative arm. It handled the correspondence and printing of publications, such as manuals and regulations. It also was in charge of personnel assignments, recruiting, the Army postal system, and historical and personnel records. For a few years before World War I, the AG was known as the "Military Secretary's Department."

The AG's office was in charge of printing all the forms and paperwork used by the Army. Army forms were known by their AGO number (i.e., AGO Form number 21). In 1946, it was renamed the Adjutant General's Corps.

The branch insignia is a red, white, and blue shield representing the shield of the coat of arms of the USA. The branch color was dark blue piped with scarlet.

The Corps of Chaplains

Chaplains provided for the spiritual needs of the men. Every unit from a regiment up has its own chaplain, and roughly one chaplain was authorized per 1,200 men. Most services were non-denominational, but the Army attempted to provide a good mix of chaplains so Jewish, Catholic, or Protestant chaplains would be available if needed. The number of Army chaplains reached its peak of 8,171 in July 1945.

A Chaplain holds a religious service in a field somewhere in France. His assistant plays a foot-powered field organ. Chaplains were allowed to wear the Red Cross armband to indicate their status as a non-combatant. National Archives

Although there were no Muslim or Buddhist chaplains in World War II, there were clergy from many of the minor Christian sects. The majority of chaplains were Roman Catholic (2,278), followed by Methodist (1,200). Some of the smaller sects represented in the war included Latter Day Saints, Christian Scientist, Unitarians, Quakers, and Greek Orthodox.[13] Chaplains were expected to provide nondenominational services for all soldiers, and provide aid and comfort to anyone, no matter what his religion.

Chaplains were graduates of a theological college or seminary, certified by their particular denomination, and ideally had at least three years of experience. Every chaplain was a commissioned officer and was at least a 1st lieutenant. No enlisted men served in the Corps of Chaplains. Chaplains also performed other morale building duties, such as running clubs and libraries. For insignia, Christian chaplains wore a cross and a Jewish rabbi wore a double tablet bearing the Roman numerals I through X. The branch of service color was black.

> BOOK NOTES
>
> *Battlefield Chaplains: Catholic Priests in World War II* by Donald Crosby, University Press of Kansas, 1996, ISBN 0-7006-0814-1

The Chemical Warfare Service

These troops originated with the use of gas warfare in World War I. Although poison gas was not used in combat during World War II, the Chemical Warfare Service (CWS) was an important part of maintaining a defense against possible enemy gas usage. Its existence posed a threat to the enemy by implication alone: if the Axis used gas, the Allies were prepared to retaliate in kind. The CWS oversaw production and distribution of more than 35,000,000 military and civilian gas masks during the war.

The main combat use of CWS troops during World War II was providing smoke screens and operating 4.2-inch chemical mortars. These weapons were designed to shoot chemical rounds and were used in combat to great effect by firing regular explosive and white phosphorus rounds. In 1946, the CWS was redesignated the Chemical Corps. Men serving in the CWS wore a blue six-sided benzene ring over a pair of retorts (chemical flasks) as their insignia, and used cobalt blue and yellow as their branch color.

In combat the two main roles of the Chemical Corps were manning the 4.2 inch mortars, and creating smoke screens as seen here. Smoke, created by burning oil, was used to conceal ground targets from aircraft, as well as providing concealment for ground operations such as river crossings. National Archives.

> BOOK NOTES
>
> *The Chemical Warfare Service: Organizing for War*, by Leo P. Brophy, *The Chemical Warfare Service: From Laboratory to Field*, by Leo P. Brophy, Office of the Chief of Military History, 1959
>
> *The Chemical Warfare Service: Chemicals in Combat*, by Brooks E. Kleber, Office of the Chief of Military History, 1959

The Corps of Engineers

One of the oldest branches of American service, the Engineers have the distinction of being the only branch of service to have their own button design. All Army officers wear the same button with the great seal of the United States except for engineer officers, who are allowed to wear the traditional Engineer design. Army Engineers played many important roles in the war. Not only were they in charge of military construction (both at home and overseas), but they also served in combat engineer units that saw heavy action and suffered high casualty rates.

Engineers built bridges, cleared and planted land mines, constructed roads and airstrips, and cleared ports. Combat engineers were often in the thick of things, lifting mines while under fire, setting demolition charges, and at times they even served as infantry. Engineer units drafted maps and developed camouflage materials. Traditionally, the top graduates from West Point were commissioned into the Engineers.

Engineers also took part in many civilian engineering activities, such as flood control and dredging inland waterways. They also oversaw the expensive and top secret projects, like building the atomic bomb. The insignia of the Engineers was a three-turreted castle and the branch color scarlet and white.

BOOK NOTES

The Corps of Engineers: Troops and Equipment, by Blanche D. Coll, Office of the Chief of Military History, 1958

The Corps of Engineers: Construction in the United States, by Lenore Fine, United States Government Printing, 1994, ISBN 0-16-001919-2

The Corps of Engineers: The War Against Germany, by Alfred M. Beck, University Press of the Pacific, 2004, ISBN 1-41020-138-4

The Corps of Engineers: The War Against Japan, by Karl C. Dod, Center of Military History, U.S. Army, 1987

The Finance Department

These were the paymasters of the Army. The Finance Department handled all the financial transactions, whether paying the troops or paying for equipment. They also handled all the paperwork involved in sending money home to a soldier's family. They checked over contracts and made sure the Army was getting the best possible deal for its money. During World War II, this department was charged with helping the government's war bonds program. In its peak year of 1943, the Finance Department sold more than $127,000,000 in bonds.[14]

It also oversaw the life insurance program, which offered soldiers a $10,000 policy—the only one that would insure a soldier in combat. In 1950, this department was renamed the Finance Corps.

The Inspector General's Department

This agency performed fact-finding missions for the Army. It did not make decisions or set policy. Instead, it inspected, investigated, and reported as required. The goal of the department was to keep the Army functioning smoothly. This office conducted investigations when an individual was accused of a crime, and conducted audits of the weapons in an armory.

The branch insignia was a laurel wreath bearing the inscription "Droit et Avant" (right and forward) superimposed upon a crossed sword and fasces. The fasces (a bundle of reeds around an axe), is a traditional symbol of law and power dating back to the Roman Empire. Its colors were dark blue and white.

The Judge Advocate General's Department

This group, whose lawyers are commonly referred to as JAGs, was (and is) the Army's legal team. Members of the department oversaw everything legal in the Army and made sure justice was done and the laws followed. They handled legal matters of all kinds, from contractual disputes with civilian companies to problems with Army real estate, criminal prosecutions and defenses, and even the patents of equipment the Army would like to adopt for use.

> **BOOK NOTES**
>
> For a fascinating look at a famous military trial regarding abuse at the 10th replacement depot in England is *Litchfield: The U.S. Army on Trial*, by Jack Gieck, University of Akron Press, Ohio, 1997, ISBN 1-884836-27-5

Military personnel were governed by an entirely different set of regulations than civilians. These regulations were found in the Uniform Code of Military Justice (UCMJ). Not every court-martial had a JAG officer present, but every such trial was reviewed by one to make sure the rules were followed and the actions taken were legal and justified. JAG officers wore the insignia of a crossed sword and pen superimposed over an open laurel wreath. The branch colors were dark blue and light blue.

Military Police Corps

Before World War II, Military Police (MPs) were locally assigned from whatever troops were available on-site. The Military Police Corps, which had been in existence since it was initially developed in World War I, was officially reformed in August 1941.

These men served as the law enforcement branch of the Army. They patrolled bases and local cities, investigated crimes, provided security forces, and guarded POWs. Provost Marshal is the military term for chief of police. The commanding officer of any MP unit is known as the provost marshal of the area under his jurisdiction. In combat zones, an MP's primary task was directing traffic and providing information to men in search of specific units. Some of the rear-echelon MP units were disliked by the troops for their insistence on fol-

Military Policemen preparing for the invasion of Normandy wear the MP armband and MP markings on their helmets.

The yellow band on the helmet signified an MP attached to a division, while a white band indicated a non-divisional MP.

National Archives

lowing regulations, but the MPs of a combat unit were generally well regarded after they were seen directing traffic or manning their posts under heavy artillery fire. Like a policeman's badge, the MP armband (white letters on dark blue) indicated the soldier's official status. From time to time, non-MPs were assigned similar duties and were authorized to wear the MP armband. Their insignia was crossed flintlock pistols and their colors were yellow piped with green (this was reversed in 1951 to accommodate armor also using yellow and green).

A group associated with the MPs but not part of the Military Police was the Counter Intelligence Corps (or CIC). The CIC often worked with MP units. It was tasked with fighting and countering enemy spying activities. Members of the CIC rarely wore official uniforms and insignia.

BOOK NOTES

For information on the Counter Intelligence Corps, see: *America's Secret Army*, by Ian Sayer, Harper Collins, New York, 1997, ISBN 0006369863

The Ordnance Department

These men designed, purchased, and fixed the Army's weapons, ammunition, and explosives. Until August 1941, the Ordnance Corps was only responsible for armed vehicles, such as tanks and armored cars.

After that date, the Army transferred authority over every type of vehicle from the Quartermaster Corps to the Ordnance Department. It oversaw the gigantic budget spent on ammunition and explosive plants during World War II, a sum that exceeded three billion dollars.

After the war, this department was renamed the Ordnance Corps. Its insignia was a flaming bomb, and the branch color was crimson piped with yellow.

The Quartermaster Corps

The Quartermaster Corps (QMC) fed, clothed, and supplied the Army. It bought the food that was cooked in Army mess halls and bakeries, designed and issued uniforms, equipment, and everything from wastepaper baskets to fire hoses. More importantly, it made sure that the needed supplies arrived and were issued where and when they were needed. In World War II, the QMC oversaw the handling of more than 70,000 different items.

Quartermasters were initially responsible for the Army's construction program of bases and facilities, but that was transferred to the Corps of Engineers early in the war. Quartermasters, however, continued to be responsible for the operation of bases and camp facilities, such as laundries and heating plants.

Quartermasters also operated bathing and delousing stations, refrigeration stations, remount depots (for the few horses and mules required), and sold off items surplus to the Army's need. The QMC was also responsible for all burial functions, which included everything from locating bodies in the field, identifying and interring them overseas, and eventually bringing many of them back to the States.

The Quartermaster insignia was a crossed sword and key superimposed on a wheel and surmounted by an eagle. The key alludes to control of supplies and the wheel to their distribution. Their branch color was buff.

BOOK NOTES

The Ordnance Department: Planning and Munitions for War, by Constance McLaughlin Green, Office of the Chief of Military History, Dept. of the Army, 1990

The Ordnance Department: Procurement and Supply, by Harry C. Thomson, Office of the Chief of Military History, Dept. of the Army, 1990

The Ordnance Department: On Beachhead and Battlefront, by Lida Mayo, Office of the Chief of Military History, Dept. of the Army, 1991

The Quartermaster Corps: Organization, Supply, And Services, Volume I & II, by Erna Risch, Office of the Chief of Military History, Dept. of the Army, 1988

The Quartermaster Corps: Operations in the War Against Japan, by Alvin P. Stauffer, Office of the Chief of Military History, Dept. of the Army, 1956

The Quartermaster Corps: Operations in the War Against Germany, by William F. Ross, Office of the Chief of Military History, Dept. of the Army, 1956

The Signal Corps

The Signal Corps ran all Army communications around the world, whether by radio, telephone, teletype, or carrier pigeon. It also oversaw the design and operation of all communications equipment, including all code machines.

Its members made sure that proper training was provided to non-Signal Corps men who would be operating communications equipment.

The US Army's radio equipment was by far the best used during World War II. Radio, however, was still in its infancy and often unreliable. The majority of communications during the war were conducted via telephone, and every unit needed a good switchboard operator.

The Signal Corps was also in charge of Army photography and cinematography. The men who served in the Signal Corps, many of whom had good civilian careers before the war, documented the war in both color and black and white photos and movies.

The insignia of the Signal Corps was a set of crossed signal flags superimposed over a flaming torch. Their branch color was orange and white.

BOOK NOTES

The Signal Corps: The Emergency (To December 1941), by Dulany Terrett.

The Signal Corps: The Test (December 1941 To July 1943), by George Raynor Thompson.

The Signal Corps: The Outcome (Mid-1943 Through 1945), by George Raynor Thompson

For info on Combat Photographers, *Armed With Cameras*, by Peter Maslowski, The Free Press, New York, 1998, ISBN 0-684-86398-7

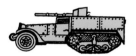

The Tank Destroyer Command

While not actually a branch of service, the Tank Destroyers (TDs) had their own insignia of a halftrack with 75mm gun (the first tank destroyer) and orange and black branch color. The TDs were initially towed anti-tank guns and grew out of the artillery. Some TD units had halftrack-mounted guns in the first part of the war, and later moved to high powered open-topped tanks designed for their specific purpose. TD battalions were designated as either being towed or self propelled (SP).

There were many Tank Destroyer units with their weapons mounted on a tracked chassis, but many of the battalions relied on towed guns, like this of the 614th Tank Destroyer Battalion (colored).

The tracked vehicles offered greater mobility, but the towed guns were cheaper and easier to produce, and packed the same punch when confronted with German tanks.　　　　National Archives

The TDs were the result of the theory that the average tank should not fight other tanks; instead, they should be used to break through enemy lines and leave anti-tank fighting to a specialist group. Substantial debate has ensued about whether this was the right idea, but it was the doctrine the Army employed during World War II. After the war, the TD concept vanished and the units were shifted into the Armor branch.

BOOK NOTES

For a short history of Tank Destroyers, *The Tank Killers*, by Harry Yeide, Casemate, Havertown PA, 2005, ISBN 1-932033-26-2

The Transportation Corps

The Transportation Division was organized in August 1942. This branch was in charge of moving men and material to where they were supposed to go. It managed all Army shipments by road, rail, or water, and operated all related facilities, such as the ports of embarkation.

In July 1942, the Transportation Division was renamed the Transportation Corps (TC). At the same time, all transport by air was transferred to the Army Air Force.

Some of the common Transportation Corps units were port battalions, which operated seaport facilities both in the States and abroad; rail units, which repaired and operated railroads overseas; and transportation companies composed of trucks that moved men and supplies over the roads.

One of the more interesting aspects of the TC involved the ocean-going transports they operated. By the end of the war, the TC was running 186 ships of various descriptions, including troopships, freighters, hospital ships, tankers, tugs, and floating warehouses.[15]

Prior to the war, Army vessels were under the jurisdiction of the Army Transport Service (which wore uniforms similar to the Navy). In 1942, however, these ships were amalgamated into the Transportation Corps.

Transport ships under the command of the Transportation Corps had the prefix U.S.A.T. (United States Army Transport). An example of this was the U.S.A.T. *George Washington*, the largest troop transport operated by the Army.

Its insignia was a shield bearing a winged car wheel on a rail, all superimposed on a ship's wheel. The branch color was brick red and yellow

Army Transport Service button worn by their ship-going personnel

---

BOOK NOTES

Life in a Port Company in the Pacific: *Between Tedium and Terror*, by Sy Kahn, University of Illinois Press, 1993, ISBN: 0-25201-858-3

For railway operations: *Steel Rails to Victory*, by Ron Zeil, Random House Value Publishing, 0-5171-4877-3

The Transportation Corps: Responsibilities, Organization, And Operations, by Chester Wardlow. Office of the Chief of Military History, Dept. of the Army, 1951

The Transportation Corps: Movements, Training, And Supply, by Chester Wardlow. Office of the Chief of Military History, Dept. of the Army, 1956

The Transportation Corps: Operations Overseas, by Joseph Bykofsky, Office of the Chief of Military History, Dept. of the Army, 1956

THE MEDICAL DEPARTMENT

World War II was the first conflict fought by the United States in which disease did not kill more soldiers than the enemy. This was due largely to the efforts of the Medical Service, not only in caring for the wounded, but in preventing all manner of illnesses.

The US Army had arguably the best medical care in the world during the war. Deaths from wounds totaled only 4.5 %, compared to 14.1% in the Civil War.[16] The senior officer of a medical unit was traditionally known as a surgeon. This was a generic term for the physician in charge, even if he was not an actual surgeon capable of performing operations. The chief medical officer of the Army was (and is) the Surgeon General.

A major task of the Medical Department was running the plethora of hospitals around the world that took care of sick and wounded soldiers. The central Army hospital was Walter Reed General Hospital, located outside Washington DC. Facilities with names like Walter Reed had fixed locations; numbered units were considered mobile, if need be.

The Medical Department was different from the other branches of service as some of its troops were assigned to units from other branches. The only non-infantrymen in an infantry regiment were the section of attached medical personnel. Most units had a few medics attached to take care of the men. In combat units, there were generally one or two medics or "aid men" per company.

The insignia of the Medical Department is the caduceus: the traditional medical insignia. It is derived from the classical winged staff of Mercury with entwined snakes. Although no one is really sure where this design came from, some believe it may have originated from an ancient remedy for a worm-like parasite that was removed from under the skin by twisting it out on a stick. The color for all sections of the Medical Department was maroon and white. The sections of the Medical Department included:

The Medical Corps

The Medical Corps was composed of the medical doctors (always an officer) and medical enlisted men. They were the basic medical personnel for the Army. The officers included general practitioners, surgeons, psychiatrists, radiologists, and other specialized physicians. These men wore a plain caduceus as their branch insignia.

> **BOOK NOTES**
>
> The best overall summary of the Medical Corps in World War II is. *Fighting for Life* by Albert Cowdry, The Free Press, New York, 1994, ISBN 0029068355
>
> An excellent book on the life of a battalion aid station. *Long Walk though War* by Klaus Huebner, Texas A&M University Press, 1987, ISBN 158544023X

The Dental Corps

The Dental Corps was just what it sounds like— the organization responsible for caring for the Army's teeth. Soldiers in combat or stationed at the front ran a large risk of developing dental problems because they could not brush their teeth regularly, if at all. Many teeth that had cavities were filled near the front lines by dentists using foot-pumped drills.

An unusual sideline of many World War II dentists was providing soldiers with replacement glass eyes. Making glass eyes was a time-consuming process. It was discovered, however, that the same skills and materials necessary for working with teeth allowed dentists to make plastic eyes better and faster than conventional glass methods. The men serving in the Dental Corps wore the medical caduceus with the letter "D."

The Veterinary Corps

These men were in charge of all the Army's animals, which were mainly horses and mules. They were also in charge of inspecting food purchased for the Army, since it was thought that a veterinarian would be the best person to inspect meat to see if it came from a sick animal. Army veterinarians wore the medical caduceus with the letter "V."

The Medical Administrative Corps

Trained doctors were scarce, so these medically trained specialists were formed to handle administrative tasks to allow the doctors to treat patients. Doctors were in such short supply that midway through the war battalion aid stations were cut from two doctors to one doctor and one medical administrative officer. These men wore the medical caduceus with the letter "A."

Army Nurse Corps

The Army Nurse Corps (ANC) provided the female nursing staff for hospitals. Until the establishment of the Women's Army Corps (WAC), this was the only way women could serve with the Army. They wore different uniforms and insignia than the WACs. Nurses are always commissioned officers; there were no enlisted women in the Nurse Corps. Included in the ANC were female dieticians and physical therapy aides. Nurses in the ANC wore the medical caduceus with the letter "N." There were 59,000 ANC nurses in World War II.

Half of them volunteered to be sent overseas and into possible combat zones. Of these, 16 were killed by enemy action and more than 70 were captured by the Japanese (most as a result of the surrender in the Philippines).[17]

BOOK NOTES:

On nurses in World War II, see:
And If I Perish, by Evelyn Monahan,
Knopf, New York, 2003,
ISBN 0375415149

Before the war, nursing ranks were considered "relative" to an officer's rank, meaning that they were not looked upon or valued in the same way. This was adjusted in December 1941 and from that point forward, nurses held standard ranks and enjoyed the same pay as men for the duration of the war and for six months afterward.

NURSE TITLE	RANK RELATIVE TO	NURSE TITLE AFTER 10 DECEMBER 1941	RANK EQUIVALENT
Head Nurse & Nurse	2d Lieutenant	Nurse	2d Lieutenant
Chief Nurse	1st Lieutenant	Chief Nurse	1st Lieutenant
Asst. Superintendent, Director	Captain	Asst. Director	Captain
Superintendent	Major	Asst. Superintendent	Lt. Colonel, Major, Captain
		Superintendent	Colonel

Pharmacy Corps

The Pharmacy Corps was created in May 1943 to handle matters relating to the development, adoption, and distribution of drugs. In 1947, it became part of the Medical Service Corps. Their medical caduceus carried the letter "P."

Sanitary Corps

Traditionally, the Medical Department of the Army was known as the Sanitary Service because of its concern with fighting disease. In the pre-war years there was still a vestige of this in the Army Reserves, which was known as the Sanitary Corps Reserve.

This was composed of health professionals and scientists who were not physicians, but involved with combating infectious disease. The Sanitary Corps Reserve was merged into the Military Administrative Corps (MAC) in 1920, but some sanitary officers were kept on the reserve rolls and shifted to the MAC when called to active duty. They wore the medical caduceus with the letter "S."

Contract Surgeons.

Civilian doctors who worked for the Army were given the title of Contract Surgeons and allowed to wear the uniform of a 1st lieutenant. This designation was primarily for female doctors who, until April 1943, were not legally allowed to hold a commission in the Army.

Medical Service Corps

This group was not active in World War II, but formed in 1947 to bring together all Pharmacy, Medical Supply and Administration, Sanitary Engineering, Optometry, and other Allied Medical Sciences.

OTHER BRANCHES

Army Air Force

Members of the AAF wore the traditional winged propeller to indicate their branch. Although often involved in combat, the AAF was not considered one of the combat arms. Organization of AAF ground units was similar to that of the rest of the Army, but the aviation units had a system all their own. (Information on the aviation elements of the AAF is found in Appendix E.)

> **BOOK NOTES**
>
> A good overview on the AAF is *Winged Victory*, by Geoffrey Perret, Random House, New York, 1993 ISBN 0679404643
>
> An excellent wartime book on the AAF is *The Official Guide to the Army Air Forces*, Army Air Forces Aid Society, 1944

The Woman's Army Corps

The Woman's Army Corps (or WAC) was one of the two female contingents in the Army (the other being the Army Nurse Corps). Many soldiers were not happy with women being allowed into the Army, but the needs of a world war called for all available manpower—even if it came in the form of a woman.

Initially, the Woman's Army Corps was known as the WAAC (Woman's Auxiliary Army Corps, established in May 1942) and was not considered part of the Army. They wore buttons with the head of Athena insignia, and their own specific officer's rank badges. Female NCOs wore a tab with "WAAC" under their rank stripes to indicate their true status. They had a peculiar hat insignia depicting an eagle, which was nicknamed the "walking buzzard."

WACs were not authorized the same pay and benefits as the men in the Army. They were considered a temporary expedient that would not continue past the

This WAAC MP wears the Walking Buzzard insignia on her "Hobby Cap."

The circular collar disks indicate an enlisted person (same as the Army) and would display the head of Athena.

Before the WAACs were brought into the Federal Army, the MP armband would be in branch colors yellow and green, as technically the woman was not a genuine soldier and thus did not have the same military police powers.

National Archives

end of the war. WACs served in many capacities, such as radio and telephone operators, photographers, lab personnel, finance specialists, and many various administrative duties. Although many served as secretaries, as the saying at the time went, every WAAC doing a job for the Army "freed a man to fight."

On July 1, 1943, the WAC was officially accepted as part of the US Army. Because the women had not enlisted into the Army, every WAC was allowed to resign and go home; few did. The head of the WACs, Col. Oveta Culp Hobby, made sure her troops were above reproach. All WAC officers were required to go through WAC Officer Candidate School. No one was allowed to gain a WAC commission on political or financial pull. There was a loophole that allowed non-US citizens to receive a direct commission. One of the handful of women given one was Kay Summersby, General Eisenhower's personal chauffeur. He arranged a WAC commission for her over the strong disagreement of Colonel Hobby.[18]

At its peak there were 100,000 WACs in uniform (6,000 of them officers). More than 17,000 WACs served overseas during the war. There were also black WAC units. The 6888th Central Postage Battalion was the only one to serve overseas, and did so with distinction in Europe.[12]

WAC insignia was the helmeted head of Athena, the Greek goddess of wisdom. The branch color was moss green and yellow.

BOOK NOTES

The Woman's Army Corps, Mattie Treadwell, Office of the Chief of Military History, Dept. of the Army, 1954

NON-BRANCH GROUPS

Some troops belonged to special groups that wore their own unique insignia in place of branch insignia on their uniforms. These men were often trained in one of the main branches, but because of their specific duties wore a different insignia. They are listed here so that they will not be confused with one of the arms or services.

Non-assigned

There were officers and enlisted men who, for one reason or another, were not assigned to a specific branch. In place of a branch insignia, they wore the seal of United States. The enlisted man's device had a solid disk backing. The officer's version was the same shape and size, but of pieced metal without a backing.

Warrant Officer

Warrant Officers were not part of a specific branch, but had their own insignia to wear on uniforms. It consisted of an eagle clutching bundles of arrows, rising from an open laurel wreath

National Guard Bureau

Formerly known as the Militia Bureau, men in the National Guard Bureau were involved in working with a state's National Guard to keep it at a high state of readiness. In March 1942, when National Guard units were federalized, this bureau was rolled into the Army Service Forces. Officers wore insignia of two crossed gold colored fasces superimposed on an eagle.

Military Intelligence Reserve

Throughout World War II, officers assigned to intelligence duties were first commissioned and trained in one of the standard branches. The insignia of a sphinx at the center of a shield was worn by the few reserve officers who had been trained in intelligence matters in World War I. They were, however, officially commissioned in one of the standard branches. The Military Intelligence Branch was created in 1952, which became the Military Intelligence Corps in 1987.

Army Bandsmen

Before the war, each regiment had its own band. This was cut to one band per division during World War II. In combat zones, these men were used for many different functions, from security troops to stretcher bearers. Army bands traditionally had their own dress uniforms, which were fancier than those worn by normal enlisted men, and wore a lyre as their branch insignia. Many units had their own semi-official band to play at functions, but the lyre was worn only by men assigned to one of the full-time official Army bands.

General's Aides

Every general was allocated a certain number of personal aides of specific rank. These men did not wear their branch insignia on their uniform, but instead wore an eagle under a red, white, and blue shield.

On the shield were one to five stars indicating the rank of the general each aide worked for. The assumption was that the aide represented the authority of the general, and this insignia made it clear to everyone that he spoke for a senior officer.

General Staff

This insignia was worn by anyone serving on the War Department General Staff. These were the officers who coordinated and conducted centralized planning for the entire Army.

U.S. Military Academy

Students and staff at West Point wore a special insignia to indicate their attachment to the school. Students at West Point were known by the rank of cadet, and expected to be commissioned as a 2d lieutenant upon graduation. They wore the shield of West Point, with helmet, scroll, and eagle above the words "duty, honor, country."

Some 8,800 graduates of the Academy took part in World War II. This number represented less than 2% of all officers who served, but 83% of all general officers.[20]

BOOK NOTES

US Military Academy: *Black '41*, by Bill Yenne, paints a portrait of the U.S.M.A. class of 1941 and what happened to those graduates in the war. Publisher: Wiley, New York, 1991, ISBN 0471541974

First Special Service Force: *Military Relations Between the United States and Canada*, 1939-1945, by Stanley Dziuban, United States Government Printing, 1991, ISBN: 0160018714 and *The Supercommandos*, by Todd Ross, Schiffer Publishing, Atglen, PA, 2000, ISBN 0764311719

First Special Service Force

Although not technically a branch, the FSSF was unique in the Army in that it had its own branch-type insignia and branch-type color. These men were a highly trained commando-like unit composed of both Canadian and American troops. Initially developed for combat in the snows of Norway, they instead saw heavy action in Italy and southern France. They wore crossed arrows (the former insignia of Indian scouts) and red, white, and blue piping (which was left over from the CMTC).

Civil Affairs

Once the fighting passed through a given area, the Army had to deal with the civilians left in the wake of combat, almost always without the benefit of a stable civilian government. Civil Affairs was not an actual branch, but rather an offshoot of the Military Police. Those involved with Military Government had their own shoulder patch.

The shoulder sleeve insignia of the First Special Service Force illustrating its combined US/Canadian origins.

Special Services Division

This was not a branch of service, although after the war it acquired its own branch-type insignia. In 1940, The Special Services Division was known as the Morale Branch, and renamed The Special Services in 1942. Men who served in the Special Services provided morale-boosting support, such as post exchanges (stores), libraries, USO galas, and motion picture shows. Special Services companies distributed music, books, and athletic equipment to the troops. Small paperback books printed specifically for the soldiers called "Armed Services Editions" were very popular with the men.

Special Services personnel helped organize anything that might boost the morale of the soldier. Their job was vastly expanded when the fighting stopped and they had to keep millions of GIs from getting bored.

Capt R.D. Rigler, of HQ Company 28th Infantry Regiment, plays ball in Luxembourg in October 1944. The Special Services troops would have been the ones to hand out the equipment for this game. National Archives

TRAINING ORGANIZATION
THE ARMY GROUND FORCE,
THE ARMY AIR FORCE AND
THE ARMY SERVICE FORCE

The Army operated on a system of strict hierarchical units. Everyone instantly knew who outranked whom, and how various sub-units fit into the big picture. Every soldier was able to trace the chain of command from himself all the way up through the War Department to the commander-in-chief—the President of the United States.

General George C. Marshall was the highest ranking Army officer in World War II. He directed the operations of the entire Army throughout the war. Marshall had a staff of officers and men to assist him in his overall decision making, but he did not directly issue orders to units in the field. The Army was structured so that decisions were made by the men best equipped to make them. This was especially important in an age where reliable worldwide communications was still in its infancy. An officer in Washington, after all, could not be expected to control every move of a unit in Germany or Japan.

To subdivide the Army into more manageable sections, the three basic non-combat components of the Army were the Army Ground Force (AGF), the Army Service Forces (ASF), and the Army Air Force (AAF). The AAF, commanded by General Henry H. ("Hap") Arnold, was in charge of developing and training all aviation elements; the AGF, commanded by General Lesley J. McNair, was in charge of developing and training the combat units; and the ASF, under General B. Brehon Sommervell, was responsible for all support functions, such as procurement, transport, supply, construction, and so on.

These three main groups were the ones that created the various units of the Army. Units inside the ZI (Zone of the Interior—the continental USA) remained under control of the AGF, ASF, or the AAF. When a unit was ready for action and

Shoulder sleeve insignia of the Army Air Forces, Army Ground Forces, and Army Service Forces.

was sent outside the USA (or to a location where possible combat might occur, such as Alaska), it was transferred to the command of that area. These three components built and trained the units, and then handed them over to someone else in a Theater of War to use in combat.

Theaters of War

Outside of the ZI, the world was divided up into three sections or theaters of war: American, Pacific, and European. These sections were further subdivided as needed into theaters of operation when combat was actually taking place in that area. Typically an area that was expected to have combat would have a command or department set up in advance to form a basis for the theater command should fighting develop there.

In the Pacific-Asiatic Theater, the three main regions included the Southwest Pacific Area commanded by General MacArthur (noted for its jungle fighting); the Central Pacific Area commanded by Admiral Nimitz (noted for its island-hopping invasions); and the China-Burma-India Theater commanded by General Joe Stillwell. The CBI held few American combat units, but was known for men building the Burma-Ledo road, flying supplies "over the hump" (the mountains between India and China), and helping to train the Chinese Nationalist forces.

The only ground combat to take place in the American theater was in the Aleutian Islands. However, anti-submarine operations took place off each coast. In the European Theater, the fighting began with the North African Theater of Operations (NATO), and then expanded to include the Mediterranean Theater of Operations (MTO). The fighting in France and northern Europe came under the European Theater of Operations (ETO).

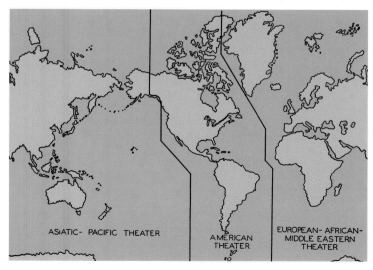

ASIATIC- PACIFIC THEATER   AMERICAN THEATER   EUROPEAN- AFRICAN- MIDDLE EASTERN THEATER

For administrative purposes the world was divided up into three main "Theaters of War."

These were broken down into Theaters of Operation as needed.

THE ARMY GROUND FORCES

Shoulder sleeve insignia of the Airborne Command.

Shoulder sleeve insignia of the Tank Destroyer Command. This patch was worn by all Tank Destroyer units in the field. There were a number of minor variations with different numbers of wheels in the track section.

Shoulder sleeve insignia of the Armored Center and independent tank battalions. This same insignia was used for Armored Corps with a Roman numeral in the top section, and for Armored Divisions with an Arabic number.

The Army Ground Forces (AGF) essentially trained units and sent them on their way to fight. Early in the war, a similar organization was known as the General Headquarters (GHQ). The GHQ was reorganized and renamed in March 1942 to become the Army Ground Forces (AGF). Once a unit was ready for action, it was sent on to another organization that would put it to use.

The easiest transfer was when a unit was sent to one of the theaters of operations (where combat was going on). An engineer battalion sent to Europe, for example, was handed over to, and followed the orders of, commanders running the ETO. If the unit remained in the USA or was sent to an area where there was no current combat, it was transferred to the control of the appropriate department.

In the ZI, a unit could be assigned to a field army designated for service in the USA, or to one of the specialist centers. For most of the war, the ZI-based armies were the 2d Field Army (based at Memphis for the Eastern part of the country), and the 4th Field Army (based at San Antonio for the western part of the country).

Specialized centers included the Mountain Training Center, Airborne Command, Tank Destroyer Center, Antiaircraft Command, Desert Training Center, the Armored Center, and the Replacement and School Command. Other commands to which a unit could be assigned included Departments (areas which may be involved in combat in the future) such as Alaska or Panama, or to one of the Service Commands within the US itself.

The Armored Center at Fort Knox, Kentucky, was where the development of tank and armored warfare took place.

The Airborne Command (primarily the Parachute School at Fort Benning, Georgia), figured out the best ways to safely land men and material via parachute from aircraft.

The Tank Destroyer Center at Camp Hood, Texas, was concerned with developing methods of destroying enemy tanks.

The Mountain Training Center was based at Camp Hale, Colorado, where snow and mountains were plentiful. This center developed and trained men how to use skis, climb mountains, live in cold climates, and use mules to move supplies across roadless terrain.

The Antiaircraft Command, based in Richmond, Virginia, was concerned with how to shoot down enemy aircraft. Not only was this center interested in antiaircraft guns, but also in barrage balloons, searchlights, and other aircraft detection techniques.

Shoulder sleeve insignia of the Antiaircraft Command.

The Desert Training Center covered a massive area in southern California and Arizona. There the officers associated with this center were free to conduct large-scale exercises without having to worry about civilians getting in the way. It did not specifically train men in desert warfare, but it was the largest (and least expensive) region where the Army could run divisions through realistic maneuvers without having to worry about broken fences or children wandering into artillery ranges.

The Amphibious Training Command was based on Cape Cod, and was used to train special brigades of engineers in how to conduct landings on an enemy shore. In late 1942, this center was moved to Camp Carrabelle, Florida, and renamed the Amphibious Training Center.

Shoulder sleeve insignia of the Army Amphibious Forces. The same design (in red) was used by Navy amphibious units.

The Replacement and School Command ran the Army schools and the replacement training centers. As soon as units left training, they needed replacements to keep them at full strength. Even in a non-combat area men were lost to illness or accident.

Without this organization, the flow of trained men would have dried up quickly. In areas where combat was possible, but not taking place, local commanders were organized to control the Army elements in the region.

Departments that became combat areas included the Philippine Department, the Hawaiian Department, and the Alaskan Command. (There was combat in the Aleutian Islands.) Other areas included the Bermuda Base Command, the Greenland Base Command, the Panama Canal Department, and Southeast Asia Command. Units could also be assigned to a temporary task force intended

Shoulder sleeve insignia of the Replacement and School Command.

Shoulder sleeve insignia of the Greenland Base Command, Bermuda Base Command, Labrador Base Command, Atlantic Base Command, and the Iceland Base Command.

for a single purpose. All of those commands, bases, theaters, and task forces reported to the Army chief of staff, and not the Army Ground Force.

Units assigned to antiaircraft work in North America were assigned to their own separate AAA commands because their job was fairly self-contained. Likewise, the various coastal artillery units along the American coasts were divided up into five defensive sectors.

There were a large number of bases, sectors, and commands, and keeping them all straight can be confusing. In essence, they were just a handy way of dividing up the work into logical geographic or functional units. For the most part, each had their own shoulder patch, which was an easy way to differentiate and identify them.

Wearing the warm weather cotton khaki uniform, you might think this photo will tell you what unit a man served in.

The swallow tailed flag is called a guidon—pronounced "guide-on"—and every company had one. The letters "RTC" stand for Replacement Training Center, and "41D" stands for a temporary unit (such as Battalion 41, Company D) that the men were assigned to while going through their training.

This designation has no connection to the unit a man would serve with after leaving the course. The only useful information is that the crossed rifles indicate this was an infantry training unit.   Author's Collection

THE ARMY AIR FORCES

The Army Air Forces (AAF) was similar to the AGF, except it prepared and trained aviation units for action. When an aviation unit was ready for duty, it was transferred to one of the commands, departments, or theaters (just like a ground unit would be). There were many different commands to oversee various functions relating to air warfare, each identified with a yellow and blue labeled tab over the shoulder patch.

Like the AGF, the AAF had US-based Air Forces (the equivalent of a field army) to control air units in the United States. When it was time to be sent to the front, air units were transferred to the various Air Forces, or some other specific air commands around the world. Because of its specialization and smaller size, the AAF was more involved with day-to-day operations of its units around the world than the AGF.

THE ARMY SERVICE FORCES

Unlike the Army Ground Forces, the Army Service Forces (formerly known as the Service of Supply) controlled units around the world and not just in the United States. The ASF was concerned with just about everything that was not directly involved in fighting. It helped develop equipment and saw that it was produced and purchased for use. It also stored supplies, transported them, and oversaw aspects of their distribution. Unless otherwise assigned to a different command, ASF men wore a red and white shoulder patch with a blue star. This gave rise to the nickname "blue star commandos."

The ASF oversaw control of the technical services (engineers, quartermasters, etc.) and the administrative services (IG, JAG etc). In theory, the ASF was supposed to provide what the local commanders needed without causing them any distraction that might interfere with ongoing combat responsibilities. Thus, from development to delivery, the ASF controlled the supply flow to the units in the field of food, weapons, uniforms, and equipment. It also ran the ports of embarkation where soldiers shipped overseas, and on the other side of the ocean reconstructed destroyed ports to unload transport ships.

The ASF divided the USA into eight geographic areas called Service Commands (with two others in Alaska and the Persian Gulf). The Service Commands were the local headquarters for all the various (non-combat related) housekeeping duties that took place in that area. These Service Commands were based on the pre-war division of the USA into corps areas of responsibility. On 2 September 1942, the corps headquarters went off to war, and Service Commands were formed to take over their military responsibilities. The Northwest Service Command, for example, was tasked with the heavy responsibility of maintaining the Army in the barren Alaskan area, and the Persian Gulf Service Command was in charge of a massive build-up of logistical units to help supply the Soviet Union across a land route through Iran.

ASF units serving in a given theater of operations normally were found behind the field armies. This rear area was known as the Communications Zone, far away from the combat.

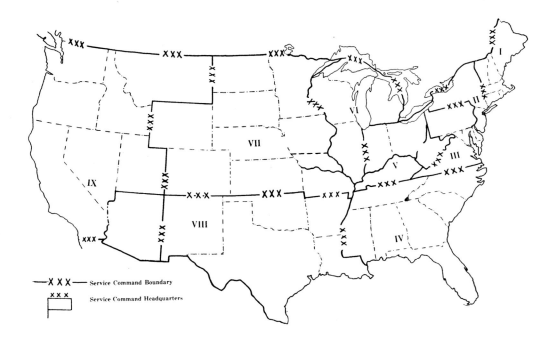

Service Command Boundaries and Headquarters.

The Service Command Headquarters are: I, Boston; II, New York; III, Baltimore; IV, Atlanta: V, Columbus: VI, Chicago: VII, Omaha; VIII, Dallas; IX, Fort Douglas, Utah; Northwest Service Command, Whitehorse, Yukon Territory, Canada.

BOOK NOTES

The Organization and Role of the Army Service Forces, by John D. Millett, Center of Military History, United States Army, 1987

RACE IN WORLD WAR II

The Army during World War II was heavily segregated. Black troops were not allowed in white units. Curiously, there was no prohibition against American Indians, Chinese, or other minorities serving in white outfits. Most of the junior, and nearly all the senior, officers in black units were white. Units to which black troops were assigned had the term "cld" or "colored" placed at the end. For example, "827th Tank Destroyer Battalion (colored)."

The vast majority of black soldiers who served during World War II did so in non-combat units. These included engineer construction units, quartermaster companies, port companies, and truck companies. However, two black infantry divisions saw action during the war: the 92d in Italy, and the 93d in the Pacific. There were also a handful of black artillery and armored units.

One amazing group of black troops was known as the Negro Volunteer Infantry. During the manpower crisis in the winter of 1944, more than 2,200 black solders volunteered to be trained and used as infantrymen. They were organized as a fourth platoon in some rifle companies and proved to be good combat troops. The

Black troops of the 92d Infantry Division are seen here on patrol in Italy. Note the shoulder sleeve insignia of a black buffalo on an olive background. This unit was the only black infantry division in the ETO, while its sister unit, the 93d Infantry Division, served in the Pacific

Library of Congress, Prints & Photographs Division, FSA-OWI Collection

BOOK NOTES

The Employment of Negro Troops, by Ulysses Lee, US Government Printing Office, 1986 & 2000

company is the standard administrative unit of the Army, and therefore these mixed companies were the first attempt at integration. Sadly, their story has never been well documented and they never received the credit they were due. At war's end they were sent back to service units—and largely forgotten.

Native Americans served in many different units of the Army. Traditionally, each tended to be nicknamed "chief." Unlike the Marine Corps, which utilized Native American languages to encode radio transmissions, the Army never did so on an official basis. In 1942 a group of Comanches was transferred to the 4th Infantry Division Signal Company to experiment with using their native tongue. The trial never went beyond this experiment, but due to the number of Comanche speakers in the unit the 4th Infantry Division unofficially used them for secure communications in Europe.

The Army was concerned, however, about enlisting Japanese-Americans in case their loyalty remained with Japan. In 1942 a group of Nisei (second generation Japanese-Americans) were formed into the 100th Infantry Battalion (separate). These men were primarily from the pre-war Hawaiian National Guard. They served with distinction in Italy, so the Army expanded the unit to form the Japanese-American 442d Infantry Regiment.

The 442d Infantry Regiment then took part in the landings in southern France. Its men fought with such tenacity that the unit is considered the most highly decorated of all US Army units in World War II. It was never an organic part of any division, but wore its own shoulder sleeve insignia. This makes it one of the only regiments to have its own shoulder sleeve insignia—it featured the Torch of Liberty.

CAMPAIGN PARTICIPATION

For the most part, the fighting in World War II was often continuous action in a large area over the course of many days, weeks, or even months. Unlike earlier wars, where men were credited with taking part in a specific battle, World War II soldiers were credited with taking part in a campaign. Every combat action was divided into campaigns covering a specific geographic area and a specific timeframe.

Every soldier who served in a particular region during a specific timeframe was credited with participation in that campaign, whether or not they saw combat.

For this reason, military records do not indicate whether a man took part in the Battle of the Bulge, Pearl Harbor, or the D-day landings. They instead indicate participation in the Ardennes-Alsace, Central Pacific, or Normandy Campaigns. Each campaign a man participated in authorized him to wear one battle, or campaign, star on that theater's ribbon.

Keep in mind that the Army and Navy have slightly different campaign lists for World War II.

Following is a list of the authorized Army campaigns in World War II. (For a short description of each campaign, see Appendix G.)

American Theater

- Antisubmarine, 7 December 1941–2 September 1945

Asiatic-Pacific Theater

- Philippine Islands, 7 December 1941–10 May 1942
- Burma, 7 December 1941–26 May 1942
- Central Pacific, 7 December 1941–6 December 1943
- East Indies, 1 January–22 July 1942
- India-Burma, 2 April 1942–28 January 1945
- Air Offensive, Japan, 17 April 1942–2 September 1945
- Aleutian Islands, 3 June 1942–24 August 1943
- China Defensive, 4 July 1942–4 May 1945
- Papua, 23 July 1942–23 January 1943
- Guadalcanal, 7 August 1942–21 February 1943
- New Guinea, 24 January 1943–31 December 1944
- Northern Solomons, 22 February 1943–21 November 1944
- Eastern Mandates, 31 January–14 June 1944
- Bismarck Archipelago, 15 December 1943–27 November 1944
- Western Pacific, 15 June 1944–2 September 1945
- Leyte, 17 October 1944–1 July 1945
- Luzon, 15 December 1944–4 July 1945
- Central Burma, 29 January–15 July 1945
- Southern Philippines, 27 February–4 July 1945
- Ryukyus, 26 March–2 July 1945
- China Offensive, 5 May–2 September 1945

European-African-Middle Eastern Theater

- Egypt-Libya, 11 June 1942–12 February 1943
- Air Offensive, Europe 4 July 1942–5 June 1944
- Algeria-French Morocco, 8-11 November 1942
- Tunisia, 17 November 1942–13 May 1943
- Sicily, 9 July–17 August 1943
- Naples-Foggia(Air), 18 August 1943–21 January 1944;
- Naples-Foggia (Ground), 9 September 1943–21 January 1944
- Anzio, 22 January–24 May 1944
- Rome-Arno, 22 January–9 September 1944
- Normandy, 6 June–24 July 1944
- Northern France, 25 July–14 September 1944
- Southern France, 15 August–14 September 1944
- Northern Apennines, 10 September 1944–4 April 1945
- Rhineland, 15 September 1944–21 March 1945

- Ardennes-Alsace, 16 December 1944–25 January 1945
- Central Europe, 22 March–11 May 1945
- Po Valley, 5 April–8 May 1945

FOOTNOTES

1   Official definitions from *The Army Dictionary* 1944 TM 20-205 18 January 1944.

2   Kent Greenfield, *The Organization of Ground Combat Troops*, p. 350.

3   Kent Greenfield, *The Organization of Ground Combat Troops*, p. 353.

4   Kent Greenfield, *The Organization of Ground Combat Troops*, p. 368.

5   *The Army Almanac*, p. 265.

6   Kent Greenfield, *The Organization of Ground Combat Troops*, p. 351.

7   Kent Greenfield, *The Organization of Ground Combat Troops*, p. 347.

8   Harvey Ford, *What You Should Know about the Army*, p. 46.

9   Robert R. Palmer, *The Procurement and Training of Ground Combat Troops*, p. 348.

10   Kent Greenfield, *The Organization of Ground Combat Troops*, p. 359.

11   According to the standards of the NOBC, The National Order of Battlefield Commissioned Officers, the veterans group for battlefield commissioned officers.

12   Development of both the GHQ and AGF is covered in *The Organization of Ground Combat Troops*, by Kent Greenfield.

13   *The Army Almanac* 1950, p. 72.

14   *The Army Almanac* 1950, 1950, p. 85.

15   *The Army Almanac* 1950, p. 148.

16   *The Army Almanac* 1950, 1950, p. 91.

17   Evelyn Monahan, *And If I Perish*, p. 6.

18   Mattie Treadwell, *The Woman's Army Corps*, p. 393.

19   Mattie Treadwell, *The Woman's Army Corps*, p. 600.

20   *The Army Almanac*, p. 340.

FINDING YOUR FATHER'S WAR

Section 2

INDIVIDUAL RECORDS

This section explains all the various Army records pertaining to an individual soldier.

It also explains the Serial Number system by which all such records are filed. This is essential information for anyone preparing to do documents research on the service of a relative in the World War II Army.

This soldier, dressed in the herring bone twill fatigue uniform, throws a hand grenade.

Once the safety pin has been pulled, the grenade is safe to hold as long as the lever is held in place. Once the lever is let loose the grenade will explode in 4-5 seconds.

Serial Numbers
Military Occupational Specialty (MOS) and
Specification Serial Numbers (SSN)
Other Individual Records: Dog Tags, Service Records,
Army Mail, Discharge Records
Death Records

INDIVIDUAL RECORDS

The Army lived for records. Everything you could ever want to know or find out about something connected with the Army was, at one time or another, put down on paper. Many of the more mundane records, such as which serial-numbered rifle a man was issued, or who was given a weekend pass on a certain date, have long since been discarded. However, a staggering number of World War II-era records are still available. They offer a wealth of information if you know where to look, what to look for, and how to read them.

Although complicated at first, most Army records are quite easy to read if you take your time and become familiar with Army terms and abbreviations. There are so many different forms that it would take a number of books to illustrate each example. Different versions of the same form also exist because the Army periodically modified them to improve the system. The forms presented below are representative samples, with the personal information on real paperwork blacked out. Some examples are from Army publications designed to train clerks and use generic information.

Army records should be divided into two main classes: individual and organization (unit) records.

SERIAL NUMBERS

Army Serial Numbers (ASN) are the key to accessing Army records. Everything in the Army revolved around a man's serial number, and for good reason. Before World War I, it was rare for a soldier to move from one unit to another. Therefore, if you knew the man's name and unit, identifying him was a relatively simple matter. John Q. Smith, 18th Infantry Regiment, was as unique as John Q. Smith, 7th Cavalry Regiment.

When the United States entered World War I, it quickly became apparent that this system would not work for a large modern army. Men were rapidly transferred from one unit to another, leaving in their wake a confusing trail of paperwork. In an effort to make it easier to keep track of a man's service (and also to deal with future veteran's benefits), the Army instituted serial numbers for enlisted men in February 1918. Number 1 was assigned to Arthur B. Cream in March 1918. Because there were relatively few officers, it was initially believed that they could continue to use their names as a means of identification. By February 1921, however, this was deemed impractical and officers were assigned serial numbers with the prefix "O-." For example, General John J. Pershing, commander of the American Forces in France, was given serial number O-1. The serial number allowed the Army to prepare records that could easily follow men from induction through wartime service, and thereafter through their civilian years when they might require veterans' services.

According to the serial number system, there were two occasions when a man might have two different serial numbers: if he made the move from enlisted man to officer, or if he was broken from officer to enlisted man. In either case the last number assigned was used, and all records were linked to that number. In some cases men left the service before the war and were given new (second) serial numbers. This was very rare, however, and always the result of Army error. It was not until 1967 that the military began using a soldier's social security number in place of a serial number. Soldiers serving before and after that date had one ASN linked to their Social Security Number, which was used from that date forward.

Serial Number Prefixes

A serial number with no letter prefix indicates an enlisted man. The prefix O-indicates a commissioned officer. Other World War II-era prefixes included:

> Warrant Officers: W
>
> Flight Officers: T
>
> Army Specialist Corps: S
>
> Army Nurse Corps: N
>
> Hospital Dietitian: R
>
> Physical Therapist: M
>
> Contract Surgeon: CS
>
> WAC officer: L
>
> WAC Warrant Officer: V
>
> WAC Enlisted Person: A

The Numbering Scheme

In July 1940, the serial number system was changed to reflect the three main sections of the army. The new army serial numbers were eight-digit numbers. Numbers starting with a "1" were assigned to enlistees, i.e., members of the Regular Army. Members of the National Guard were given serial numbers beginning with the number "2." "Draftees," i.e., men who served with the National Army, were given serial numbers beginning with a "3." By the end of the war, some draftees were given serial numbers beginning with "4."

A few longtime soldiers had shorter serial numbers that had been issued to them before the war. It is not uncommon to find seven digit numbers starting with a 5 or 6 that had been issued to men who enlisted in the 1930s.

The second digit in a man's serial number corresponded to the region of the country where he entered service (either for the Regular Army or as a draftee). This number reflected the geographic region of the corps assigned to the area he enlisted or was drafted from. For National Guardsmen, the third digit of a serial number corresponded to the region. After 1942, the Corps areas were re-designated as service commands, but the second digit designations stayed the same.

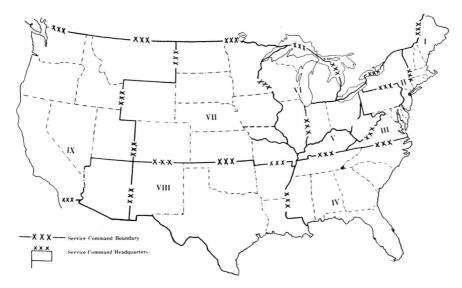

The pre-war Field Army boundaries were redesignated Service Command boundaries in 1942. The Service Commands took care of all the housekeeping duties in their region of the United States.

First Corps Area (Maine-New Hampshire-Vermont-Massachusetts-Rhode Island-Connecticut) HQ: Boston, Massachusetts.

Second Corps Area (New Jersey-Delaware-New York) HQ: Governors Island, New York.

Third Corps Area (Pennsylvania-Maryland-Virginia-District of Columbia) HQ: Baltimore, Maryland.

Fourth Corps Area (North Carolina-South Carolina-Georgia-Florida-Alabama-Tennessee-Mississippi-Louisiana) HQ: Atlanta, Georgia.

Fifth Corps Area (Ohio-West Virginia-Indiana-Kentucky) HQ: Ft. Hayes, Ohio

Sixth Corps Area (Illinois-Michigan-Wisconsin) HQ: Chicago, Illinois.

Seventh Corps Area (Missouri-Kansas-Arkansas-Iowa-Nebraska-Minnesota-North Dakota-South Dakota) HQ: Omaha, Nebraska.

Eighth Corps Area (Texas-Oklahoma-Colorado-New Mexico-part of Arizona) HQ: Ft. Sam Houston, Texas.

Ninth Corps Area (Washington-Oregon-Idaho-Montana-Wyoming-Utah-Nevada-part of Arizona-California-Alaska attached) HQ: Presidio of San Francisco, California.

The U.S. overseas possessions named as Departments were Hawaii, the Panama Canal Zone, Puerto Rico, and the Philippines

Unfortunately, this is all the information that can be obtained from a man's serial number. There is no way to tell a World War II soldier's unit from his serial number.

(Note: for World War I, it is sometimes possible to determine the unit a man was assigned to when he was first given a serial number.)

Shoulder Sleeve Insignia of the 1st through 9th Service Commands, and the Northwest (Alaska) Service Command.

*Shoulder sleeve insignia
of the Panama,
Philippine, Puerto Rico
and Hawaiian,
Departments.*

Regular Army Serial Number Ranges

REGION	RANGE STARTS	RANGE ENDS
HAWAIIAN DEPARTMENT	10,100,100	10,199,999
PANAMA CANAL DEPARTMENT	10,200,100	10,299,999
PHILIPPINE DEPARTMENT	10,300,100	10,399,999
PUERTO RICAN DEPARTMENT	10,400,100	10,499,999
FIRST CORPS AREA	11,000,000	11,499,999
SECOND CORPS AREA	12,000,000	12,499,999
THIRD CORPS AREA	13,000,000	13,499,999
FOURTH CORPS AREA	14,000,000	14,499,999
FIFTH CORPS AREA	15,000,000	15,499,999
SIXTH CORPS AREA	16,000,000	16,499,999
SEVENTH CORPS AREA	17,000,000	17,499,999
EIGHTH CORPS AREA	18,000,000	18,499,999
NINTH CORPS AREA	19,000,000	19,499,999

National Guard Serial Number Ranges

REGION	RANGE STARTS	RANGE ENDS
HAWAIIAN DEPARTMENT	20,010,000	20,019,999
PUERTO RICAN DEPARTMENT	20,020,000	20,029,999
FIRST CORPS AREA	20,100,000	20,199,999
SECOND CORPS AREA	20,200,000	20,299,999
THIRD CORPS AREA	20,300,000	20,399,999
FOURTH CORPS AREA	20,400,000	20,499,999
FIFTH CORPS AREA	20,500,000	20,599,999
SIXTH CORPS AREA	20,600,000	20,699,999
SEVENTH CORPS AREA	20,700,000	20,799,999
EIGHTH CORPS AREA	20,800,000	20,899,999
NINTH CORPS AREA	20,900,000	20,999,999

Army of the United States Serial Number Ranges

REGION	RANGE STARTS	RANGE ENDS
HAWAIIAN DEPARTMENT	30,100,100	30,199,999
PANAMA CANAL DEPARTMENT	30,200,100	30,299,999
PHILIPPINE DEPARTMENT	30,300,100	30,399,999
PUERTO RICAN DEPARTMENT	30,400,100	30,499,999
FIRST CORPS AREA	31,000,000	31,499,999
SECOND CORPS AREA	32,000,000	32,499,999
THIRD CORPS AREA	33,000,000	33,499,999
FOURTH CORPS AREA	34,000,000	34,499,999
FIFTH CORPS AREA	35,000,000	35,499,999
SIXTH CORPS AREA	36,000,000	36,499,999
SEVENTH CORPS AREA	37,000,000	37,499,999
EIGHTH CORPS AREA	38,000,000	38,499,999
NINTH CORPS AREA	39,000,000	39,499,999

WAC—First digit indicates Service Command

SERVICE COMMAND	RANGE STARTS	RANGE ENDS
FIRST SERVICE COMMAND	A-100,000	A-199,999
SECOND SERVICE COMMAND	A-200,000	A-299,999
THIRD SERVICE COMMAND	A-300,000	A-399,999
FOURTH SERVICE COMMAND	A-400,000	A-499,999
FIFTH SERVICE COMMAND	A-500,000	A-599,999
SIXTH SERVICE COMMAND	A-600,000	A-699,999
SEVENTH SERVICE COMMAND	A-700,000	A-799,999
EIGHTH SERVICE COMMAND	A-800,000	A-899,999
NINTH SERVICE COMMAND	A-900,000	A-999,999

To mark an individual's clothing and equipment, a standard marking was used by the Army. This consist-ed of the first letter of the soldier's last name, followed by the last four digits of his serial number.

This jacket was hand marked with "K-1742" (last name starting with K; the last four digits of his serial number were 1742). The solder later obtained a small rubber stamp, such as that on the left, and remarked it above the 42S size marking. The lines through these numbers indicate the jacket was reissued to another soldier.

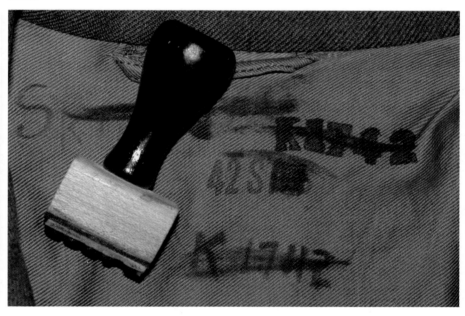

DOG TAGS

Dog Tags are synonymous with serial numbers. Every soldier's serial number was stamped on his dog tags. Dog tags were to be worn at all times when in service. They were never to be taken off. The history of dog tags dates from the American Civil War, when men purchased identification tags with their own money. The tags would help identify them should they be killed or otherwise incapacitated. In 1906, the Army decided to officially issue identification tags. The first type was a hand-stamped aluminum disk marked with name, rank, and unit. In 1916, the Army authorized two tags per man: if he was killed one would stay with the body and the other would mark the grave. When serial numbers later came into use, they were also stamped on the tags.

In 1940, the simple aluminum disk was replaced by what we now traditionally think of as a "dog tag." Initially made of brass, the dog tags held five lines of information: name, serial number, religion, blood type, and the address of next of kin. The notch that appears on these tags was put there for the sole purpose of keeping it aligned and held securely in stamping equipment. Various ghastly tales of the use of the notch have surfaced over the years, but they are all myths.

For the rest of World War II, dog tags were made in various metals, including stainless steel. The most common was a silver colored non-corrosive alloy called Monel. Little information can be gleaned from the type of metal used in a man's dog tags. Generally speaking, brass tags were used early in the war, but some were held back in supply depots and used later during the conflict.

The embossed information on the tags was done in a carefully prescribed manner. Although there are minor variations, dog tags break down into two main types. The first, which was used from 1940 until July 1943, had the following information:

  Line 1: Name

  Line 2: Serial number, tetanus inoculation, blood type

  Line 3: Name of next of kin

  Line 4: Street address of next of kin

  Line 5: Town and state of next of kin, religion code

The tetanus inoculation is more important than it might seem because it provides an idea of when the man entered service. The two numbers following the "T-" indicate the year the shot was administered. A second set of numbers indicate the year a tetanus booster was administered. Thus, "T-43" on a dog tag is a good indication the soldier entered service in 1943 (the first inoculation was generally given as soon as a man entered the Army). Positive and negative blood typing was not in use during World War II.

The religion code was a single letter denoting the man's religion. For example, P for Protestant, C for Catholic, H for Hebrew, or no letter if a man had no religious preference. There were only three official religious codes, but it was not uncommon to find others used on an unofficial basis. NP, for example, indicated "no preference."

In July 1943, an abbreviated dog tag form was authorized that deleted information about the next of kin. This tag offered the following information:

The temporary grave markers at this overseas cemetery bear the casualty's dog tag near the top of the cross. The Graves Registration personnel have had enough time to make a more permanent metal tag now attached to the center.

When the war ended the body would be shipped home, or buried in a permanent cemetery under a marble cross.

National Archives

> Line 1: Name
>
> Line 2: Serial number, tetanus inoculation, blood type
>
> Line 3: Religion

The reason sometimes given for the elimination of the next of kin information is that it might aid the enemy if a man was captured. An unscrupulous enemy might use the information for some nefarious purpose. The official reason provided in quartermaster files was that the five lines of information embossed on the tag weakened the metal to the point that it bent and broke more easily. The Army had been considering eliminating the information for that very reason as early as 1941, but did not act on it until 1943.

One of the great myths of World War II is that dog tags were removed from the dead. Dog tags were not removed because that would only make it more difficult to identify the bodies. The official procedure called for leaving both tags on the body until someone from Graves Registration arrived to collect the corpse. These men used the tags, as well as other methods of identification, to identify the body. Once identified, one tag was left on the body and the other was nailed to the cross as a temporary grave marker.

BOOKS

For a complete history of dog tags, see the self published book *Dog Tags*, by Paul Braddock, 2003

THE ARMY SERIAL NUMBER DATABASE

Until recently it was impossible to trace a serial number to a specific man. However, in 2004 the National Archives made available a searchable database of the majority of World War II enlisted serial numbers. This database is officially known as the "Electronic Army Serial Number Merged File, 1938–1946." It will allow you to find basic information on a soldier by name or serial number. The database is not perfect, however, because it was converted to computer files from a series of cards. Some errors have been reported, and not every enlisted man's record is present. It does not include information on officers. This National Archives' description of its database reads as follows:

> This series contains records of approximately nine million men and women who enlisted in the United States Army, including the Women's Army Auxiliary Corps. Although incomplete, the records contain data for a majority of the enlistments in the United States Army during World War II. The bulk of the records conform to the format found on War Department Adjutant General's Office (WD AGO) Form 317 (Enlistment Card) for the period ca. 1941–1945, and WD AGO Form 372 (Enlistment Card) for ca. 1945–1946. Additional records contain data originally recorded on Enlisted Reserve Corps (E.R.C.) Statistical cards. In general, the records contain the serial number, name, state and county of residence, place of enlistment, date of enlistment, grade, Army branch, term of enlistment, longevity, nativity (place of birth), year of birth, race, education, civilian occupation, marital status, height and weight (before 1943), military occupational specialty (1945 and later), component, and box and reel number of the microfilmed punch cards.[1]

> WEBSITE
>
> The serial number database is available on the AAD (Access to Archival Database system) at www.nara.gov

MILITARY OCCUPATIONAL SPECIALTY (MOS) AND SPECIFICATION SERIAL NUMBERS (SSN)

To help assign the right man to the right job, the Army developed a system of job classification known as "Military Occupational Specialty," or MOS. Every position in the Army was categorized as to what MOS was required to do the job. Each man was given an MOS indicating what he was qualified to do. As soldiers were promoted or changed jobs, they could acquire new skills that would allow them to be qualified in a new and more difficult MOS.

The term MOS actually referred only to the title and description of the job. The numbers given to these job categories were technically known as SSN's (Specification Serial Numbers). However, in common usage, MOS came to be identified with both.

Generally speaking, a man had to finish a training program to be classified with an MOS. In some cases he could be given an MOS based upon what he had done in civilian life. Soldiers could also gain a new MOS classification after sixty days of satisfactory performance in a new position. For a man qualified to be an instructor for a specific MOS, the term "instructor" was added after the number. Qualifying as a parachutist or horseman was considered an extra specialty and handled by adding a prefix of "7" for parachutists and "9" for horsemen. Thus, a rifleman (MOS 745) who was also parachute qualified became an MOS 7745.

There were hundreds of MOS classifications and each one had a definition of what that individual should be able to do. MOS numbers under 500 were directly linked to civilian occupations, such as cook, radio repairman, or truck driver. MOS numbers above 500 indicated a job that was specific to the Army, such as rifleman or tank gunner.

One specific MOS that is confusing is number 521-Basic. This is the MOS of a man who was not assigned to any specific position but, given a reasonable amount of training, could take on and learn any job with a little assistance. Basics were the built-in replacements in every unit. At the start of the war, units had roughly 10% of their strength in basics, but this was cut to 5% midway through the war to better utilize available manpower.

An example of a basic would be a soldier assigned to an infantry regiment. He had a general military understanding and had been given basic instruction in many areas. When needed, he could be assigned to the job of 745 Rifleman, 746 Automatic Rifleman, 761 Scout, or 667 Message Center Clerk. In theory, an experienced man in the unit would help him get up to speed. After sixty days in the new job, the basic was officially assigned that MOS.

As the war progressed, some MOS designations were eliminated and new ones added. Therefore it is important to keep in mind that a man may have held one MOS early in the war and another MOS later, but without any actual change in his duties. Because the Army worked hard to make the most out of its limited manpower, the tendency was to combine as many similar jobs as possible. Combat experience quickly demonstrated that one could not always be picky about who was given what job in a unit, and MOS designations began to contain all the jobs in a given small unit. For example, the MOS Antitank Gun Crewman (SSN 610) allowed any man so qualified to also serve as a Cannoneer, Gunner, Driver, Radio Tender, or Antitank NCO.

A major change in the MOS system occurred in 1944 when the MOS and SSN used for positions of command rank (such as "platoon leader" or "first sergeant") were changed to better reflect that these men were a more highly trained version of the men they commanded. For example, let's assume an Antitank Gun Crewman (SSN 610) who demonstrated leadership and other personal supervisory qualifications was promoted to the position of Antitank Noncommissioned Officer. In his case, the MOS "Antitank Gun Crewman" (SSN 610) was not changed except that the alternate title of "Antitank NCO" (SSN 610) should be used and accordingly posted in the item.

Other common titles used throughout the Army to indicate the supervisory nature of a duty assignment were also used as alternate titles. Examples of this are sergeant major, first sergeant, platoon sergeant, chief of section, section leader, and squad leader. However, the SSN used in each case will be the SSN that represents the MOS of that NCO.

Examples: A platoon sergeant of a rifle company should be shown as Platoon Sergeant, SSN 745 if he was assigned to a Rifle Platoon; or 1812 if assigned to an Infantry Platoon employing 60-mm mortars and light machine guns; a platoon sergeant of an antitank company should be shown as Platoon Sergeant SSN 610; a first sergeant whose duties required that he be an administrative specialist should be shown as First Sergeant, SSN 502; and a first sergeant whose duties required a tactical specialist should be shown with the SSN covering his tactical specialty. For example, the first sergeant of an infantry rifle company should be shown as First Sergeant, SSN 1812. The first sergeant of a tank destroyer company (firing) should be shown as First Sergeant SSN 610.2

In the 1944 changes in an infantry company, the platoon sergeant and platoon guide (both MOS 651) became MOS 745 (Rifleman). The rifle squad leader and assistant squad leader (both MOS 653) also became MOS 745 (Rifleman).

The Weapons Platoon Sergeant MOS 651 (Platoon Sergeant) became MOS 1812 (Light Weapons NCO). In his machine gun sections, the Section Leader MOS 651, MOS 653 (Squad Leader) and MOS 504 (Ammo Bearer) all became MOS 604 Light Machine Gunner). In the mortar section, the Section Leader (MOS 652), Squad Leader MOS 653 and (Ammo Bearer) MOS 504 became MOS 607 Light Mortar Crewman.

BOOKS

Technical Manual -12-427 contains a full listing of MOS description and SSN numbers.

A list of common MOS definitions is available at www.fatherswar.com.

The company First Sergeant position was converted from MOS 585 to MOS 1812(Light Weapons NCO). This was because as the top NCO in the company, he was expected to know not only rifle platoon weapons but also the light mortars and machine guns in the weapons platoon.

OTHER INDIVIDUAL RECORDS

There were many different records generated on individual soldiers during the war. They range from classification cards to records of marksmanship. Most paper records were only valuable for a short period of time and then discarded, so only the more commonly found records are described here.

In general terms, a serviceman's personnel records are known as his "201 file." This is because in the Army decimal classification system (much like the Dewey Decimal System), the number 201 is what personal records are filed under.

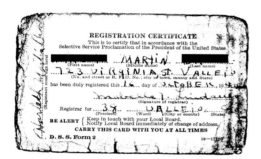

A well worn draft card issued in 1940. All eligible males had to carry their card on them at all times. This explains why most of those still in existence are in poor shape. It is really more of an identification card allowing authorities to ascertain if a man had complied with the draft regulations and registered for selective service.

The first records of a man's service were his Selective Service registration and qualification cards, i.e., his draft record. These records are fairly self-explanatory; every man eligible for the draft had to register with his local draft board. Once he did so, he was given a physical exam to determine his suitability for military service. His ranking ranged from 1-A (suitable for military service) to 4-F (not suitable for military service). The standards varied over time. Later in the war, when the need for more men increased, those who had initially been given lower grades were passed through the system, even if they had minor physical problems.

Most selective service or draft records contain little information on a man's military service. These records were designed only to collect information about him as a civilian and his ability to perform as a soldier. Draft notices were often kept as souvenirs because they were originally mailed to a man's house and remained there until he finally came home.

Draft records contain personal information and fall under the Federal Privacy Act, which limits their access to family members. However, registration cards from the Fourth Draft (April 1942) are available. They are organized by state in Record Group 147 in the National Archives regional branch serving that state. These registration cards contain information on the man's civilian life before he entered service. Scanned examples of these from Ohio are available on the National Archives website.

The front and back of a sample registration card from the NARA collection for the 4th Draft.

The front indicates the man's name, birthday, address, work place, and next of kin.

The back indicates his race, height, weight, complexion, and that he is hard of hearing.

Processing Records

One of the first records kept by the Army was a man's Soldier Qualification Card. This record originated at a reception center and was a large cardboard card with holes punched around the edges. The card provided a listing of a man's qualifications in an easily searchable format. By recording a man's specific talents (hobbies, languages, sports, training, or talents), the army could use a McBee Keysort selector device to quickly find someone with the proper skills needed.

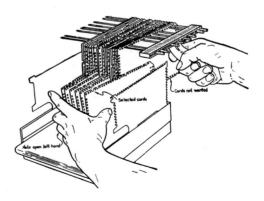

The qualification cards could be sorted to quickly locate a man with a certain skill or background. This allowed the Army to best utilize its manpower.

Another form that was important to the Army was Form Number 43:
the Personal Addressee and Property Card. This was effectively the
next of kin registry, and told the Army who to notify if anything happened to the soldier. If a man was injured or killed, notification was
automatically sent to this address.

No insurance company in its right mind would issue life insurance policies to
men entering combat. Because of this, the government created National
Service Life Insurance and made it available to everyone who served in the
armed forces. The cost of a $10,000 policy for a 20-year-old soldier was sixty-
five cents a month. This sum, which was considered substantial at the time,
was taken out of his monthly pay.

The Service Record

The main record of information
kept on a specific solder was the
Service Record (AGO form 24).
This multi-page booklet contained
all the information on a soldier
and tracked his service from start
to finish. The ultimate goal of anyone attempting to find out what a
man did during the war is to find
this booklet. Unfortunately, the
vast majority of World War II-era
Army service records were burned
in a 1973 fire, so most of this information has been lost.

The Service Record covers induction, immunizations, beneficiar-
ies, qualifications, any special
duty, when he was read the arti-

cles of war, promotions, assignments, furloughs, overseas service, medals and decorations, time lost in service (AWOL, etc.), courts-martial, allotments, insurance, and deposits.

BOOKS

Everything you could want to know about the minutiae of Army paperwork can be found in the field manual FM 12-250 The Army Clerk.

The Service Record remained with the Army and was not given to the soldier upon his discharge. During the war it was kept and maintained by the company clerks and was never in the soldier's possession. Once the man was discharged the record was officially closed. It could not be altered thereafter without permission from the Secretary of War

Officer Records

Records of commissioned officers were slightly different from those of enlisted men. They were considered highly confidential because no one wanted enlisted men reading about the history of their officers. Their files contained much the same kind of information as the enlisted men—with one significant exception. Officers were rated by their commanders every year at the end of June, whenever they were transferred to a new unit, or whenever their commander was transferred to a new unit.

The Efficiency Report was a critical record for an officer hoping to be promoted. Mediocre reports could block a promotion; excellent ones could speed them up. If a man was rated as unsatisfactory in any category, he was allowed to see the report and comment on it. Otherwise, it was up to the commander to allow the officer to see his report when it was filed. The report was also checked by the unit personnel officer and the next higher commander in case the report offered an unfair evaluation.

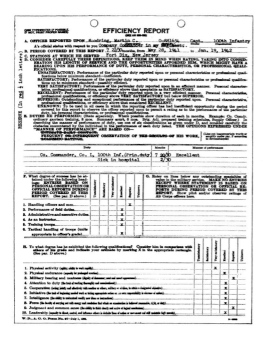

Efficiency Reports were not kept in the 201 file, but instead were sent immediately to the Adjutant General's office in the War Department. If an officer was in Washington, he could request permission to see his reports. Once the officer retired or left the service, his reports were no longer needed in Washington for future promotion evaluations, and so were transferred to his 201 file at the Personnel Records Center. Unfortunately, if an officer's file was lost in the 1973 fire, so were all his Efficiency Reports.

ARMY MAIL

APOs

Mail sent to soldiers overseas was sent to an Army Post Office Number (APO). This made it much easier for the Army to get mail to the correct place, as well as keep information on what unit was located in what area a secret. An APO corresponded to either a specific unit or a group of units based in a specific place.

There were more than 1,000 APO numbers used during World War II. Some numbers were assigned for a reason, while others were just the next unused number on the list. Infantry divisions usually had their division number as their APO. The list of APO numbers and what they meant was kept secret for obvious reasons.

> **WEBSITE**
>
> In 1949, a list of World War II Army APOs was published, but this list is quite rare and until recently the only available copy was located at the Military History Institute in Carlisle, Pennsylvania. It is now available on their website as the *Alphabetical listing of APO's, January 1942 – November 1947*. It was published by the Army Postal Service and Strength Accounting Branches, AGO, 1949.
>
> www.carlisle.army.mil/ahec/index.htm

Censor Stamps

Every letter sent by a soldier was censored by an officer. The only exception was when the soldier had something very personal to convey. In these cases, a special blue envelope was provided that passed unread to a rear area and an anonymous censor. Soldiers turned their mail over to their officers, who had to find the time to read each piece, stamp it with their censor stamp, and initial it as having been read. A sampling of these censored letters was doubled checked before they were delivered to make sure the officers were doing their job.

Censor stamps were numbered, but there is little that can be derived from that number. The initials or signature on the stamps can often be identified as the soldier's commanding officer at the time. There was very little soldiers could write home about.

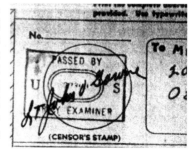

This is a censor's stamp placed on a piece of V-mail being sent home from the ETO in 1944. Each stamp was numbered so its use could be tracked.

Technically each item was also to be signed by the officer doing the censoring, but some mail was just stamped, and some just signed with no stamp.

They were forbidden from mentioning their location or what had been happening to their unit. Although nearly devoid of interesting information, most World War II-era mail offers a good look at just how homesick many of these young men were.

V-Mail

These two V-Mails sent from Europe show how it was used. On the left an artist has drawn a nice cartoon as part of the message, and on the right the space was used for a short one page letter.

Courtesy Oscar Olen and Bernie Mason

No discussion of Army mail would be complete without a mention of V-Mail. This was a special type of mail designed to save shipping space. A one page form was sent to a special photographic laboratory, where all the mail destined for a specific location was collected and microfilmed. The roll of film, containing a large number of V-Mails, was then sent via the fastest available route to its destination. When it arrived overseas, the film was reprinted and sent on to the final destinations. There were many jokes about the final copies being small, but the whole process saved an enormous amount of tonnage on ships and planes during the war.

It was not just letters that were sent this way; cartoons and drawings were frequently put on V-Mails and used as cards for a variety of occasions. Some units found their best artists and put them to work making V-Mail designs that were printed up for anyone who wanted to send them.

THE DISCHARGE

A soldier's discharge is the single most important piece of paper you can find. It is his final resume of what he did in the Army. On one side is a certificate that some men framed. On the reverse is his enlistment history of what he did in the service. This is similar to today's form DD-214, which replaced the reverse of the discharge in the 1950s.

The most common type of discharge is AGO Form 55, an honorable discharge printed on white paper. AGO Form 56 was printed on blue paper and was given to men who would have been able to serve except for "ineptitude or lack of adaptability to military service."

This "blue discharge" was given for fraudulent enlistment or desertion if no trial had been held. Other reasons were ineptness, undesirable habits, and deleterious character taints. Finally, the "blue discharge" could be given if a man's company commander believed he had not served honestly and faithfully and was thus not entitled to a character rating of good or better. A yellow-colored discharge (AGO Form 57) was a dishonorable discharge and was only given to men who had been discharged due to the actions of a courts-martial. Most soldiers kept multiple copies of their discharges, and a common form of copying in 1945 resulted in poor copies with a negative white text on a black background. This was the standard pre-Xerox form of copying.

Before war broke out in 1941, a soldier could buy his way out and purchase his discharge after a period of one year. This was suspended for the duration of World War II. There were a number of reasons why some men were given an honorable discharge during the war. Some were considered more valuable to industry; others were released for service to a reserve unit; others were discharged because of a chronic illness. Enlisted men receiving a commission were officially discharged before receiving their lieutenant's bars. They were then brought back into the Army as an officer. Soldiers under the age of 18 could be discharged at the request of their parents (but not their own desire). In some rare cases a man could be discharged if someone in his family died and it would cause undue hardship to his family if he stayed in uniform.

There were two main types of discharge forms used in World War II. The first was the Regular Army Discharge used during the early years of the conflict. Until the war brought about the formation of the Army of the United States (combining Regular, Reserve, and National Guard troops), only Regulars received a discharge. Reserve and guardsmen received a "Certificate of Service." After the war a man would receive a certificate of service if he was being returned to reserve status and not completely leaving the military. His final discharge would arrive when he reached the end of his military service.

The front of the discharge was a certificate suitable for framing and indicated the unit the man was discharged from. The reverse of the discharge held information about his service. The discharge shown below was prepared for a hypothetical soldier and used to train Army clerks.

ENLISTED RECORD OF

Kelsey	Michael	J.	30766766	Pvt.1cl.Specl.4c)
Enlisted or inducted	June 1	19 41	of New York, New York	

Completed _O_ years, _6_ months, _15_ days service for longevity pay.

Prior service: * None

Noncommissioned officer: Never
Qualification in arms: † ER, July 25, 1941, RO #56, 100th Infantry, July 25/41
Horsemanship: Not mounted   Army specialty: Clerk
Attendance at: None
Battles, engagements, skirmishes, expeditions: None

Decorations, service medals, citations: None

Wounds received in service: None
Date and result of smallpox vaccination: † June 2, 1941—Vaccinoid
Date of completion of all typhoid-paratyphoid vaccinations: † June 16, 1941
Date and result of diphtheria immunity test (Schick): † None
Date of other vaccinations (specify vaccine used): † None
Physical condition when discharged: Poor   Married or single: Single
Character: Excellent mcw Efficiency Rating: Excellent mcw
Remarks: Time lost under 107th A.W.: July 1/41 to July 2/41 incl., 2 days.
Soldier entitled to travel pay.

Signature of soldier: *Michael J. Kelsey*
James M. Perkins
JAMES M. PERKINS,
Capt., 100th Inf.
Commanding Assistant Adjutant.

Honorable Discharge
from
The Army of the United States

TO ALL WHOM IT MAY CONCERN:

This is to Certify, That * _____ JOHN O. GAWNE _____
† _____, Cpl. 14th Co. 2nd Stu Tng Regt, I&C, Fort Benning, Georgia
THE ARMY OF THE UNITED STATES, as a TESTIMONIAL OF HONEST AND FAITHFUL SERVICE, is hereby HONORABLY DISCHARGED from the military service of the UNITED STATES by reason of ‡ __CONVENIENCE OF THE GOVERNMENT TO ACCEPT APPOINTMENT AS 2ND LIEUT., ARMY OF THE US AND ACTIVE DUTY__
Said _____ JOHN O. GAWNE _____ was born
in _____ Albany _____, in the State of _____ New York _____
When enlisted he was 27 10/12 years of age and by occupation a Executive Secretary Assistant
He had __Blue__ eyes, __Blonde__ hair, __Light__ complexion, and was __5__ feet __8__ inches in height.
Given under my hand at _____ FORT BENNING, GEORGIA _____ this
22nd day of __February__, one thousand nine hundred and __Forty-three__

Edward B Jackson
COLONEL INFANTRY
Commanding

See A.R. 345-CO.
*Insert name as, "John J. Doe."
† Insert Army serial number, grade, company, regiment, or arm or service; as "ASSN00," (Corporal, Company A, 1st Infantry," "Sergeant, Quartermaster Corps."
‡ If discharged prior to expiration of service, give number, date, and source of order or full description of authority therefor.
W. D., A. G. O. Form No. 55
April 28, 1941

Honorable Discharge
from
The Army of the United States

TO ALL WHOM IT MAY CONCERN:

This is to Certify, That * _____ Michael J. Kelsey _____
† __30766766 Private First Class, Specl. 4th cl., Company L, 100th Infantry__
THE ARMY OF THE UNITED STATES, as a TESTIMONIAL OF HONEST AND FAITHFUL SERVICE, is hereby HONORABLY DISCHARGED from the military service of the UNITED STATES by reason of ‡ __C. D. D.__
__3rd Ind., Hq.,20th Inf. Div., Dec. 12, 1941__
Said _____ Michael J. Kelsey _____ was born
in _____ New York _____, in the State of _____ New York _____
When enlisted he was 26 11/12 years of age and by occupation a Clerk
He had __Blue__ eyes, __Black__ hair, __Ruddy__ complexion, and was __Five__ feet __Eight__ inches in height.
Given under my hand at _____ Fort Dix, New Jersey _____ this
__15th__ day of __December__, one thousand nine hundred and __forty-one__.

John O. Atwater
JOHN O. ATWATER
Colonel, 100th Infantry
Commanding

Private Kelsey (above left and above) was discharged from the Army after only six months for medical reasons. This relatively simple form was replaced by the Army of the United States Discharge used for the majority of men in World War II.

This Army of the United States discharge (left) shows the man served as an enlisted man who was discharged for the convenience of the government to accept appointment as 2d lieutenant. His unit was listed as a student training regiment at the Infantry School at Fort Benning. Training regiments and companies were temporary organizations serving as holding units for students. They have no further meaning and are not linked to any actual unit.

The reverse of his discharge (right) indicates his enlisted rank as corporal. Since all enlisted men accepted to officer's candidate schools were promoted to corporal, he did not necessarily hold that rank in his previous unit.

He had been serving as a General Clerk MOS 055 from 5/1/42, and had served as an enlisted man for 22 months.

The only school he attended during this time was the Infantry Officers Candidate School. His basic and advanced training were all handled in the unit he had joined upon enlistment. He had actually served on Christmas Island in the Pacific, but no indication of this is made except for a remark that he had returned from the North Pacific.

This early form of the discharge was similar to the pre-war Regular Army form. It would later be revised to allow for more information to be included.

Later in 1945 he received another discharge (right), this time as an officer but again from the Army of the United States (AUS). His commission was in the AUS and not in the Regular Army. He was discharged in Florida while on his way home to New York.

The reverse of the new discharge (see top of next page) is War Department Form 53. This is a Report of Separation and contains a capsule history of the man's service including wounds, campaigns, and medals. This record indicates that he took part in two campaigns (Normandy and Northern France) and was thus authorized two service stars.

Curiously, a later check of his records discovered that his service in the Pacific

---

ENLISTED RECORD

OF

Gawne   John   O.   ▮▮▮▮   Cpl.
(Last name)   (First name)   (Middle initial)   (Army Serial No.)   (Grade)

Enlisted–Inducted: April 18, 19 41, at Albany, New York

Completed 1 years, 10 months, 5 days service for longevity pay.

Prior service: None

J. H. McFall,
Finance Officer,
Fort Lessing, Georgia
Final Statement
Paid in full this date 37.5 43

Agent Finance Officer, Jack W. Mahler, Capt Inf   Computations made by:
Noncommissioned officer: Corporal 8/25/42   H. C. Amack,   Lt., F. D.
Qualification in arms: None   Agent Finance Officer,
Horsemanship: NOT MOUNTED   Army specialty: Gen Clk, 055, 5/1/42
Attendance at: INFANTRY OFFICER CANDIDATE SCHOOL (Name of service announced officers or special service school)
Battles, engagements, skirmishes, expeditions: NONE

Decorations, service medals, citations: NONE

Wounds received in service: NONE
Date and result of smallpox vaccination: 1/15/42
Date of completion of all typhoid-paratyphoid vaccinations: 2/5/42
Date and result of diphtheria immunity test (Schick): LOCAL
Date of other vaccinations (specify vaccine used): Tetanus 1/25/42, Pneumonia 11/2/42, Yellow Fever 1/15/42
Physical condition when discharged: GOOD   Married or single: Single
Character: Excellent JWM
Remarks: NOT ENTITLED TO TRAVEL PAY NO ITM. LOST UNDER AW 107
Returned to Ft. McDowell, Calif fr North Pacific, on Sep 14/42.

Signature of soldier: *John O. Gawne*

2nd Lieut, Infantry
Assistant Adjutant

Army of the United States

CERTIFICATE OF SERVICE

This is to certify that

JOHN O GAWNE ▮▮▮▮ 1st LIEUTENANT
Infantry

*honorably served in active Federal Service
in the Army of the United States from*

23 February 1943   *to*   22 November 1945

Given at SEPARATION CENTER Camp Blanding Florida

on the 22nd   *day of*   November   19 45

W. R. McClintock
W. R. McCLINTOCK
Lieutenant Colonel AGD

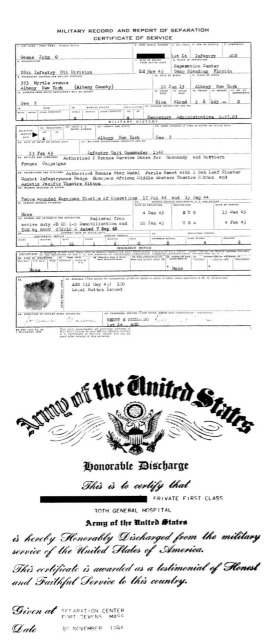

put him inside the geographic boundary and timeframe for a service star on his Pacific Theater ribbon.

It is also interesting that the report does not credit him with the American Theater ribbon, to which he would have been entitled, for serving one year in the USA.

These are good examples of the sloppy clerical work that was performed at the time of discharge, when men just wanted to get home.

A later request to the government corrected the records and authorized the missing decorations with updated paperwork.

His decorations and wounds are mentioned, although months after the war a second bronze star citation, for the second time he was wounded, finally made its way through channels and arrived in the mail.

The reason for discharge was demobilization, and it was noted that he was issued his lapel button. This was the Honorable Discharge lapel button known as the ruptured duck.

The discharge on the left was for an enlisted man who had served in a hospital unit. It is important to know that this may not have been the unit with which the man served most of his time during the war; apparently men were given some choice as to which unit they served with should appear on their final paperwork. There is no importance to the location of discharge or to the officer who signed it; it was just whoever happened to be on duty at that time.

On the reverse of the discharge is his WD Form 53. Boxes 1–21 contain general information, including name, date of birth, serial number, hair color, civilian profession, and so forth (right). Military information starts in the second section with Box 22. This records his enlisted dates and his last MOS (in this case SSN 409- medical technician).

Box 32 lists the campaigns he was credited with. This man's record indicates Normandy, Northern France, and the Rhineland, which meant he could wear three bronze battle stars on his ETO ribbon. Box 33 lists the medals and decorations he was entitled to wear: ETO Service Ribbon, Victory Medal, and Good Conduct Medal. Box 34 indicates that he was not wounded in action.

The next section deals with the length of his Army service, how long overseas, and records his major inoculations. This particular man left the USA on 27 May 1943, and returned home on 25 November 1945, a total credited time overseas of two years, five months, and 29 days. This meant he was entitled to wear four overseas bars on his uniform, for each six-month period, but narrowly missed out on his fifth bar. Because he served only four months in the continental limits of the USA, he was not awarded the American Campaign medal.

The report mentions that he had more than four years of prior service in the Army before he was inducted in the Army for World War II. The reason for discharge was given as demobilization. There were a number of reasons a man could be discharged, from medical reasons and age, to the rather vague description that it was "for the convenience of the government."

An important thing to notice about these discharges is that they were filled out at one sitting, so only one typeface should appear on it. They were not updated, with decorations added as they were earned.

If it looks as though someone has gone back and added on a record in a slightly different typeface or at a slight angle, it is more than likely fraudulent.

In the 1950's the record of service found on the reverse of the discharge was found on form DD-214 (Department of Defense form 214). This DD-214 dates from 1950 but contains information of an engineer officer that served during WWII and remained in the Reserves. When looking for information on men who remained in the service, the form DD-214 is the one to look for.

Articles of war

The Articles of War are the laws by which the Army governs itself. Some soldier records refer to disciplinary action under a specific article number. A reference to time lost under AW 61, for example, indicates the soldier you are researching was punished for being AWOL (Absent Without Leave). It is important to keep in mind that any time spent in a stockade for a violation of the Articles of War was not credited toward the total time a soldier served in the Army.

VIOLATIONS UNDER THE ARTICLES OF WAR			
AW 54	Fraudulent enlistment	AW 73	Releasing a prisoner without proper authority
AW 58	Desertion	AW 77	Improper use of password
AW 59	Aiding another to desert	AW 81	Aiding the enemy
AW 61	Absent without leave	AW 82	Spying for the enemy
AW 64	Assault or willfully disobeying a superior officer	AW 85	Drunk on duty
AW 66	Mutiny or sedition	AW 86	Misbehavior
AW 67	Failure to suppress mutiny or sedition	AW 92	Murder or rape
AW 75	Misbehavior before the enemy	AW 93	Manslaughter, burglary, robbery, forgery or embezzlement
AW 76	Trying to get a commander to surrender	AW 94	Frauds against the Government

The Official Army Officer Register

The Army published a listing of all Regular Army officers, information on their background, and where they were serving each year. These books list only those officers with commissions in the Regular Army. A similar volume was published listing officers who held National Guard and Reserve commissions, but it did not include anyone who was an officer only in the Army of the United States.

Here is the 1943 entry for General Patton.

Patton, George S., jr. (O2605). B— Calif. 11 Nov. 85. A—M. A., Calif. **D. S. C. D. S. M. S. S. P. H.** B. S., U. S. M. A., 09. G. S. C. 2 July 24 to 21 Feb. 28; 9 July 35 to 12 June 37. Grad. Army War. Coll. 32. Hon. grad. C. and G. S. Sch. 24. Grad.: Mtd. Serv. Sch. 14, Second Year Course, 15, Cav. Sch., Advanced Course, 23.

Lt. col. Tank C., N. A. 30 Mar. 18; accepted 3 Apr. 18; col. Tank C., U. S. A. 17 Oct. 18; accepted 18 Oct. 18; hon. dis. 30 June 20; brig. gen. A. U. S. 1 Oct. 40; accepted 2 Oct. 40; maj. gen. A. U. S. 4 Apr. 41; accepted 19 Apr. 41.——Cadet M. A. 16 June 04; 2 lt. of Cav. 11 June 09; 1 lt. 23 May 16; capt. 15 May 17; maj. (temp.) 26 Jan. 18 to 2 Apr. 18; maj. 1 July 20; lt. col. 1 Mar. 34; col. 1 July 38.

The left hand column lists his serial number, background, decorations, and military schools attended. The right hand column details his progression through the ranks. The first section describes his temporary ranks in both the World War I National Army and the World War II Army of the United States. His current rank is listed as major general in the A.U.S. as of 19 April 1941. However, his permanent rank in the Regular Army was colonel as of 1 July 1938.

The Officer Register also lists who has retired or died, and who was on the retired list. As an official publication, the Officer Register can be found in many major military research libraries. Similar publications exist listing officers who were members of organizations (such as the Army-Navy Club) in various regions. Those non-official directories are rare and it is difficult to find them today.

PAY RECORDS

Records frequently mention a man's pay, so it is useful to have an understanding of how the Army paid the troops. Each month the company was assembled to be paid, either by a finance officer or the company commander. Every rank had a base rate of pay that was paid monthly (see Section 1, pages 52–54). After three years of service this base pay increased over time (but stopped increasing after 30 years of service). Before the war, soldiers were paid extra for proficiency in arms (being a good shot), but this was suspended during World War II.

An additional $2.00 of "distinguished service" pay was added each month for men who had earned the Medal of Honor, Distinguished Service Cross,

Payday in Alaska with the company commander counting out each man's pay. The men were paid in strict order by rank, and then alphabetically.

Note the loaded .45 pistol at his right elbow in case someone considers robbery.

Author's Collection

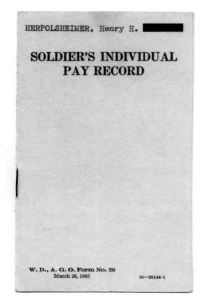

HERPOLSHEIMER, Henry H. ■■■■■

SOLDIER'S INDIVIDUAL PAY RECORD

W. D., A. G. O. Form No. 28
March 26, 1942   16—28144-1

Distinguished Flying Cross, or Soldiers Medal. Multiple medals earned an additional $2.00 apiece.

Hazardous duty pay included flight pay if the soldier was regularly and frequently in flight. This was considered to be the case if the man made 10 flights per month or spent three hours in the air each month. Hazardous duty pay was substantial—a 50% bonus on their base pay. Men on parachute duty earned an extra $50.00 each month for enlisted men and $100.00 for officers. Service outside the continental USA and Alaska added an additional 20% for enlisted men and 10% for officers. If a man was not being fed or housed by the Army, he could draw extra money to cover his food and lodging.

Deductions were taken before the soldier was paid. For example, soldiers were charged for lost or damaged equipment, and for expenses incurred at a Post Exchange or laundry. Deductions were also made for a company fund, and if the soldier was Regular Army, twenty-five cents a month was subtracted to help fund the Soldier's Home in Washington DC, where they might someday retire.

Voluntary and regular deductions from pay were called "allotments." These funds were withdrawn to cover the cost of the $10,000 government life insurance policy, to be deposited in a bank, or sent home to the family. The Army allowed men to send money home each month, and in some cases added extra funds. For example, $22.00 sent to a wife earned an extra $28.00 from the Army for her, or $40.00 if she had a child.

Soldiers were also strongly encouraged to allocate money each month to buy war bonds. These were purchased by enlisted men in multiples of $1.75, and $3.75 by officers. The bonds helped pay for the war and were redeemable with interest.

The Soldier's Individual Pay Record

In theory, soldiers had to be with their company to be paid. This posed a problem when men were sent on temporary duty (TDY). They could be detached on a special detail, away at school, in a hospital, or be involved in any number of legitimate activities. For this reason the Army developed the "soldier's pay record," a small paper booklet that allowed soldiers to apply at any Army paymaster for their monthly pay.

When a soldier returned to his regular unit, he would present his pay book for inspection so the entries therein could be examined to make sure he was not being double paid. These booklets generally do not provide much useful information. However, in some cases they may prove a man was away from his unit on a specific date. Some soldiers held onto the books after the war, but if they did not there is little hope of finding them in any official records collection.

DEATH RECORDS

A separate file of records was generated if a soldier was killed while serving in the Army. His service record was closed, and a new file opened that traced his remains and personal effects. The Army went to great lengths to ensure that every body was properly identified and its location recorded. Personal items found on the body or in his baggage were returned to the next of kin. The body was normally buried in a temporary grave until the war ended, at which time family members decided whether they wanted it returned to the United States for burial or permanently interred in one of the official military cemeteries overseas.

The War Department published a series of books in 1946 listing the name, rank, and serial number of every American who was killed in action. The World War II Honor List of Dead and Missing contains the names of every Army and Air Force casualty. Each state has its own volume, and the names are listed alphabetically by county. The Navy published its own version called State Summary of War Casualties, which lists casualties of the Navy, Coast Guard, and Marine Corps. These records are available on the Internet at the National Archives web site. Although they were not yet posted on the Internet when this book went to press, the National Archives also has files listing World War II Army casualty information arranged by the division in which each man served.

Individual Personal Death Files

Perhaps the hardest records of all to read are those found in the Individual Deceased Personnel File (IDPF), which was generated when a soldier died. The IDPF documents record what happened to the body from the time the soldier was killed until it was placed in a permanent cemetery. The contents vary depending upon the situation. If a soldier's body was quickly picked up by the Graves Registration unit (such as a battalion aid station), the IDPF may only contain a signed report of how he was identified (dog tags, name on clothing,

personal documents, etc.). There might be a record of his burial in a temporary cemetery, followed by paperwork indicating that his personal effects had been returned to his family.

Remains picked up long after the fighting ended (and they continue to be found to this day) generate more paperwork. The location and conditions of the body were carefully noted, as was any evidence about its identity. Records often noted the type of wounds visible on the corpse. Reading this today may cause some emotional distress for family members.

In many cases the remains were found after the soldier had been declared missing in action. The date and exact location where the body was recovered was recorded, which was especially important in case the identity of the remains was in question. Records were carefully kept documenting every movement of a body to prevent later confusion as to which body was in which grave. The Army did everything it could to avoid mistakes in this regard. Undoubtedly some errors were made, but given the magnitude of the task at hand the Army did a very good job overall.

Most casualties had two sets of personal possessions returned home. The first package contained the articles found on the body when it was recovered. The second shipment contained what was found in his duffel bag or footlocker. Enlisted men overseas possessed only what they could carry on their person or store in a duffel bag. The majority of these items were G.I. (Government Issue). If still useable, they were put back into quartermaster stocks and reissued. The usual personal items returned to the family included photos, watches, letters, money, or rings. These items were turned over to the Army Effects Bureau for return to next of kin.

In some cases a court-martial was held to determine the proper next of kin (father, wife, child, etc.). This did not indicate anything out of the ordinary; it is just an army term for an official hearing. The IDPF records list the items returned home. These records can be a valuable confirmation of a family history; for example, that "this watch was worn when he was killed."

Often these items were not returned home until well after the war.

Officers had to purchase most of their uniforms from their own funds, and were allowed a footlocker for their storage. Material not issued by the government was supposed to be returned to the family. It is sad to think that there may well still be footlockers of deceased soldiers sitting in someone's attic which have never been opened since they arrived home 60 years ago.

Although diaries were forbidden by Army regulations, many soldiers kept them anyway. Personal items such as diaries, which might have been useful to enemy intelligence, were retained by the government until the end of the war.

Blood-stained or other gruesome items were prohibited from being sent home. This was done to spare the family from having to look at a bloody jacket or an ID bracelet or watch torn apart by shrapnel. IDPFs often contain letters from the family asking for a specific item, such as a ring or a fountain pen. The usual reply was that the Army did not have the item in question. There were several reasons for this reply. If the item was being carried in a backpack covered with blood, the entire backpack might have been discarded by the Graves Registration troops. Many soldiers were killed by artillery shells or other high explosives, and little if anything was found. In other cases the item had been lost, sold, or traded by the soldier before he was killed.

								ARMY EFFECTS BUREAU			P. O. W.	
	WILL OR POWER OF ATTY.										ABANDONED	
X	TALLY IN FORM 43										UNKNOWN	
	BAGS, CLOTH OR TRAVEL		BELT			OVERCOATS						
	BELT, MONEY (NO MONEY)		BOOKS, ADDRESS			PAPERS, PERSONAL						
	BILLFOLD (NO MONEY)		BOOKS, PILOT LOG			PENCIL, MECHANICAL						
	BOOKS		BRUSHES			PEN, FOUNTAIN						
/	BRACELET, IDENT.		CASE			PHOTOS						
	CAMERAS		CLOTH, WASH			PIPES						
	CLOTHING		COATS			RINGS						
X	MISC. ARTICLES		FOOTLOCKER			SCARFS						
	RELIGIOUS ARTICLES		FOOTWEAR, PR.			SHIRTS						
	RIBBONS, DECORATION		GLASSES			SOCKS, PR.						
	SHORT SNORTER		GLOVES, PR.			STATIONERY						
	SOUVENIR MONEY		HANDKERCHIEFS			TIES						
	SOUVENIRS		HEADWEAR			TOBACCO						
	TESTAMENTS		JACKETS			TOILET ARTICLES						
	TOWELS & WASHCLOTHS		KITS			TOWELS						
	U. S. MONEY (AMOUNT)		KNIVES			TROUSERS, PR.						
	WATCH		LETTERS			TRUNKS, PR.						
	WINGS		LIGHTERS			UNDERWEAR						
	CONTAINERS ADDRESSED TO									INFORMATION		

For example, the effects taken from the body of an officer killed near the end of the war were sent home in September 1945. These included an identification bracelet, a gold wedding ring, infantry collar insignia, and two lieutenant colonel insignia. Unlike enlisted men who were issued what they needed, officers purchased their own insignia. Also listed among the effects sent

This is the form used to identify articles being sent home as personal effects. Officers, having to buy their own uniforms, could have such items sent home, while clothing issued to enlisted men was put back into stocks if still serviceable.

home were his Purple Heart's Oak Leaf Cluster (which represented his mortal wound) and a copy of the award from the 298th General Hospital, where his body had been taken after it was recovered from the field.

The second shipment home, in June 1947, included the officer's footlocker. Its contents: one bag (cloth or travel), books, miscellaneous articles, ribbons and decorations, souvenir money, brushes, letters, one overcoat, personal papers, one mechanical pencil, photos, one shirt, socks, stationary, two trousers, and underwear. The condition of the items, if damaged, was also noted as follows: "lock on footlocker broken, undershirts slightly stained, overcoat slightly stained and greasy, stop watch not running and crystal missing."

By way of comparison, the records of a private killed in September 1944 listed only one item sent back to his family: a 100 Franc note. Because this was an Allied occupation bill, it was technically not worth anything in the United States and thus was returned as "souvenir money." Any salvageable items found on his person or in his baggage were deemed either Government Issue, or not suitable for return to the family.

The report of burial form has an outline of a dog tag on it that held all the information from the man's actual dog tag. In some cases the information is type-written, but in others the Graves Registration personnel used a special tool to copy the actual embossed letters from the dog tag to the paper.

In theory, one of the dog tags was supposed to remain with the body, while the other was used as a temporary grave marker. To prevent any questions from arising in the future about the identification of the body, a paper form was filled out with information on the casualty and placed with the body inside a small green bottle. These bottles were not always available, however, so an accepted alternative was to place the information inside a used .50 caliber shell casing. The second dog tag was sometimes discarded after a more permanent marker was made, but in a small percentage of cases it is still paper-clipped to the burial form in the government records.

IDPFs are now considered public information and can be requested by anyone under a Freedom of Information Act request. The request should include the name and serial number, as well as either your relation to the deceased or that it is a FOIA request. It usually takes a long time to process these requests, so patience is required.

Requests should be sent to:

U.S. Army Total Personnel Command
ATTN: TAPC-PAO
200 Stovall Street
Alexandria, VA 22332-0404

On this Death Record the original embossed dog tag was used to transfer the information directly to the form to prevent transcription errors

Cemeteries

After World War II ended, the next of kin was asked whether he or she wanted the body returned to the USA for burial, or interned in one of the permanent cemeteries overseas. Records were kept documenting every step of the way to prevent any later confusion as to who was in what grave. Because temporary cemeteries were often consolidated, some remains were moved many times before they reached their final resting place.

Today, the American Battlefield Monuments Commission (ABMC) operates a number of cemeteries related to World War II around the world. They are kept in immaculate condition and stand as a wonderful memorial to the dead. The ABMC maintains a database on the Internet listing every man buried in their cemeteries. This database does not contain information on those men returned home for burial. The ABMC will also supply a photograph of the grave to next of kin, if requested.

> WEBSITE
>
> More information on the ABMC can be found at http://www.abmc.gov/

FOOTNOTES

1   National Archives website: www.nara.gov

2   TM-12-427 12 July 1944, p. 4.

3   TM-12-427 12 July 1944, p. 157.

4   Unless otherwise specified, such documents are from the author's collection.

5   The Official Army Officer Register 1943, p. 690.

FINDING YOUR FATHER'S WAR

Section 3

ORGANIZATIONAL RECORDS

This section explains all the various unit and organizational records.

It will provide you with more information on what a man and his unit actually did, once in the service.

General George Patton is often quoted as saying the Army is a team. While an individual soldier may not know anyone beyond his immediate squad or platoon, unit histories are rarely kept below regimental or battalion level.

To understand what a man did in the war, you have to understand how he fit into the unit, or team, as a whole.

National Archives

Army Time and Date — Maps
Classified Materials — Company Records
Organizational Records
Army Publications — T/O&Es
Code Names — Unit Histories
Other Records

ORGANIZATIONAL RECORDS

By regulation, every unit in the army had to keep specific records of their activities. Records of men coming into, and leaving the unit were all handled on a company level. Records of awards or decorations were handled at battalion, regiment, or division level, depending upon a number of factors. The smallest unit that was required to keep records on its overall activities was the regiment, or a battalion if it was an independent battalion.

It is important to determine the exact name and number of the unit you wish to research. This will be a regiment for an infantry unit, and a numbered battalion for almost everything else. In some very specialized cases it will be a numbered company, although those were often so small they did not keep many records and more info on them can often be found by searching the group they were attached to.

These unit records were required by the Adjutant General's office, which specified the bare minimum of what was to be documented. Some units saved everything, including daily logs from battalions and companies. Some filed away photos, propaganda leaflets dropped on them by the enemy, map overlays, and every possible piece of paper you could think of. Other units kept almost nothing. Some records were lost or misfiled in the years before they were transferred to the National Archives. You will not know how much exists until someone actually examines their files.

ARMY TIME AND DATE

The Army used the 24-hour method of telling time. Thus one o'clock in the afternoon is 1300 (stated as "thirteen hundred hours"). Time is generally stated with the full four digits, such as 1657 hrs. or 2300 hrs.

To identify a specific time and date, Army records will sometimes use a six-digit number with the first two digits being the date and the last four the time. An example would be "at 200645 the company landed." This simply means the

20th of the month at 0645 hours (6:45AM). This notation is commonly seen showing a period of time such as "from the period 150800 through 162300." Which would indicate from 0800 hrs. on the 15th through 2300 hrs on the 16th. The month and year are always made clear either after the notation, or as the specific subject of the record (i.e. "report for June 1944").

Different lettered suffixes were used to indicate what kind of time was being used. Much like EST today indicates Eastern Standard Time. Greenwich Mean Time is indicated by the suffix "Z." The other lesser used suffixes are "A" which meant normal summer time (Z-time +1 hour). The suffix "B" meant summer daylight saving time (Z time +2 hours). "Z" time was generally used for large scale operations; the British areas used "A" time, and occupied countries used "B" time.

MAPS

Maps can be important in finding exact locations of military units. Army records use grid coordinates to identify a specific location on a map. World War II military maps are essentially the same as civilian contour maps used by hikers today. There are many good books and websites that can explain how to read these maps. The two military-specific things that are different are the use of military grid coordinates and military unit symbols.

Grid coordinates are a way to give a numeric address to any place on the map, even if there is no identifiable feature nearby. A numbered grid is laid over the map. In this example (taken from FM 21-25, Elementary Map Reading, 1944), the vertical grid lines are numbered along the bottom 46, 47,and 48. The horizontal grid lines are numbered along the left side 32, 33 and 34. Grid coordinates are read to the right then up. The mnemonic is "read right up."

Thus, the four-digit coordinate 47 by 34 would be the intersection next to the words "Furlough Farm." Simple enough, but as each grid line is a thousand yards apart this works only to bring you within a thousand yards of the target site. If you break each grid into imaginary tenth lines, as seen in the second example, you can pinpoint a location to within 10 yards. The letter "S" in Liaison Field would be six-digit grid coordinate 479 by 334. Most records will use a six digit coordinate number, as that tends to be close enough for most purposes. The Army just uses the string of four or six numbers so the above would be called 479334.

To speed up the process the Army also labels each map in an area with a letter. This makes it easier to find if the location is near the junction of two maps. Locating the coordinate T477336 is faster if you know to first look at the "T"

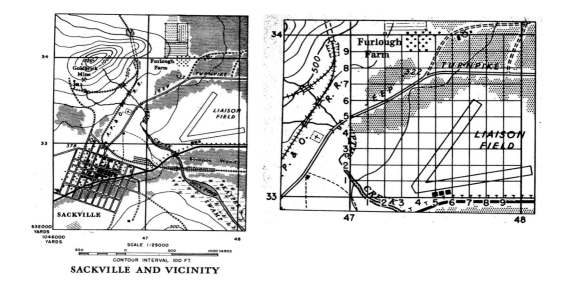

SACKVILLE AND VICINITY

labeled map, then find the grid coordinate. The letter is not necessary, but helpful. Section letters will be found noted on the edges of maps and sometimes printed as a larger shaded letter at the center of that section.

Standard map symbols such as roads, woods, streams, or bridges are the same as on a civilian map. Most include a key for these along the side. To identify the location of military units, a series of standard map markings was developed. These are not the same in every nation's Army, but it was a standard for the US Army in World War II and is still in use today.

Units are identified by type (infantry, artillery, engineer), starting with a rectangle. A symbol in the rectangle indicates what type of unit it is. A vertical line at the lower left, like a flagpole, indicates it is a headquarters unit. The end point of this line is the exact location of the headquarters. Non-headquarters units are larger and are considered to be in the general location of the symbol. Sometimes an oval is drawn around the unit symbol to better identify the area it is occupying.

To identify the size of the unit, a code is placed above the rectangle. These can range from a single dot (squad), to XXXX (a Field Army). To identify the specific unit, its number or company letter is placed to the left side. A number to the right side indicates what parent organization the unit comes from, although this is not always needed.

Maps in combat were valuable items and not always easy to replace. They needed to be kept free from marks or would eventually become useless. To

CHART SHOWING UNIT SYMBOLS

SQUAD	●	REGIMENT	III
SECTION	●●	BRIGADE	X
PLATOON	●●●	DIVISION	XX
COMPANY / TROOP / BATTERY	I	CORPS	XXX
BATTALION	II	ARMY	XXXX

⊠ .... INFANTRY UNIT

⃠ .... ARMORED FORCE UNIT

⋈ .... AIR CORPS UNIT

⊡ .... ARTILLERY UNIT (FIELD ARTILLERY AND COAST ARTILLERY OTHER THAN ANTIAIRCRAFT).

⃔ .... CAVALRY UNIT.

G .... CHEMICAL WARFARE UNIT.

⃔ .... COAST ARTILLERY ANTIAIRCRAFT UNIT.

E .... ENGINEER UNIT.

P .... MILITARY POLICE UNIT.

⊞ .... MEDICAL UNIT.

⋎ .... VETERINARY UNIT.

⊡ .... ORDNANCE UNIT.

Q .... QUARTERMASTER UNIT.

S .... SIGNAL CORPS UNIT.

A chart of common World War II map symbols for various styles of military units.

A⊠48 .... ONE SQUAD, COMPANY A, 48TH INFANTRY.

IA⊠48 .... IST PLATOON, COMPANY A, 48TH INFANTRY.

A⊠48 .... LIGHT MACHINE-GUN SECTION, COMPANY A, 48TH INFANTRY.

D⊠48 .... MACHINE-GUN PLATOON, CALIBER .30, COMPANY D, 48TH INFANTRY.

A⃔16 .... TROOP A, 16TH CAVALRY.

SpW⃔16 .... SPECIAL WEAPONS TROOP, 16TH CAVALRY.

⃔16 .... MACHINE-GUN TROOP, CALIBER .50 16TH CAVALRY.

A⃠IL .... COMPANY A, IST ARMORED REGIMENT (L).

B⊡5 .... BATTERY B, 5TH FIELD ARTILLERY.

B⃔104 .... BATTERY B, 104TH COAST ARTILLERY (AA)

B⃠68 .... BATTERY B, 68TH FIELD ARTILLERY(ARMORED).

2⊠48 .... 2d BATTALION, 48TH INFANTRY.

⋈7obsn .... 7TH OBSERVATION SQUADRON.

Q6 .... 6TH QUARTERMASTER REGIMENT.

⊡8 .... COMMAND POST, 8TH FIELD ARTILLERY.

+ .... MEDICAL UNIT IN OPERATION.

Ⓐ⊠48 .... AREA OCCUPIED BY COMPANY A, 48TH INFANTRY.

preserve these maps, most were placed under a clear plastic sheet and wax pencils were used for any notations. To document positions, map overlays were made. To make an overlay, a sheet of thin translucent paper is placed over the map. The desired information is traced on the paper and two grid intersections are drawn and labeled. The result makes little sense until you place it on the correct scale of map and align the two grid intersections.

To make sure a grid coordinate is properly read it is important that you have the correct map. It is important to use a wartime military map, the same as the troops during the war would have had.[2] Most unit records will contain the actual maps used in the war and numerous overlays showing the local situation. Some of these maps will have been refolded and taped up many times, and all will have been stored over 60 years ago. Coupled with the brittle wartime paper it is almost impossible to unfold and read them.

Thankfully, the Cartography Branch of the National Archives has a good collection of World War II military maps. These have been stored flat, and can be more easily copied. The Cartography staff can help you find the correct map, working from the general latitude and longitude of the area. If unknown, this can be determined from the nearest large town or city. It's also important to know the scale of the map (such as 1:250,000).

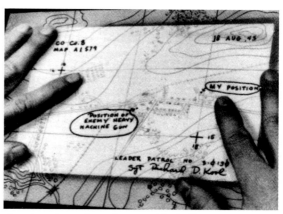

A map overlay as drawn by a patrol leader.[1]

Another important reason to use original World War II military maps is that they do contain some errors. Some foreign towns may get misspelled, or have been renamed over time. One of the most famous errors on any World War II map is the railroad shown running just behind Omaha Beach. Almost every period (Allied) map shows this, but the railroad had actually never been built.

Infantrymen in Normandy transfer material from a large overlay onto the smaller maps they will carry up to the front lines. Using overlays preserved the maps (which were often in short supply) and made it easy for information on troop locations to be transferred from unit to unit.   National Archives

CLASSIFIED MATERIALS

There are five types of classifications for information the Army wanted to keep secret. These were typed or stamped on the top and bottom of each page to indicate the level of classification. Almost all material classified in World War II has now been declassified and should be freely available. The only problem is knowing where to look for it.

The lowest class of secrecy is "RESTRICTED." This term is for material that is for official use only and not meant for the general pubic. Circulation is limited for reasons of administrative privacy. The next higher classification is "CONFIDENTIAL," which limits distribution only to those who need it to carry out their duties. [3]

The highest form of classification normally found is "SECRET." This level is for documents that might endanger national security, cause serious injury to government activity, or be of great advantage to the enemy, such as cryptographic information. The term "TOP SECRET" was adopted late in the war and was one level higher, used for upcoming operations, technological developments, or counterintelligence information.

There was still a higher form of classification referred to as "CODE WORD SECRET." At this high level of secrecy no one was allowed to share such code word classified information with anyone that was not specifically cleared to that specific code word. The most famous example of this is the code word "BIGOT" which concerned information about the Normandy invasion. Even the meaning of the code word was secret and only those cleared for Normandy information knew what the word BIGOT meant.

The Army did not hide events by not producing paper records for matters deemed SECRET, or destroy those records afterward. Documents with secretive information may have dates, names, and places blacked out on copies that were not kept in a secure location. The originals would contain the full information and should still be readily available, with the exception of those still involving national security, in the appropriate files.

There were no secret or classified missions that went unrecorded by the Army in World War II. The Army ran on paperwork and even the most sensitive missions needed to account for men and materiel. Anyone claiming a fanciful account that does not have the paperwork to back it up because the mission was "secret" should be taken with a grain of salt.

Almost every document from the World War II era has now been declassified. Some, considered to hold information that might embarrass another nation, endanger a former agent, or give away some desirable secret may still be classified. One of the last areas to be heavily classified is that dealing with crypto-graphic systems because even knowing how a nation used to think about codes and ciphers can help a foreign nation think along the same path.

Interestingly enough, it is prohibited to classify a document to conceal viola-tions of law, inefficiency, or administrative error, as well as to prevent embar-rassment to a person, organization, or agency.[4]

It is very unlikely that anything related to an average World War II soldier would still be classified. If, in the extremely unusual case that records are still classi-fied, it is possible to ask the government if they can be opened up. Sometimes, things will sit in classified status only because no one ever asked to see them. You will need to know the exact records and the agency which holds them. If it is the Army, information on classification and declassification is available from the Army Records Management and Declassification Agency.

<table>
<tr><td>

BOOKS

An important examination of military secret paperwork and missions from the Viet Nam era, but applicable to World War II, is: *Stolen Valor*, by B. G. Burkett, Verity Press Publishing, 1998, ISBN 096670360X

</td><td>

WEBSITE

The Army Records Management and Declassification Agency.
www.rmda.belvoir.army.mil/rmdaxml

</td></tr>
</table>

COMPANY RECORDS

Rosters and Morning Reports

In the Army, the company (or battery or troop) was the administrative home to a soldier. Every soldier in the Army had a company (or equivalent) he was assigned to.

To track his comings and goings, every morning each company would file a Company Morning Report. The Morning Report also indicated the total strength of the company so that it would receive the correct amount of rations.

The Morning Report is a daily history of the unit and accounts for every officer and enlisted man assigned to that company. This report indicated any changes in personnel in the last 24 hours. They did not contain a full roster of every man in the company, just those that had arrived, had a status change (such as a pro-motion), or left (gone to the hospital, been wounded, gone AWOL, or been transferred). AR 345-400 describes how the morning reports were to be done.

Morning Reports were useful not just for tracking where every man in the army was, but important for keeping track of how many effective men were in the company and how much food was needed for it. The Morning Report covered a midnight to midnight time period, and the company commander signed off on

SOME OFFICIAL ABBREVIATIONS

Resgn	RESIGNED	EPTE	EXISTED PRIOR TO ENLISTMENT
Asgn	ASSIGNED	ar	ARREST
Reld	RELIEVED	ret	RETIRED
Comd	COMMAND	qrs	QUARTERS
Fr	FROM	fur	FURLOUGH
Jd	JOINED	lv	LEAVE
Jn	JOIN	AWOL	ABSENT WITHOUT LEAVE
Sk	SICK	SD	SPECIAL DUTY
Trfd	TRANSFERRED	Conf	CONFINED
Co	COMPANY	Disch	DISCHARGED
aptd	APPOINTED (PROMOTION)	LWA	LIGHTLY WOUNDED IN ACTION
gr	GRADE (RANK)	SWA	SERIOUSLY WOUNDED IN ACTION
rd	REDUCED	KIA	KILLED IN ACTION
NLD	NOT IN LINE OF DUTY	MIA	MISSING IN ACTION

it, after which it was sent on to the personnel section of the regiment. They were to be done in ink and never changed once submitted. Only specific authorized abbreviations (shown in the chart above) were to be used.

"Fr duty to lv 5 days" meant going from his normal duty to a 5 day leave.

"Fr AWOL to conf" meant a man previously listed as AWOL was now confined in a guard house or jail.

"Fr duty to sk" indicated a man had gone from active duty to the sick list.

"Fr duty to Ab Sk indicates the man was sick but absent as he was sent off to a hospital.

The reports were also used to give the location of the company (the "station"), marches, and an abbreviated mention of anything of major interest. If the unit remained in the same location it only had to mention where they were every 10 days.

In combat, the location indicated was normally the position of the Regimental headquarters where the regimental personnel section (and company clerks) was located. The actual Morning Report form changed slightly over the war years, but essentially it provided the same information.

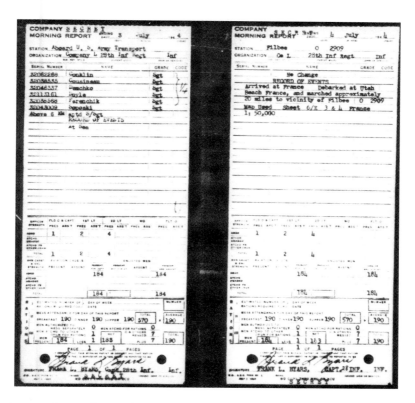

The image above shows the company Morning Reports from Company L, 28th Infantry Regiment for 3 and 4 July 1944. The unit landed in France on 4 July 1944. On the 3d it can be seen the unit is listed "at sea" with 184 men (all present or absent). Five Sergeants were appointed S/Sgt. (Staff Sergeant). This would have been done to make sure the unit landed with all positions properly filled. Listed in the unit are one Captain, two 1st Lieutenants and four 2d Lieutenants.

The rations section indicates that out of the 184 enlisted men, one is attached to another organization for rations. It is unclear who this is, but probably the company clerk attached to the regimental headquarters. Total strength for the company is 190 soldiers.

The form is signed by Captain Frank Byers, the Regimental Personnel Adjutant and not the company commander. This is because in combat the company clerks worked out of the regimental headquarters and a company commander would not have the time to journey every day back from the front to sign the paperwork. A company HQ in combat was normally little more than a hole in the ground, so it would be hard to type up and file reports in such a location.

On 4 July 1944, the Record of events indicates: "arrived at France. Debarked at Utah Beach France and marched approximately 20 miles to vicinity of Filbee O 2909. Map used Sheet 6/E 3&4 France 1:50,000."

This means the company landed at Utah Beach and marched inland to a bivouac site near the town of Filbee. The map sheet is given, and the rough coordinate of O 2909 (Map sheet O, grid coordinate 2909).

This location is also mentioned in the top section. The total numbers are the same, and no one was listed as sick, wounded, or missing.

Skipping ahead a few days to 12 July (see image below left), the company first entered combat at La Haye du Puis. This is the fourth sheet of five for the day. The location of the unit is listed as being Rauville La Place—Map sheet T coordinate 2195. Again, this is most likely the location of the regimental headquarters where the company clerk was—not the actual company location, although they would be reasonably close to one another.

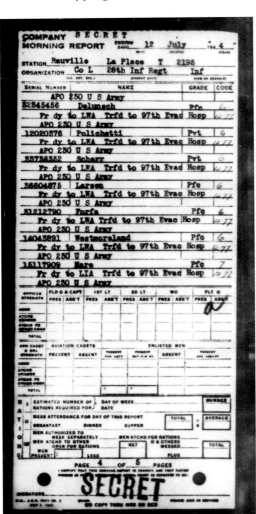

This page lists seven men wounded—"fr dty LWA" indicates that the men's status is changed from his current duty due to being Lightly Wounded in Action. They are then transferred to the 97th Evacuation Hospital (trfd to 97th Evac Hosp).

The Morning Report on this date lists only 7 men wounded with 156 men left for duty. This was because at this point the clerk only knew of the men that had definitely left the unit and been sent to the hospital.

The fighting at this time was very confusing and on the next day the report lists only three men transferred to the hospital (two for non-battle reasons—sick, shock, etc.).

It is not until the 14th that any troops are listed as killed. 5 are WIA and 12 KIA.

On the 15th the former First Sgt. is finally listed as KIA (he was one of the first few casualties on the 12th). His position would not be filled until the 17th. On the 16th the company Commander, Captain Patty, was listed as KIA. He was actually one of the first men in the unit to be killed, and yet it took from the 12th until the 16th for him to be officially listed as KIA.

The report for July 16th also indicates 10 men listed as MIA (missing in action) as of 12 July, and another 4 men MIA as of 13 July. The final total for the unit on the 16th leaves them with only four 2d lieutenants. as officers (one having been transferred in from Company K) and 141 enlisted men.

Totaling up the numbers from 12–16 July one can find that the company lost 4 officers KIA, 2 WIA, and received two new officers as replacements. The enlisted men lost 16 men KIA, 43 WIA and 14 MIA. To replace these losses, 31 men were assigned to the company from a replacement battalion.

Why did it take so long for the KIAs and MIAs to be listed on the official report? The answer is that the unit knew that as soon as they were listed as casualties the Army paperwork machine would be put into action. Telegraphs would be sent to their next of kin with the information. Unless there was definite proof a man was dead no one wanted to put his family through getting that telegram needlessly.

Combat was a confusing thing and there was always a chance that a man thought to be dead or missing would turn up alive in a hospital or wander back into the American lines.

On to July 17 (see right). The company lists some promotions as it reorganizes after its initial losses. Pvt. Lambo is made company First Sergeant. Four Technical Sergeants, seven Staff Sergeants, and and an additional seven were made buck Sergeant .

This is combat as seen through Morning Reports. Men are killed and wounded. Replacements are assigned, and men are promoted to fill the necessary posts. The cycle repeated for months until there were very few men left in the company who had originally landed with it.

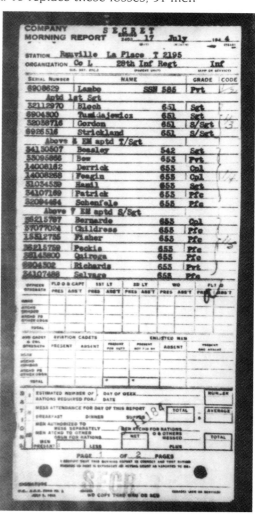

Monthly Personnel Rosters

With such a system it would be easy for men to get lost in the shuffle, so every month a roster of every company was prepared as a double check against errors. This meant that with the roster, the changes in the Morning Reports would only have to be tracked from the start of the month.

Sadly, almost all of the wartime monthly unit rosters are missing. The National Personnel Records Center holds what remains, but the years 1944, 1945 and 1946 were destroyed (supposedly in the fire of 1973). For those interested in an earlier time frame the company roster would provide a starting place to begin the addition and subtraction of men mentioned in the Morning Report to determine exactly who was in the company on a specific day.

Each company was supposed to keep a copy of their roster in their files, but these rarely turn up in unit records. Most rosters in existence today from the lost 1944–46 period were copies kept by a soldier as a souvenir or in order to keep track of the men in his unit for future reunions.

Duty Rosters and Company Orders

Duty Rosters (AGO Form 6) were used in non combat areas to assign men to various fatigues, or non-combat related tasks. It was kept by the company first sergeant who had the power to assign men to a number of good, or bad, jobs that needed to be done. Ordinary drill and training is not included. Duties were separated into guard duty and all others, like Kitchen Police (KP), latrine orderly, fatigue details (cleaning, digging, moving materials, etc). All non-combat related tasks to be done were known as fatigues because they tired you out.

NCOs technically did not perform fatigues, but could be assigned to oversee a group of men on a job, or be given "CQ" (charge of quarters) which meant he was in charge of an organization's headquarters, generally at night or when everyone else was away training.

In theory these jobs were to be given in rotation—the man who had been the longest off that duty was the first available for it. In practice it was used as an unofficial punishment to enforce the authority of the sergeants. Duty Rosters were published the day before and posted on the company bulletin board. They were signed by the First Sergeant "by order of the company commander." There was no reason to keep duty rosters once the day was over, so few survive. They are mentioned here as some soldiers may have kept them as souvenirs, or mentioned them in letters.

The other type of company level orders that might be found are Company General Orders, numbered starting with "General Order Number 1" every year. The most common company order is used to promote a private to private first class. This is the only promotion handled inside the company.

Also handled on the company level was the record of individual clothing or equipment record. This tracked what items had been issued to the soldier. If he lost or damaged anything the cost was taken out of his pay.

In true Army fashion, a man who was short something on his list might turn first to "moonlight requisitioning" rather than pay the cost. This was a nice term for stealing from someone else (always in another company, not your own). It was often justified, as someone had probably stolen the missing item in the first place, and the soldier was just passing the bad luck on.

ORGANIZATIONAL RECORDS

The Adjutant General's office required all organizations to submit periodic records for historical purposes. According to AR 345-105, each unit had to submit a standardized record indicating the following items:

- Original unit
- Changes in organization
- Strength
- Stations of units (or parts thereof)
- Marches
- Campaigns
- Battles
- Commanding officers in important engagements

Obviously this list makes more sense for a 19th century unit, but it formed the basis for the historical records that units submitted monthly with a yearly summary to the Adjutant General's office.

These are the basis of the main historical records kept by the Army, and which can be found in the National Archives under Record Group 407.

Thankfully, most units recognized that this was not a significant amount of information for modern warfare and included far more than these bare basics in the files they submitted. General orders, field orders, operations reports, logs, and just about every possible type of record made its way into the historical files.

At the end of the war some units discarded everything that was not required by the regulations; others sent their entire files in to the AG's office.

General Orders and Field Orders

General and special orders are documents that publish information, of a permanent nature, that needs to be disseminated and kept on record. One example is a general order indicating that a new commander has taken over a unit. More commonly found are orders indicating promotions or awards to men. When such an order specified a specific individual he was given a copy of it. Often the copies made during the war blanked out dates or places for security reasons. The originals in the unit files would have the unaltered version.

DECLASSIFIED PER EXECUTIVE ORDER 12356, SECTION 3.3, NND PROJECT
NUMBER *NND 733017*, BY *RB/VSw*   , DATE *9/22/94*

R E S T R I C T E D

GENERAL ORDERS)   HEADQUARTERS 8TH INFANTRY DIVISION
              :   APO #8, U. S. Army,
NUMBER   21   )   12 July 1944 /ftk

        In accordance with Army Regulations 600-20, 1 June 1942, as
amended, the undersigned hereby assumes command of the 8th Infantry
Division effective this date.

                        Donald A. Stroh
                        DONALD A. STROH,
                    Brigadier General, U. S. Army,
                            Commanding.

Dist: A & C

                        - 1 -

                R E S T R I C T E D

Orders were always numbered starting at 1, with a new series each year. This is the 8th Infantry Division's General Order number 21 for 1944, in which General Donald Stroh assumes command of the division. Note that even a simple item like this was considered "restricted." The tag at the top of the order is the declassification information.

General Order number 47 of the Department of the Army (from 1949; see image opposite) contains some World War II-era awards that had only just then been approved. Aside from a current change at Toole Air Force Depot, the 829th Engineer Aviation Battalion was awarded the meritorious Unit Commendation for its efforts In Iceland in 1944, and Company I, 28th Infantry Regiment is cited for a "Battle Honor" for their efforts in the Hurtgen Forest in 1944, resulting in what is today known as a Presidential Unit Citation. Many unit citations were not made official until years after the war ended.

GO 47

DEPARTMENT OF THE ARMY\
WASHINGTON 25, D. C., *19 October 1949*

Section

TOOELE ORDNANCE DEPOT, TOOELE, UTAH—Tooele Sub-Depot of Ogden
Arsenal and Ogden Arsenal redesignated_____ I

MERITORIOUS UNIT COMMENDATION—Award_____ II

BATTLE HONORS—Citation of unit_____ III

I__TOOELE ORDNANCE DEPOT, TOOELE, UTAH.—1. *Effective 1 November 1949*, The Tooele Sub-Depot of Ogden Arsenal, Ogden, Utah, will be redesignated Tooele Ordnance Depot, Tooele, Utah, a class II installation under the jurisdiction of the Chief of Ordnance.

2. *Effective 1 November 1949*, Ogden Arsenal, Ogden, Utah, will be redesignated the Sub-Depot of Tooele Ordnance Depot, Tooele, Utah.

[AG 680.1 (14 Oct 49)]

II__MERITORIOUS UNIT COMMENDATION.—By direction of the Secretary of the Army, under the provisions of paragraph 14, AR 260–15, the Meritorious Unit Commendation is awarded to the following unit of the Army of the United States for exceptionally meritorious conduct in the performance of outstanding service during the period indicated. The citation reads as follows:

The *824th Engineer Aviation Battalion* is commended for exceptionally meritorious conduct and performance of outstanding services in Iceland from January to July 1944. Given the mission of preparing airfield facilities at that important base, the unit constructed and maintained Meeks and Patterson Fields during unusually trying weather conditions. In addition, the battalion performed many other essential engineer tasks on the island. The consistent high standard of operating efficiency, leadership, and teamwork reflects great credit on the *824th Engineer Aviation Battalion*, the Air Corps, and the Army of the United States.

III__BATTLE HONORS.—As authorized by Executive Order 9396 (sec. I, WD Bul. 22, 1943), superseding Executive Order 9075 (sec. III, WD Bul. 11, 1942), the following unit is cited under the provisions of AR 260–15 in the name of the President of the United States as public evidence of deserved honor and distinction. The citation reads as follows:

Company I, 28th Infantry Regiment, is cited for outstanding performance of duty in action against the enemy on 23 November 1944 in the Hurtgen Forest, Germany. Given the mission of reducing a well-fortified and supported enemy position, the company launched two attacks which were repulsed. Determined to take the position, the company commander deployed his entire company and ordered a bayonet assault. Springing to their feet, shooting and yelling, the men were upon the enemy before they could bring down defensive fire. This ferocious attack so disorganized the defenders that they were driven from their emplacements and surrendered in groups. Over 100 prisoners were taken in addition to many killed and wounded. The extraordinary courage, initiative, and determination to close with the enemy exhibited by the personnel of *Company I, 28th Infantry Regiment,* reflect great credit on this unit and the Armed Forces of the United States.

BY ORDER OF THE SECRETARY OF THE ARMY:

OFFICIAL:\
EDWARD F. WITSELL\
Major General\
The Adjutant General\
AGO 827B—Oct. 851714°—49

J. LAWTON COLLINS\
Chief of Staff, United States Army

U. S. GOVERNMENT PRINTING OFFICE: 1949

R E S T R I C T E D

GENERAL ORDERS)

NUMBER   80)

HEADQUARTERS- 8TH INFANTRY DIVISION
APO #8, U. S. ARMY
9 October 1944   /ctp

E X T R A C T

SECTION III - AWARD OF BRONZE STAR MEDAL

By direction of the President, under the provisions of AR 600-45, 22
September 1943, as amended, the Bronze Star Medal is awarded to:
*   *   *   *   *   *   *

Corperal William T. Dowd, ■■■■■■, Field Artillery, Headquarters Battery,
43rd Field Artillery Battalion, for heroic service in connection with military operations against the enemy on 2 September 1944 in the vicinity of
* * * * *, France. Then an infantry regiment was being subjected to a heavy
enemy artillery barrage, a direct hit severed communications with the supporting artillery battalion. Corporal Dowd, with the aid of another soldier,
advanced several hundred yards to locate the break and repair the line while
subjected to concentrated enemy fire. His voluntary and courageous action
and untiring devotion to duty on numerous other occasions merits the highest
of praise. Entered the military service from New Jersey.

First Lieutenant John O. Gawne, ■■■■■■, Infantry, Company L. 28th Infantry Regiment, for heroic service in connection with military operations
against the enemy on 15 September 1944 in the vicinity of * * * * *, France.
While Lieutenant Gawne was leading his company in an attack, the right platoon
was held up by heavy enemy machine gun fire. With complete disregard for
his own safety, Lieutenant Gawne moved to that position, reorganized the
platoon, and led it against the enemy. Wounded during this action. his continued examples of personal courage were an inspiration to his men. Entered
the military service from New York.

*General Order 80 (1944) from the 8th
Infantry Division showing two Bronze
Star awards.*

*To save the clerks from typing a long
document many times, only extracts of
the full document were copied and given
to the individual soldiers.*

*There might be dozens of awards listed
on one General Order, and there was no
need for every man to get a copy of every
other man's information.*

This extract of orders (above)—AR 600-45, 22
September 1943—refers to the army regulation
concerning the award of the Bronze Star medal.

The actual details of the incident might be fairly
sketchy to the clerk assigned to write the citation,
so they should not always be taken as absolute
truth.

Some citations can list incorrect dates, places, or
events, but they do provide a great starting place to
put the action into perspective.

Cpl. Dowd's citation for fixing severed telephone lines under enemy fire was
perhaps one of the most common ways a signalman was given such an award.
It takes a brave man to go out under enemy fire to splice the lines together.

The locations of the action were deleted so that these copies could be sent
home and used in the local newspaper without giving away a unit's location.

Stock phrases such as "voluntary and courageous action and untiring devotion to duty," and "examples of personal courage were an example to his men" were commonly used to round out a short blurb. Keep in mind that clerks sometimes had to write up dozens of similar citations and they quickly learned the standard phrases used by the Army in such situations. All such phrases should be taken with a healthy dose of skepticism.

Field orders, abbreviated as FO, were combat orders issued in the unit directing some action to be taken.

There is a specific format for such orders. The first paragraph contains information about enemy and friendly troops. The second paragraph contains direction on what the commander wants done. This is a statement of what, where, how, and when a force is to operate. The third paragraph assigned definite missions to each of the elements. The 4th paragraph covers administrative details (supply, medical evacuation, etc.) which often remained the same as they normally were. The 5th paragraph covers locations of command posts and instructions on methods of communication such as radio frequencies.

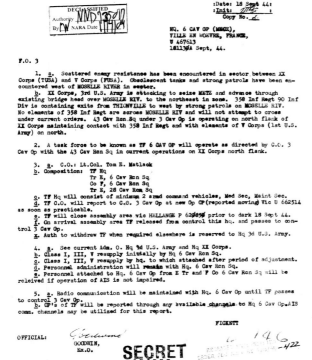

Field Order number 3 for 1944 of the 6th Cavalry Group (mechanized).

This order details the formation of a task force (who commands it, what it's composed of, where it will assemble, and where it will get supplies from).

As it details a future combat operation, it is automatically classified as SECRET.

Staff Reports

The Personnel (S-1) Intelligence (S-2) Operations (S-3) and Supply (S-4) sections regularly produced reports on their areas of interest. Of these, the S-3 operations reports are the most useful as they indicate what the unit was doing, or planned to do. The S-3 (or G3) section maintained the maps and overlays indicating where the various elements of the unit were.

Logs were kept by the operations section of all messages or other important matters that transpired at their headquarters. Not all of these logs survive in the files but they give a minute by minute description of what the unit's headquarters witnessed. It is also possible to find such files of messages and major incidents at battalion level.

The S-3 Journal for the 6th Cavalry Group, dated 19 Sept. 1944.

Some are messages to be sent via messenger or via radio. Some officers are mentioned by name, but it would be rare to find an enlisted man mentioned in this kind of record.

These types of records are useful for finding out details about a particular day; especially for when the headquarters received specific orders or news.

DECLASSIFIED
Authority NND735212
By CW NARA Date 1/1/01

```
                                          S-3 JOURNAL
      TIME    :SERIAL   TIME   :        WHO TO & FROM              :ACTION
   IN  : OUT  :  NO    :SIGNED :                                   :TAKEN
        :     :        :(18 Sep):         19 SEPT 1944             :
 1200A  :     :   1    : 1826A :C.O.6th Cav Sq V C.O. 6th Cav Gp.  : File
        :     :        :       :information Dets now committed except :
        :     :        :       :E-2 will be relieved approx. 1200B 21 :
        :     :        :       :Sept.  Dets have been instructed to assem
        :     :        :       :ble by troops and return to Sq. assembly
        :     :        :       :area in this vicinity.  You will re-   :
        :     :        :       :connoiter and select appropriate bivouac
        :     :        :       :areas in this vicinity.  Guides will be
        :     :        :       :held available any time after 211200B to
        :     :        :       :take troops to areas.  Locations of areas
        :     :        :       :selected will be reported to this Hq.  :
        :1252A:   2    : 1252A :CO's All Troops TASK FORCE 6th Cav Gp V: Msgr.
        :     :        :       :C.O. Task Force Effective at once all  :
        :     :        :       :civilians will be kept out of the camp :
        :     :        :       :area.  This includes children.  It is  :
        :     :        :       :the responsibility of every individual :
        :     :        :       :to see that order is enforced.         :
        :     :        :(18 Sep):                                      :
        :     :   3    : 2255A :C.O. 6th Cav Rcn Sq V C.O. 6th Cav Gp  :
        :     :        :       :You will issue instructions to Lt. Heath, File
        ::    :        :       :Tr C your command to report to Maj. F.L.
        :     :        :       :Martin, senior Ln O this Hq at G-3 Opns:
        :     :        :       :TUSA within 24 hrs after his release   :
        :     :        :       :from current AIS assignment.           :
        :1305A:   4    : 1302A :S-1, 6th Cav Rcn Sq V C.O. Task Force  : Rad.
        :     :        :       :6th Cav Gp.  Task force located 830028.:
        :     :        :       :Have maint secure one set half tracks  :
        :     :        :       :this date am sending in for them.      :
        :1512A:   5    : 1510A :CO's All Troops TF 6th Cav Gp V C.O. TF: Msgr.
        :     :        :       :Until further notice troops will furnish
        :     :        :       :water detail of three (3) men and one(1)
        :     :        :       :Half Track as follows: 20 Sept - Troop :
        :     :        :       :E 6th Cav Rcn Sq, 21 Sept - Troop E 28th
        :     :        :       :Cav Rcn Sq, 22 Sept - Troop F 6th Cav :
        :     :        :       :Rcn Sq.  Detail report to Capt. Taylor :
        :     :        :       :0830 for instructions.                 :
        :1600A:   6    : 1555A :Comm O, 43 Sq V C.O TF 6th Cav Gp.     : Msgr.
        :     :        :       : Push Button   XTAL         NET        :
        :     :        :       :   1           41       Fwd and Rr Ech.:
        :     :        :       :   2           --           --         :
        :     :        :       :   3           --           --         :
        :     :        :       :   4           4          Tr A         :
        :     :        :       :   5           44          "  B        :
        :     :        :       :   6           6           "  C        :
        :     :        :       :   7           26          "  E        :
        :     :        :       :   8           62          "  F        :
        :     :        :       :   9           4       Sq Tact will con-
        :     :        :       :                       tact Fwd and Rr Ech
        :1605A:   7    : 1600A :CO's E-6, F-6, E-28 V CO TF 6th Cav Gp : Msgr.
        :     :        :       :for our operation, FM PB #9 will not be:
        :     :        :       :used for tactical net.  Tactical net   :
        :     :        :       :will be on PB #10 crystal # 60.        :
        :     :        :       :          20 SEPT.                     :
 1004A  :     :   1    : 0840A :CO's E-6, F-6 V S-4 6th Cav Rcn Sq.    : File
        :     :        :       :Draw sand bags from NAN Four as soon   :
        :     :        :       :as practicable                         :
 0852A  :     :   2    : 0851A :CO 6th Cav Gp TF V CO E-6.  Departed   : File
        :     :        :       :Biv 0850.                              :
```

When documenting the events of a unit it would be impractical for the Army to do so at a message-by-message level. Operations Periodic Reports allowed the information to be condensed into a more easily readable form. All the staff sections produced periodic reports to summarize their activities, but the operations section contains the most information on what the unit was actually doing.

C O N F I D E N N T I A L

G-3 PERIODIC REPORT   FROM: 200001A Sept 44
                      TO : 202400A Sept 44

HQ T.F., 6th CAV GP
HELLANGE, LUXEMBOURG
Coordinates: P-830028
201900A Sept 44

No. 1

Maps: 1/100,000 Europe, NUENKIRCHEN SHEET.

1. Our Front Line: Does not apply

2. All units this organization assembled in biv in vic HELLANGE, LUXEMBOURG (P830028).

3. C.P. 43rd Cav Rcn Sq at P832026 with Tr A 43rd Cav at P932122, and C.P. Tr C 43rd Cav at P900000. Foward elements along line P945000 north to P945113.

4. Weather and Visibility: Execellent.

5. Our Operation for the Period 200800A Sept 44 to 201630A Sept 44.
   a. At 1110A, Co F 6th Cav Sq launched the initial attack on Obj 1, which was the high ground south of BOUS at P988054, from which point we were to establish an OP for the two Assault Gun Troops, Obj 1 was taken at 1320A.

   b. Tr E 6th Cav Sq and Tr E 28th Cav Sq were in direct support of the tanks throughout the entire action. By 1400A the OPs had been set up and fire was laid on the Bridge across the MOSELLE RIVER at REMICH.

6. The efficiency with which the operation was carried out was very satisfactory.

7. Results of Operation: Our mission was accomplished successfully.

OFFICIAL: MATLACK,
        McKENZIE,   Lt.Col.,
        Maj, S-3.   Comdg.

The G-3 Periodic Report for a Task Force of the 6th Cavalry Group for 20 September 1944.

Note that all proper place names are typed in capital letters.

This helped soldiers unfamiliar with the region to readily recognize an unfamiliar word as a location.

Overlays were used to indicate locations on a map. By aligning up the two grid coordinates the overlay could be perfectly placed on the proper map to illustrate locations of units, supply routes, front lines, etc.

Most overlays from the war were drawn on thin translucent paper that has not always held up to 60 years in storage. A good tip is to photocopy them, and have a local copy shop recopy them at the same size onto transparency material. Then they can be aligned on a copy of the proper map.

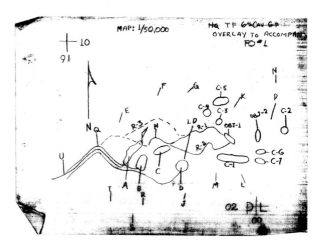

Paper was always in short supply, and so it is quite common to find unusual types of paperwork in the files. As the Army captured more enemy stocks the men used whatever was handy. This stationary was originally printed for the German Labor Office in Diedenhofen, Germany. It was used by the Americans (see example below) to record artillery concentrations fired on 28 Sept. 1944. It records the target, the grid coordinate and how many shells were fired (HE means high explosive).

Der Leiter des Arbeitsamtes Diedenhofen

Anschrift des Absenders:

Arbeitsamt Diedenhofen Schlageterstraße	Fernsprecher 43 u. 85	Bankkonto Kreditkasse Diedenhofen 151	Postscheckkonto 10 131 Saarbrücken

Nebenstellen: Hayingen, Bahnhofstraße 30, Fernsprecher 81 – Mövern, Adolf-Hitlerstraße 4, Fernsprecher 13 – Deutsch-Oth, Adolf-Hitlerstraße 29, Fernsprecher 7 – Sierk, Bahnhofstraße 20, Fernsprecher 4

Gesch. Z. _____

(In der Antwort gefl. angeben)

Diedenhofen, den   28 SEPT

RESUMME OF DAYS ACTIVITIES T&E 6 Cav

Relieved E 28TH Cav 0840

Reg on Targets of 28TH Cav (9 Registrations)

Fired on five targets of opportunity.

1. Tank Concentration (U865835)   72 HE

    One hit, probable damage to others

2. Tank Concentration (U879834)   56 HE

    Scattered personnel

3. Personnel along R.R. _ _ (U876859)   94 HE

    Report stated area well covered

4. Personnel & automatic (U875862)   46 HE

    weapons along River,

    Neutralized their fire

5. Fired Mission for 135E (U873858)   129 HE

    They reported excellent Results (after dark

B. Changed three sets of tracks

C. Unloaded 1026 Rds ammo.

After Action Reports

The most useful of all organizational records are the After Action Reports (A/A or AAR) mandated by the Adjutant General's office. These are a compilation of all the individual reports packaged to provide an overview of what a unit did in a given month. Most of the time, only senior officers or men who were singled out for a specific reason are mentioned. However, in the first few weeks a unit was in combat some clerks were more likely to make mention of a specific soldier. When a unit was new to combat everyone knew everyone else and each incident was important. As replacements began to fill up the companies, the new faces become only names and numbers to the clerks.

RESTRICTED

```
:Auth:    CG, VIII Corps,
:Date:    1 June, 1945,
:Init:    WHF
```

HEADQUARTERS 28th CAVALRY RCN SQUADRON (MECZ)
APO 403, U. S. Army

1 June, 1945.

SUBJECT: Action Against Enemy, Report After.

TO   : The Adjutant General,
           War Department,
           Washington 25, D. C.

THRU   : The Commanding Officer,
           6th Cavalry Group (Mecz),
           APO 403, U.S. Army.

SECTION I - Introduction
SECTION II - Narrative of Operations
SECTION III - Recommendations

SECTION I - INTRODUCTION

1. **Authority:** This report is submitted in compliance with paragraph 10 (Change 3) AR 345-105. It is the tenth such report of its kind submitted by this headquarters. The report covers the period 1 May to 090001B May, 1945.

2. **Command:** From 1 May to 090001B May the 28th Cavalry Reconnaissance Squadron (Mecz), commanded by Lt. Col. WALTER E. DAY, was attached to Col. EDWARD M. FICKETT's 6th Cavalry Group (Mecz), under VIII U.S. Corps, commanded by Maj. Gen. TROY H. MIDDLETON. The Squadron was assigned to First U. S. Army, commanded by Lt. Gen. COURTNEY HODGES.

SECTION II: NARRATIVE OF OPERATIONS

1 May 1945: The Squadron was maintaining a holding position in zone awaiting the approach of the Russian troops. The limiting line was well organized and an officer "squealer patrol" from Troop A was operating in the rear of the enemy lines. A patrol from Troop C pushed forward at 1130B and occupied a position at (K210022) but was forced to withdraw to its original position

- 1 -

RESTRICTED

DECLASSIFIED
DOD Dir. 5200.9, Sept. 27, 1998
NWM by _____ date _____

HEADQUARTERS, 747TH TANK BATTALION
APO 339, U. S. ARMY

4 April 1945

SUBJECT: After Action Report for the Month of March 1945.

TO   : The Adjutant General, Washington, 25, D. C.

THRU   : Commanding General, 29th Infantry Division, APO 29, U. S. Army.

I - Taking of Munchen-Gladbach, Germany

1. This battalion continued the drive on Munchen-Gladbach, Germany on 1 March 1945 with Company "A", commanded by 1st Lieutenant Lester J. Clauer; four (4) Assault Guns, commanded by Staff Sergeant Kendal T. Van Pelt; and one (1) platoon of Company "D", commanded by 1st Lieutenant Arnold Dryer, attached to the 175th Infantry Regiment pushing on OLENKIRCHEN (F-1082) by employing one platoon and two (2) Assault Guns in a flanking movement up the left of the railroad track (F-099842) and one (1) platoon and two (2) Assault Guns moving up on the right of the railroad while the platoon of light tanks of Company "D" followed straight into the town mopping up as they came. These elements then pushed toward Rheydt and Munchen-Gladbach.

2. Meanwhile, one (1) platoon of Company "C" and one (1) platoon of Company "D" left their positions at Jackerath, Germany (F-103715), joined the 2d Battalion of the 115th Infantry Regiment at Wickrathberg, Germany (F-075803) and prepared to move out at 1600 to assault Rheydt, Germany (F-1086) and Munchen-Gladbach, Germany (F-1089). Before this team could move out, the Company "A" team pushed uncontested into Munchen-Gladbach before dark on 1 March 1945 and set up defensive positions for the night.

3. At 0900 hours on 2 March 1945, all units of this battalion were detached from the 29th Infantry Division and brought under battalion control in Rheydt. The CP moved from Holzweiler, Germany (F-067733) and closed in Rheydt at 1035 hours, at which time the battalion was attached to the 29th Infantry Division Artillery for administrative purposes. From 2 March 1945 until 5 March 1945, the battalion remained in Rheydt and conducted a period of rehabilitation and tank maintenance.

4. During this period, the following units were encountered by this battalion: 901st PGR; 902d PGR; 130th Artillery Regiment; Replacement Battalion Z.B.V. Berta; 673d Tank Destroyers; 799th Engineer Battalion; and troops of the military police and Volkssturmers.

5. Enemy casualties inflicted by this battalion during this period are as follows: Three men killed.

6. As a result of this action, the following casualties were sustained by this organization: One (1) Officer and two (2) enlisted men killed in action; one (1) officer and five (5) enlisted men wounded in action.

After Action Report of the 747th Tank Bn, attached to the 29th Infantry Division, covering the month of March 1945.

It details the actions of the battalion, what enemy troops it fought, and how many casualties it took.

Men are not named in the record unless they were singled out for an important reason.

ARMY PUBLICATIONS

There are a number of official publications printed by the Army that are important to know about. Many of these are now considered collectors items and are readily available only in a few archives and museums.

"AR" is the abbreviation for Army Regulations. These are the rules of the Army and dictate how the Army is to function. These were published as a series of numbered pamphlets designed to be filed in loose-leaf note books so that changes could easily be added. During World War II it took five thick notebooks to hold them all. They are numbered by "group number" and then subdivided for the specific topic. The group number 600 covers personnel regulations and AR 600-35 covers the wearing of the service uniform.

An entire library of books was printed during the war to provide information on just about anything a soldier might need to know. These are known as Field Manuals (FMs) and Technical Manuals (TMs). Today they are prized by collectors, and the best public collection of them is housed at Carlisle Barracks, PA.

Field manuals contain information relative to the tactics and techniques of one branch of service. Basic field manuals contain information applicable to several branches. Technical manuals describe equipment and how to operate or maintain it.

These manuals have a prefix determined by the appropriate branch of service. Much like every branch has its own color, they also have a number that readily describes who the manual is for (see chart opposite for a breakdown). Numbers 21–31 were for the basic field manuals.

Best known of all the manuals was FM 21-100 The Soldier's Handbook, which provides information that every enlisted man might want to know, from how to wear the uniform, how to drill and march, to how to get paid. The second number identifies the unique books. FM's were numbered 1–100, and TM's from 200 on.

FM 100, Field Service Regulations was a special title providing the basis for how all units were expected to fight. It contains the basic doctrines of the Army at the time. Once printed it was a major undertaking to revise these books. Thus changes were issued as needed on separate pages that could be glued or stapled into the previous edition. When a new edition was brought out it had the same number, but a different publication date on the cover.

Information that did not fit into any of the field manuals was issued in the form of a bulletin (considered permanent) or circular (information of a general, but temporary nature).

BRANCH NUMBERS FOR PUBLICATIONS			
1	ARMY AIR FORCES	13	INSPECTOR GENERAL'S DEPARTMENT
2	CAVALRY	14	FINANCE DEPARTMENT
3	CHEMICAL WARFARE SERVICE	15	JUDGE ADVOCATE GENERAL'S DEPARTMENT
4	COAST ARTILLERY CORPS	16	CHAPLAINS
5	CORPS OF ENGINEERS	17	ARMORED FORCES
6	FIELD ARTILLERY	18	TANK DESTROYERS
7	INFANTRY	19	MILITARY POLICE
8	MEDICAL DEPARTMENTS	20–31	BASIC FIELD MANUALS
9	ORDNANCE CORPS	100	FIELD SERVICE REGULATIONS
10	QUARTERMASTER CORPS	101	STAFF OFFICER'S FIELD MANUAL
11	SIGNAL CORPS	105	UMPIRE MANUAL
12	ADJUTANT GENERAL'S DEPARTMENT		

All Army documents are dated, and it is imperative that one knows what is the latest version published for the time period you are interested in.

When a document replaced a previous version it will say which version it replaces, but a 1941 edition may or may not be the edition in use in 1944.

WEBSITE

The Military History Institute at Carlisle Barracks has begun putting copies of many field and technical manuals on the digitized Document System of its website.
http://www.carlisle.army.mil/usamhi/index.htm_

Designation: Company †------, ‡------ Infantry

(Sideways text at right:) INFANTRY RIFLE COMPANY

	1	2	3	4	5	6	7	8	9	10	11	12	13	14	15	16	17	18
						Weapons platoon							3 rifle platoons (each)					
							60-mm mortar section		Light machine gun section									
1	Unit	Specification serial No.	Technician grade	Company headquarters	Platoon headquarters	Section headquarters	3 squads (each)	Total section	Section headquarters	2 squads (each)	Total section	Total platoon	Platoon headquarters	3 rifle squads (each)	Total platoon	Total company	Enlisted cadre	Remarks
2	Captain, including			1												1		†Insert letter of company.
3	Company commander	1542		(1)												(1)		‡Insert number of regiment.
4	First lieutenant, including			1	1							1				2		ᵃ Also classification specialist (275).
5	Executive	1542		(1)								(1)				(1)		ᵇ Armed with rifle, automatic, cal. .30.
6	Platoon commander	1542			(1)											(1)		ᶜ Armed with carbine, cal. .30.
7	First lieutenant) including											1			1	2		ᵈ Battalion headquarters company is responsible for the company maintenance of vehicles assigned this organization.
8	Second lieutenant∫															1		
9	Platoon commander	1542										(1)			(1)	(3)		
10	Total commissioned			ᶜ2	ᶜ1							1	ᶜ1		1	6		
11	First sergeant	585		ᶜ1												1	1	
12	Technical sergeant, including				1							1	1		(1)	4	4	Second echelon maintenance provided by service company.
13	Platoon	651			(ᶜ1)							(1)	(1)		(1)	(4)	(4)	ᵉ Armed with pistol, automatic, cal. .45.
14	Staff sergeant, including	824		2		1		1	1		1	2	1	1	4	16	4	ᶠ Armed with rifle, cal. .30, M1, unless otherwise indicated. One individual per rifle platoon, as designated by rifle platoon leader, will be armed with rifle, cal. .30, M1903A4.
15	Mess	824		(ᶜ1)									(1)			(1)	(1)	
16	Platoon guide	651											(1)		(1)	(3)		
17	Section leader	652				(1)		(1)	(1)		(1)	(2)				(2)	(2)	
18	Squad leader	653												(1)	(3)	(9)	(1)	
19	Supply	821		(ᶜ1)												(1)		
20	Sergeant, including			(1)												15		
21	Communication	542		(1)				3		1	2	5			3	(1)		
22	Squad leader	653				(1)	(3)		(1)	(2)	(5)					(5)		
23	Squad leader, assistant	653												(1)	(3)			For specification serial numbers shown in column 2, for enlisted men, see AR 615-26; for officers, see TM 12-406 and 12-407.
24	Corporal, including			1												1	1	
25	Clerk, company	405		(ᶜ1)												(1)	(1)	
26	Technician, grade 4															2	2	
27	Technician, grade 5 ⟩including			28	4	1	4	13	1	4	9	26	2	10	32	104	3	
28	Private, first class ⟩															40		
29	Private ⟩																	
30	Ammunition bearer	504	5	(1)			(ᶜ2)	(6)		(ᶜ2)	(4)	(10)		(1)	(3)	(19)	(1)	
31	Armorer-artificer	511	5	(ᶜ1)												(1)		
32	Bugler	803		(ᶜ1)												(1)		
33	Cook	060	4	(2)												(2)	(2)	
34	Cook	060	5	(2)												(2)	(2)	
35	Cook's helper	521		(2)												(2)		
36	Driver, truck, light	345	5	⟩	(2)							(2)				(1)		
37	Driver, truck, light	345		⟩												(1)		
38	Gunner, machine gun	604							(ᵇ1)	(2)	(2)					(2)		
39	Gunner, machine gun, assistant	604							(ᵇ1)	(2)	(2)					(2)		
40	Gunner, mortar	607				(ᵇ1)	(3)				(3)					(3)		
41	Gunner, mortar, assistant	607				(ᵇ1)	(3)				(3)					(3)		
42	Messenger	675		(ᶜ3)	(ᶜ2)	(ᶜ1)		(1)	(ᶜ1)		(1)	(4)	(2)		(2)	(13)		
43	Rifleman	745												(7)	(21)	(63)		
44	Rifleman, automatic	746												(ᵇ1)	(3)	(9)		
45	Rifleman, automatic, assistant	746												(1)	(3)	(9)		
46	Basic	521		(17)												(17)		
47	Total enlisted			33	5	2	5	17	2	5	12	34	4	12	40	187	15	
48	Aggregate			35	6	2	5	17	2	5	12	35	5	12	41	ᶠ193	15	
49	O Carbine, cal. .30			9	4	1	3	7	1	3	5	16	1		1	28		
50	O Gun, machine, cal. .30, light, flexible								1	2	2				2		
51	O Gun, machine, HB, cal. .50, flexible			1								1				1		
52	O Launcher, rocket, AT, 2.36-inch			5								3				5		
53	O Mortar, 60-mm						1	3				3				3		
54	O Pistol, automatic, cal. .45						2	6		2	4	10				10		
55	O Rifle, automatic, cal. .30													1	3	9		
56	O Rifle, cal. .30, M1			26	2	1	1	4	1	1	3	9 ⟩	4	11 ⟩	36	143		
57	O Rifle, cal. .30, M1903A4														1	1		
58	O Trailer, ¼-ton			ᵈ2								2				2		
59	O Truck, ¼-ton			ᵈ2								2				2		

Table of organization for the Infantry Rifle Company. This edition is dated 26 February 1944 and indicates the authorized ranks and positions for all of the 6 officers and 187 enlisted men in the company, as well as weapons and vehicles.

WEBSITES

http://www.militaryresearch.org sells copies of T/O&Es

Carlisle Barracks MHI website:
http://www.carlisle.army.mil/usamhi/index.htm

T/O & Es

During World War II almost every Army unit of the same type and size was organized along the specifications put forth in a Table of Organization (T/O). Later in the war the T/O was expanded to include the major equipment authorized for that type unit, and renamed the T/O&E (Table of Organization and Equipment).

Every infantry company was organized as directed by T/O 7-17; likewise, every 105mm truck-drawn artillery battalion was governed by T/O 6-27. These listed the number of men allotted to the unit by rank and specialty. The T/O also dictated how the unit was subdivided (if at all). Also included in the T/O were major items of equipment such as weapons and vehicles. The addition of the equipment lists added in such items as entrenching tools, binoculars, tents, tool kits, and so forth.

T/Os were periodically changed as needs demanded. Some stayed the same through the war, but in some types of units there were frequent changes. Thus a T/O is only good for the specific time period it was authorized. Units generally took some time to make the necessary alterations and acquire the proper equipment after a new T/O was issued.

The Army did experiment with headquarters units that did not have permanently attached sub-units. Before the war, a brigade was a specific size with its own T/O. During the war the brigade was, for the most part, relegated to having only a headquarters section as its permanent troops. Other battalions, companies and regiments could be put under that brigade's command. This allowed for maximum flexibility in the field. The largest public collection of historical Army T/Os is housed at the Military History Institute library at Carlisle Barracks. They have started to make some of them available on their website. The Military Research Service also sells photo copies of specific T/Os.

Publication Changes

The Army was constantly striving to become more efficient. If a minor change in a manual or regulation was made, one not great enough to warrant reprinting the entire thing, a "change" was issued. These were numbered—change 1 change 2, etc., from the last main printing of the publication. Thus if the letter "C" followed by a number appears underneath the main heading (AR 10-101, or T/O&E 7-17) it is the latest revision. Some publications had many changes before being reprinted, others had none. It is important to be sure to check for any changes to an Army publication when dealing with a specific time frame.

CODE NAMES

The Army used code names for many things in World War II. These are some-times found in unit documents and can be confusing if one is not aware of them. The most common code names were those of operations (Overlord for the invasion of Normandy, or Torch for the invasion of North Africa). Every Army unit had its own code name so that it did not have to use its numbered designation in messages or on signs.

These code names are found in orders, or seen on signs directing traffic to "Lucky Forward" (Third Army Forward Headquarters). No master list of these names has been located. The names also allowed for some level of security in radio and telephone conversations. As a rule, every divisional element will have code names starting with the same letter.

As an example, the 8th Infantry Division was known as "Granite." Its three Infantry Regiments were the 13th (Greyhound), 28th (Grasshopper) and the 121st (Grapefruit). The divisional artillery was known as "Grindstone" with the Headquarters battery known as "Gorilla." The four artillery batteries were the 28th (Gunshot), the 43d (Gopher), the 45th (Greenback), and the 56th (Goldenrod).

In the Division Special Troops, there was the HQ Company (Grandmother), the 8th Signal Company (Goat), the 8th Quartermaster Company (Gobbler), the 708th Ordnance (Governor), and the 8th Recon Troop (Gypsy). Other main units were the 12th Engineer Bn. (Gondolas) and the 8th Medical Bn. (Guillotine). Attached units would have a "G" name only by chance. For this division some were the 445th AAAW Bn. (Mayfair 445), the 709th Tank Bn. (Healthy), the 644th Tank Destroyer Bn. (Hazard), and the 86th Chemical Mortar Bn. (Lobster).

These unit code names could be used to identify specific officers in a unit. In a regiment the battalions were known by the colors "red," "white," and "blue" for the first, second, and third battalions. The 3d Battalion of the 28th Infantry Regiment was thus "Grasshopper Blue," while the 1st Battalion of the same regiment would be called "Grasshopper Red."

To identify the key officers in a unit the numbers 1through 6 were used. 1–4 were used for the staff officers (S1, S2, S3, and S4). The number 5 indicated the executive officer, and 6 was used for the commander. The commander of the 3d Battalion would be known as "Grasshopper Blue Six" but within the unit only the term "six" needed to be used to identity the position. Keep in mind that these were code names for positions and not specific individuals. Anywhere in the Army, a mention of "Blue Six" meant the commanding officer of the local 3d battalion.

The same system went down to company level. In an infantry regiment all that was needed to identify a company was the phonetic name for the letter. The battalion number was not needed as every regiment was set up the same way (1st battalions were always companies A, B, C, and D, etc.). So the correct code name for the commander of Company L, 28th Infantry Regiment would be "Grasshopper Love Six."

The phonetic names for the alphabet vary from country to country and have changed through the years. The most commonly used phonetic names for the World War II period are shown in the following chart.

CHART SHOWING PHONETIC NAMES USED IN WORLD WAR II		
1st Battalion (Red)	2d Battalion (White)	3d Battalion (Blue)
A – ABLE	E – EASY	I – ITEM
B – BAKER	F – FOX	K – KING
C – CHARLIE	G – GEORGE	L – LOVE
D – DOG	H – HOW	M – MIKE

UNIT HISTORIES

Every unit was expected to maintain its own basic history of its activities, but at the end of the war just about every major unit had someone write an official history of its wartime role. The bulk of these were published by 1947 and made available to veterans of the unit for a nominal cost.

Many of these histories are rare and can fetch high prices from collectors. The largest public collection of unit histories is at the Carlisle Barracks library, which has a listing of them available on line.

The most complete listing of known unit histories is a reference volume, *United States Army Unit and Organizational Histories: Vol. 2, World War I to the Present*, by James T Controvich. This book lists the known published unit histories, although previously unknown privately printed works are still being discovered. It is a useful place to start when investigating what published works on a specific unit exist.

Unit histories range from large hardbound books filled with photos and colored maps, to small stapled pamphlets printed on a German press in 1945. Generally, the smaller the unit the rarer the book.

Divisional histories are relatively easy to find in one form or another (some veterans associations have begun making them available on the web), but company and battalion histories can be almost impossible to find. Some unit associations have reprinted their histories, and the Battery Press (www.battery-press.com, or Battery Press, P.O. Box 198885, Nashville, TN 37219) is a publisher that has specialized in reprinting these books.

A number of books have been published since the war containing a history of a specific unit. To be truly considered a "unit history" the unit, or its veteran's association, must accept or sponsor the book. Otherwise it remains simply a book about a specific unit. It may still be a very good book, but to collectors of unit histories, the support or authorization of the unit members is required.

More recently some publishers have produced "commemorative volumes," in which a brief history of the unit is printed, followed by biographies and photos of any known veterans that wish to take part. Some of these are well done; others may not be as interesting. It is good to check with a unit association first, as some sell the books to raise money for their organization.

OTHER RECORDS

There are many smaller sets of specific records that exist in various archives. The National Archives has a file for former POWs who recalled atrocities committed during their imprisonment. The Office of Air Force History has a file with information on all missing aircrew members.

The list of potential types of records is vast, but almost without exception most will be found in the unit records collected by the Adjutant Generals Office (Record Group 407) and held in the National Archives. There are a few other record groups that may hold some unit-specific information, such as interviews done with soldiers about their combat experience, or records of logistical plans for a specific operation, but RG 407 is the primary source for information about a World War II Army unit.

FOOTNOTES

1 *Ordnance Soldier's Guide*, 1944. p 61.

2 Correspondence with Sherry Dowdy, Cartographer USA-CMH, 4 May 2004.

3 TM-20-205 *Dictionary of Army Terms*.

4 Executive Order 12958, *Classified National Security Information*, 17 April 1995.

FINDING YOUR FATHER'S WAR

Section 4

FINDING
RECORDS

This section explains the many and varied places
around the country where you can find records
of your soldier's service.

It provides great detail on the National Archives where
many researchers have to go, explains what you can
expect when you visit, and how to make the most of
your research there.

M3 medium tanks in the desert.

*Although phased out of combat units as soon as the
Sherman M4 tank came into production, many tank
crews were first trained on this model with its distinctive
side mounted main gun.*

Next of Kin and the Freedom of Information Act
Records, Records Everywhere – Finding Records at Home
Local Newspapers – State Records – Church Records
The National Archives – The National Personnel Records Center
Official Army Military History Sources
Veteran's Affairs Records – Military Museum and Base Records

FINDING RECORDS

NEXT OF KIN AND THE FOIA

Federal privacy laws protect individuals by limiting the personal information the government can disseminate to others. During a veteran's lifetime, he is the only one who can request any of his own personal information. Once the veteran is deceased, however, the government allows the next of kin to request this information. Next of kin is specifically defined as an unmarried widow or widower, son, daughter, father, mother, brother, or sister. Nephews, nieces, and grandchildren are not allowed access to this data.

If you are not a next of kin, it doesn't necessarily mean you can't get any information. Many records are considered public domain and available to anyone. This includes things like name, serial number, rank, records of promotions, decorations, and basic dates of service. You will not, however, be able to get a serviceman's full record. The privacy laws exclude such information as the man's education, financial transactions, medical history, criminal or employment history, and even his fingerprint. If the man is dead, they will also release place of birth, date and location of death, and geographical location of burial.

Until the Freedom of Information Act (FOIA) was passed, government agencies were under no obligation to provide any non-classified or personal information. The FOIA means that anyone requesting Federal information under the act must be replied to within a reasonable timeframe. Unless you are requesting material as the next of kin, you need to state that your request is being submitted under the Freedom of Information Act.

The military personnel record was created to be an administrative record. It documents enlistment/appointment, duty stations and assignments, training, qualifications, performance, awards and medals, disciplinary actions, insurance, emergency data, administrative remarks, separation/discharge/retirement, and other personnel actions. The DD Form 214, Report of Separation, or equivalent is filed in the Official Military Personnel File. It is not an easily read narrative of a man's service and may need deciphering and explanation.

RECORDS, RECORDS EVERYWHERE...

The military generated billions of paper records during World War II. At one point anything you could ever wish to know about anything related to our military was written down. However, because storage space was (and remains) limited, most of these records were discarded or lost; only the most important files were retained. The Army placed the major burden upon individual soldiers to keep a copy of their own files, with the other copy going into a main storage facility at the National Personnel Records Center (NPRC) in St. Louis, Missouri. Military records from the pre-20th century era (Revolutionary War, Civil War, etc.) are held at the National Archives in Washington.

The principal reason the military retained personnel records was to support Veterans Administration claims for disabilities that occurred while on duty. Few expected anyone would ever examine these records in any historical context. Since veterans were supplied with records upon their discharge, no one in the government thought ahead about how much interest there might be in these documents, and so kept staffing at the facility to a minimum.

Unfortunately, on 12 July 1973, a fire at the NPRC destroyed approximately sixteen to eighteen million Military Personnel Files. The following chart describes the losses.

NPRC RECORDS LOSSES		
BRANCH	PERSONNEL AND PERIOD AFFECTED	ESTIMATED LOSSES
ARMY	PERSONNEL DISCHARGED NOVEMBER 1, 1912, TO JANUARY 1, 1960	80%
AIR FORCE	PERSONNEL DISCHARGED, SEPTEMBER 25, 1947, TO JANUARY 1, 1964 (With names alphabetically after Hubbard, James E.)	75%

This loss made it much more difficult for researchers to find relevant information. Over the years many tales have been spread about the fire and of phantom duplicate record sets stored elsewhere. The facts are simple: the fire occurred, and there were no duplicate records kept anywhere.[1] Fortunately for non-Army types, no records of the Coast Guard, Navy, or Marines were lost..

The rumors of duplicate records originated in 1988 when a collection of ten million hospital and treatment facility admission records on computer tapes were obtained by the NPRC. After extensive efforts to convert the old code into a readable format, nearly eight million records were salvaged. These records include Army and Air Force personnel who served between 1942 and 1945, active duty Army personnel serving between 1950 and 1954, and a few Marine, Navy, and Air Force records for 1950–54.

The NPRC states:

The admissions records are not specific or detailed medical documents, but summarized information indexed by military service number. They contain limited medical treatment information, but diagnosis, type of operation, and dates/places of treatment or hospitalization are frequently included. Although no names are shown, patients are identified by military service number and certain personal data including age, race, sex and place of birth. THESE RECORDS ARE NOT DUPLICATES OF THE ORIGINAL MEDICAL TREATMENT FILES LOST IN THE 1973 FIRE AT NPRC (MPR). They were created using data sampling techniques for statistical purposes. Therefore, the listings are not complete and many admissions were skipped during the sampling process. Nevertheless, the information is useful as proof to support certain benefit claims . . . . [2]

FINDING RECORDS AT HOME

With luck, most of what you need will be found at home or with family members. The critical items are name and serial number, but the first item to look for should be the soldier's discharge. This will provide a framework for the veteran's service and give you some direction where to look.

Every veteran was presented with a copy of his discharge (and frequently with copies made on an early copy machine that produced white on black copies). The discharge was an important item to have when applying for jobs in the post–World War II era, and many veterans obtained a miniature copy of it to carry around with them to prove they had served their country.

Discharges were required to be shown for many reasons, and in some cases copies were either requested or required to be deposited at a local courthouse. Some towns gave veterans tax benefits or other services if they could prove they had served, and the discharge was the proof required.

The Army specifically recommended that the serviceman deposit a copy of his discharge with his local county clerk or county recorder's office. That way, a certified copy of the discharge would be easily available if the veteran lost his personal copy.

While you are looking for the discharge, it is important that you collect every scrap of evidence on a serviceman you can find. You never know when some seemingly minor name or location will become an important piece of the research puzzle.

LOCAL NEWSPAPERS

Do not ignore local newspapers. Most newspapers delighted in printing material about hometown boys in the service. In some small towns, the papers printed entire letters written home so that the whole town could see how "Johnny" was doing overseas. Larger towns or cities ran regular columns with patriotic names such as "With the Colors." These columns provided news of interest on local servicemen (and women). Often the only remaining letters or photographs of a soldier are those printed in his local paper. Due to censorship rules, a soldier's unit or location was not always mentioned. As the war progressed, however, more information was allowed to be printed. In the weeks following D-Day, many newspapers ran items on local soldiers involved in the landing operation. As a rule, specific units were not mentioned, and this can be frustrating for researchers. However, the print articles often provide enough pieces of the puzzle to work out where and what a man was doing.

Reading wartime papers is always interesting and is an education all its own. Because of a national paper shortage, most newspapers were shorter during the war and thus had limited space. Reading through notices about Boy Scout scrap drives, ads for ashtrays, and war bond drives provides a better appreciation for what the home front was like during that period of our history. Even with reduced space, society and fashion pages were still included. It's always good to check postwar newspaper editions on important anniversaries like VE-Day, VJ-Day, or D-day. Especially in the years immediately after the war, papers liked to run information and veteran reminiscences.

STATE RECORDS

Some states were better than others at collecting information on their veterans. This is particularly true of states with a strong tie to a National Guard unit. Every state is different, but it is worth checking with yours to see if there are any records that may be of help to you. Many states paid a bonus to returning servicemen to help them get back on their feet. These records can provide valuable information, including a copy of your soldier's discharge.

Check and see if there is a state office of Veteran's Services or an official state military museum. If your veteran served in a National Guard unit, you may find a great deal of information without even leaving the state. Those records are maintained by the State Adjutant General's Office. If you are unable to find out where these records are kept, call your elected state representatives. They should be happy to help you locate the correct offices.

CHURCHES, SCHOOLS, AND COLLEGES

Religion played a more important role in many families in the 1940s than it does today. If you know what church a soldier or his family attended, it may prove worthwhile to contact the church about any wartime records. Some churches printed bulletins with information about how "their boys" were doing overseas. If a man was killed, wounded, or missing, the church may have had a special service to pray for him.

Do not overlook any school or college a soldier attended before the war. Many men left school to join the Army, and they frequently stayed in touch with their alma maters. Some schools kept meticulous records about their men in serv- ice. This could include not just a mention of what he was doing and where he was serving, but photographs and letters back to the school as well.

If a man had been at one of the country's military schools, the chances are good that they hold some information on him. If your soldier attended the U.S. Military Academy at West Point, information on him will be found in its records. At a minimum, his photo and school biography will be found in the annual yearbook, "The Howitzer."

Other schools that had major military programs include The Citadel, Norwich University, Virginia Military Institute, Clemson University, and Texas A&M. A check in the school archives may turn up some interesting information.

THE NATIONAL ARCHIVES

Most roads in research will inevitably lead you to the National Archives.

The National Archives and Records Administration (NARA) is a group of archives scattered across the country and include presidential libraries.

For the purposes of World War II research, there are two key sites with which you should become familiar. The National Archives Building 2 at College Park, Maryland, and the National Personnel Records Center (NPRC) in Missouri.

Every year the Federal government makes more records available on the World Wide Web. Recently, records of World War II soldiers missing in action, as well as the database of World War II enlisted serial numbers were placed on their website.

It's a good idea to routinely check the Archives' website, as you never know what new records or documents may go up next.

The College Park Archives building (shown above) is located just outside Washington DC and is generally one of the best sources of information for Army units. At some point in time every dedicated researcher will have to make the pilgrimage. Visits to this facility are almost always rewarding and frustrating—at the same time!

The National Archives is charged with storing and maintaining government records of all types. At College Park you will find not only textual records but maps, photographs, films, and even computer records on magnetic tape. Unlike a library that holds only one of many copies of a book, the National Archives often holds the only copy of a record. For that and other reasons, its staff is very careful about protecting its valuable holdings. Keep in mind that thousands of people use the Archives every week, and the intent is to keep these records for hundreds of years to come. While you may be the only person to ever look at specific documents since the time they arrived, many other records are heavily used and the wear on them is considerable.

The main National Archives building inside Washington DC still has some historical records, but the bulk of the military holdings have been transferred to Archives 2 in College Park. This is a newer and far nicer building than the original. It can be reached by a shuttle bus, or you can drive there and park free in its parking garage. The facility has a nice cafeteria and some extended late night hours.

The first floor is the reception area and cafeteria. The second floor holds the textual records research room. The third floor houses motion picture and audio recordings. The fourth floor holds microfilm records, and the fifth floor contains still photographic records. There is a sixth floor for classified and electronic records.

Since 9/11, security has been greatly increased, and all visitors are checked thoroughly upon entering. Everyone must pass through a metal detector. A photo ID is needed to enter the grounds and also to obtain a researcher ID card. This card is used to scan you in and out of the building and the various research rooms.

Don't be intimidated by any of this. It is paid for with your tax dollars, so don't feel you have to be a world famous researcher to get access to these records. In theory, every visitor—foreign and domestic, neophyte or world renowned scholar—is supposed to be treated the same. A study of the NARA website is highly recommended before any visit (www.nara.gov). Policies, procedures, and opening hours can and do change, so again, check the website.

It is important to keep a few things in mind. First, you cannot take anything into the research rooms except (almost literally) the clothes on your back. All bags, coats, purses, folders, and so forth must be left in the researcher lockers in the basement. These lockers are free, but you will need a quarter to operate them (the quarter is returned when you open the locker). No pens are allowed in the research rooms because of the chance they might leak ink on valuable papers.

On the plus side, NARA provides free pencils and note-taking paper. If you have notes you want to bring in with you, they will need to be approved and stamped when you enter so they will not be mistaken for archival property when you leave. Laptops, scanners, and cameras can be brought in, though there are certain rules governing their use.

The main military collections of interest are the Army records from World War II in the Textual Branch, The Signal Corps collection of photographs in the Still Photo Branch, the Signal Corps film collection in the Motion Picture Branch, and the aerial photograph and map collections.

It is important to keep in mind that the policies and procedures at these facilities change. Be sure to check websites for information on the current policy, and do not be afraid to call and double check if you have questions.

One suggestion is that you photocopy anything you find of interest. As you become more knowledgeable about military records you may find that what was once an obscure abbreviation takes on new meaning. You might run into someone with an interest in the same unit who would love some copies in your possession. While it is tempting to just take some notes about what you find, it's always a good idea to photocopy anything of specific interest. It may cost a few dollars, but in the long run it is almost always worth it. Always make notations on your copies about which Record Group and box the original was found in so you can return to it if necessary.

One term you will keep hearing at NARA is "finding aid." A finding aid is anything that helps you find the location of the records you want. It can be a list of what's in the boxes of a Record Group or a series of notebooks cataloging the files in it. The Archives staff is always working on new finding aids for frequently requested material.

National Archives: Textual Records

In the Textual Records Branch, most research into unit records will be in Record Group 407. These are the World War II unit records held by the Adjutant General's Office. They are so heavily used that they are well indexed with finding aids. The typical request of unit records from World War II can be done from the research room without any special appointment.

NARA obtains so many groups of records from the government (and throughout America's past) that the cataloging system can initially be very daunting. Every type of record from a specific office or bureau is given a "Record Group" number. The Army Signal Corps, for example, is RG 111. Records of the Army Air Force are RG 18. RG 247 holds records of the Chief of Chaplains. Navy

The Textual Records room at the National Archives, College Park, MD.

National Archives

records are in RG 38. Material on the Japanese, Italian, and Germans interned in camps during the war will be found in RG 389: The Office of the Provost Marshal General. The list of Record Groups and what is in them is quite staggering. Always be sure to mention to the staff your exact topic of interest, because many know the holdings very well and can provide good suggestions where to look.

The most common Record Group used for World War II is RG 407: The Adjutant General's Office. This collection contains unit historical records. This is where you look to track a specific unit. RG 332 contains records of theaters of war from World War II, but this holds theater-level records such as studies, overviews, and plans. RG 407 is sorted by unit and branch. There is a notebook listing information for each type of unit (armor, infantry, engineer, etc.) and then by numerical designation. Units that were permanently attached to a specific division are filed under that division.

What you will probably be seeking is the specific numbered regiment, battalion, or in some cases, company, in which your soldier served (for example, the 121st Regiment, 308th Artillery Battalion, or 602d Light Equipment Company). Looking for "company B" or "1st battalion" won't work. Likewise, if all you know is a division name or number, you can find some information, but little more than you would by reading a general book on the unit. For these specific num-

308-FA(28)-0 28th Field Artillery Bn		8th Infantry Division
308-FA(28)-0	Hist. - "Gunshot" On the Way	1944
308-FA(28)-0.1	History	1940-Oct.45
308-FA(28)-0.3	A/A Report	Jul 44-May 45
308-FA(28)-0.7	Journal	28 Jun 44-Aug 45
308-FA(28)-0.8	Journal File	Jul 44-9 May 45
308-FA(28)-0.20	"Cannoneers Marching Song"	Undated
308-FA(28)-1.13	General Orders	1942-45
308-FA(28)-26	Annual Report - Med Det	1941-42

A sample card from RG 407. This card is for the 28th Field Artillery Battalion.

The left hand column is the file number, followed by a brief description of the file's contents and the dates it covers.

The first line, file 308-FA (28)-0 contains a copy of the period unit history "Gunshot On the Way," published in 1944.

The third file contains the official After Action Reports (A/A or AAR) for July 1944–May 1945.

Files are of different sizes and there may be only one, or many in each box. Unless there is an index to which files are in which box number, you'll need to request these according to the Record Group and file number.

Heavily used records are better indexed, such as these for the 8th Infantry Division.

This finding aid is located in the notebook for the 8th Infantry Division, and lists the unit, the box numbers those files are in, and the location of those boxes.

Knowing the location of the boxes makes it faster and easier for the Archives staff to retrieve the records.

Division Records, Entry 427, Record Group 407

Division	File#	Inclusive Boxes	Inclusive Location
8th Infantry	308	7175-7324	270/55/11/2-55/14/2
Histories (-0/-0.1/-0.2)		7175	
AARs/Ops Reports (-0.3)		7176-7177	
General Orders (-1.13)		7179-7181	
G-2 Journal (-2.2)		N/A	
G-2 Journal/File (-2.3)		N/A	
G-3 Journal (-3.2)		7182-7183	
G-3 Journal/File (-3.3)		7184-7210	
Component Units			
ART		7212-7239	
CAV		7240	
CIC		N/A	
ENG		7241	
FABN- 28		7242-7251	
FABN- 43		7252-7264	
FABN- 45		7265-7267	
FABN- 56		7268-7280	
INF RGT-13		7281-7290	
INF RGT- 28		7291-7316	
INF RGT- 121		7317-7321	
MED/MP/ORD/QM/SIG-		7322-7324	

bered units, each subsection of information has a decimally numbered file. Files are put into numbered boxes. Some indexes will tell you what is in the box; others will just mention the folder number. All of these documents are stored in carefully controlled secure areas where the public is not allowed.

In order to obtain these documents, you must request them on a "Reference Service Slip." These request forms are always referred to as "pull slips" because the staff uses them to go into the holdings and pull out the records you are requesting. You have to fill one out for every folder or box you want to see.

One nice exception is that if you want a sequential series of boxes, such as boxes 45, 46, and 47, you can use one slip for all three. The staff leaves a copy of the slip in the gap created by the pulled boxes, so as long as they are sequential boxes one slip will do.

A sample pull slip, requesting three boxes (7179, 7180, 7181) from RG 407 containing the 8th Infantry Division's General Orders.

Here, one slip is used for three boxes, as they are sequential. Instead of calling for specific file numbers, the box numbers are known from the Division finding aid notebooks. It's always good to add a short description of the records you want to eliminate any confusion.

One of the most frustrating aspects of working in the Archives is the concept of "pull times." To keep some order on how the institution is run, the staff will only pull records at specific times of the day. This is generally done about five or six times each day, and each branch has different times. The pull times are clearly labeled at each branch desk, and they are important to know. If you miss a pull time it could take a few hours before the next pull time arrives.

You are allowed to have one full cart of material pulled at a time, but two carts out of the storage area at any time. This means you need to plan ahead and have your next set of pull slips turned in so that when you finish with your current cart your next one is ready and waiting for you. You can have the carts held for a few days before the documents need to be re-shelved, but you will only have access to one cart at a time. You are also only supposed to have one box off the cart at a time, and only one folder out of the box at a time.

This is to prevent documents from being accidentally put into the wrong box and being lost forever. Of course, no food or drink is allowed in the research rooms at any time.

This is the standard sized box used for World War II Army records.

Each of the folders inside is a file. Some boxes contain only one file, while others, like this one, house a number of files.

A paper tab, as seen here, is used to mark the location of the file taken from the box.

Only one box is allowed on the table at a time, and only one file can be taken out at a time.

Papers put pack into the wrong file or box are potentially lost forever.

As previously mentioned, RG 407 is the collection of World War II unit records. These vary considerably. Some divisions have many boxes of documents, while some smaller units will have only a thin file. Some units saved every scrap of paper they ever produced, while others put only the bare minimum into their files. Unfortunately, some units, specifically the smaller ones, have no records in the Archives at all. If you are interested in an independent (as in non-divisional) unit, it may be better to have someone check the file before you make a long trip to Washington only to discover that it contains a few scraps of uninteresting paper.

Normally, these records contain monthly after-action reports indicating what happened to the unit during the time period covered. These reports will list locations, unit strength, whether it was in combat, and any incidents of importance (such as bridges built for engineer units). Units that took part in combat will normally (but not always) have a day-by-day record of their experience. These vary considerably in detail, but it is very rare for an enlisted man's name to appear in these unit records.

Some files contain photos, copies of various paperwork, maps, overlays, and even propaganda leaflets picked up on the battlefield. It's always a bit of an adventure to look in these files as you never know what you are going to find.

Many files will have copies of a unit's General Orders. These will indicate which men received medals and decorations. Unfortunately, a great many decorations were not awarded until after the war, and so never made it into the unit's General Orders. However, these General Orders do contain names, ranks, and serial numbers (which can be used in other ways to track specific soldiers), so they are very important. It is sometimes possible to recreate the roster of a company when it entered combat by listing all the men who were awarded purple hearts (wounded and dead) and then all the men who were awarded the combat infantryman's badge.

For medals, these files usually include a short description of the action that earned the soldier his specific award. As noted previously, however, the detail in these records varies considerably. For instance, the General Orders for the 28th Infantry Regiment only cover two of its three battalions. For reasons that are unclear, medal awards from some units serving in France after D-day were not written up, so the typical short description of the action for which the medal was awarded will not be found. No one knows why this is or whether the records were simply misplaced.

To have unit records pulled for you, you must first locate the information about the correct files in a series of notebooks. These notebooks list unit records by branch and then by unit number. There is an exception, however, if the unit was part of a division. In that case, an infantry regiment or artillery battalion that was part of the 3d Infantry Division, for example, will be found as a subsection of the 3d Infantry Division files. In cases where a unit such as a tank battalion was technically independent, but spent a lot of time with a specific division, it can be useful to check in both the armored notebook by unit number and the division's notebook.

The staff at NARA is generally helpful and will help you fill out the pull slips. Once you've done that you wait until the appointed time and ask for them (under your last name) at the desk. After signing for the records, you are free to start poring through them on one of the research tables. Just be sure to do your best to keep them in good shape (some are very brittle). When you are finished with everything on the cart, sign them back in at the desk. A staffer will ask you whether you want them for future work, or if you are finished and they can be filed back into the bowels of the Archives.

Most researchers prefer to photocopy records rather than try to copy them by hand. There are a number of good photocopiers available in the research rooms, and they take a debit copy card that you can buy in the research rooms. The copiers are often very busy in the Textual Records research room. The staff is supposed to check each record you want to copy to be sure it is strong enough to withstand the handling.

If any of your records were at one time classified (secret, top secret, or classified), you will have to get a "declassification" tag from the desk to put on the photocopier and be made a part of every copy you make. Also, every photocopy will automatically include a notation "copied at the National Archives." This is very important because when you leave the building a guard will make sure all your photocopies have this notation or they will not leave the building.

Routines and policies have changed over time at NARA, so it is always best to ask how you are supposed to do something. Ask how to fill out the forms for unit records. Once you have turned it in, if you have time before the next pull, ask about photocopier policies, where you should sit, or where the copy card machines are located. Many staffers are human repositories of valuable information and often come up with outstanding and helpful suggestions. Of course, being polite and friendly to the staff goes a long way.

If you are just interested in what one specific soldier did during the war, that unit's RG 407 file will probably be all you care about. There are, however, vast numbers of other military files that may be of some interest in case the soldier was involved in some other aspect of the war. If he was assigned to the staff of a base anywhere in the world, there are records of military bases and camps (these will only be of interest for background information or if he was a permanent member of the camp staff). If he worked in the development of a weapon, ration, or any item of equipment, there are records for those activities.

If there is something unusual in his service record, it might be useful to speak to one of the military archivists to determine if they have any ideas for other places you should check.

National Archives: Photographic Records

Everyone would like to find photographs of their relatives in the Army. In most cases you will not be able to do so unless you are very lucky or there was a special reason why he was photographed. There were millions of men in the armed forces in World War II, and most of them never saw an official photographer. In addition, the majority of official photographs never made it into the final Signal Corps collection. Thousands of photos were taken of soldiers receiving awards or special passes. Copies were given to the soldiers but never added to the main photo collection. Photos at every level were weeded out. As a result, many good official overseas shots will not be found in the Archives today.

Each of the services has its own photo collection in the Archives. The Army's collection is in Record Group 111-SC. These are almost all in the 4" x 5" format. The negatives for all the photos are in cold storage and staffers will only bring them out for special reasons. Researchers are allowed to view a 4 x 5 copy print with the caption on the back. If you find a photo you would like copied, you can do one of the following: bring a camera and use one of the copy stands in the research room; pay for a third party company to make a copy for you; make a photocopy or instant print yourself on equipment available in the research room; or bring in a scanner and scan the print yourself.

White cotton gloves, freely available in the research room, are required when handling any photographs, as the natural oils found on everyone's hands slowly deteriorate the chemistry of photographic prints.

The still photos research room on the 4th floor of Archives 2 at College Park. The card catalog in the background contains a partial index to military photographs from World War I through Viet Nam.

It is estimated that the Signal Corps collection contains more than one million photographs. Of those, nearly 500,000 are from World War II. Before this collection reached NARA it was held by the Department of Defense, which did not properly care for it. Images and index records are missing from that period. .

The first step in searching for a photo of a specific person is to check in Record Group 111-PX. This is the personality index, which contains a listing of names of people in specific photos. It is not complete. Only a fraction of the individuals photographed are listed in this index, most of whom held higher rank. However, it is the first resource you should consult.

If a man is not mentioned in the personality index, finding a photo of him will be difficult and largely a matter of luck. The next thing to do is check the massive card catalog for listings of his unit. While there may be thousands of photos from a unit in the collection, you may find listings for only a handful in the card catalog.

You can also try specific locations or investigate any topic you think your soldier was involved with. Say, for example, you are seeking a photo of someone who served in the 23d Infantry Division. Images from this outfit might be listed generically under "military police," "men eating," "men training," or not even cataloged at all, waiting instead for someone to weed through the hundreds of boxes and stumble upon it accidentally.

There is a collection of bound Signal Corps albums (RG 111-SCA) containing prints of specific units, places, and types of activities. These are perhaps the most commonly reproduced photos in the collection because they were selected and placed in the albums by the Army, and are therefore easy to access.

A word of warning regarding photographs: it is very common to mistake one man for another from the same time period.

All too often someone believes he has found a photo of his veteran, only to discover the captioning information makes it impossible for it to be so. A man who did not leave the United States until late 1944 cannot show up in a photo taken in North Africa in 1943. Still, the misidentification of soldiers is quite common. Even the men themselves make mistakes (in one case no less than three veterans claimed to be the same soldier in a photograph). Remember to check to see if the location, timeframe, and subject of the photo line up with what you know about the soldier you are researching.

National Archives: Motion Picture Records

Another floor of the Archives contains motion picture records of all kinds. These include films taken during World War II. No index of individuals is available for these films, but there is a listing by location, unit, and subject description.

This floor has a good collection of World War II-era training films and bulletins. The holdings contain the original "as shot" film taken by Signal Corps cameramen during the war. This is particularly interesting because some footage has never have been used in any documentary. It is amusing to watch film of men in combat rushing out from cover, stopping, turning to face the camera, and then mouthing the words, "How was that?" Sometimes multiple takes of an "action scene" were required before the cameraman believed it looked right.

Given the large number of men who served during World War II, and the relatively small amount of footage taken, the chances that a specific man will appear in a film are slight. However, if you know his exact unit and the time-frame in which he served, it is always worth a few hours of searching.

There is a viewing room where you can view copies of the 16 and 35mm films. You can set up a video camera to copy these films from the viewing screen. Some have been transferred to videotape, and playback equipment is available to view them in the research room, or to use as a source to copy to your own video recording equipment. Video recording decks are available to rent at the facility if you do not bring your own, but do not count on these without checking the Archives' current policy.

National Archives: Maps and Aerial Photographs

The cartographic records at College Park are quite extensive. As previously mentioned, most unit records contain the maps the unit used while in the field, but these are often torn, stained, brittle, and include 60-plus years of tape and adhesives. Some are nearly impossible to copy or even open.

Before attempting to have one of these folded maps copied, be sure to check with the cartographic records staff to see if they have a better copy of the map they can run through one of their special oversize photocopiers. If there is a small area with original markings on a map you need to copy, it may be much easier to use a hand-held digital camera to photograph the specific section.

Aerial photographs are housed on the same floor as the maps. To find out if there is an aerial photo of an area, you need to know the approximate longitude and latitude. Then check an overlay of a map to see where the photo reconnaissance missions in that area were conducted and on what date they were taken. With this information you will be able to obtain a roll of large-format negatives that contain the shot. Keep in mind that not every aerial photograph is in this collection, and coverage of some areas will be very limited.

Finding aerial photos in this collection is not hard, but initially it can be confusing. Just tell the staff exactly what you are looking for, such as "aerial photos covering the area around Avranches, France, around the period August 15 1944." They will be happy to explain the procedure and guide you through it.

Although the detail on these photos will not always be of use, they can help identify buildings, roads, and trenches mentioned in reports, or give you an idea of the terrain in which your soldier's outfit operated. In one case a researcher knew the exact location where his father's tank had been knocked out. He located a photograph taken days after the action in which the tank could be seen next to a hedge just as his dad had described it. Such finds, however, require knowing exactly where to look, and a great deal of luck.

National Archives: German Records

The Allies captured many German military files at the end of the war. The originals were eventually returned to the German government after microfilm copies of them were made. These copies, available in the National Archives, are of varying quality. Some are nearly illegible because of the poor quality of the originals and/or improper copying. A large number of files were destroyed or captured by the Russians and are not available.

While it may seem like a good idea to look into the German records to see "the other side of the story," be warned that not only were they written in German, but in 1940s technical military German. Many of the abbreviations and terms do not make sense even to native Germans.

The microfilm research room in the Archives has a listing of all its foreign records holdings. There are photocopiers available to make reproductions from the microfilm. If a specific reel is of great interest to you, it may be worthwhile to purchase a copy of it. It is not that expensive and the staff will be able to help you with the proper forms

NPRC—THE NATIONAL PERSONNEL RECORDS CENTER

Although many records were lost in the fire of 1973, the NPRC can play an important role in tracking a man's service. Requests should be made to see if the soldier's records are still available, and if not, ask the staff if they can officially reconstruct them. Additionally, the NPRC maintains the remaining collection of unit rosters and company morning reports.

Before you initiate a search for individual records at the NPRC, keep in mind that the facility was built and staffed to handle official requests. The surge of interest in World War II has stretched the staff to the limits. It is not uncommon to have to wait months before someone can consider your request.

The proper way to initiate a request is to submit a signed Form 180 by mail. These forms are available on the NPRC website. You can also send a signed letter providing as much information about the serviceman as possible; name and serial number are the critical pieces of information they will need to effectively help you. The NPRC will allow servicemen or their next of kin to make a request directly from its web site, which speeds up the process for everyone involved.

One of the most popular reasons to request a veteran's paperwork is to claim any medals that may not have been presented before the serviceman left the Army. Because service medals were only issued as a ribbon until after the war, many men never received them. There were also decorations that, for some reason, never caught up with a discharged veteran on the move.

As the World War II veteran population grew older and anniversaries of the war became more popular, many soldiers began requesting replacement medals. The deluge of requests overwhelmed the NPRC. At that time medals were not allowed to be sold on the private market. If a veteran wanted to replace a lost or stolen medal, he had to get a form from the NPRC stating he was allowed it, and then submit the form to another government agency. Because of the massive backlog at the NPRC, the government changed the law to allow all but the Medal of Honor to be made available commercially without any paperwork.

Because so many medals were never issued to the soldiers during the war, or the paperwork was not finalized until after a man had been discharged, many veterans filed paperwork with the NPRC to determine if there were any "forgotten" awards they deserved. Many were surprised to learn they were due a Bronze Star for no apparent reason (a 1947 decision was made to award Bronze Stars to every combat infantryman).

The other files held at the NPRC that may be of interest to researchers are the Company Morning Reports. These are available if you get permission in advance and set up an appointment for the specific files you want to see. If you ask to see different records at the last minute, the staff will not get them for you. Be warned that the Morning Reports are kept on microfilm of varying quality, so some days may no longer be legible. It is almost impossible to obtain Company Morning Reports unless you wade through endless layers of red tape and then either personally visit the facility or hire a freelance researcher to make the visit for you.

WEBSITE

for information on World War II veteran's records:

http://www.archives.gov/facilities/mo/st_louis/military_personnel_records.html
and http://vetrecs.archives.gov

OFFICIAL ARMY MILITARY HISTORY SOURCES

For many years the Military History Institute at Carlisle Barracks in Pennsylvania has been the primary library of historical Army material. Its library maintains the best collection of published Army material, including unit histories, field and technical manuals, and tables of organization. It also houses a good collection of Army-related photographs and the personal papers of many well known (and unknown) soldiers.

This collection—which spans the whole of Army history from the American Revolution through the Civil War and up to the present day—contains more than eleven million items, including books on nearly every imaginable military subject.

The Army is currently making a change regarding how it handles its history. The Carlisle Barracks facility is being moved to a new and updated building that will house both the Military History Institute and a new US Army Heritage & Education Center. This facility will house the library and information aspect of the Army's history. A second new facility, The National Museum of the US Army, is being constructed at Fort Belvoir, Virginia, to house the tangible artifacts of the Army.

Both the Heritage Center and National Museum, although official in nature, are not funded by the US government. They rely instead upon memberships and private donations for their funding. If you are looking for a way to commemorate someone's service in the Army, there is no better way to do so than to donate to these fine organizations.

If you have any items that you think may be of interest to future researchers, consider donating them to these institutions. Written materials such as books, diaries, manuals, and orders, as well as photographs, films, or any other printed memorabilia are of interest to the Military History Institute. Of particular interest are entire collections of papers from long-serving soldiers.

Artifacts such as uniforms, insignia, or equipment would be of interest to the National Museum of the US Army. Items donated to this facility would be available for loan to any of the Army's officially recognized museums. Before sending anything, you should write the facility a letter describing what you have and ask if it is something of interest.

The Army's Center for Military History (CMH) is the central office for studying Army history and learning lessons from the past. Although currently in Washington DC, the CMH will be moving to Fort Belvoir at some point in the future. The CMH oversees every official Army museum; a list of those currently in operation is on their website.

The CMH is the organization that writes the official histories of the Army. It has a small library (mostly duplicating what is located at the MHI), but in recent years has been putting many of its publications on the Internet. Many of the official World War II histories ("the green books") are now on their website.

The CMH has also made available a series of small brochures describing specific World War II campaigns.

WEBSITES

Military History Institute:
http://www.carlisle.army.mil/ahec/index.htm

National Museum U.S. Army: http://www.army.mil/nmusa/

Army Heritage Center: http://armyheritage.org/

Center for Military History: http://www.army.mil/cmh-pg/

Institute of Heraldry:
https://www-perscom.army.mil/tagd/tioh/tioh.htm

The Institute of Heraldry regulates the use of Army medals, decorations, awards, and insignia. Most of this information is now on its website and includes colored images of insignia and ribbons.

This organization is geared toward supporting the current forces, but also has some useful historical information. The section on unit insignia provides the official description of the symbolism behind each insignia.

VETERANS AFFAIRS RECORDS

If a veteran was wounded or injured in the service, the odds are that he has a file at the office of Veterans Affairs (VA). These records are only available to the individual or his next of kin, but they often contain interesting information. To find out if such a file exists, call the VA at 800-827-1000 and ask. A staff person should be able to help you if you can supply either his serial number or social security number. If a file exists, you can ask how to go about getting a copy.

The VA can also help you find a soldier by forwarding a letter to his last known address. This can help you track down a friend of your veteran. Unfortunately, those days are quickly drawing to a close. In order to do this, you will need the man's Army serial number. Call your local VA office for assistance because you will have to send your letter with the man's name and serial number on it. If the VA has an address for the man (and keep in mind it does not have everyone's address on file), someone will check the letter you submit to make sure it is appropriate before forwarding it to the last known address.

MILITARY MUSEUM AND BASE RECORDS

Military Base records would probably only be of interest if a soldier was directly assigned to that base for a long period of time. In that case, things like base newspapers or histories might have useful information. Most of the wartime bases have been closed down, and all of their official records should have long since been transferred to the National Archives.

The Army has a number of museums scattered across the country that tell the story of a base, unit, or branch. Most of their information will be limited to the specific focus of their museum and not on specific units. For instance the Patton Museum at Fort Knox will have extensive records on tank development, but may be able to provide only a very brief summary of operations of a specific tank unit. The US Army Woman's Museum at Fort Lee, Virginia may be able to provide more details because of the limited number of female units in World War II.Keep in mind that the staff at these museums is limited, but will generally take the time to answer a specific request. Likewise, if you have materials that might be of specific interest to their museums' focus, the official Army museums are the place to make donations. Private museums can eventually shut down, but once something is in the Army Museum system, with its new and improved inventory system, it will be maintained for future generations.

WEBSITE
List of current Army Museums: http://www.army.mil/cmh-pg/Museums/links.htm

DEATH RECORDS

As previously mentioned, the Individual Personnel Death Files are not available for researchers to look through. Specific files may be requested either as a next of kin, or under the Freedom of Information Act, by sending a request to:

> Commander,
> Total Army Personnel Command,
> ATTN TAPC-PAO (FOIA),
> 200 Stoval Street
> Alexandria, VA 22332-0404

HIRING A RESEARCHER

Not everyone is able to make a trip to the National Archives. Thankfully, there are active freelance researchers available for hire. In many cases it is far more cost efficient to hire someone who knows the Archives' system intimately than to make the trip yourself. The Archives has a listing on its website of researchers available for hire, or you can call the Archives to inquire. The staff does not have any say about who is on this list, but will promptly remove anyone with a track record of complaints.

Because there is no set standard for being on this list, be sure to look for someone who lists World War II military records as a research specialty. Be sure to lock down all the details in writing before going forward, including mailing and copy costs, hourly fees, how long he/she should search for you, exactly what you are looking for, and so forth. Like any private contractor, some are better than others. Most who have worked around the Archives for any length of time will probably be fine, but it is always best to be careful.

Most researchers charge by the hour, not including expenses. Having your researcher make copies of everything he finds can quickly run up your tab, so make sure he knows exactly what you are seeking and what you are willing to spend. A good researcher charges about $50 an hour. Some highly skilled and experienced researchers charge more, some charge less. Be very careful about hiring inexperienced researchers; even though they may charge less an hour (and sometimes substantially less), they often end up costing you more because they are learning about how to research military records on your dime. Tell the researcher specifically what you are looking for, and ask how much similar work they have done.

When you factor in the cost of a trip to Washington, hotels, meals, and car rental, it is often much cheaper to hire someone to do it all for you. However, there is nothing like the thrill of opening a 60-year-old record and reading the original papers. Somehow, seeing that original document with the name of the man you are interested in makes almost any cost worthwhile.

A number of Internet-based companies have sprung up offering to search for veterans' information for a fee. Many have slick ads and look very professional. Most of these companies check only public databases, which you can easily do yourself. Further, most have very limited experience working with older military records. The best way to check on researchers is to be sure they do work in the National Archives and the Military Personal Records Center. If they do not, or someone tells you there is no need to do so, look elsewhere—fast!

COPYRIGHT

It's worth mentioning that any document, film, map or photograph produced by the US government is considered to be in the public domain and you can freely copy, sell, or publish it. They assume that as a taxpayer, you have paid for the item to be made. Some companies make a good living by collecting public domain government records, repackaging, and selling them.

Most archives will ask that you properly cite any records you publish. This makes their life easier if someone requests a copy for themselves; a proper citation will allow an archives employee to go right to the correct box. The National Archives has available a small pamphlet on proper citation for their files.

One word of caution, however. There are records in the archives that have been obtained from other sources, such as a collection of photographs from a private photo agency, which were donated to the archives but with copyrights held by the original owners. Likewise, just because a map was used by the Army and left with the unit records does not mean it wasn't originally a commercially purchased map (such as from the National Geographic Society) that the Army found easier to purchase than to produce themselves.

FOOTNOTES

1.	Information on the NPRC comes from the official NPRC Website: http://www.archives.gov/facilities/mo/st_louis/military_personnel_records.html

2.	NPRC Website

Soldiers attract children and dogs and this GI in Germany is no exception.

The leather cuffs stitched to the top of his books replaced the older style canvas leggings late in the war.

His rifle is the M1 Garand, the most commonly found weapon of the US Army.

National Archives

FINDING YOUR FATHER'S WAR

Section 5

TANGIBLE EVIDENCE OF SERVICE

What is in your wardrobe, closet or attic? An entire uniform or part of one? A box of medals? Some patches—or something else?

This section will help you identify what you have and what it can tell you about your relative's service.

Engineers in camouflage uniforms attack a pillbox with a flamethrower. This weapon would not only burn any combustible material, but also suck oxygen out of the air and suffocate anyone trapped inside the burning structure.

FINDING RECORDS

Uniforms and Insignia

Members of the military carry their service history around with them as if wearing a resume on their chest. Those able to read and understand the wide array of insignia and decorations can tell at a glance what specialties a soldier has been trained in, and where and for how long he has served. Insignia and decorations are thus an easy way for men and women to immediately grasp and appreciate another's background and service without having to say a word.

Combat uniforms in World War II were either wool or cotton, and either khaki (for warm areas) or standard Army Olive Drab (commonly referred to as OD). OD was a greenish-brown color the Army used on everything from toothbrushes to truck paint. It blended in well with just about any background. Insignia were rare on combat uniforms. It was possible to find rank or a unit patches, but for the most part combat clothing tended to be devoid of such markings.

An enlisted man's uniform showing placement of disks, DIs, ribbon bar, and marksmanship badges.

Combat is one of the filthiest jobs there is, and in all probability few uniforms ever worn in action ever came back to the States.

Most were washed and recycled a few times before they became too worn out and were discarded.

It was not unusual for a soldier to go for weeks, if not months, without a shower.

National Archives

This group of soldiers wears a mixture of the olive drab fatigues, and the cotton khaki summer uniform. The cotton khaki uniform was supposed to serve as the hot weather combat uniform, but the darker herring bone twill fatigues were found to be far superior for field use.

National Archives

Captain Frank Orville Gray is seen here in Northern Ireland wearing the officer's dress uniform, with web belt and carbine for parade use. On his left shoulder is the patch of the 8th Infantry Division and the red and green French Fourragere earned by his regiment (the 28th Infantry) in WW1. The sole ribbon bar over his left breast pocket is for the ETO ribbon, awarded as soon as he was assigned to a unit in that Theater.

Photo courtesy of Frank Orville Gray

On maneuvers Captain Gray now wears almost exactly the same uniform as an enlisted man: field jacket, wool pants, and leggings.

Once in combat the tie, helmet rank, and collar insignia, although regulation, would vanish from many front line combat officers.

Photo courtesy of Frank Orville Gray

The reason for there being so few markings on combat uniforms is that, in the field, men turned in their dirty clothing when they entered a shower tent and received a different set of clean clothing (taken from a previous group and washed) when they exited. Most veterans did not keep their combat clothing, and were issued a complete set of dress items when they left the service, including all authorized insignia.

During World War II, officers and enlisted men wore basically the same uniform in combat, but their dress uniforms were quite different. The enlisted man wore his standard OD wool field trousers and shirt, but added on a tie and a four-pocket coat for dress purposes. The color of the trousers did not match the shirt and jacket and so offered a two-toned look. During the summer months, men wore a cotton khaki shirt and trousers. Enlisted men did not have a dress jacket to wear in hot weather, and would just add a tie. They wore the same boots for dress and field use. In the field they added canvas leggings.

Officers had a completely different dress uniform. During the summer they wore a thin wool khaki four-pocket coat with matching trousers. In cooler seasons they wore a sharp outfit known by its nickname "pinks and greens." This was a dark chocolate-colored coat worn with trousers a shade of khaki that had a distinctive pink coloring to it. This was worn up until 1957, when the current Army green dress uniform replaced it.

Near the end of the war a new short jacket was developed. Nicknamed the "Ike jacket" after General Eisenhower, this was supposed to be part of a combat uniform layered for warmth in cold climates.

Officers of Company G, 28th Infantry Regiment, wear their Ike jackets upon return to the USA. Wearing this jacket over the cotton khaki uniform was not typical, but one of many variations found in the period immediately after the war.

The company commander, Captain Phil Emerson, proudly holds the "Combat Infantry Company" streamer attached to the company guidon.

This was given to any company from which more than 65% of the men had been awarded the CIB.

Photo Courtesy Frank Orville Gray

The soldiers preferred to keep it in good shape for dress use, so the quartermasters decided not to issue it until the end of the fighting. Because they had to buy their own uniforms, some officers purchased Ike jackets privately. Officers also had a similar short Ike jacket made in the chocolate brown color of their standard dress uniform, and also had shirts and caps made in both the pink trouser color and the chocolate jacket color.

For work details, such as KP, digging latrines, cleaning, etc., the men had thin OD cotton uniforms made from herring bone twill (HBT) material. This was easily washed when dirty and was cut larger than normal so it could be worn over wool uniforms to keep them clean. The term "fatigues" in relation to military clothing comes from these because all non-combat forms of labor in the Army are known as "fatigue duties." These HBTs, or fatigues, were frequently worn as a combat uniform in hot climates. Before the war, fatigues were actually made of blue denim, which was used up to about mid-1941.

Most uniforms remained fairly standard throughout the war, but a man's tie can provide a clue as to when a specific photo was taken. Since World War I, the Army tie had been black. In February 1942, however, it was officially changed to a khaki color for both officers and enlisted men. Therefore, any photo showing a black tie was probably taken before February 1942.

To further distinguish officers from enlisted men, the former wore braid on the sleeves of their jackets and coats.

Officers wore a one-half inch OD braid three inches from the sleeve end. Warrant officers did not wear this braid. However, if a warrant officer or enlisted man had served honorably as an officer in World War I and been reduced in rank following the war, they were allowed to wear a similar forest green color braid. General officers sported two bands of braid on the sleeves of their overcoats.

BOOKS

The World War II GI: US Army Uniforms 1941–45 in Color Photographs, by Richard Windrow, Tim Hawkins, Crowood Press, 2000, ISBN 1-86126-302-3

This photo holds three clues to the time period it was taken. The men wear breeches instead of trousers, which would indicate either it is well before the war, or that they were in a cavalry unit during the first period of the war. The leather enlisted man's garrison belt was eliminated as a standard item in 1942, although some men may have worn them up through 1943 as a private purchase item.

The main clue is the black tie, which would date the photo to pre-February 1942. The photo is in fact of a Massachusetts National Guard unit and was taken in 1939.

National Archives

In the early 1960s, the US army did away with olive drab as its primary uniform color and changed to the dark green still worn today.

Insignia sewn on the uniform was also changed at this time to better blend with the new uniforms.

Some, like this Meritorious Unit Citation, were drastically changed, while most patches only had their outer edging color changed from the brownish olive drab to this green color.

INSIGNIA

There were many different types of insignia worn by Army personnel. These included national insignia (indicating a soldier of the USA), branch and rank insignia, unit insignia, and badges (denoting special training or skill), decorations for unit or individual actions, and service medals to indicate where a soldier had served.

Standard Button   *Engineer's Button*   *WAAC Button*

The most basic form of insignia in the army was the button. Most buttons were made out of plain plastic, but on dress uniforms they bore the coat of arms of the United States. Engineer officers were the only Army troops with their own special uniform buttons. Engineer officer buttons (which were not worn by enlisted men), bore the design of a flying eagle holding in its beak a banner with the word "Essayons" (French for "let us try").

Due to a shortage of brass, some dress buttons were also produced in OD plastic. The Navy used buttons with an eagle atop a horizontal anchor, while the Marine Corps button was an eagle atop a diagonally placed fouled anchor. The Woman's Auxiliary Army Corps (WAAC) also had its own design (see above) for the period before it was accepted into the Army (when it moved to standard buttons.)

Rank insignia (described in Section 1) was worn by enlisted men on the sleeves, and by officers on the shoulders or on the shirt collar. An enlisted man's rank stripes came in two different versions: OD stripes on dark blue wool, or lighter khaki stripes on dark blue cotton. There was no real difference between the two varieties, but in theory the cotton stripes were for washable uniforms while the wool ones were for the dry-cleanable wool. In practice, they were used interchangeably.

In the Korean War era, the World War II dark blue backing (almost black in appearance) was changed to a medium blue. In the 1950s, rank insignia were reduced in size and made yellow on blue for combat personal, and blue on yellow for non-combat troops. Enlisted rank during World War II was always represented by stripes worn on the sleeves; placing the rank of an enlisted man on the collar began during the Vietnam era.

A major difference between an officer's and enlisted man's insignia was that the latter was always on a circular background, while the former was cut out without any background. This was true on branch insignia, the letters "U.S.," and the national seal on headgear.

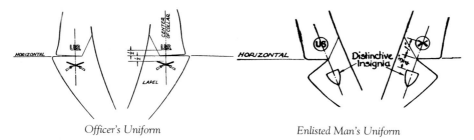

| *Officer's Uniform* | *Enlisted Man's Uniform* |

Officers and enlisted men wore insignia in a slightly different way. Officers wore the national letters "U.S." on both lapels, while enlisted men wore their "U.S." on a one-inch brass disk on their right lapel only. Officers displayed a pair of branch insignia (crossed rifles for infantry, etc.) below their "US" letters; enlisted men wore one branch insignia on a one-inch brass disk on the left lapel. Enameled distinctive insignia were worn on the lower lapel by enlisted men and on the shoulder by officers.

Officers wore their rank insignia pinned to the epaulets of their uniform jackets, along with their enameled distinctive insignia. When they wore just a shirt as an outer garment, their rank and branch insignia was displayed on the collar. Enlisted men wore their rank stripes on the sleeves of their jackets and shirts (sewn halfway between elbow and shoulder).

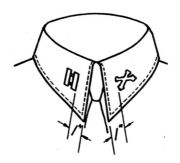

Officer's Shirt

There were many ways that a soldier's uniform identified his unit. At the top of the left sleeve an embroidered patch was worn indicating his main attachment. This was primarily the division, corps, army, department, or command he was serving in at that time. Enameled crests, known as distinctive insignias or "DIs," indicated a smaller unit that was a part of the unit represented on the shoulder patch. This was almost always either a regiment or battalion. Officers wore DIs on their shoulder straps; enlisted men wore them on their lower lapels. Late in the war enlisted men had their DIs moved from lapel to shoulder. When this happened, some but not all soldiers adopted the practice of wearing four collar disks on their lapel: two US and two branch disks.

The number of their regiment or battalion could also be worn on both an officer's or enlisted man's branch or national insignia. This was very common before the war, but was seen less frequently as the war progressed. The reason was obvious: wearing such numbers was considered a security risk because it provided casual observers information on what unit was in which area. Once the war ended, however, this once again became a popular private purchase item. Likewise, the company letter could also be worn on the branch insignia if a soldier desired.

REGULAR ARMY

WITHOUT REGIMENTAL NUMBER

WITH REGIMENTAL NUMBER

NATIONAL GUARD

WITHOUT REGIMENTAL NUMBER

WITH REGIMENTAL NUMBER

Before the federalization of the National Guard, it was also common to find the letters of the unit's state superimposed on the national "U.S." This indicated the state to which the soldier technically reported. Some men continued wearing them while in federal service for the first few months out of pride for their National Guard origin, or until they obtained the regulation insignia.

Sleeve Insignia

Sleeves were used not only for the unit patch and rank stripes, but also bore insignia indicating how long a man had been in the Army. Short horizontal gold stripes on the lower left sleeve were overseas bars. One was worn for each six-month period the man had served outside the USA. An OD diagonal stripe was called a service stripe (or hash mark) and indicated one three-year term of enlistment in the Army.

Some older soldiers who had been in World War I still wore chevrons indicating a wound on the lower left sleeve, and service chevrons on the left sleeve indicating six months of overseas service during that earlier conflict. A single red chevron worn halfway up the arm was a discharge stripe from World War I,

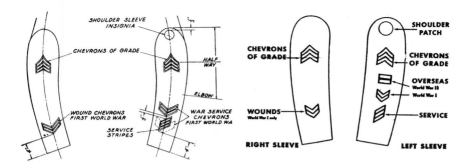

but would not have been worn on any serving soldier during World War II. Officers wore these same chevrons and stripes indicating overseas and World War I service, but did not wear the hash marks for enlistment unless they had earned them as an enlisted man.

Depending upon personal taste and finances, both officers and men could purchase bullion insignia to wear instead of the standard cotton embroidery. Bullion insignia used either gold or silver thread, which some soldiers felt was more stylish. Bullion is most commonly found in the various sleeve service stripes and officers' rank.

The Colonel on the right has just been awarded the Legion of Merit (note it is the only full medal on his chest, the rest being just ribbons).

From his left sleeve we can tell he is currently assigned to the ETO Headquarters, has served two years overseas during World War II, and another one and a half years overseas in World War I.

Officers of this rank rarely fought in the front lines, but this man earned the CIB as an infantry regimental commander early in the campaign.   National Archives

Left: A bullion shoulder sleeve insignia of the Army Air Force. Such custom-made insignia were quite popular in some units.

Hand embroidered insignia were particularly inexpensive in the China-Burma-India area.

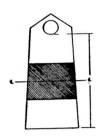

Combat Leader Marks

There were far more officers and men serving in non-combat duties behind the lines than in combat units on the front lines. To help set these combat troops apart from a similar-ranked man who may never have heard a shot fired in anger, the Army adopted combat leader markings.

An officer commanding a combat unit wore a dark green strap on his shoulder board. NCOs in command of a combat unit (such as a squad) wore a dark green horizontal stripe, three inches by a quarter-inch. Not every unit adopted these markings, and the use of the NCO mark was stopped at the end of the war. Most examples on surviving uniforms appear to have been simply cut from whatever dark green cloth was at hand.

HEADGEAR

In the Army, headgear with a brim was called a hat; headgear without a brim was called a cap. Both officers and enlisted men wore a gold colored national seal on their peaked service caps. The difference was that enlisted men had a circular brass backing to their insignia, while the officers did not have this backing. Warrant officers had their own distinctive cap insignia.

The service cap was hard to store when traveling, so the Army developed the garrison cap (also known as the overseas cap). This was easy to fold and store. Enlisted men wore colored braid in their branch of service color on this cap; warrant officers silver and black braid; company and field officers gold and black braid; and general officers solid gold braid.

The majority of enlisted men did not bring their service caps overseas with them because it was prone to be crushed in their duffel bag. Thus, most photos showing an enlisted man in a service cap were probably taken in the USA. Members of the Army Air Force took great pride in removing the stiffener from the service cap and making it look as though it had been crushed down by the pressure of headphones after flying a number of missions. The "50 mission crusher" (as the style was known) was an unofficial but universally seen component of the AAF officer's uniform.

Not every enlisted man's cap bore the colored piping. Most were made without the piping sewn on; it was left to the soldier to add the correct color when he was assigned to a branch. For whatever reason, many overseas caps never received the piping. One common variation to officers wearing gold and black piping was officers in paratroop units. Some wore either light blue (infantry) or

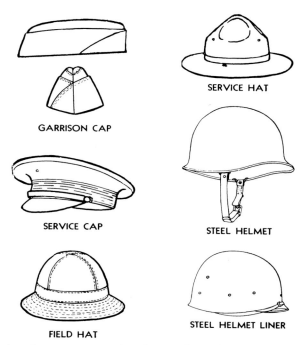

GARRISON CAP

SERVICE HAT

SERVICE CAP

STEEL HELMET

FIELD HAT

STEEL HELMET LINER

This illustration from Army quartermasters' regulations indicates the official terminology for the various types of headgear used in the Army.

OFFICERS' INSIGNIA
(Service Cap)

WARRANT OFFICERS' INSIGNIA
(Service Cap)

SERVICE CAP

ENLISTED MEN'S
INSIGNIA
(Service Cap)

Location
of Insignia

Army service cap insignia: officers, warrant officers, and enlisted men (all gold colored).

red (artillery) on their caps to distinguish themselves from the noncombat elements of their unit.

Another piping oddity is the red, white, and blue worn by the First Special Service Force. This tri-colored piping was originally produced for trainees at the Civilian Military Training Camps held every summer.

When these camps were suspended for the war, the surplus red/white/blue piping was adopted by the elite First Special Service Force. This explains why men who never served in that specialized unit had that piping in their possession.

COLORS WORN ON THE OVERSEAS CAP	
General Officers	Gold
Officers	Gold and Black
Warrant Officers	Silver and Black
Infantry	Light Blue
Cavalry	Yellow
Armored Command	Green piped with White
Artillery (both coast and field)	Scarlet
Tank Destroyer Forces	Orange and Black
First Special Service Force	Red, White and Blue
WAC	Yellow with Moss Green
Medical Department	Maroon piped with White
Engineer Corps	Scarlet piped with White
Ordnance Department	Crimson piped with Yellow
Finance Department	Grey piped with Yellow
Air Corps	Ultramarine Blue piped with Orange
Militia Bureau	Dark Blue
Chemical Warfare Service	Cobalt Blue piped with Yellow
Adjutant General's Department	Dark Blue piped with Scarlet
Quartermaster Corps	Buff
Transportation Corps	Brick Red with Yellow
Military Police	Yellow piped with Green
Unassigned	Green
National Guard Bureau	Dark Blue
Signal Corps	Orange piped with White
First Special Service Force / C.M.T.C	Red, White and Blue

NOTE: Members of the General Staff, Chaplains, Inspector General's Department, Judge Advocate General's Department, United States Military Academy Professors, Specialist Reserve and Military Intelligence Reserve were almost exclusively officers. They would wear the gold and black piping of an officer rather than a branch color

WAAC and WAC Insignia

When the Women's Auxiliary Army Corps (WAAC) was organized, it was not officially part of the Army. It had its own button and cap insignia. Brass was in short supply while the WAACs were forming, so the majority of their cap badges and buttons were OD plastic.

It was illegal for anyone not in the US Army to wear the rank insignia of an Army officer if he had not received a commission in the Army. To indicate officer rank, the few WAACs who held such positions wore the standard WAAC uniform, but with an added special shoulder board pointed over (instead of along) the shoulder. The Army ranks of captain, 1st lieutenant, and 2d lieutenant were officially called first officer, second officer and third officer, respectively. The commandant of the WAACs was the only WAAC major.

Branch insignia for both officers and enlisted WAACs were the head of Athena, and their branch colors were gold and green. WAAC military police wore the MP armband in yellow and green, and not the standard Army white and blue. WAAC NCOs wore the same rank stripes as their male counterparts, but because they were not technically part of the Army, they wore a small embroidered title saying WAAC in green letters on a gold background underneath the stripes.

When the WAAC became part of the US Army in September 1943, the special WAAC buttons and insignia were discarded and standard Army insignia was used. A service medal was issued to those women who honorably served in the WAAC from July 1942 to August 1943, or in the WAC from September 1943 to September 1945. This medal was never awarded to any man. Keep in mind that WAACs were not part of the Army Nurse Corps and vice versa; they were separate branches.

BADGES

MARKSMAN   **SHARPSHOOTER**   **EXPERT**

The three weapons qualification badges with rifle bar, shown in order of skill from lowest to highest.

This studio photograph tells us that this technician 5th grade (or tech/corporal) was assigned to the Army Ground Forces (red/white/blue patch on shoulder. The design on his collar disk indicates he is in a quartermaster unit.

The sole ribbon is the Good Conduct medal, and the lack of a theater ribbon indicates he has not been stationed outside the USA.

On his pocket are the Marksman's badge for rifle, and Expert's for two other weapons (lettering not visible). Soldiers generally would not wear two shooting badges but he probably wanted to dress up his somewhat bare uniform for the photo.

Badges in the Army were insignia indicating a specific skill or training. The most common were silver shooting badges. These came in three grades (increasing in skill): Marksman, Sharpshooter and Expert. After training and practice, a soldier "shot for record" and his score determined which badge he was allowed to wear until the next year when he again "shot for record." This was very important in the pre-war Army when soldiers were paid extra if they did well on the rifle range. The extra payment was eliminated during World War II, but being able to wear one of these badges was its own reward for many young soldiers. A soldier had to continue to requalify each year if he was to continue to wear these badges.

The regulations called for a man to be awarded a second bar for every three years of continuous qualification, and to have the dates of the following two yearly qualifications engraved on the back of the previous bar, but this was rarely done during the war.

At the bottom of the badge were two loops to which bars could be attached to indicate which weapons the man had qualified with. There was a list of almost 30 different weapon types that bars were made for, ranging from rifle to 60mm mortar to 75mm TD (for Tank Destroyer crews). These badges, like many others, were issued to the men. Higher quality metal, or sterling silver versions, were available for private purchase. There were also badges for shooting champions in various corps and Army matches, but these are quite rare and generally clearly marked as to what they represent.

Driver's Badge

Location of the ribbon bars with shooting badge underneath on pocket, such as this regional shooting award.

The same pocket flap location was used for the driver/mechanic badge and the diver badge.

The silver driver's and mechanic's badges were authorized in July 1942 for men who passed a qualification test. Like the weapons qualification bars, these bars could be attached to this badge to indicate driver-W (for wheeled vehicles), driver-T for (tracked vehicles), driver-M (for motorcycles), and mechanic (for automotive or similar mechanics). A similarly styled badge with hanging bars was used by Air Force personnel for some of their specialties. This, along with flight crew badges, will be discussed in the AAF section.

Diver's Badge

While small in number, the Army had its own divers to help with salvage, bridge construction, and port repair. This was in the days of the brass hard helmet and before the invention of SCUBA. Four different levels of silver diver's badges were authorized in February 1944: second class diver, first class diver, and master diver. These were silver badges of a diver's helmet. The forth category was salvage diver, which had the letter "S" on the font.

Parachutist Badges

The silver parachutist badge was authorized in March 1941 and awarded to men who had successfully made five training jumps or one actual combat jump. Most paratroops went through a tough training course before making their jumps; however, when specialists were needed in a hurry, some made all five jumps on one day after a short period of instruction. The parachutist badge was worn by the jumper for the rest of his Army career. During the war, a tradition was started by some paratroops when they drilled holes in their wings and attached a small bronze star for each combat jump. This is now an accepted practice in the Army.

Some airborne units developed an embroidered oval worn behind this badge. Known as a parachute oval (or backing), the colors indicated what airborne unit the man was attached to. Not every unit had these ovals until after the war.

| Senior Para Wings | Master Para Wings | Glider Wings |

Master and senior parachutist badges were not authorized until 1949. The senior wings had a star above the canopy and were awarded for 30 jumps; the master wings had a wreath around the star and were awarded for 65 jumps. A similar silver badge was authorized for glider troops in June 1944. It was awarded for either passing a qualification course or making a combat landing in a glider.

Combat Infantryman's Badge

The most respected badge awarded by the Army was the Combat Infantryman's Badge (CIB). Many soldiers felt this was the single most important decoration a man could wear. The CIB was a silver musket on a light blue background. It was awarded for successful participation in combat as an infantryman. No other branch could qualify for this award. It was first authorized in October 1943 and brought with it extra pay. There was no real length of time a man had to spend in combat, but generally the awards started coming

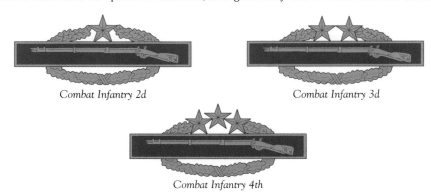

Combat Infantry 2d   Combat Infantry 3d

Combat Infantry 4th

through about one month after a man entered a combat unit. He was due this coveted award even if he was wounded or killed on his first day at the front.

Expert Infantryman's Badge

At the same time the CIB was created to help boost the morale of the infantryman, a non-combat version called the Expert Infantry-man's Badge (EIB) was also authorized. This was awarded to any infantryman (below the rank of colonel) who passed a series of proficiency tests. It also brought with it a small amount of extra pay.

Only one of these awards could be worn, with the CIB taking precedence. As the most important award in the Army (to an infantryman, at least) it was displayed on the left breast above any ribbons.

Medical Badge

Medics assigned to the infantry had to deal with the rough life of the frontline without a weapon. Because they were not infantrymen, they did not qualify for the CIB. Most troops believed this was a grave injustice, and in January 1945 a silver Medical Badge was authorized specifically for any medical personnel (colonel or below) who had been assigned to a company-sized unit of infantry during combat operations. This was specifically intended for company aid men who daily risked their lives on the battlefield to help others.

In 1951, silver stars were added to both the CIB (see left) and the medical badge (see below) to indicate the wearer had served in more than one war. Until recently this meant that a "three-star man" had served in World War II, Korea, and Vietnam.

Combat Medic 2d

Combat Medic 3d

Combat Medic 4th

It is not unusual to find a uniform with insignia in the wrong place. In this photograph the Combat Infantry Man's Badge is in not in the right position in relation to the ribbons (it should be above them.) Many soldiers were more interested in getting out of the Army than they were in making sure all their insignia were in the correct location.

There was no Army aviator insignia during World War II, but a large number of qualified pilots flew small observation or liaison aircraft as part of every artillery battalion.

These pilots (technically called liaison pilots) were authorized to wear flight wings with a superimposed "L." There were a number of other flight wings used by the AAF that will be discussed in Appendix E.

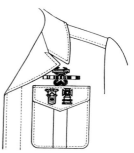

Location of ribbons and badges.

General Staff Identification Badge

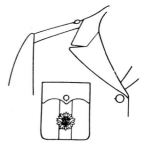

Serving on the War Department General Staff was considered a great honor because only the best men were selected for this duty.

Officers assigned to the General Staff for at least one year were allowed to wear the General Staff Badge.

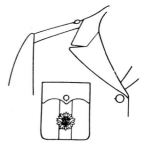

Location of General Staff Badge on jacket.

This is a large gold and green enameled badge worn on the right side pocket of the dress uniform coat.

FASTENINGS

There are three main types of fasteners used on metal insignia. A "screwback" insignia had a threaded post on the back. The post was pushed through a hole in the cloth and a nut (normally a round disk) was screwed on to hold the insignia firmly in place. Screwback insignia were used throughout World War II, but were more common in the early years of the conflict. The necessity to punch a hole in the cloth made soldiers look for a better way to fasten their insignia to their uniforms.

"Pin Back" insignia used a safety pin style attachment. It did not leave a permanent hole and started becoming popular during the early months of the war. However, it was a bit tricky to get the insignia aligned properly. Pin back insignia was generally from the World War II years.

"Clutch back" insignia solved the alignment problem by having two prongs on the back of the insignia held in place by two clutches held on by friction. Clutch back insignia came into use late in World War II, but quickly surpassed all other types in popularity and are still in use today. It is possible to date the period in which the clutches themselves were made, but because they were replaced when they wore out and thus no longer held the insignia firmly in place, it is not uncommon to find old insignia with post-World War II clutches. If the tops are smooth it is a wartime production; if the top has a series of small bumps, it is postwar production.

The three major varieties of insignia attachment.

Left: The screwback type, held in place with a single threaded nut. Screwback insignia were most popular before World War II, but died out during the war because a hole had to be cut in the uniform for the threaded post. Center: Pinback insignia were held in place with a hinged pin. These came into fashion in World War II, as no hole had to be cut into the uniform, but they were awkward to attach. Right: The clutch back attachment appeared near the end of World War II and was quickly adopted because no hole had to be made, and it was easy to put the insignia on at the exact spot. The two pins sticking up from the bottom were held in place by clutches. Shown here is a post World War II clutch with small bumps on the flat surface. A true World War II clutch had no such bumps.

Unit Insignia

Soldiers indicated the unit to which they were attached in a number of ways. The most common was an embroidered shoulder patch (known officially as an SSI, or shoulder sleeve insignia) worn half an inch below the seam of the left shoulder. This was typically the division, corps, army, service command department, or other similar large-sized unit to which the soldier was assigned.

Before World War II, many SSIs were sewn from wool by hand. The vast majority of World War II-era SSIs were embroidered with cotton thread. Some were privately purchased with elaborate metallic bullion embroidery or manufactured from local esoteric materials. These odd patches are eagerly sought after by insignia collectors as "theatre made" patches, and are worth far more than the standard embroidered versions.

A large number of patch designs were used in World War II. The most common are shown in Appendices A, B, C & D. There were many variations depending upon where and when they were made; World War II-era SSIs have been reproduced in recent years.

Units assigned to a corps or army wore that insignia, but many non-combat units reported to higher organizations, such as the Army Service Forces or Army Ground Forces, and also wore those patches. Perhaps the most common SSI worn in World War II was the blue star on red and white worn by the Army Service Force. These were non-combatant troops serving in support positions.

While some of the designs on patches are easy to understand, such as the red number one worn by the 1st Infantry Division, some represent the history of the unit or have a clever connection to it. For example, the 4th Infantry Division wore a patch with four ivy leaves (the roman numeral for 4 is IV, which was morphed into "ivy"); the 27th Infantry Division was originally commanded by a man named O'Ryan, so that unit wears the constellation of Orion on its patch.

One of the most confusing aspects of trying to understand a World War II uniform is keeping in mind that the left shoulder patch was not always the patch of the unit the man served with. This began in World War I, when units were sent home in a reverse order of their arrival. Therefore, men who had just entered France were sent home long before the men who had been serving overseas since the beginning of the war. This was rectified in World War II by making sure the first men to go overseas were the first to come home via a point system.

At the end of the war, anyone with 85 or more points was sent home (with the exception of those volunteering for overseas duty or those with scarce and required skills). In combat units, the troops were a mixture of both low point and high point men (newer men sent in as replacements had fewer points). To get the right men home as quickly as possible, soldiers were transferred (sometimes multiple times) to sort them into groups of similar points.

These high point units eventually contained men who had served for a long time with a different combat unit; most were very proud of their former units. Many soldiers refused to remove the patch of their combat unit and replace it with one they had no respect for. The Army wisely relented and allowed soldiers to wear the patch of the unit they had served with overseas on their right shoulder. This has become known as the combat patch, but it could be any unit the man served in overseas—even it if never actually saw any fighting. It also could be the reserve unit a man was assigned to when he came home.

For example, many men of the veteran 29th Infantry Division were sent overseas long before D-Day and were sent home as part of the 69th Infantry Division, which had only been in France since December 1944. In this case, the men wore the 69th Division patch on their left shoulder, and a 29th Division patch on their right shoulder. The left shoulder patch would continue to change if the man remained in the service, but the right shoulder patch displayed the unit to which the soldier felt most closely associated. If a man served overseas with more than one unit he was allowed to choose which one he wore on his right sleeve.

BOOKS

A very detailed history of Army insignia, with information on how to date the various types is: *The Encyclopedia of United States Army Insignia and Uniforms,* by William Emerson. University of Olklahoma Press, 1996, ISBN 0-8061-2622-1

An introductory book on World War II patches is: *U.S. Military Patches of World War II,* by Christopher Brown. Turner Publishing, KY, 2003, ISBN 1-56311-830-0

This solder can be identified as an infantryman by the crossed rifles on his collar brass.

The Enameled insignia with the letter "5" in it is the divisional insignia of the 175th Infantry Regiment: a Maryland National Guard unit that served with the 29th Infantry Division.

His tie is black, indicating this photograph was taken before February 1942.

The total absence of ribbons on his uniform is a good indication this was taken very early in his service, possibly when he initially joined the Army. If it had been taken after his initial training period he would have probably at least had one marksmanship badge.

Yannick Creach Collection

DISTINCTIVE INSIGNIA

This soldier wears a typical early war dress uniform, showing the regulation two-collar disks with unit DIs underneath. Clues to when the photo was taken are the service cap (which was rarely seen on enlisted men outside the USA) and the white shirt and black tie. He is Staff Sergeant Alvin Casey, who earned the Medal of Honor in Brittany in 1944.
National Archives

Each regiment and even some battalions had their own unit crest or distinctive insignia (DI). These were enameled pins about one inch tall whose design told the story of the unit. Before the war, every unit had its own DI, but most were made of brass. Because this metal was considered critical to the war effort, after January 1943 DIs were no longer made or officially approved. Soldiers with existing DIs were permitted to keep wearing them.

These insignia are sometimes called "crests," although technically the crest is a smaller insignia that appears on the top of the shield of the full unit insignia. The crests were not always included on the DI, but were part of the unit's official insignia. National Guard units used the crest of their home state, and reserve units used the Minuteman. Regular Army units had unique crests normally taken from something in its history.

Some men had insignia custom-made from silver, plastic, and even fabric. The end of the war brought forth a flood of DIs because many were made overseas or sold to returning servicemen once brass was no longer restricted.

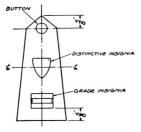

The proper position of insignia on an officer's shoulder loop or board.

The Distinctive Insignia is centered with the rank insignia near the edge. If the officer has no DI then the rank insignia is centered.

Literally thousands of DI designs have been produced over the years, and some of them are today quite rare. Many designs were never officially recognized by the Army's Institute of Heraldry, but instead were something the men made up on the spot. No single book shows every DI, but the American Society of Military Insignia Collectors (ASMIC) publishes catalogs of DIs from various branches, along with listings by motto or major devices on the design.

A clue to the branch of the unit represented on a DI can sometimes, but not always, be taken from the major color of the insignia. As a general rule, the major color was that of the branch's service (see piping color charts, pg. 101). Blue was usually infantry, red was artillery, red and white was medical, green was armor, yellow was cavalry, and so forth. Although not always the case, this can help you to focus in on a specific branch.

More typical of the middle to late war period is Sgt. Sherwood Hallman who wears the more easily transported garrison cap, standard wool shirt and khaki tie. He wears only standard US and infantry collar disks and an ETO ribbon with no campaign stars.

This probably indicates the photo was taken in England before he went into combat (and also earned a Medal of Honor in Brittany).   National Archives

Some DIs contained the unit motto, which ranged from famous quotes of the unit like "Keep up the Fire" (13th Infantry Regiment), "Hit 'em First" (109th Cavalry Regt), or "Don't kick our Dog" (203d AAA Battalion). Mottos were in English, Latin, French, or any language deemed appropriate.

In theory, every element of a DI was supposed to indicate something of the history of the unit it represented. The massive increase in the size of the Army, however, caused many of the official rules to be thrown out the window in World War II. Since no new designs were approved by the Army for the duration of the war, some units had one of their artistic men come up with a design.

WEBSITES

A number of the most common DIs appear on the Institute of Heraldry's website: http://www.tioh.hqda.pentagon.mil/

www.asmic.org is the website for ASMIC, the association for anyone interested in collecting military insignia.

The 45th Field Artillery Battalion used a red shield (red being the branch color of artillery).

On it is a mule kicking an artillery shell, indicating the power behind its weapons.

The DI of the 102d Infantry Regiment has a lion indicating its service in the Revolutionary War.

The blue cross indicates Civil War, the prickly pear cactus at top right denotes service on the Mexican border in 1916, and the Fleur de Lys at top left means it served in France in World War I.

The motto, "Stand Forth," is taken from a speech made to the men in 1776.

The DI of the 16th Infantry Regiment.

The official Army heraldry statement for this insignia is, "The shield is blue and white (blue being the color of infantry, and white being the 19th-century color of infantry). The background design is taken from the arms of Fleville in France, where the unit fought during World War I. The crossed arrow and bolo indicate service in the Philippine insurrection. The red fort below represents service with the 5th Corps in Cuba."

UNIT AWARDS

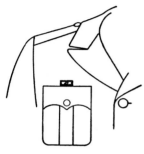

Top: The Distinguished Unit Citation award.

Above: Its proper location on the jacket above the right hand pocket flap.

The Distinguished Unit Citation

There were two Army unit awards used in World War II. One was for combat units (the Distinguished Unit Citation), and the other for non-combat units (the Meritorious Service Unit Plaque).

The award was made as if every member of the unit was considered to deserve the DSC or the DSM. These awards were made to both the unit and the individuals who were in the unit when it was earned. All future members of the unit were authorized to wear the award as long as they were assigned to the unit, but those who actually earned the award could wear it no matter what unit they were later assigned to serve in.

The Distinguished Unit Citation (sometimes referred to in orders as a "battle honor") is a blue ribbon with gold frame worn on the right breast.

This was renamed the Presidential Unit Citation in 1966. More than one such award was indicated by the addition of a 5/16 inch bronze oak leaf cluster affixed to the ribbon.

The citation awarding the Distinguished Unit Citation to a company of the 69th Tank Battalion reads as follows:

> Company C, 69th Tank Battalion (Reinforced), is cited for extraordinary heroism and outstanding performance of duty in action against the enemy during the period 5 to 11 January 1945 near Bastogne, Belgium. After having taken Positions 2,000 yards to the east of Mageret, Belgium, Company C, 69th Tank Battalion (Reinforced), was on January 1945 ordered to withdraw to Hill 510, a distance of 500 yards north of Mageret, and assume defensive positions in preparation for expected German counterattacks. The positions were assumed on 5 January 1945. For the following 6 days, the enemy, with massed infantry and heavy tanks, attempted to drive the company from its positions and seize the hill. Each attack was preceded by a violent artillery preparation by 150-mm guns, was mounted in such strength that the enemy's superiority in numbers ranged from two to five times the company's strength, and was supported or led by from four to eight tanks, the majority of which were Mark VI Tigers or Mark V Panthers. Despite the enemy's superiority and the bitter cold weather which froze men's

feet and hands even as they were fighting, the company gallantly and tenaciously held its positions and beat off every attack with casualties to the enemy in men, armor, and guns which far exceeded our own. The collective heroism displayed by the officers and men of Company C, 69th Tank Battalion (Reinforced), in bolding this vital position against the fiercely fighting and determined enemy was largely responsible for maintaining the line protecting Bastogne and is in keeping with the finest traditions of the military service. (General Orders 298, Headquarters 6th Armored Division, 3 August 1945, as approved by the Commanding General, European Theater (Main).)[1]

The Meritorious Service Unit Commendation

The Meritorious Service Unit Commendation was actually awarded as a plaque to the entire unit (see photo on next page).

Soldiers in that unit wore a gold wreath embroidered on an OD background on the lower left sleeve. It was quickly nicknamed "the toilet seat."

This plaque became the Meritorious Unit Commendation (MUC) and was awarded to units for exceptionally meritorious conduct in performance of outstanding services for at least six continuous months during the period of military operations against an armed enemy occurring on or after 1 January 1944.

Top left and above: The gold wreath on olive drab sleeve insignia (the "toilet seat"), the post war version indicating three such awards.

MUC's were worn on the sleeve of the jacket.

Service in a combat zone was not required, but the service must have been directly related to the combat effort. Units stationed in the United States were not eligible.

Only one MUC patch could be worn on the uniform and no provision for multiple awards existed during the war.

In 1946, embroidered numbers in the center of the wreath were authorized to indicate multiple awards. In the early 1960s, the MUC was renamed the

Meritorious Unit Award (MUA) and changed to a red ribbon with a gold frame worn on the right breast similar to the Distinguished Unit Citation.

A Meritorious Unit Plaque presented to the 110th Quartermaster Bakery Company in Italy, 1943.

Lieutenant General Mark Clark's Fifth Army had somewhat customized the design to include the Army insignia.

Of special interest is that the two bakery officers wear the highly desirable paratrooper boots and the winter combat jacket with knitted cuffs.

National Archives

Foreign Unit Awards

While many soldiers earned foreign decorations and awards during the war, two of the most common were the Fourragere from France and Belgium, and the Orange lanyard from Holland. These were braided cords or ropes worn around the left shoulder. The Fourragere rope was worn with a brass tip and indicated that the unit, or individual, had been cited more than once for bravery in official reports. The French used a very complicated system of different versions for different numbers of awards, but the Americans reduced this to two basic awards: a red and green rope for two French citations, and yellow and green for four or more French citations. The Belgium Fourragere was always scarlet and green.

Illustration showing how the Fourragere was worn.

Fourrageres awarded during World War I have the color broken up along the cord, while those issued in World War II show a continuous line of red or yellow. The yellow/green Fourragere is extremely rare, and only one unit was authorized to wear it for service in World War I (the 646th Ambulance Service Section). These were mainly unit awards and so the same principle as other unit awards applied. The men who won the award could continue to wear it no matter what unit they were later assigned to, but anyone joining the unit afterward could wear it only as long as he was assigned to that unit.

Most soldiers in World War II wore the Fourragere due to its award to their unit in World War I. A few men, however, actually earned the award for being cited for bravery as an individual. In this case they could continue to wear the Fourragere no matter what unit they served with. A Fourragere won as an individual was to be worn with a small enameled insignia of the last unit the soldier was with when he was cited.

Like the Fourragere, the Netherlands Orange lanyard was a unit award worn on the left shoulder, but it had no brass tip. One end of the lanyard was buttoned to the top left pocket button.

France and Belgium also awarded the Croix de Guerre medal as both an individual award (in which a medal was issued to the soldier, with a citation specifically naming him) and as a unit award (no medal or ribbon was issued and the citation names the unit only). Veterans are often confused about the Croix de Guerre as a unit award. This authorized their unit to bear a Croix de Guerre streamer on their unit flag, but does not allow the soldiers to wear the Croix de Guerre ribbon. If the Croix de Guerre was awarded to an individual, he was presented with the actual medal and an award certificate, and could wear the ribbon on his uniform.

Illustration showing how the Belgian lanyard was worn.

INDIVIDUAL DECORATIONS

Decorations were earned by an individual's specific actions, while medals (service or campaign) were earned by participating in an event or campaign. This can sometimes be confusing, since a "decorated" soldier is generally the recipient of medals, for example the Medal of Honor or the Silver Star. A Decoration was traditionally engraved on the reverse with the name of the person receiving it to indicate that he had performed a specific action to earn it. By way of contrast, service medals were not engraved.

Both types of awards were commonly referred to as medals. The traditional medal is an ornament hung from a brightly colored suspension ribbon. It's not practical to wear these medals every day, so, with the exception of important occasions, most soldiers wore only the ribbon of the decoration. These ribbons were worn in rows on the left breast in a specific order of precedence. These were known as "ribbon bars." No miniature medals were made during World War II; however, each medal presentation box contained not only the full medal and the ribbon bar, but also a small enameled lapel pin made as a miniature of the ribbon for use on civilian clothing.

Some awards existed only as a ribbon; no hanging medal was ever made for them. This was because during the war there was a dire shortage of metal. The medals were not made until after the war. The first ETO medal wasn't presented, to General Eisenhower, until July 1947.

It is quite common for a World War II soldier who did not stay in the military to have the ribbons on his uniform out of the correct order of precedence. Many men did not get their decorations until they were ready to be discharged, or they arrived in the mail after they got home. Under those circumstances, many veterans simply stuck them on the uniform and did not bother to arrange them in the proper order.

Only one of each type of medal or decoration was allowed to be worn on the uniform. To indicate multiple awards of the same decoration, a 5/16th inch bronze oak leaf cluster device was attached to the metal ribbon. All of the small metal devices attached to the ribbon were called appurtenances.

The Bronze Star

There were many decorations awarded to soldiers for bravery. The most common of these was the Bronze Star (not to be confused with the small bronze campaign stars) with almost 400,000 being awarded in World War II. The Bronze Star was awarded for acts of heroism deemed of lesser degree than required for the award of the Silver Star. Awards could be made to recognize single acts of merit or for long-term meritorious service.

Left: the "V" for valor device worn on the Bronze Star ribbon bar and suspension ribbon.

Bronze Star ribbon with "V" for valor device and one Oak Leaf Cluster, indicating a second Bronze Star award.

Bronze Stars could be awarded for any meritorious non-combat service ranging from being an outstanding cook to running an extensive telephone cable system for a few weeks. Bronze Stars awarded for valor (battlefield heroism) had a small bronze "V" device on them. Unless the award included the "V" for valor device, the bronze star was not combat-related.

In 1947, an Army study concluded that men who had been awarded the Combat Infantryman's Badge deserved more recognition. The theory was that anyone who had been in combat could have done something worthy of a decoration, but no one may have witnessed it or the act could have gone unreported. There was also some concern that the Air Medal (the Air Force equivalent to the Bronze Star) had been given out in far greater quantities than the Bronze Star to the ground combat troops.

Consequently, Congress voted to retroactively award a Bronze Star to every man who had ever been awarded the CIB. The legislators also decided that anyone who had served in the Philippines from December 7, 1941 until General Wainright surrendered them to the Japanese deserved a Bronze Star as well—even if they were not originally in a combat unit. Many combat veterans were against this because they believed it devalued the Bronze Stars actually earned during World War II. More importantly, they believed the CIB was by itself its own award and the most important any man could earn.

This postwar award of the Bronze Star has mystified many families. They learn that their soldier was awarded a Bronze Star, but no citation or reasons for it (other then "meritorious actions against the enemy") are ever found. These CIB-awarded Bronze Stars have no specific citation describing specific actions, nor were they written up in the units' general orders.

The Silver Star

The next step for an award of bravery above the Bronze Star is the Silver Star (not to be confused with a silver campaign star). This was an award for gallantry in action only, but one that did not warrant the Distinguished Service Cross or the Medal of Honor.

The design is a silver star with the words "For Gallantry in Action" on the reverse. Silver Stars were not passed out too often during World War II, and a man had to certainly stand out in a combat action to receive one.

The Distinguished Service Cross

Next in line was the Distinguished Service Cross (DSC). This was the nation's second highest award given for bravery in the Army.

A DSC was awarded for extraordinary heroism against an armed enemy. The design is a bronze star with an eagle on it and the words "For Valor." The Air Force had its own version of the DSC known as the Distinguished Flying Cross.

The Medal of Honor

The most important award in the Army was the Medal of Honor (often erroneously referred to as the Congressional Medal of Honor). This was a five-pointed star surrounded by a laurel wreath bearing the words "For Valor." It was an award worn around the neck on a pale blue ribbon with small white stars.

The Army awarded only 289 of these medals during World War II (the Air Force awarded only 37). Of these 289, 220 were awarded to infantrymen and almost 60% were presented posthumously. In contrast, 4,696 DSCs were awarded in World War II, of which 65% were awarded to infantrymen.

The Legion of Merit

Non-combat awards included the Legion of Merit (which came in four different classes: Legionnaire, Officer, Commander, and Chief Commander) for "exceptionally meritorious conduct in the performance of outstanding services and achievements."

This was an award frequently given to foreign officials, with the Chief Commander class (a large breast pin) being reserved only for heads of state and Commander (a neck decoration) for foreign military chiefs of staff.

Some 20,000 Legions of Merit were awarded during World War II.

The Distinguished Service Medal

The Distinguished Service Medal was for an individual who "distinguished himself or herself by exceptionally meritorious service to the Government in a duty of great responsibility.

The performance must be such as to merit recognition for service which is "clearly exceptional." This was similar to a DSC, except it was for merit and not for combat heroism.

The Soldier's Medal

There were also a number of decorations awarded for specific actions performed by an individual not considered strictly acts of combat heroism or merit. The Soldier's Medal was given to a soldier who distinguished himself in an act not involving combat.

Traditionally, this was awarded to someone who put his own life at risk to save another (rescuing a drowning man, for example). More than 12,000 Soldier's Medals were awarded during World War II.

Following is one example of the award of a Soldier's Medal taken from War Department GO 80, 1945.

"Private First Class Marie Lavrich (A312647), WAC Detachment, Army of the United States, stationed at the Army Service Forces Convalescent Hospital, Camp Upton, New York, went to the aid of a drowning fellow WAC who was being carried out in rough water by a strong undertow at West Hampton Beach, New York, on 22 July 1945. Swimming through the high waves and surf for approximately 100 feet, she reached the helpless WAC and pulled her safely to shore, after two others had made gallant but unsuccessful attempts to save the drowning woman. Private Lavrich's heroic act reflects great credit on herself and the Women's Army Corps."

The Air Medal

The Air Medal was an award for meritorious service in aerial flight. It could be awarded for a single action, but the Air Force used a point system. Men acquired points for making successful flights, shooting down enemy planes, and so forth. After so many points were earned, the man was awarded an Air Medal. It is not uncommon to find a number of oak leaf clusters on ribbons (indicating multiple awards) for soldiers who served on flight duty.

The only men awarded these medals in a ground unit were the liaison pilots in artillery outfits. More than one million Air Medals were awarded during World War II.

The Army Commendation Ribbon

The Army Commendation Ribbon was authorized in 1945 as an award for men who deserved something for their outstanding deeds, but were not eligible for a Bronze Star because they had not served in a combat area. This remained a ribbon-only award until 1950, when a full-sized medal was designed.

The Purple Heart

The Purple Heart is the oldest decoration in the US Army and dates back to the era of George Washington. It was awarded to any man wounded or injured due to enemy action. The award was also made posthumously to any man killed in enemy action.

Unlike some countries that have different awards for different wounds, there was no differentiation for severity of wounds. For example, it was considered a single award even if a man was wounded multiple times in one engagement. If he was wounded a second time while being brought back to the hospital, it was also considered just one wound for award purposes.

If an injury was an accident, self-inflicted, or inflicted by friendly fire, no Purple Heart award was made. Many light wounds were never reported (and thus no Purple Heart awarded). Many of the men who felt it was not important to report a wound during the fighting sang a different tune when the war ended, once they realized that each Purple Heart was worth five more points toward their discharge.

The Good Conduct Medal

The Good Conduct Medal was only awarded to enlisted men (as opposed to officers). Officers were considered to always be on their best behavior or they would lose their commission.

The Good Conduct Medal was initially awarded for three years of good service at the discretion of the company commander. In March 1943, the qualifications were lowered to one year of service after December 7, 1941 (while the country was at war). Soldiers killed in the line of duty were eligible for the award even if they had not completed the necessary time.

Unlike other decorations, the Good Conduct Medal did not use Oak Leaf clusters to indicate multiple awards. A bronze attachment to the ribbon of a clasp with loop was used instead. Multiple loops indicated multiple awards. This was a form of Army humor because the "loops" could be considered a "hitch" in a rope, and a hitch is the Army word for one three-year term of service. Thus, soldiers could literally wear their "hitches" on their uniform.

The Good Conduct Medal was not an automatic award. A soldier's commanding officer had to authorize it, which meant any man who had caused enough trouble (even if not on the records) could have the medal withheld from him.

Some soldiers thought it was a badge of honor to NOT have a Good Conduct Medal. Officers who had served as enlisted men felt some pride in being able to wear a decoration that indicated they had risen from the ranks.

President Harry Truman awards the Medal of Honor to Private William Soderman. From this photo one can tell Soderman is an infantryman (Combat Infantry Badge above the breast pocket). He is assigned to the 2d Infantry Division (shoulder sleeve insignia), and has served overseas more then 6 months, but less than 12 (one service stripe on the lower sleeve).   National Archives

AWARDING MEDALS

Decorations were not given lightly. While some may have been awarded to officers as part of an arrangement with friends in high places, the Army took awards seriously and tried to see they went to the right men. Memoirs abound with stories of senior officers visiting the front for a moment, only to have one of their friend's submit them for a decoration for their actions in some vague frontline activity such as directing the actions of the men during an artillery bombardment, or showing great courage and leadership while under fire. Certainly this happened, but for every officer who claimed he had rallied the troops under enemy fire, there was another officer who did put his life on the line to rally troops during a genuine enemy attack.

Recommendations for decorations had to be submitted by an officer who, in theory, should have witnessed the event in question. Once the recommendation was submitted there was a chance it could be downgraded to a lower award or sent to a higher headquarters for consideration of a more appropriate decoration. It was always better to ask for an award that fit the action, and this led to many soldiers being able to say they had been put in for a DSC, but it was downgraded to a Silver Star.

The senior awards (DSC and MOH) were taken extremely seriously. In the case of a Medal of Honor recommendation, everyone involved in the action was interviewed. The area of the action was photographed, if possible, and men were often transported to the site so they could retrace their steps and demonstrate exactly what had transpired. It was very rare for a high level medal recommendation to be lost, as some soldiers claim, but they were often downgraded or simply turned down if they did not meet the criteria necessary for the award. It is beyond a reasonable doubt that any action deemed worthy of a high level medal would have resulted in the award of something—even if only a Bronze Star.

Being awarded medals in World War II was often a hit or miss proposition. An award might have a chance if an officer witnessed the event, if there was some-one with the time to write up the recommendation, or if there was someone to polish it up before it was forwarded to higher headquarters. Decorations were always announced in a unit's general orders, which provided a brief synopsis of who, where, and how the award was earned. The higher the award, the greater the detail of how a soldier earned it.

There has been substantial interest in recent years to make sure no one was denied a Medal of Honor on racial grounds. A careful examination of wartime records has revealed that seven Medals of Honor were awarded to African-Americans for World War II service. In the year 2000, 22 more Medals of Honor were awarded for World War II. These were primarily awards that had been approved as DSCs, but in hindsight the Army believed were more appropriate for a Medal of Honor award.

An old soldier once commented that no one should take much stock in medals given to senior officers; contrarily, it really meant something if an enlisted man or lieutenant was given such a decoration. A good example is the following citation given to an enlisted man who was posthumously awarded the Medal of Honor:

> "Corporal Horace M. Thorne (Army serial No. 32012364), Troop D, 89th Cavalry Reconnaissance Squadron (Mechanized), Army of the United States, was leader of a combat patrol on 21 December 1944 near Gruhlingen, Belgium, with the mission of driving German forces from dug in positions in a heavily wooded area. As he advanced his light machine gun, a German Mark III tank emerged from the enemy position and was quickly immobilized by fire from American light tanks supporting the patrol. Two of the enemy tank men attempted to abandon their vehicle but were killed by Corporal Thorne's shots before they could jump to the ground. To complete the destruction of the tank and its crew, Corporal Thorne left his position and crept forward alone through intense machine-gun fire until close enough to toss two grenades into the tank's open turret, killing two more Germans. He returned across the same fire-beaten zone as heavy mortar fire began falling in the area, seized his machine gun and without help dragged it to the knocked-out tank and set it up on the vehicle's rear deck. He fired short, rapid bursts into the enemy positions from his advantageous but exposed location, killing or wounding eight. Two enemy machine gun crews abandoned their positions and retreated in confusion. His gun jammed, but rather than leave his self-chosen post he attempted to clear the stoppage.

Enemy small-arms fire concentrated on the tank killed him instantly. Corporal Thorne, displaying heroic initiative and intrepid fighting qualities, inflicted costly casualties on the enemy and insured the success of his patrol's mission by the sacrifice of his life." [2]

Keep in mind that all medal and decoration awards were labeled with at least the "Restricted" classification. This was done as the actual award paper indicated names, ranks, units, locations, and specific actions.

The use of such classification does not in any way mean the award was anything that had to be kept a secret. Recipients of most wartime awards received copies of the orders with the locations of the event blanked out with a string of asterisks. This prevented a local newspaper from printing the information which, if seen by an enemy agent, would identify the location of the specific unit. In the unit records a copy of the same order should exist with the full information.

The higher up in rank, the easier it seemed to be to get awards.

Here, General Patton decorates one of his corps commanders. The ranking officers not only tended to know one another, but realized that decorations were necessary for one's career.

While many officers were indeed justifiably awarded medals they deserved, it was much harder for an enlisted man to be singled out for his actions.

National Archives

WEBSITES

Information on all American medals, badges and decorations can be found at: http://www.tioh.hqda.pentagon.mil/

More detailed information on the Medal of Honor can be found at www.homeofheroes.com or http://www.cmohs.org

SERVICE MEDALS

Service medals and their ribbons tell the story of where a soldier served. At the start of the 20th century, the Army created service medals for actions dating back to the Civil War. To indicate World War I service, a World War I Victory Medal was awarded to all participants. To indicate participation in a specific World War I battle, brass clasps bearing the name of the battle was worn on the suspension ribbon, while small bronze campaign stars were worn on the ribbon. In World War I, a small silver star on the victory medal indicated the man had been mentioned for bravery and was the equivalent of a Silver Star medal (which had not yet been authorized). Other World War I-related service medals that appear on the uni-

Mexican Service   *Occupation of Germany*

forms of older soldiers are the Mexican Service and Mexican Border Service medals, or the World War I Occupation of Germany Medal (for service in Germany from 1919 to 1923).

In World War II, the U.S Military divided the world up into three main theaters of war: the American Theater; the European, African, Middle Eastern Theater;

American Theater   *European, African, Middle Eastern Theater*   *Asiatic-Pacific Theater*

and the Asiatic-Pacific Theater. One medal was authorized for service in each of these three areas. For the Pacific and European theaters, a soldier only had to be officially assigned to a unit in the theater to be eligible for the medal.

There was almost no combat in the American Theater, so that ribbon was handled differently. Men were not authorized the American Theater medal unless they had been stationed in the theater, but outside the continental US—men stationed in Canada or the Caribbean, for example. Crews of ships or planes that made regular trips out of the US also earned this medal, as did anyone who had engaged in combat in the theater, or anyone who had served for one year inside the USA. There was only one campaign that Army personnel could have participated in: the Antisubmarine Campaign.

To indicate what battles a soldier had participated in, the fighting in the ETO was divided into 19 main campaigns with specific times and geographic areas. The Sicily Campaign ran from May 14, 1943 through August 17, 1943, and the Normandy Campaign lasted from June 6, 1944 to July 24, 1944. Any man in the designated geographic area during that time was allowed to wear one small 3/16-inch bronze star on his theater ribbon to indicate his participation.

These small stars are known officially as "campaign participation stars," but are also referred to as battle stars. These were often mistaken in documents for Bronze Star medals. When the Army is denoting a man with more than one Bronze Star medal, it always does so this way: "Bronze Star with 'X' Oak Leaf Clusters." Only one Bronze Star is ever awarded to a soldier—each additional award is an Oak Leaf Cluster worn on the ribbon.

In the Pacific Theater, there were 21 campaigns for which campaign participation stars, or battle stars, could be earned. Again, do not confuse these small bronze stars for the Bronze Star medal awarded for specific valor or meritorious service. When five bronze campaign stars were reached, they were represented by a single silver star. It was very common for soldiers to cram as many bronze stars on their campaign ribbons as possible because it looked a lot more impressive than one silver and one or two bronze stars.

If a man took part in an amphibious, parachute, or glider assault, he was also allowed to wear a small bronze arrowhead on the ribbon. By regulation, only one arrowhead should be worn, no matter how many assaults were made, but is was not uncommon for soldiers to wear multiple arrowheads to denote multiple assaults. The arrowhead was always worn point up.

To reward those who had been in the Army before Pearl Harbor, the American Defense Service Medal was awarded to anyone who had been on active federal service between September 8, 1939, and December 7, 1941. The few men who had served in overseas posts during this time were authorized a metal clasp for the medal indicating "Foreign Service." When only the ribbon is worn, the clasp is represented by a single bronze star.

Every soldier who participated in the war was given the World War II Victory Medal. The timeframe for participation ran from December 7, 1941 until President Truman officially ended the state of hostilities on December 31, 1946. Those men remaining in occupied areas after the fighting ended were also authorized the Army of Occupation Medal. A clasp of "Germany" indicated occupation service in Europe, while "Japan" meant occupation service in the Far East.

The end of occupation duties differed from country to country. For Italy it was 1947; Korea, 1949; Japan, 1952; and Germany,

American Defense Service   *World War II Victory*

1955. A small bronze airplane worn on the ribbon indicated service during the Berlin Airlift, for 90 consecutive days between June 26, 1948 and September 30, 1949.

Men who remained in the military or had been recalled to service for the Korean War were also awarded the Korean War Medal. It was not a World War II decoration, but enough soldiers served in World War II and also fought in Korea that it was deemed important to recognize service in that later conflict.

The Prisoner of War Medal was not designed or authorized until 1985. It was awarded to any serviceman held as a prisoner by an enemy combatant. It will not be found on any World War II uniform unless the veteran lived until 1985 and specifically requested it from the government. Proof of having been held prisoner was required for it to be authorized, but many World War II-era soldiers who were held as a POW may be unable to find enough documentation to prove their status.

Korean War Service   *Prisoner of War Medal*

FOREIGN DECORATIONS

An American soldier must receive permission to wear a foreign award on his uniform. With the exception of the French, Belgian, and Dutch lanyards, mentioned previously, few foreign awards were approved for display without individual permission.

Most of the Allied nations made it a point to issue some of their decorations to servicemen from other nations to improve inter-service relations. This, of course, meant that many high ranking officers in their armies could be awarded American decorations. Some of the Allied senior officers were awarded American decorations almost automatically as a display of friendship. However, the method of awarding the lower ranking soldiers (below colonel) is something of a mystery. In some cases the American officer worked with the other nation on a temporary assignment; in others, a foreign liaison officer spotted a citation of an American soldier and decided he should also get a decoration from their country.

Foreign service medals, such as the British battle stars awarded to men who took part in specific campaigns, were not eligible for display on American uniforms. Only decorations earned for specific actions were authorized to be worn on the uniform.

While it is possible to find World War II soldiers with just about every possible decoration from around the world, there are a few that are fairly common. The Croix de Guerre was bestowed mainly as a unit award, but also as an individual medal to a number of Americans serving in France. The French had a very complicated system (a series of metal palms on the ribbon) indicating both the quality and quantity of the Croix de Guerre.

In the Pacific Theater, the most common foreign award was three campaign ribbons given to soldiers who fought in the Philippines. One was for a man's participation in the defense the Philippines in 1941–42. If he took part in an engagement, he was authorized a star for the ribbon. The Philippine Liberation Medal was authorized for anyone who took part in the 1944–45 liberation of the islands. A third award, The Philippine Independence Medal, was authorized for every man who was present in the Philippines on July 4, 1946—Philippine Independence Day. Because of the close ties between the Philippines and the USA, the Philippine government convinced the American Army to authorize the wearing of these service ribbons on its uniforms.

BOOKS

One of the best books on the history of American military awards and decorations is *The Call of Duty*, by John Strandberg and Roger Bender, R. James Bender Publishing, San Jose, CA, 1994, ISBN 0-912138-54-8

PURCHASING DECORATIONS

The Army is supposed to provide one decoration or award to each man who earned them. This was not always possible in the confusion of demobilization. Other men lost or had their medals stolen over the ensuing years. Once a man's paperwork has been located or reconstituted by the NPRC, he can submit a form that allows him to obtain any replacements for medals he had already been given for free, or he can purchase replacements at a low price. Unfortunately, it can take a long time to get medals from the government.

It is important to note that collectors value original World War II-issue decorations far more than those manufactured today. To the average person the differences are slight, but to the experienced eye it is another matter. The differences in price can therefore be substantial. Most Army medals can be obtained for $10–$40 from a company that buys them directly from an official government contractor. These companies will also sell the ribbon bars and appurtenances, miniature medals, and hat pins. Decorations for bravery as well as the Good Conduct Medal have a location on the reverse for the soldier's name to be engraved. If obtained from the government, these will be engraved; otherwise, you will have to pay extra for a private company to engrave them.

COMMEMORATIVE MEDALS

In recent years it has become trendy for private firms to design and issue commemorative medals to sell to veterans. These generally commemorate a specific battle or the anniversary of an event. Some include the Disabled Veterans of the Korean War Medal, Iwo Jima Veterans Commemorative Medal, Commemorative Medal for the Liberation of Belgium, 50th Anniversary of Victory in Europe Medal, and the D-Day Commemorative Medal.

These are not official US Military awards and technically cannot be worn on the uniform. In essence, they are nothing more than novelty items that some people want to own to better illustrate their service in the war. Unfortunately, some veterans have been compelled to feel as if they "earned" these medals in the war and thus should purchase them to complete their correct set of decorations.

There were official commemorative medals issued by the government in the 19th century, but none have been authorized for World War II. The last commemorative medal with official sanction was the 75th Anniversary of World War I Medal given, free of charge, to any living veterans of that war on the 75th anniversary of the war by the McCormick Foundation.

THE RUPTURED DUCK

The last badge a soldier put on his uniform was the Honorable Discharge Badge. This was an eagle with its wings outstretched inside a circle. It was worn as an embroidered cloth badge over the right top pocket to indicate the man had been discharged, and as a small metal pin on civilian clothes to indicate the man had served honorably. The eagle had its head turned sideways in the typical "turn your head and cough" position that doctors use to check for hernias, which in turn prompted its famous nickname: the ruptured duck.

The Ruptured Duck on this Staff Sergeant's uniform indicates he was honorably discharged from the service. A close examination indicates he was in the Ordnance Dept. (from the collar disk). This would mean the cap piping would be crimson piped with yellow. The two ribbons are the Good Conduct Medal, and the ETO ribbon with two campaign stars.

There is no way, without knowing his exact unit or having his paperwork, what two campaigns they were for.

National Archives

The ruptured duck was normally embroidered on the basic color of the uniform (OD or khaki). Some examples were silk-screened to help speed up production when millions of these were needed. The last thing a man would do in the Army before his discharge was have the "ruptured duck" sewn on. He wore it on his uniform on his way home to indicate he was no longer part of the army, and thus no longer subject to its rules and regulations. Each discharged solder received a small gold lapel pin of the same insignia to wear on civilian clothing.

AFTER THE WAR

A number of soldiers stayed in the Army, the Army Reserves, or the National Guard after World War II ended. These men would have kept their uniforms up to date with the appropriate insignia. Other men went home, took off their uniforms and either put them in a footlocker or threw them out, vowing never to wear one again.

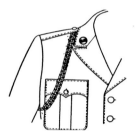

One of the common elements added to Army uniforms after the war were some light blue additions to help develop pride in the infantry.

Infantrymen were authorized to wear a light blue braided cord around the right shoulder, and light blue plastic backings to their collar disks. These were not used during the World War II period, but are common on postwar uniforms.

OTHER SOUVENIRS

Almost every souvenir from the war years can help add some piece of information to a soldier's story. A weekend pass left in a pocket offers a clue as to where a man was stationed at a specific time. Postcards from France or from the Philippines are a good indication of which theater he served in. Even with heavy censorship, letters home can provide small clues as to what the soldier was up to when he wrote them.

Photos often provide clues by showing insignia and vehicle markings. Always check the back of every photo to see if there is any information written on it. If the photos are in an album, make sure to replace them in the same original position you found them. It can be helpful to photocopy the page before trying to remove them so you have a handy reference as to how they were initially placed.

Everything a man has that is at all associated with the war should be examined for clues. Books in his home collection should be checked to see if he penciled in margin notations about his part in a specific battle.

However, do not assume that everything military is from a man's service. Vast quantities of surplus items have been sold since World War II. There are few houses in this country that do not have something military-related in them. Boy Scout troops used a number of military items, as did average families going camping.

Radio enthusiasts often bought World War II surplus transmitters, even though they never touched a radio in the war. A man who served in the Pacific Theater may have been given a German decoration as a souvenir by a friend who fought in France. A Navy veteran may have his brother's Army insignia in a box in the basement. Keep an open mind if you find something that does not seem to fit the story of the man or men you are researching.

FINDING ARMY BUDDIES

The ultimate tangible reminder of someone's service would be to find an Army buddy. This is becoming harder to do because many hundreds of World War II veterans pass away each day. Almost all the higher ranking officers have now died, leaving behind mostly those who served as privates, sergeants, and lieutenants.

While certainly not impossible, it can be very hard to find someone who knew a specific man in the Army. In order to do so, it is imperative that you identify the company he served in and the dates he was there. It is relatively easy to find someone who was in the same division or regiment, but unless he served in the same company, the chances are they did not know your soldier or have forgotten him. Keep in mind that some units—primarily combat outfits—experienced constant roster changes. A man who joined a platoon or even a squad would not know anyone who had been killed, wounded, or transferred prior to his arrival.

Tracking down someone who knew a specific soldier in a combat unit is vastly harder than in a non-combat unit. The turnover in combat units means that you not only have to find someone from the right company, but from the right time period. In a non-combat unit, such as a quartermaster company, the same men may have served together for years and are more likely to recall a number of men from the outfit.

There are two ways to go about looking for survivors of a unit. The first is to find a list of names. These might be written on a souvenir flag, inside a book, or even on a roster in the National Archives. The easiest method to find the right pool of men is to use the many telephone listings available on the Internet. It is especially helpful to know that anyone listing a middle initial in the phone book is generally older and more likely to be from the World War II generation. This is obviously a hit or miss procedure, but if you know a town or locality a man was from, you can narrow it down a bit. There are still veterans living in the same house they came home to in 1945.

Serial numbers for men from a company can be found on many unit records, but specifically the company morning report. With the serial number you can have the Veteran's Administration determine if it has a current address for an individual, and if so they will forward it to you. This is particularly useful for combat units, where men were more likely to get wounded and therefore file for a VA claim.

The procedure to do this is simple. Write the soldier a letter, explain that you are trying to find old comrades who knew your relative, and ask if the fellow would contact you. Address the letter with the man's name and serial number. Do not seal the envelope because the VA must check the letter to make sure it is appropriate to forward. Put a stamp on that envelope and send it, along with a written request to forward the letter to the last known address of the noted individual. Find the address of the local regional VA office and send it to them. It is a long shot, but just one can hit pay dirt for you.

The other method of finding veterans is to look for a unit association. Some unit associations have held annual reunions every year since 1946. Some never organized once they were sent home. For many years Ben Myers has been keeping the best list of unit associations and contact addresses. This is the best place to start.

It is also useful to search the Internet using various search engines looking for any reference to the specific unit. You might turn up someone else who has an interest in the unit. As the veteran community dies out, many sons and daughters of veterans have taken to carrying the torch to keep their unit memory alive. There are some very active discussion groups at places like Yahoo Groups, where people trade information and help those just starting their search.

Within a few short years it will be all but impossible to find World War II veterans. However, locating the relative of someone who served with your own soldier can also be a valuable event. You never know when they will have something relating to your subject—a photo of the two men leaning against a barracks, or a signature of your dad in a souvenir book, for example. Tracking down relatives can be hard and generally means calling everyone with a certain last name in a given area. Posting a notice on one of the many World War II unit sites on the Internet can lead to some lucky discoveries.

If you cannot find a website for a specific World War II unit, start one! It is not hard to find someone who knows the basics of setting up a simple and inexpensive website. Put in whatever information you have found, and one day someone else looking for that unit may well find it and contact you.

The National World War II Memorial maintains an on-line registry of World War II veterans both living and deceased. The author once looked up information on a friend of his father's who had been killed late in the war. Fortunately, the deceased's next of kin had put his information and a photo of the soldier in the registry. Calling everyone with the last name in the town listed resulted in an unusual reunion between the son and niece of two one-time Army friends. It's not common, but with perseverance and a little luck, good things can happen.

WEBSITES

Ben Myers Association List: http://www.military-network.com

The National World War II Memorial: http://www.wwiimemorial.com

---

FOOTNOTES

1.   p. 4 *General Order 80*, War Department. 19 September 1945.

2.   p. 1 *General Order 80*, War Department 19 September 1945.

APPENDIX A

The Infantry and Airborne Divisions in World War II

This Appendix gives detailed information on each of the Infantry and Airborne divisions in World War II, together with their insignia. We begin with a series of tables showing the number designations of the organic elements of each Infantry and Airborne division during the war.

COMPONENT ELEMENTS OF THE INFANTRY DIVISIONS IN WORLD WAR II

Division	Infantry Regiments			Division Artillery and Field Artillery Battalions				Signal Company	Ordnance Company	Quarter-master Company	Reconn-aissance Troop	Engineer Battalion	Medical Battalion	CIC Detachment
1	16	18	26	5	7	32	33	1	701	1	1	1	1	1
2	9	23	38	12	15	37	38	2	702	2	2	2	2	2
3	7	15	30	9	10	39	41	3	703	3	3	10	3	3
4	8	12	22	20	29	42	44	4	704	4	4	4	4	4
5	2	10	11	19	21	46	50	5	705	5	5	7	5	5
6	1	20	63	1	51	53	80	6	706	6	6	6	6	6
7	17	32	184	31	48	49	57	7	707	7	7	13	7	7
8	13	28	121	28	43	45	56	8	708	8	8	12	8	8
9	39	47	60	26	34	60	84	9	709	9	9	15	9	9
10	85	86	87	604	605	616	—	110	710	10	10	126	10	10
24	19	21	34	11	13	52	63	24	724	24	24	3	24	24
25	27	35	161	8	64	89	90	25	725	25	25	65	25	25
26	101	104	328	101	102	180	263	39	726	26	26	101	114	26
27	105	106	165	104	105	106	249	27	727	27	27	102	102	27
28	109	110	112	107	108	109	229	28	728	28	28	103	103	28
29	115	116	175	110	111	224	227	29	729	29	29	121	104	29
30	117	119	120	113	118	197	230	30	730	30	30	105	105	30
31	124	155	167	114	116	117	149	31	731	31	31	106	106	31
32	126	127	128	120	121	126	129	32	732	32	32	114	107	32
33	123	130	136	122	123	124	210	33	733	33	33	108	108	33
34	133	135	168	125	151	175	185	34	734	34	34	109	109	34
35	134	137	320	127	161	216	219	36	735	35	35	60	110	35
36	141	142	143	131	132	133	155	36	736	36	36	111	111	36
37	129	145	148	6	135	136	140	37	737	37	37	117	112	37
38	149	151	152	138	139	150	163	38	738	38	38	113	113	38
40	108	160	185	143	164	213	222	40	740	40	40	115	115	40
41	162	163	186	146	167	205	218	41	741	41	41	116	116	41
42	222	232	242	232	292	402	542	42	742	42	42	142	122	42
43	103	169	172	103	152	169	192	43	743	43	43	118	118	43

COMPONENT ELEMENTS OF THE INFANTRY DIVISIONS, CONTINUED

Division	Infantry Regiments			Division Artillery and Field Artillery Battalions				Signal Company	Ordnance Company	Quarter-master Company	Reconn-aissance Troop	Engineer Battalion	Medical Battalion	CIC Detach-ment
44	71	114	324	156	157	217	220	44	744	44	44	63	119	44
45	157	179	180	158	160	171	189	46	700	45	45	120	120	45
63	253	254	255	718	861	862	863	563	763	63	63	263	363	63
65	259	260	261	720	867	868	869	565	765	65	65	265	365	65
66	262	263	264	721	870	871	872	566	766	66	66	266	366	66
69	271	272	273	724	879	880	881	569	769	69	69	269	369	69
70	274	275	276	725	882	883	884	570	770	70	70	270	370	70
71	5	14	66	564	607	608	609	571	771	251	71	271	371	71
75	289	290	291	730	897	898	899	575	775	75	75	275	375	75
76	304	385	417	302	355	364	901	76	776	76	76	301	301	76
77	305	306	307	304	305	306	902	77	777	77	77	302	302	77
78	309	310	311	307	308	309	903	78	778	78	78	303	303	78
79	313	314	315	310	311	312	904	79	779	79	79	304	304	79
80	317	318	319	313	314	315	905	80	780	80	80	305	305	80
81	321	322	323	316	317	318	906	81	781	81	81	306	306	81
83	329	330	331	322	323	324	908	83	783	83	83	308	308	83
84	333	334	335	325	326	327	909	84	784	84	84	309	309	84
85	337	338	339	328	329	403	910	85	785	85	85	310	310	85
86	341	342	343	331	332	404	911	86	786	86	86	311	311	86
87	345	346	347	334	335	336	912	87	787	87	87	312	312	87
88	349	350	351	337	338	339	913	88	788	88	88	313	313	88
89	353	354	355	340	341	563	914	89	789	405	89	314	314	89
90	357	358	359	343	344	345	915	90	790	90	90	315	315	90
91	361	362	363	346	347	348	916	91	791	91	91	316	316	91
92	365	370	371	597	598	599	600	92	792	92	92	317	317	92
93	25	368	369	593	594	595	596	93	793	93	93	318	318	93
94	301	302	376	301	356	390	919	94	794	94	94	319	319	94
95	377	378	379	358	359	360	920	95	795	95	95	320	320	95
96	381	382	383	361	362	363	921	96	796	96	96	321	321	96
97	303	386	387	303	365	389	922	97	797	97	97	322	322	97
98	389	390	391	367	368	399	923	98	798	98	98	323	323	98
99	393	394	395	370	371	372	924	99	799	99	99	324	324	99
100	397	398	399	373	374	375	925	100	800	100	100	325	325	100
102	405	406	407	379	380	381	927	102	802	102	102	327	327	102
103	409	410	411	382	383	384	928	103	803	103	103	328	328	103
104	413	414	415	385	386	387	929	104	804	104	104	329	329	104
106	422	423	424	589	590	591	592	106	806	106	106	81	331	106
Americal	132	164	182	245	246	247	221	26	721	125	21	57	121	182

COMPONENT ELEMENTS OF THE AIRBORNE DIVISIONS

Airborne Division	Glider Infantry Regiment	Parachute Infantry Regiment	Glider Field Artillery Battalion	Parachute Field Artillery Battalion	Airborne Anti-aircraft Battalion	Parachute Maintenance Company	Special Troops			Airborne Engineer Battalion	Airborne Medical Company
							Airborne Signal Company	Airborne Ordnance Company	Airborne Quartermaster Company		
11	187 88	188 511	472 675	457 674	152	11	511	711	408	127	221
11	187	188 511	472 675	457 674	152	11	511	711	408	127	221
13	88 326	515	676 677	458	153	13	513	713	409	129	222
13	326	515 517	676 677	458 460	153	13	513	713	409	129	222
17	193 194	513	680 681	466	155	17	517	717	411	139	224
17	193 194	507 513	680 681	464 466	155	17	517	717	411	139	224
82	325	504 505	319 320	376 456	80	—	82	782	407	307	307
82	325	504 505	319 320	376 456	80	82	82	782	407	307	307
101	327 401	502	321 907	377	81	—	101	801	426	326	326
101	327	502 506	321 907	377 463	81	101	101	801	426	326	326

NOTE: *The Parachute Infantry Regiments listed above were organic to these divisions. This table does not include attached units, for example, the 501st PIR (101st Airborne) and the 508th (82d Airborne)*

In the table above, you will see each Airborne division listed twice. The first row for each division shows its organization prior to 1 March 1945, and the second (lighter colored) row shows its composition after that date. All units omitted in the lighter rows were inactivated or disbanded on 1 March 1945, and all additional units listed were activated or assigned on that date.

For both tables, the particular division is listed in the first column and you should read across to learn what the constituent parts of each division were. For example, if you take the first line of the table opposite, you will be able to learn that the 44th Infantry Division consisted of the 71st, 114th and 324th Infantry Regiments, the 156th, 157th, 217th and 220th Artillery Battalions, and so forth.

The reason the divisions don't follow a strict numerical sequence (in other words there are gaps – there's no 50th Infantry Division, for example) is that those numbers were reserved for other units in the Army.

INFANTRY AND AIRBORNE DIVISIONS
ACTIVATION AND CAMPAIGNS

1st INFANTRY DIVISION
The Big Red One

Arrived overseas: 7 August 1942. Days of Combat: 443.

Campaigns: Algeria-French Morocco, Tunisia, Sicily, Normandy, Northern France, Rhineland, Ardennes Alsace, Central Europe.

2d INFANTRY DIVISION
The Indian Head Division

Overseas: 10 October 1943. Days of combat: 303.

Campaigns: Ardennes-Alsace, Central Europe, Normandy, Northern France, Rhineland.

3d INFANTRY DIVISION
Rock of the Marne (earned at Chateau Thierry in july 1918)

Arrived overseas: 27 October 1942. Days of combat: 233.

Campaigns: Tunisia, Sicily, Naples-Foggia, Rome-Arno, Southern France, Rhineland, Central Europe.

4th INFANTRY DIVISION
The Ivy Division

Activated: 3 June 1940. Overseas: 18 January 1944. Days of combat: 299.

Campaigns: Normandy, Central Europe, Northern France, Rhineland, Ardennes-Alsace.

5th INFANTRY DIVISION
The Red Diamond Division

Activated: 2 October 1939. Arrived overseas: 30 April 1942. Days of combat: 270.

Campaigns: Normandy, Northern France, Rhineland, Ardennes-Alsace, Central Europe.

6th INFANTRY DIVISION
The Red Star Division

Activated: 12 October 1939. Overseas: 21 July 1943. Days of combat: 306.

Campaigns: Luzon, New Guinea.

7th INFANTRY DIVISION

Activated: 1 July 1940. Arrived Overseas: 24 April 1943. Days of combat: 208.

Campaigns: Aleutian Islands, Leyte, Eastern Mandates, Ryukyus.

8th INFANTRY DIVISION
The Golden Arrow Division

Activated: 1 July 1940. Arrived Overseas: 5 December 1943. Days of combat: 266.

Campaigns: Normandy, Northern France, Rhineland, Central Europe.

9th INFANTRY DIVISION
The Varsity

Activated: 1 August 1940. Arrived Overseas: 11 December 1942. Days of combat: 264.

Campaigns: Algeria–French Morocco, Tunisia, Sicily, Normandy, Northern France, Rhineland, Ardennes-Alsace, Central Europe.

10th MOUNTAIN DIVISION
The Mountain Division

Activated: 15 July 1943. Overseas: 6 January 1945. Days of combat: 114.

Campaigns: North Appennines, Po Valley.

11th AIRBORNE DIVISION
The Angels

Activated: 25 February 1943. Overseas: 8 May 1944. Days of combat: 204.

Campaigns: New Guinea, Southern Philippines, Luzon.

13th AIRBORNE DIVISION

Activated: 13 August 1943. Overseas: 25 January 1945.

Campaigns: Central Europe. The 13th AB did not see combat in World War II, having been kept in strategic reserve in the ETO. It was then transferred to the Pacific just prior to the Japanese surrender.

17th AIRBORNE DIVISION
Thunder from Heaven

Activated: 15 April 1943. Overseas: 17 August 1944. Days of combat: 45.

Campaigns: Ardennes-Alsace Rhineland, Central Europe.

24th INFANTRY DIVISION
The Victory Division

Activated: 1 October 1941. Overseas: 1 October 1941. Days of combat: 260.

Campaigns.: New Guinea, Southern Philippines, Luzon.

25th INFANTRY DIVISION
The Tropic Lightning Division

Activated: 1 October 1941. Overseas: 1 October 1941. Days of combat: 260.

Campaigns: Guadalcanal, Luzon.

26th INFANTRY DIVISION
The Yankee Division — New England National Guard

Activated: 16 January 1941. Arrived Overseas: 26 August 1944. Days of combat: 210.

Campaigns: Northern France, Rhineland, Ardennes-Alsace, Central Europe

27th INFANTRY DIVISION
The New York Division — New York National Guard

Activated: 15 October 1940. Arrived Overseas: 10 March 1942. Days of combat: 110.

Campaigns: Various elements participated in several campaigns in the Pacific but not the entire division.

28th INFANTRY DIVISION

Keystone Division — Pennsylvania National Guard

Activated: 17 February 1941. Arrived Overseas: 8 October 1943. Days of combat: 196.

Campaigns: Normandy, Northern France, Rhineland, Ardennes-Alsace, Central Europe.

29th INFANTRY DIVISION

The Blue and Gray Division — Maryland and Virginia National Guard

Activated: 3 February 1941. Arrived Overseas: 5 October 1942. Days of combat: 242.

Campaigns: Normandy, Northern France, Rhineland, Central Europe.

30th INFANTRY DIVISION

Old Hickory Division — North Carolina, South Carolina, Georgia, and Tennessee National Guard

Activated: 16 September 1940. Arrived Overseas: 11 February 1944. Days of combat: 282.

Campaigns: Normandy, Northern France, Rhineland, Ardennes-Alsace, Central Europe.

31st INFANTRY DIVISION

The Dixie Division — Alabama, Florida, Louisiana, and Mississippi National Guard

Activated: 25 Nov. 1940. Arrived Overseas: 12 March 1944. Days of combat: 245.

Campaigns: New Guinea. Southern Philippines.

32d INFANTRY DIVISION

The Red Arrow Division — Michigan and Wisconsin National Guard

Activated: 15 October 1940. Overseas: 14 May 1942. Days of combat: 654.

Campaigns: New Guinea, Southern Philippines, Luzon.

33d INFANTRY DIVISION

The Prairie Division — Illinois National Guard

Activated: 5 March 1941. Arrived Overseas: 7 July 1943. Days of combat: 139.

Campaigns: New Guinea, Luzon.

34th INFANTRY DIVISION

The Red Bull Division — North Dakota, South Dakota, Iowa, and Minnesota National Guard

Activated: 10 February 1941. Arrived Overseas: May 1942. Days of combat: 500.

Campaigns: Tunisia, Naples-Foggia, Rome-Arno, North Apennines, Po River.

35th INFANTRY DIVISION

The Santa Fe Division — Kansas, Missouri and Nebraska National Guard

Activated: 23 December 1940. Arrived Overseas: 12 May 1944. Days of combat: 264.

Campaigns: Normandy, Northern France, Rhineland, Ardennes-Alsace, Central Europe.

36th INFANTRY DIVISION

The Texas Division — Texas National Guard

Activated: 25 November 1940. Arrived Overseas: 2 April 1943. Days of combat: 400.

Campaigns: Naples-Foggia, Rome Arno, Southern France, Rhineland, Central Europe.

37th INFANTRY DIVISION

The Buckeye Division — Ohio National Guard

Activated: 15 October 1940. Arrived Overseas: 26 May 1942. Days of combat: 592.

Campaigns: Northern Solomons, Luzon.

38th INFANTRY DIVISION

The Cyclone Division — Indiana, Kentucky, and West Virginia National Guard

Activated: 17 January 1941. Arrived Overseas: 3 January 1944. Days of combat: 210.

Campaigns: New Guinea, Southern Philippines, Luzon.

40th INFANTRY DIVISION
The Sunshine Division — National Guard Division from California and Utah

Activated: 3 March 1941. Arrived Overseas: 23 August 1942. Days of combat: 265.

Campaigns: Bismarck Archipelago, Southern Philippines, Luzon.

41st INFANTRY DIVISION
The Jungleers — Idaho, Montana, Oregon, Washington, and Wyoming National Guard

Activated: 16 September 1940. Overseas: 4 March 1942. Days of combat: 380.

Campaigns: New Guinea, Southern Philippines, Papua.

42d INFANTRY DIVISION
The Rainbow Division

Activated: 14 July 1943. Overseas: November 1944. Days of combat: 106.

Campaigns: Rhineland, Central Europe.

43d INFANTRY DIVISION
The Winged Victory Division — Maine, Vermont, Connecticut, and Rhode Island National Guard

Activated: 24 February 1941. Overseas: 1 October 1942. Days of combat: 370.

Campaigns: New Guinea, Northern Solomons, Luzon.

44th INFANTRY DIVISION
New Jersey and New York National Guard

Activated: 16 September 1940. Overseas: 5 September 1944. Days of combat: 190

Campaigns: Northern France, Rhineland, Central Europe.

45th INFANTRY DIVISION

The Thunderbird Division — Arizona, Colorado, New Mexico, and Oklahoma National Guard

Activated: 16 September 1940. Overseas: 8 June 1943. Days of combat: 511.

Campaigns: Sicily, Naples-Foggia, Anzio, Rome-Arno, Southern France, Ardennes-Alsace, Rhineland, Central Europe.

63d INFANTRY DIVISION

The Blood and Fire Division

Activated: 15 June 1943. Overseas: 25 November 1944. Days of combat: 119.

Campaigns: Rhineland, Central Europe.

65th INFANTRY DIVISION

 The Battle Axe Division

Activated: 16 August 1943. Overseas: 10 January 1945. Days of combat: 55.

Campaigns: Rhineland, Central Europe.

66th INFANTRY DIVISION

The Black Panther Division

Activated: 15 April 1943. Overseas: 1 December 1944. Days of combat: 91.

Campaigns: Northern France.

69th INFANTRY DIVISION

The Fighting Sixty-Ninth

Activated: 15 May 1943. Overseas: December 1944. Days of combat: 86.

Campaigns: Rhineland, Central Europe.

70th INFANTRY DIVISION

The Trailblazers

Activated: 15 June 1943. Overseas: 8 January 1945. Days of combat: 83.

Campaigns: Rhineland, Central Europe.

71st INFANTRY DIVISION
The Red Circle Division

Activated: 15 July 1943. Overseas: 26 January 1945. Days of combat: 62.

Campaigns: Rhineland, Central Europe.

75th INFANTRY DIVISION

Activated: 15 April 1943. Overseas: 14 November 1944. Days of combat: 94.

Campaigns: Rhineland, Ardennes-Alsace, Central Europe.

76th INFANTRY DIVISION
The Onaway Division

Activated: 15 June 1942. Overseas: 10 December 1944. Days of combat: 107.

Campaigns: Ardennes-Alsace, Rhineland, Central Europe.

77th INFANTRY DIVISION
The Statue of Liberty Division

Activated: 25 March 1942. Overseas: 24 March 1944. Days of combat: 260.

Campaigns: Western Pacific, Southern Philippines, Ryukyus.

78th INFANTRY DIVISION
The Lightning Division

Activated: 15 August 1942. Overseas: 14 October 1944. Days of combat: 125.

Campaigns: Rhineland, Ardennes-Alsace, Central Europe.

79th INFANTRY DIVISION
The Cross of Lorraine Division

Activated: 15 June 1942. Overseas: 7 April 1944. Days of combat: 248.

Campaigns: Normandy, Northern France, Rhineland, Central Europe.

80th INFANTRY DIVISION
The Blue Ridge Division

Activated: 15 July 1942. Overseas: 1 July 1944. Days of combat: 239.

Campaigns: Northern France, Rhineland, Ardennes-Alsace, Central Europe.

81st INFANTRY DIVISION
The Wildcat Division

Activated: 15 June 1942. Overseas: 3 July 1944. Days of combat: 166.

Campaigns: Western Pacific, South Philippines.

82d AIRBORNE DIVISION
The All American Division

Designated an airborne division on 15 August 1942. Overseas: 28 April 1943. Days of combat: 422.

Campaigns: Sicily, Naples-Foggia, Rome-Arno, Normandy, Ardennes-Alsace, Rhineland, Central Europe.

83d INFANTRY DIVISION
The Thunderbolt Division

Activated: 15 August 1942. Overseas: 6 April 1944. Days of combat: 244.

Campaigns: Normandy, Northern France, Rhineland, Ardennes-Alsace, Central Europe.

84th INFANTRY DIVISION
The Railsplitters

Activated: 15 October 1942. Overseas: 20 September 1944. Days of combat: 170.

Campaigns: Rhineland, Ardennes-Alsace, Central Europe.

85th INFANTRY DIVISION
The Custer Division

Activated: 15 May 1942. Overseas: 24 December 1943. Days of combat: 260.

Campaigns: Rome-Arno, North Apennines, Po Valley.

86th INFANTRY DIVISION
The Blackhawk Division

Activated: 15 December 1942. Overseas: 19 February 1945, ETO; 24 August 1945, Pacific. Days of Combat: 34.

Campaigns: Central Europe.

87th INFANTRY DIVISION
The Golden Acorn Division

Activated: 15 December 1942. Overseas: 17 October 1944. Days of combat: 154.

Campaigns: Rhineland, Ardennes-Alsace, Central Europe.

88th INFANTRY DIVISION
The Blue Devil Division

Activated: 15 July 1942. Overseas: 6 December 1943. Days of combat: 307.

Campaigns: Rome-Arno, North Apennines, Po Valley.

89th INFANTRY DIVISION
The Rolling W

Activated: 15 July 1942. Overseas: 10 January 1945. Days of combat.: 57.

Campaigns: Rhineland, Central Europe.

90th INFANTRY DIVISION
The Tough 'Ombres

Activated: 25 March 1942. Overseas: 23 March 1944. Days of combat: 308.

Campaigns: Normandy, Northern France, Ardennes-Alsace, Rhineland, Central Europe.

91st INFANTRY DIVISION
The Powder River Division

Activated: 15 August 1942. Overseas: 3 April 1944. Days of combat: 271.

Campaigns: Rome-Arno, North Apennines, Po Valley.

92d INFANTRY DIVISION
The Buffalo Division

Activated: 15 October 1942. Overseas: 22 September 1944. Days of combat: 200.

Campaigns: North Apennines, Po Valley.

93d INFANTRY DIVISION

Activated: 15 May 1942. Overseas: 24 January 1944. Days of combat: 175.

Campaigns: New Guinea, Northern Solomons, Bismarck Archipelago.

94th INFANTRY DIVISION
The Neuf-Cats

Activated: 15 September 1942. Overseas: 6 August 1944. Days of combat: 209.

Campaigns: Northern France, Rhineland, Ardennes-Alsace, Central Europe.

95th INFANTRY DIVISION
The Victory Division

Activated: 15 July 1942. Overseas: 10 August 1944. Days of combat: 151.

Campaigns: Northern France, Rhineland, Central Europe.

96th INFANTRY DIVISION
The Deadeye Division

Activated: 15 August 1942. Overseas: 23 July 1944. Days of combat: 200.

Campaigns: Ryukyus, Southern Philippines.

97th INFANTRY DIVISION
The Trident Division

Activated: 25 February 1943. Overseas: 19 February 1945, for the ETO; 28 August 1945, for the Pacific Theater. Days of combat: 41 (ETO).

Campaigns: Central Europe.

98th INFANTRY DIVISION
The Iroquois Division

Activated: 15 September 1942. Overseas: 13 April 1944.

The 98th ID saw no combat in World War II. It served in Hawaii until occupation duty in Japan, arriving 27 September 1945.

99th INFANTRY DIVISION
The Battle Babies

Activated: 15 November 1942. Overseas: 30 September 1944. Days of combat: 151.

Campaigns: Rhineland, Ardennes-Alsace, Central Europe.

100th INFANTRY DIVISION
The Century Division

Activated: 15 November 1942. Overseas: 6 October 1944. Days of combat: 163.

Campaigns: Ardennes-Alsace, Rhineland, Central Europe.

101st AIRBORNE DIVISION
The Screaming Eagles

Activated: 15 August 1942. Overseas: 5 September 1943. Days of combat: 214.

Campaigns: Rhineland, Central Europe, Normandy, Ardennes-Alsace.

102d INFANTRY DIVISION
The Ozark Division

Activated: 15 September 1942. Overseas: 12 September 1944. Days of combat: 173.

Campaigns: Rhineland, Central Europe.

103d INFANTRY DIVISION
The Cactus Division

Activated: 15 November 1942. Overseas: 6 October 1944. Days of combat: 147. Campaigns: Rhineland, Central Europe.

104th INFANTRY DIVISION
The Timberwolf Division

Activated: 15 September 1942. Overseas: 27 August 1944. Days of combat: 200.

Campaigns: Northern France, Rhineland, Central Europe.

106th INFANTRY DIVISION
The Golden Lion Division

Activated: 15 March 1943. Overseas: 10 November 1944. Days of combat: 63.

Campaigns: Northern France, Rhineland, Ardennes-Alsace.

AMERICAL (INFANTRY) DIVISION

Activated: 27 May 1942 in New Caledonia. Overseas: 24 May 1942. Days of combat: 600.

Campaigns: Northern Solomons, Southern Philippines.

The division was formed from three regiments rushed from the States to New Caledonia (thus the name Americal) after the onset of Japanese offensives in the Pacific.

PHILIPPINE DIVISION

Activated: 8 June 1921. Overseas: 8 June 1921. Days of combat: 124.

Campaigns: Philippine Islands.

By the time of World War II, except for the 31st Infantry Regiment, the Philippine Division consisted primarily of native enlistees called Philippine Scouts. The Division was lost with the fall of Bataan in the spring of 1942.

APPENDIX B

ARMORED AND CAVALRY DIVISIONS IN WORLD WAR II

This Appendix gives detailed information on each of the Armored and Cavalry Divisions in World War II. As with Appendix A, we begin with a table showing the number designations of the organic elements of Armored divisions during the war and then proceed to the activation, campaign details and insignia of the divisions.

The table below should be read in the same way as the table in Appendix A. The first column is the division. So taking the first line (the 1st Armored Division) it can be seen that this division was comprised of the 6th, 11th and 14th Armored Infantry Battalions, the 1st, 4th and 13th Tank Battalions and so forth.

COMPONENT ELEMENTS OF THE ARMORED DIVISIONS IN WORLD WAR II

Division	Armored Infantry Battalions			Tank Battalions			Division Artillery Armored Field Artillery Battalions			Cavalry Reconnaisance Squadron	Armored Engineer Battalion	Armored Medical Battalion	Armored Ordnance Battalion	Armored Signal Company	Combat Command	CIC Detachment
1	6	11	14	1	4	13	27	68	91	81	16	47	123	141	A-B-R	501
2	41*	63*	67*	—	—	—	14	78	92	82	17	48	2	142	A-B-R	502
3	32*	33*	36*	—	—	—	54	67	391	83	23	45	3	143	A-B-R	503
4	10	51	53	8	35	37	22	66	94	25	24	4	126	144	A-B-R	504
5	15	46	47	10	34	81	47	71	95	85	22	75	127	145	A-B-R	505
6	9	44	50	15	68	69	128	212	231	86	25	76	128	146	A-B-R	506
7	23	38	48	17	31	40	434	440	489	87	33	77	129	147	A-B-R	507
8	7	49	58	18	36	80	398	399	405	88	53	78	130	148	A-B-R	508
9	27	52	60	2	14	19	3	16	73	89	9	2	131	149	A-B-R	509
10	20	54	61	3	11	21	419	420	423	90	55	80	132	150	A-B-R	510
11	21	55	63	22	41	42	490	491	492	41	56	81	133	151	A-B-R	511
12	17	56	66	23	43	714	493	494	495	92	119	82	134	152	A-B-R	512
13	16	59	67	24	45	46	496	497	498	93	124	83	135	153	A-B-R	513
14	19	62	68	25	47	48	499	500	501	94	125	84	136	154	A-B-R	514
16	18	64	69	5	16	26	393	396	397	23	216	216	137	156	A-B-R	516
20	8	65	70	9	20	27	412	413	414	30	220	220	138	160	A-B-R	520

*These units were armored regiments during World War II, as the 2d and 3d Armored Divisions were not reorganized, as the others were, on Sept. 15, 1943

ARMORED DIVISIONS
ACTIVATION AND CAMPAIGNS

1st ARMORED DIVISION
Old Ironsides

Activated: 15 July 1940. Overseas: May 1942. Days of combat: 360.

Campaigns: Tunisia, Naples-Foggia, Rome-Arno, North Apennines, Po Valley.

2d ARMORED DIVISION
Hell on Wheels

Activated: 15 July 1940. Overseas: CC "B" 27 October 1942 ; remainder 12 December 1942. Days of combat: 280.

Campaigns: French Morocco, Sicily, Normandy, Northern France, Rhineland, Ardennes- Alsace, Central Europe.

3d ARMORED DIVISION
The Spearhead Division

Activated: 15 April 1941. Overseas: 15 September 1943. Days of combat: 231.

Campaigns: Normandy, Northern France, Rhineland, Ardennes-Alsace, Central Europe.

4th ARMORED DIVISION
Breakthrough

Activated: 15 April 1941. Overseas: 29 December 1943. Days of combat: 230.

Campaigns: Normandy, Northern France, Rhineland, Ardennes-Alsace, Central Europe.

5th ARMORED DIVISION
The Victory Division

Activated: 10 October 1941. Overseas: 11 February 1944. Days of combat: 161.

Campaigns: Normandy, Northern France, Rhineland, Ardennes-Alsace, Central Europe.

6th ARMORED DIVISION
The Super Sixth

Activated: 15 February 1942. Overseas: 11 February 1944. Days of combat: 272.

Campaigns: Normandy, Northern France, Rhineland, Ardennes-Alsace, Central Europe.

7th ARMORED DIVISION
The Lucky Seventh

Activated: 1 March 1942. Overseas: 7 January 1944. Days of combat: 172.

Campaigns: Northern France, Rhineland, Ardennes-Alsace, Central Europe.

8th ARMORED DIVISION
Tornado

Activated: 1 April 1942. Overseas: 7 November 1944. Days of combat: 63.

Campaigns: Rhineland, Ardennes-Alsace, Central Europe.

9th ARMORED DIVISION
The Phantom Division

Activated: 15 July 1942. Overseas: 26 August 1944. Days of combat: 91.

Campaigns: Rhineland, Ardennes-Alsace, Central Europe.

10th ARMORED DIVISION
The Tiger Division

Activated: 15 July 1942. Overseas: 13 September 1944. Days of combat: 124.

Campaigns: Rhineland, Ardennes-Alsace, Central Europe.

11th ARMORED DIVISION
Thunderbolt

Activated: 15 August 1942. Overseas: 29 September 1944. Days of combat: 96.

Campaigns: Rhineland, Ardennes-Alsace, Central Europe.

12th ARMORED DIVISION
The Hellcat Division

Activated: 15 September 1942. Overseas: 20 September 1944. Days of combat: 102.

Campaigns: Rhineland, Ardennes-Alsace, Central Europe.

13th ARMORED DIVISION
The Black Cat Division

Activated: 15 October 1942. Overseas: 18 January 1945. Days of combat: 16.

Campaigns: Rhineland, Central Europe.

14th ARMORED DIVISION
The Liberator Division

Activated: 15 November 1942. Overseas: 14 October 1944. Days of combat: 167.

Campaigns: Rhineland, Central Europe.

16th ARMORED DIVISION

Activated: 15 July 1943. Overseas: 5 February 1945. Days of combat: 3.

Campaigns: Central Europe.

20th ARMORED DIVISION

Activated: 15 March 1943. Overseas: 6 February 1945. Days of combat: 8.

Campaigns: Central Europe.

CAVALRY DIVISIONS
ACTIVATION AND CAMPAIGNS

COMPONENT ELEMENTS OF THE 1ST CAVALRY DIVISION IN WORLD WAR II														
Cavalry Division	1st Cavalry Brigade	2d Cavalry Brigade		Field Artillery Battalions				Medical Squadron	Signal Troop	Engineer Squadron	Quarter master Squadron	Ordnance Company	Reconnais sance Troop	Light Tank Company	CIC Detach ment
1	5	12	7	8	61	82	99	271	1	1	8	16	27	302	603	801

1st CAVALRY DIVISION
The First Team

Activated: 31 August 1921. Overseas: 23 May 1943. Days of combat: 521.

Campaigns: New Guinea, Bismarck Archipelago, Leyte, Luzon.

2d CAVALRY DIVISION

Originally activated 1 April 1941, elements of the Division were transferred and inactivated 15 July 1942; inactive elements were reactivated 25 February 1943, with Negro enlisted personnel.

Campaigns: None. Inactivated: 10 May 1944, in the North African Theater of Operations

1st Cavalry Insignia

2d Cavalry Insignia

The Crew of an M3 halftrack prepares their vehicle for the invasion of Normandy. The weapon being loaded is a .50 caliber machine gun which fires a round with a slug as big as a man's thumb.

The pipe on the left hand side allows the engine to run underwater during the beach landing.

APPENDIX C
ARMY GROUPS, ARMIES AND CORPS IN WORLD WAR II

THE ARMY GROUPS

6TH ARMY GROUP

 Headquarters, 6th Army Group, was organized in the Mediterranean at Bastia, Corsica, on 1 August 1944 to provide overall operational direction and control for the combined French and American forces charged with the invasion of southern France. General Jacob L. Devers was in command during the entire period of its combat operations.

6th Army Group Headquarters moved to France on 31 August 1944 and became operational at Lyons on 15 September 1944. Its main mission was to furnish right (south) flank support and protection to the Allied Expeditionary Forces' drive to destroy the German forces in the west. In addition, it had the responsibility of protecting the lines of communication from the Southern Mediterranean ports along the Italian-French border and of eliminating German pockets of resistance on the Atlantic coast in the vicinity of the Gironde Estuary.

When the 6th Army Group first became operational, it had approximately 293,000 troops under its command; this number, however, eventually increased to 750,000, of which 405,000 were French. Its principal combat commands were the Seventh United States Army, Lt. Gen Alexander M. Patch, Jr., commanding, and the First French Army, Gen. d'armeé Jean de Lattre de Tassigny, commanding. Its command also included the First Allied Airborne Task Force, of which the First Special Service Force, later replaced by the Forty-fourth Antiaircraft Brigade, was a part. Later, the French Army Detachments of the Alps and the Atlantic were placed under its control. On 15 September 1944, the two armies included one United States and two French corps, and three United States and seven French divisions.

By May 1945, the 6th Army Group's order of battle listed 3 United States and 2 French corps, and 16 United States and 10 French divisions. The VI Corps and the 3d, 36th, and 45th Infantry Divisions, United States Army, served with the 6th Army Group continuously throughout its period of combat. Other American units that may be considered as an integral part of the 6th Army Group were the XV and XXI Corps, the 42d, 44th, 63d, 70th, 100th, 103d Infantry Divisions, and the 12th and 14th Armored Divisions. American divisions that served under the command of the 6th Army Group for varying periods of time were the 4th, 28th, 35th, 71st, 75th, 79th, 86th, and 87th Infantry Divisions; the 6th, 10th, 13th and 20th Armored Divisions; and the 101st Airborne Division.

The French Army corps and divisions in the 6th Army Group were the I and II French Army Corps, 1st, 2d, and 3d DB (Armored Divisions), 1st DMI (March Infantry Division), 2d DIM (Moroccan Infantry Division), 3d DIA (Algerian Infantry Division), 4th DMM (Moroccan Mountain Division), 9th DIC (Colonial French Infantry Division), 14th DI (Infantry Division), and the 27th DA (Alpine Division).

Fighting side by side for 265 days as combat comrades, the American and French forces of the 6th Army Group achieved a partnership that played a major role in winning from the German forces a final and unconditional surrender. Their combined achievements included the assault landings on the Riviera, the swift liberation of southern and western France, the winter-long battle to free Alsace and the Vosges (including the defense of approximately one-half of the Allied western front during the von Rundstedt offensive), the breaching of the Siegfried Line, the crossing of the Rhine River, the sweep through the German midlands, the mopping up of the so-called National Redoubt, and joining up with the Allied forces in Italy.

Unlike other Allied headquarters involving combined operations, the 6th Army Group did not have an integrated French and American staff, but was purely American in organization and personnel. This was done out of necessity and not with any desire to deny the French representation; the French were hard put at this time to find sufficient experienced staff officers to meet their own requirements. They were entirely dependent on the Americans for logistical support, were not conversant with our methods, and time was not available to teach them.

Coordination between the French and American commands was assured by the creation in the headquarters of a special liaison group which was supplemented by a French military mission of staff officers. By 4 May 1945, units of the 6th Army Group had driven into western Austria and had rendered the German forces opposing it incapable of further opposition. Its forces along the Italian-French border had penetrated within striking distances of Turin when ordered to cease their advance. The German positions on the Gironde Estuary, which had denied the Allies the use of the post of Bordeaux, had been taken by 1 May 1945. Since the landing in southern France, elements of the 6th Army Group had advanced over 900 miles and in so doing captured 948,500 enemy prisoners, freed some 71,400 Allied prisoners of war, and liberated some 779,000 displaced persons.

The cost to the American and French forces in casualties was less than might have been expected for an operation of this magnitude. Some idea of the scope of the operations can be gained from the fact that from 15 September 1944 to 2 May 1945, the various elements comprising the 6th Army Group required 411,000 tons of artillery ammunition, 410,000 tons of rations, and 650,000 tons of petroleum, oil, and lubricants.

General Devers relinquished command of 6th Army Group on 30 June 1945 to become the Commanding General, Army Ground Forces, and was succeeded by his Chief of Staff, Maj. Gen. David G. Barr. Lt. Gen. Wade H. Haislip assumed command on 18 July 1945, and two days later the 6th Army Group was ordered inactivated. The Headquarters closed on 23 July 1945.

12TH ARMY GROUP

12th Army Group was originally activated as the First United States Army Group (FUSAG) in London, England, under command of Lt. Gen. Omar N. Bradley, on 19 October 1943. 1st United States Army Group was charged with operational planning for OVERLORD and RANKIN (operations in the event of a German collapse before OVERLORD). This planning was carried out in close cooperation with the British 21st Army Group. On 14 July 1944, FUSAG was superseded by 12th Army Group. All units and individuals assigned or attached to FUSAG were transferred on that date to Headquarters, 12th Army Group, Lt. Gen. Omar N. Bradley continuing in command. Headquarters moved to the continent on 22 July 1944, opening that date in an orchard near Colombieres, France, and moving eastward as the fighting progressed.

On 1 August 1944, 12th Army Group assumed operational command over First United States Army (Lt. Gen. Courtney H. Hodges) and Third United States Army (Lt. Gen. George S. Patton), itself remaining under the operational control of 21 Army Group (British) until 1 September 1944, when it was placed under the direct command of Supreme Headquarters, Allied Expeditionary Force (SHAEF). 12th Army Group effected a breakthrough at Avranches, cleared much of the Brittany Peninsula, drove swiftly eastward liberating Orleans, Chartres, and Dreux, and crossed the Seine, Marne, and Aisne Rivers by the end of August.

On 5 September 1944, Ninth United States Army (Lt. Gen. William H. Simpson) became operational, and continued the attack on Brest, which was liberated 18 September. The First United States Army liberated Luxembourg on 10 September, crossing the border into Germany the following day, and took Maastricht on the 14th. Third United States Army captured Nancy on the 16th. In October the First United States Army attacked and captured Aachen (21

October) after a long siege; the Third United States Army remained on the defensive, building up for its big drive in November; the Ninth United States Army shifted from Brittany to positions between the First and Third Armies.

In November there was a general assault on the Siegfried Line, the Third Army launching an attack on 8 November which resulted in the establishment of a bridgehead across the Moselle north of Metz. Metz was surrounded and fell on the 22d of the month. First and Ninth Armies attacked on the 16th of November, reaching the Roer and Inde Rivers. In December the general attack toward the Rhine was interrupted by the enemy winter offensive in the Ardennes, launched 16 December 1944.

Allied strategic reserves were committed at Bastogne and Stavelot to stop and turn the enemy drive; First and Ninth Armies were placed under the operational control of 21 Army Group (British). The Third Army, halting its offensive in the Saar sector, swung north to launch a successful counterattack on the south flank of the enemy salient. The bulge was reduced in January, St. Vith falling on the 24th.

Meanwhile, Fifteenth United States Army became operational on 6 January 1945 (Maj. Gen. Ray E. Porter until 15 January; and Lt. Gen. Leonard T. Gerow, beginning 16 January) with the mission of supervising the staging, training, and equipping of 12th Army Group units.

In February the Siegfried Line was breached. In March the First Army crossed the Roer and drove across the Rhine on the Remagen Bridge, captured intact 8 March 1945. Third Army cleared the area around Trier, attacked north across the Moselle, and established bridgeheads across the Rhine between Mainz and Worms, 22–23 March.

April witnessed the encirclement of German forces in the Ruhr pocket by First and Ninth Armies. Attacks were launched which brought Allied forces to the banks of the Elbe and Mulde Rivers by the middle of the month. Third Army continued to race toward Austria, crossing the border on 3 May 1945. All offensive operations ceased on 9 May upon German surrender. 12th Army Group was dissolved 31 July 1945, operational control over all United States Forces in Germany passing to USFET (United States Forces, European Theater).

At various times during the campaign on the continent, the following American Divisions were assigned to 12th Army Group: 1st Inf, 2d Inf, 4th Inf, 5th Inf, 8th Inf, 9th Inf, 17th A/B, 26th Inf, 28th Inf, 29th Inf, 30th Inf, 35th Inf, 42d Inf, 44th Inf, 65th Inf, 69th Inf, 70th Inf, 71st Inf, 75th Inf, 76th Inf, 78th Inf, 79th Inf, 80th Inf, 82d A/B, 83d Inf, 84th Inf, 86th Inf, 87th Inf, 89th Inf, 90th Inf, 94th Inf, 95th Inf, 97th Inf, 99th Inf, 100th Inf, 101st A/B, 102d Inf, 104th Inf, 106th Inf, 2d Armd, 3d Armd, 4th Armd, 5th Armd, 6th Armd, 7th Armd, 8th Armd, 9th Armd, 10th Armd, 11th Armd, 12th Armd, 13th Armd, 14th Armd, 16th Armd, and 20th Armd Divisions.

15TH ARMY GROUP

The 15th Army Group was activated and made operational at Algiers, North Africa, on 10 July 1943, the date of the Allied landing in Sicily, whose invasion the group had planned under another task force designation. The Army group was commanded at this time by British Gen. Sir Harold L.G. Alexander and comprised the Seventh U. S. Army under Gen. George S. Patton, Jr., and the British Eighth Army under Gen. Sir Bernard L. Montgomery.

The Sicilian landings were made south of Syracuse by the British and west of Licata by the American forces. This campaign was marked by the successive captures of Syracuse, Primosole Bridge, Enna, Palermo and Leonforte (both on 22 July), Catania, Agira, Troina, Torrenova, and Randazzo. On 15 August, Taormina was occupied and on 17 August the capture of Messina ended effective resistance. Only about half of the enemy escaped to the Italian mainland. Sicily had been conquered in 38 days. After the end of the Sicilian campaign, the Fifth U. S. Army in North Africa under the command of Gen. (then Lt. Gen.) Mark Wayne Clark, replaced the Seventh U. S. Army for the invasion of Italy. On 3 September 1943, two divisions of the British Eighth Army crossed the Straits of Messina into the toe of Italy, occupying Reggio and San Giovanni. On 8 September, while the Fifth U. S. Army was en route by sea to make the principal assault on the Italian mainland, the surrender of the Italian Government was announced.

On 9 September, the Fifth U. S. Army, which included British elements, landed on the beaches along the Gulf of Salerno in the first major invasion of the continent of Europe by United States troops. After fighting off strong German counterattacks, they pushed on to capture Naples on 1 October. Meanwhile, the British Eighth Army advanced along the Adriatic and joined forces with the Fifth U. S. Army along the general line of the Volturno River east to the Adriatic. The Volturno was crossed in October, and the advance continued until the winter line was reached. In December 1943 and early January 1944, the German winter line was breached and parallel advances were made on the east coast. On 19 January 1944 the Headquarters 15th Army Group was redesignated as Headquarters Allied Central Mediterranean Force, and on 12 March 1944 it was renamed Headquarters Allied Armies in Italy.

In mid January 1944, the Fifth U. S. Army attacked the Gustav Line, which was anchored on Cassino and the heights above the Garigliano River. A few days later, an amphibious force of the Fifth Army landed at Anzio behind the enemy lines to turn the German flank and force the main enemy forces on the Cassino front to withdraw. In spite of heavy losses, the enemy contained the beachhead force at Anzio and held on to the Gustav Line. In May 1944, a new attack was launched against the Gustav Line, breaching the German positions and forcing the enemy to retreat toward Rome. Fifth Army captured the Ausoni Mountains and exploited rapidly to outflank the Hitler Line in the Liri Valley. Eighth Army captured Cassino and pursued the retreating enemy up the Liri Valley. The Anzio garrison broke out of its beach-head on the 23d of May, joining the main body of the advancing Fifth Army. The Germans retreated north and the Fifth Army entered Rome on 4 June—the first Axis capital to fall to the Allies in World War II.

The Fifth and Eighth Armies pushed on in pursuit of Field Marshal Kesselring's forces until the Arno River was reached. The British Eighth Army launched a general attack in late August, capturing Pesaro, the eastern anchor of the Gothic Line. In September, the Fifth U. S. Army attacked, outflanking Futa Pass and pushing to within 9 miles of Bologna. Terrain, weather, shortage of ammunition and troops prohibited continuation of a general assault into the Po Valley, forcing the Fifth Army to halt at the northern edge of the Apennines. However, during the winter, the Eighth Army captured Forli and Ravenna and the Senio River Line northwest of Faenza, while the Fifth Army took Mounts Grande, Belvedere, and Castello. In December 1944, Headquarters Allied Armies in Italy was redesignated again as the Headquarters 15th Army Group and General Clark was designated as its commander. At the same time, Lt. Gen. Lucian K. Truscott was given command of the Fifth U. S. Army. The Eighth Army was under command of Lt. Gen. Sir Richard L. McCreery.

In April, the final offensive was launched. Mountain and river defenses were stormed and the breakthrough into the Po Valley plain was achieved as Bologna fell on 21 April. Bridgeheads were established over the Po River by 25 April. Genoa, Brescia, Vicenza, Padua, Milan, and Venice fell in rapid succession; and finally, in order to escape annihilation, the entire German army in Italy surrendered on 2 May 1945. This was the first major surrender of Nazi forces to the Allied Armies in Europe.

Throughout the Italian campaigns the 15th Army Group was a polyglot fighting force, composed of fighting soldiers from the six continents of the world. These included Americans, British, Australians, New Zealanders, Poles, South Africans, French, Canadians, Indians, Brazilians, Palestinians, Moroccans, Greeks, Italian troops, and Italian partisans. In spite of these divergent nationalities and races, their great uniformity of purpose and action was an outstanding example of Allied unity of effort.

The 15th Army Group was disbanded on 5 July 1945. Its commander, General Clark, was appointed U. S. High Commissioner for Austria, and the bulk of the combined staff of the 15th Army Group Headquarters moved north to Austria, where the American element formed the headquarters of the United States Forces in Austria and many of the British elements joined the British Forces of Occupation in Austria.

THE ARMIES

FIRST ARMY

When the Eastern Defense Command was set up for the protection of the Atlantic seaboard on 21 June 1941, the new headquarters was joined to that of First Army, giving General Hugh A. Drum the additional command, in which he continued until 7 October 1943. During this period First Army became a well-trained field unit, participating in wide-scale maneuvers in North Carolina in the fall of 1941 and otherwise preparing for its World War II combat role.

On 8 October 1943, Lt. Gen. George Grunert took command of Eastern Defense Command and First Army, and when, two days later, First Army was separated from EDC, General Grunert retained command of the Army until 28 January 1944, at which time Gen. (then Lt. Gen.) Omar N. Bradley succeeded him.

First Army Headquarters embarked on 12 October 1943, established headquarters at Bristol, England, on 20 October, and began intensive preparations for the cross-Channel assault of the Normandy beaches on 6 June 1944.

Thereafter, until VE-day, First Army was in action continuously in the following campaigns: Normandy, Northern France, Ardennes, Rhineland, and Central Europe. Utah Beach, Omaha Beach, Cherbourg, St. Lo, Mortain, Falaise-Argentan Pocket, Liberation of Paris, Aachen, Hurtgen Forest, Ardennes, Roer River Crossing, Cologne, Remagen Bridgehead, Ruhr Pocket—all were important way-stops in First Army's push into Germany.

Gen. Courtney H. Hodges, who had been the First Army Deputy Commander, assumed command on 1 August 1944. On 28 March 1949, Lt. Gen. Walter Bedell Smith assumed command of First Army.

First Army established the following firsts during the course of World War II operations in Europe: First on the beaches of Normandy; first to break out of the Normandy Beachhead; first to enter Paris; first to break through the Siegfried Line and enter Germany; first to cross the Rhine; and first to contact the Russians.

The V and VII Corps under First Army fought continuously from D-day to VE-day (337 days of combat); and the III, VIII, XV, XIX Corps and the XVIII Airborne Corps—making a sum total of 38 United States divisions and 2 foreign divisions—fought in the Army for varying periods of time.

The maximum number of corps under First Army at one time was 4, and the maximum number of divisions was 19.

Contact with the Russians on 25 April 1945 brought to a close, combat operations of First Army in Europe, but the Army's period of inactivity was short-lived. On 21 May 1945, Headquarters, First Army embarked at Le Havre under redeployment orders, via the United States to the Pacific theater with an assault mission in the Tokyo Bay area for the then-planned final offensive operation against Japan. Plans by the Army commander and the advance party which accompanied him by air to Manila for this operation were not used, however, due to the Japanese surrender on 2 September 1945. The advance detachment again returned to the United States.

SECOND ARMY

On 20 October 1940 the Second Army became a training army with the primary mission of preparing tactical units to take the field promptly and to operate effectively in combat. As part of this training, the Second Army, then under command of Lt. Gen. Ben. Lear, participated in the Louisiana maneuvers of 1941. These maneuvers marked the first time in the history of American military exercises that one field army had been pitted against another.

Between the time of separation from the Sixth Corps area and the conclusion of hostilities in World War II, 1 army headquarters, 10 corps headquarters, 57 divisions, and hundreds of smaller units were assigned to Second Army either for activation or training, or both, before their dispatch to the fighting fronts.

THIRD ARMY

The Third Army was reactivated on 9 August 1932 as one of four field armies created within the continental limits of the United States, with an area comprising the Fourth and Eighth Corps areas and additional missions dealing with the region of the Gulf of Mexico and the southern frontier. From the time of its reactivation until its departure for oversea duty on 26 January 1944, the location of Third Army headquarters alternated between Fort Sam Houston, Texas (the headquarters of the Eighth Corps area), and Atlanta, Georgia (headquarters of the Fourth Corps area), depending upon the senior commander at the time. This period is further characterized by the growth of Third Army from meager beginnings to a headquarters prepared for field operations. Worthy of note were the first command post exercises in October 1936 and the 1938 maneuvers, both of which provided valuable proving grounds.

On 12 January 1944 the advance detachment of Third Army headquarters, comprised of 13 officers and 26 enlisted men, left for the port of embarkation; and the Fourth Army relieved the Third Army at Fort Sam Houston, as of midnight,

25–26 January. Gen. George S. Patton, Jr., assumed command of Third Army in England where it remained until July when the headquarters moved to the Cotentin Peninsula in Normandy, France. Under General Patton's command, Third Army's campaigns in Europe, which were continuous from 1 August 1944 until VE-day, included a sensational dash across France and the forcing of the Rhine River, thence across Germany and over the Danube River, and finally down into Czechoslovakia. At various times throughout the war six corps (III, V, VIII, XII, XV, and XX) operated under the Third Army; and a total of 40 United States divisions and 1 French division were assigned to Third Army for varying periods.

FOURTH ARMY

The Fourth Army was activated in August 1932 when the War Department announced the creation of four field armies within the continental limits of the United States. At its inception the Army encompassed the Seventh and Ninth Corps areas and its mission "dealt with the Pacific coast." The senior corps area commander, Maj. Gen. Johnson Hagood, commander of the VII Corps area, assumed command of the Fourth Army on 15 August 1932, with headquarters at Omaha, Nebraska.

The headquarters was moved to the Presidio of San Francisco, California on 18 June 1936. Maj. Gen. George S. Simonds commanded the Army from October 1936 until 24 May 1938 when he was succeeded by Maj. Gen. Albert J. Bowley.

Following the organization of General Headquarters, United States Army, in 1940, the Fourth Army was assigned to the field forces during the autumn of that year under the command of Lt. Gen. John H. DeWitt. The Army was assigned the following units: IX Corps, consisting of the 3d and 41st Divisions; III Corps, later made up of the 7th and 40th Divisions; and the Ninth Coast Artillery District, stretching from the Puget Sound to San Diego, Calif.

The Army was assigned a training mission which culminated during the summer of 1941 in an extensive command post exercise held at Hunter Liggett Military Reservation, Calif., and Army maneuvers held in the Pacific Northwest.

Prior to the outbreak of World War II the Fourth Army was assigned the mission of constituting the Western Defense Command prepared to establish defense of the Pacific coast, including Alaska. These plans were implemented when Pearl Harbor was attacked: the Western Defense Command became an active organization and, using the personnel of the Fourth Army, became known as the Western Defense Command and Fourth Army. At this time the Fourth Air Force was added, as were additional ground force units, to provide defense of Kiska and Attu Islands.

Fourth Army was separated from the Western Defense Command on 18 September 1943, and reorganized at San Jose, Calif., with Lt. Gen. William H. Simpson assuming command of the Army on 13 October 1943. Seven weeks after arrival at San Jose the Army Headquarters moved back to the Presidio of Monterey, and in January 1944, it moved to Fort Sam Houston, Texas, to assume the duties of the departing Third Army. For the first time the Fourth Army had reached full operating status, having under its command the XVIII, XXI and XXIII Corps. In addition to training and administering 282,000 troops, Fourth Army was responsible for the Louisiana maneuver area.

In April 1944 General Simpson and the bulk of the Fourth Army staff were ordered overseas to establish the Ninth Army. Maj. Gen. John P. Lucas assumed command and selected a new staff. The following August the process was repeated when the Fourth Army staff was alerted for overseas shipment to organize the Fifteenth Army; thus the Fourth Army had furnished the staffs for two additional field armies, and had trained and equipped at least half of the combat units shipped overseas. By September 1944, the Fourth Army had absorbed all of the Second Army's duties west of the Mississippi River.

FIFTH ARMY

In accordance with a War Department directive, Fifth Army was activated by the Commanding General, European Theater of Operations, in G.O. No. 67, dated 12 December 1942. Lt. Gen. Mark W. Clark, the Fifth Army's first commander, opened his headquarters at Oujda, Morocco, on 5 January 1943; the Army at this time included the I Armored Corps and VI Corps. For the following eight months the Fifth Army was limited to a training role, eventually sending its original corps components to Operation Husky, the invasion of Sicily.

Fifth Army's first combat assignment was Operation Avalanche, the invasion of Italy at Salerno, which took place 9 September 1943. Taking part were the United States VI Corps (3d, 34th, 36th and 45th Infantry Divisions, 82d Airborne Division, Rangers, 13th Field Artillery Brigade and other Field Artillery units) and the British X Corps, which consisted of the British 46 and 56 Infantry Divisions and 7 Armoured Division. By 20 September, Fifth Army was prepared to start its long, hard drive up the peninsula of Italy.

Naples fell on 1 October. The VI Corps made its famous "left-hook" amphibious landing at Anzio-Nettuno, the Gustav line (including Cassino and the Rapido River) was breached, and Rome was taken on 4 June 1944.

From here the Army pushed on to the Arno River, the Gothic line, and across the rugged Apennines. At this point (December 1944) Lt. Gen. Lucian K. Truscott, former VI Corps commander, became the Fifth Army commander.

The final major assault was launched in the spring of 1945, leading the Fifth Army across the Po Valley and on to the unconditional surrender of the German forces in Italy on 2 May 1945. This date marked the end of 604 days of continuous combat for the troops of the Fifth Army, under particularly trying conditions of climate and terrain. A characteristic of the Fifth Army throughout its combat history was the heterogeneity of its composition—French, Brazilian, British, New Zealand, and Indian troops fought side by side at various times and for varying periods with American soldiers.

SIXTH ARMY

Sixth Army was activated at Fort Sam Houston, Texas on 25 January 1943, the original cadre being drawn from Third Army Headquarters. Lt. Gen. (Later Gen.) Walter Krueger, who had been Third Army commander when the Sixth Army was activated, assumed command of the Army on 16 February 1943, 8 days after the advance echelon (which left San Francisco 3 February) had arrived in Australia. Gen. Krueger commanded during its entire period of combat in World War II. The size of the Sixth Army varied with the availability of forces and the requirements of successive missions. Its corps composition ranged from one to three, including at various times the I, X, XIV, and XXIV Corps. Operations from late in April 1943 to 25 September 1944 were carried out by Task Force Alamo, the headquarters of which was the same as that of the Sixth Army; in other words, units assigned to the Sixth Army comprised the Alamo force, and the two were identical.

The first victory was the seizure of Kiriwina and Woodlark Islands in July 1943. Thereafter, the Sixth Army's 2,700-mile advance to the Philippines was marked by the following: capture of the western end of New Britain and of Saidor (15 December 1943–10 February 1944); seizure of the Admiralty Islands (29 February–18 May 1944); Hollandia-Aitape Operation (22 April–25 August 1944); clean-up of Wakde-Toem area (17 May–2 September 1944); seizure of Biak (27 May–20 August 1944) and of Soepiori Island on 7 September 1944; capture of Noemfoor Island (2 July–31 August 1944); final New Guinea landings (Sansapor, Middleburg, and Amsterdam Islands, 30 July–31 August 1944); occupation of Morotai (15 September–4 October 1944); occupation of Leyte (17 October–25 December 1944); occupation of Mindoro (15 December–31 December 1944); occupation of Luzon (9 January–30 June 1945). For the participating corps, divisions, and combat teams, many of these operations overlapped, but for Sixth Army all fitted together into an overall strategic plan.

Sixth Army Headquarters landed at Wakayama, Honshu, Japan, on 25 September 1945, and carried on occupational duties until 28 January 1946 when the headquarters was inactivated at Kyoto.

SEVENTH ARMY

The Seventh Army, the first United States field army to see action in World War II, was activated at sea, 10 July 1943, on the invasion convoy off Sicily, by the redesignation of I Armored Corps (Reinforced) under Lt. Gen. George S. Patton, Jr., on authority of North African Theater of Operations, United States Army.

Seventh Army (consisting of the 1st, 3d, 9th, and 45th Infantry Divisions, the 82d Airborne, and the 1st and 2d Armored Divisions, grouped into II Corps and a Provisional Corps) on 10 July 1943 assaulted the beaches of southern Sicily in the Licata, Gela, and Pozzallo area, with the British Eighth Army on its right. In the following weeks the American forces fanned out to the north and west, conquering all of western Sicily and capturing Palermo on 22 July. The two Allied armies then pressed the Germans and Italians into northeastern Sicily, to complete the conquest of the island with the capture of Messina on 16 August 1943. Seventh Army, with a total strength of 195,617, had killed or captured 113,000 enemy troops, against losses which were light by comparison.

Seventh Army remained at Palermo, Sicily, and Algiers, North Africa, until the summer of 1944. Its commander and divisions were transferred elsewhere. On 1 January 1944, Lt. Gen. Mark W. Clark assumed command and the staff began planning for an invasion of southern France. On 2 March 1944 Lt. Gen. Alexander M. Patch, veteran of Guadalcanal and later commander of IV Corps, assumed command. The Army moved to Naples, Italy, on 4 July 1944.

Seventh Army (consisting of 3d, 36th, and 45th U. S. Infantry Divisions in VI Corps, the First Airborne Task Force, and five French divisions under French Armee "B") assaulted the beaches in the St. Tropez-St. Raphael area of southern France on 15 August 1944. Within 30 days the Seventh Army and their French contingent advanced 400 miles to the Vosges Mountains, liberating Marseilles, Toulon, Lyon, and all of southern France by junction with the Normandy forces. The French forces became an independent command as French First Army on 15 September.

During the fall and early winter, Seventh Army crossed the Meurthe River, forced the German defenses in the Vosges Mountains, and broke into the Alsatian plain to capture Strasbourg and reach the Rhine. During the Battle of the Bulge, it went on the defensive and extended to cover much of the Third Army frontage in order to permit that Army to counterattack. With the cooperation of First French Army, Seventh Army regained the offensive and eliminated the enemy pocket in the Colmar area in February 1945. Seventh Army then advanced north into the Saar Palatinate. On 26 March 1945 Seventh Army crossed the Rhine near Worms and drove into the heart of Nazi Germany to capture Nuremberg and Munich. On 4 May 1945, less than 9 months after leaving Italy, Seventh Army troops crossed the Brenner Pass and made junction with United States Fifth Army on Italian soil, having, by 262 days of continuous fighting, advanced over 1,000 miles from the beaches of southern France.

Twelve United States Infantry divisions (3d, 4th, 36th, 42d, 44th, 45th, 63d, 70th, 71st, 79th, 100th, and 103d), five United States Armored divisions (10th, 12th, 13th, 14th, and 20th), and two United States Airborne divisions (1st ABTF and 101st AB) served extensively with the three corps (VI, XV, XXI) of Seventh Army. Seven French and various other United States divisions also fought at different times under the Seventh Army during the campaign.

EIGHTH ARMY

Activated on 10 June 1944 at Memphis, Tennessee, with a staff drawn almost entirely from the Second Army, Headquarters Eighth Army was immediately ordered overseas, arriving at Hollandia, New Guinea, on 4 September 1944. Lt. Gen. Robert L. Eichelberger, who had commanded the I Corps in the Southwest Pacific since August 1942, assumed command on 7 September 1944.

By 12 October 1944, Eighth Army had received and carried out its first mission, assuming control of all operational areas in New Guinea, New Britain, the Admiralties, and Morotai, involving approximately 200,000 troops dispersed in more than 20 localities, including Australia.

Following swift strikes at the islands of Mapia and Asia, the Eighth Army moved to Leyte, Philippine Islands, and on 26 December took over the responsibility for the completion of the Leyte operation. This action began the liberation of the Philippines south of Luzon.

Late in January 1945, Eighth Army, in support of Sixth Army (already engaged on Luzon) struck two blows at the west coast of that island: The first, north of Subic Bay toward Olongapo and Bataan; the second, at Nasugbu in southwestern Luzon, followed by a rapid drive into south Manila.

During February, March, and April 1945, Eighth Army executed a series of amphibious landings to clear the Verde Island Passages and the San Bernardino Straits. Simultaneously, the five Victor operations were launched in rapid succession.

The earliest of these operations was Victor III which opened on Palawan on 28 February; Zamboanga and the Sulu Archipelago were assaulted on 10 March in what was known as the Victor IV operation; this was followed on 18 March by drives against Cebu, Bohol, Pansy, and Negros in the Victor I and II operations; the last of these operations, Victor V, was launched on 17 April, and its successful conclusion was officially announced on 30 June 1945.

Eighth Army assumed control of the entire Philippines on 1 July 1945, when it was directed to take over the Luzon operation. By 15 August, enemy resistance was declared at an end and final preparations for the invasion of Japan were under way.

In the first 7 months of 1945 the Eighth Army had not only performed its tactical mission of clearing the southern Philippines but had set up bases on Leyte which equipped and supplied major units for the Luzon and Okinawa campaigns.

Operation Coronet, in which the Eighth Army was to make the main assault against the Tokyo plain, was obviated by the surrender of Japan. With the mission changed from one of assault to one of occupation, General Eichelberger arrived at Atsugi Airdrome on 30 August 1945 with the advance elements of Eighth Army, to set in motion the occupation of Japan in accordance with the provisions of the Potsdam Declaration.

NINTH ARMY

The Ninth Army was activated at Fort Sam Houston, Texas, on 22 May 1944. It had been originally activated on 15 April 1944 as the Eighth Army, but was re-designated the Ninth on 22 May, 10 days after the arrival of its advance party in the United Kingdom, in order to avoid confusion with the British Eighth Army, then active in Europe.

Commanded by Lt. Gen. William Hood Simpson, who was to remain in command throughout its operational life, Ninth Army drew its initial staff and headquarters personnel from the Fourth Army, which, with new personnel, remained at Fort Sam Houston to carry out the training mission of that army.

On 29 June 1944, Ninth Army established headquarters at Bristol, England, preparatory to active participation in operations on the continent of Europe. On 5 September 1944, under command of Twelfth Army Group, it became operational, taking over the mission of reducing the besieged city of Brest, containing German forces pocketed in Lorient and St. Nazaire, and protecting the southern flank of the Army group along the line of the Loire River as far east as Orleans.

All United States combat forces then located in the Brittany Peninsula, including the VIII Corps, five divisions, and supporting troops, came under Ninth Army command.

The reduction of Brest was completed on 20 September and early in October Ninth Army moved east to take up a position on the Siegfried Line in the Ardennes between First and Third Armies. Less than a month later it moved to the northern flank of the United States Forces in Europe.

As a result of its sudden and distant displacements, portions of the Army were operating simultaneously, for a time, in five different countries—France, Belgium, Luxembourg, the Netherlands, and Germany. However, Ninth Army maintained this relative position, with the First Army on its right and British forces on its left, until the German capitulation in May 1945.

During the Ardennes counteroffensive (the Battle of the Bulge), the Rhine crossing, and the envelopment of the Ruhr, Ninth Army served under Field Marshal Montgomery's 21 Army group (British). During the heavy fighting of November 1944 and during the rapid advance across the plains of northern Germany, Ninth Army served under General Bradley's 12th Army group.

Ninth Army's November offensive, exploiting a gap in the German Siegfried Line defenses north of Aachen, ended on the banks of the flood-threatened Roer River in early December 1944. Resuming the offensive in February, Ninth Army advanced from the Roer River to the Rhine in February and on 24 March 1945, made an assault crossing of the Rhine just north of the Ruhr industrial area, in cooperation with the British Second Army.

It sealed off the northern face of the Ruhr and advanced rapidly eastward to join the First United States Army at Lippstadt, Germany, on 1 April, thereby completing, with First Army, the greatest double envelopment in military history. Concurrently with the reduction of the Ruhr area, Ninth Army participated in the advance eastward. Driving 230 miles in 19 days, the Ninth was the first Allied Army to reach and cross the Elbe River. On 12 April, when orders to cease further advance were received, the Army's forward elements held a firm bridgehead across the Elbe and were preparing to advance the last 53 miles to Berlin.

On 9 May, when the war in Europe ended, Ninth Army, carrying out a role of occupation and military government, had under its command 5 corps (the VII, VIII, XIII, XVI, and XIX), 17 infantry divisions (the 9th, 29th, 30th, 35th, 69th, 70th, 75th, 76th, 78th, 79th, 83d, 84th, 87th, 89th, 95th, 102d, and 104th) and 5 armored divisions (the 2d, 3d, 5th, 6th, and 8th), reaching a peak strength of over 650,000 men on 21 May 1945.

In its campaigns in Northern France, the Rhineland, and Central Europe, Ninth Army captured 758,923 enemy prisoners. It liberated nearly 600,000 Allied prisoners of war, and more than 1,250,000 displaced persons. During its relatively short operational life, 8 corps and 37 divisions (including 2 British) came under its command for varying lengths of time.

Ninth Army completed its mission in Europe on 15 June 1945, and returned to the United States where preparations were begun for reembarkation to the Pacific Theater. With the surrender of Japan, plans were halted and the Army was inactivated at Fort Bragg, North Carolina, on 10 October 1945.

TENTH ARMY

Although activated on 20 June 1944, the Tenth Army really had its beginning on 6 June 1944. It was on that day that Lt. Gen. Simon Bolivar Buckner, Jr., then commanding the Alaskan Department, received War Department orders to proceed to Honolulu to organize and command the Tenth Army. After conferences in Washington, General Buckner arrived in Honolulu on 21 June 1944 and set up his headquarters at Schofield Barracks.

Operating directly under the Commander in Chief, Pacific Ocean areas, with administrative support by the Commanding General, United States Army Forces, Pacific Ocean areas, the Tenth Army started planning the operation to seize Formosa. However, late in September a directive was received changing the objective from Formosa to Okinawa and certain other islands in the Ryukyus Group.

The XXIV Corps (7th, 77th, 96th, and 27th Divisions), Maj. Gen. John Hodges, USA, commanding, and III Marine Amphibious Corps (1st and 6th Marine Divisions and one RCT, 2d Marine Division), Maj. Gen. Roy Geiger, USMC, commanding, comprised the Tenth Army's combat elements, which were supported by service troops, Pacific Fleet units, and Army and Marine air units.

The Army commander and staff flew to Guam early in March where they boarded Vice Admiral Kelly Turner's command ship, the *Eldorado*, and sailed to Leyte. There the XXIV Corps was picked up, having been re-equipped after the Leyte campaign.

Following preliminary landings on 26 March at Kerama Retto (to secure sheltered anchorage for fleet elements) and on 31 March at Keise (to secure positions for supporting artillery), the main landings were made on Easter Sunday, 1 April 1945, over the Hagushi beaches (southwestern coast of Okinawa), feint landings having been executed off the southeast coast of the island. While the XXIV Corps was severing the island and pushing southward against increasing opposition, the III Marine Phib Corps explored northern Okinawa. Little opposition was encountered, and by the end of April it was apparent that the bulk of the force would be committed in the south. During this period the 77th Division, having secured Kerama Retto, was reembarked and on 16 April landed on Ie Shima, a small island off northwest Okinawa. After 6 days of severe fighting, this island and its airfield were captured. The 77th Division then prepared to move to Okinawa and join the XXIV Corps which by then had developed the main Japanese positions north of Shuri.

Early in May the III Phib Corps moved southward and took position abreast and on the right of the XXIV Corps. Throughout May and most of June the Tenth Army continued to attack against fanatical enemy resistance from positions which were organized in great depth and included mutually supporting caves in rugged terrain. After the Shuri positions were taken on 31 May, the enemy's defenses deteriorated rapidly; organized resistance ended 21 June, but mop-up continued throughout the remainder of the month.

The Army Commander, Lieutenant General Buckner, was killed by enemy shell-fire on 18 June 1945 while observing a Marine infantry and armor attack. Gen. Joseph W. Stilwell assumed command on 23 June. After Okinawa was captured, the Tenth Army set about occupying the Island and preparing for the invasion of Japan. The war ended before this proposed operation took place, and the Army was inactivated on 10 October 1945.

FIFTEENTH ARMY

The Fifteenth United States Army was activated 21 August 1944 at Fort Sam Houston, Texas, from personnel of headquarters, Headquarters Company, and Special Troops, Fourth United States Army. These officers and men continued to train in various Fourth Army sections.

Col. Louis Compton, Army Artillery officer, was named commanding officer 2 November 1944, and on 3 and 6 November 1944, the headquarters sailed from New York to Scotland and thence to Doddington Hall near Nantwich, Cheshire, England.

Army Headquarters was established at Chateau d'Ardennes, near Dinant, Belgium, 14 December 1944, and on 24 December 1944 moved to Suippes in France. Maj. Gen. Ray E. Porter became Acting Army Commander on 8 January 1945. Lt. Gen. L. T. Gerow assumed command on 16 January 1945.

During the period 15 January 1945 to 31 March 1945, Fifteenth Army rehabilitated, re-equipped, and trained various units of the 12th Army Group that had suffered heavy losses during the Ardennes campaign, processed all units arriving at northern European ports through the staging areas to their 12th Army Group assignments, surveyed and prepared plans for the defense of the Meuse River south of Liege, prepared detailed plans for the organization of headquarters and occupation of the Bremen-Bremerhaven enclave and the Berlin District, and exercised operational control of the 12th Army Group units in the SHAEF reserve. On 31 March 1945, Fifteenth Army assumed command of the 12th Army Group Coastal Sector and the responsibility for containing the enemy forces in Lorient and St. Nazaire, France.

The Lorient forces surrendered 17 May 1945. The formal surrender of the St. Nazaire Pocket took place at 1000 hours 11 May 1945 on the outskirts of Bouvron, France. Concurrent with the Coastal Sector Defenses Mission, Fifteenth Army assumed the defense of the west bank of the Rhine River from Bonn to Homberg on 1 April 1945. The XXII Corps was employed in this sector.

In April 1945, Fifteenth Army progressively occupied, organized, and governed the Rhine Province, Saarland, Pfalz, and that portion of Hesse, west of the Rhine, employing the XXII Corps in the north and the XXIII Corps in the south sector. Additional functions of major importance during this period included the processing of prisoners of war and displaced persons. On 10 June 1945, the XXII Corps area was transferred to British control, and on 10 July 1945, the XXIII Corps area was transferred to French control.

FIRST ALLIED AIRBORNE ARMY

The First Allied Airborne Army was originally established as the Combined Airborne Forces, effective 2 August 1944 (per G.O. No. 81, ETOUSA, dated 10 August 1944), with Lt. Gen. Lewis H. Brereton in command (8 August). Combined Airborne Forces was redesignated First Allied Airborne Army, effective 18 August 1944, and included British and American airborne units.

The mission of the First Allied Airborne Army was to plan and mount such airborne operations as the changing situation on the continent might require, and to control such air and ground forces as might be involved in the execution of those operations until such time as transfer to suitable ground force commanders might be feasible. The commanding general was further given the responsibility of training the component units and maintaining them in readiness.

Headquarters was originally established in Sunninghill Park, near Ascot, England. An advance headquarters, authorized on 12 October 1944, was established at Hotel Royal, Maisons-Laffitte, on the outskirts of Paris. This headquarters was gradually expanded in the fall and winter, and became main headquarters on 20 February 1945. A rear headquarters was maintained at Sunninghill Park until 20 May 1945, when the First Allied Airborne Army was disbanded.

Numerous operations were planned and readied for execution, but the exigencies of war required only a few to be carried out. Operation MARKET was executed 17–26 September 1944, when the First Allied Airborne Army lifted, dropped, and resupplied more than three divisions in an operation involving the seizure of bridges and vantage points at Arnhem, Nijmegen, and Veghel in Holland.

Operational control passed to ground force commanders on 26 September 1944. The next major operation occurred during the Battle of the Bulge, when the First Allied Airborne Army supplied the besieged 101st A/B Division at Bastogne by air and also transported the 17th A/B Division by air from England to the continent, 16–28 December 1944. The next and last operation (Operation

VARSITY) was the dropping of the British 6th A/B and the U.S. 17th A/B Divisions 5 miles due north of Wesel, to seize and hold high ground in the area and to assist in the establishment of a bridgehead across the Rhine, 24 March 1945. Troops passed to ground force control upon landing. Planning for probable future operations continued until 20 May 1945, when the First Allied Airborne Army was disbanded at the direction of SHAEF.

Meanwhile, on 15 May 1945, the Berlin District, U.S. Element was organized by SHAEF, with Lieutenant General Brereton in command (20 May 1945). Headquarters organization of the Berlin District was substantially the same as that of the First Airborne Army (the U S. element in the headquarters of the First Allied Airborne Army, the two organizations existing simultaneously). In the absence of General Brereton, Maj. Gen. Floyd L. Parks assumed command on 22 May 1945, discharging the functions of the office temporarily until 3 June 1945 when he assumed permanent command.

Headquarters of the Berlin District and the First Airborne Army remained at Maisons-Laffite, near Paris, until 1 June 1945, when it opened at Bielefeld. On 24 June 1945, headquarters moved to Halle, and on 2 July 1945, an advance echelon was established in Berlin. On 6 July 1945, the main headquarters of the Berlin District and First Airborne Army opened in Berlin and occupation of the United States Sector of Berlin was officially effected.

The First Airborne Army carried out military occupation duties in the Berlin area. Among other duties, it made preparations for the "Big Three" Conference at Potsdam in July 1945. Maj. Gen. Floyd L. Parks was relieved of command 10 October 1945 and replaced by Maj. Gen. Ray W. Barker, who retained command until 31 December 1945 when the First Airborne Army was inactivated.

Blood was vitally important to the war effort.

Blood drives in the USA collected both whole blood and plasma, which were flown over the Atlantic for use in WTO hospitals.

The round insulated container is the same as used by troops to bring hot food up to the front line.

National Archives.

CORPS IN WORLD WAR II

I CORPS

Activated: 1 October 1940. Overseas: 24 September 1942. Campaigns: East Indies, Papua, New Guinea, Luzon. Commanders: Maj. Gen. Charles F. Thompson (10 October 1940–June 1942), Lt. Gen. Robert L. Eichelberger (June 1942–August 1944), Maj. Gen. Innis P. Swift (August 1944–November 1945).

I ARMORED CORPS

Activated: 15 July 1940. Overseas: The I Armored Corps became part of Task Force A for the North African invasion in November 1942, was reactivated 1 December 1942 and assigned to Fifth Army, and was inactivated in July 1943, after participating in the invasion of Sicily. Commanders: Maj. Gen. Charles L. Scott (April 1941–January 1942), Lt. Gen. George S. Patton, Jr. (January 1942–July 1943).

II CORPS

Activated: 1 August 1940. Overseas: 30 June 1942. Campaigns: Algeria-French Morocco, Tunisia, Sicily, Naples-Foggia, Rome-Arno, North Apennines, Po Valley. Commanders: Maj. Gen. H. Conger Pratt (1 August 1940), Maj. Gen. Lloyd R. Fredendall (14 August 1941), Maj. Gen. Mark W. Clark (1 July 1942), Maj. Gen. Lloyd It. Fredendall (10 October 1942), Maj. Gen. George S. Patton, Jr. (5 March 1943), Maj. Gen. Omar N. Bradley (16 April 1943), Maj. Gen. John P. Lucas (9 September 1943), Maj. Gen. Geoffrey Keyes (18 September 1943–8 September 1945). Inactivated: 10 October 1945 in Europe.

II ARMORED CORPS

Activated: 17 January 1942. Redesignated the XVIII Corps at Presidio of Monterey, Calif., on 10 October 1943. Commanders: Maj. Gen. Alvan C. Gillem, Jr. (January 1942-May 1943), Maj. Gen. W. H. H. Morris, Jr. (May 1943–October 1943).

III CORPS

Activated: 18 December 1940. Overseas: 5 September 1944. Campaigns: Northern France, Rhineland, Ardennes-Alsace, Central Europe. Commanders: Maj. Gen. Walter K. Wilson (18 December 1940–25 July 1941), Maj. Gen. Joseph W. Stilwell (26 July 1941–21 December 1941), Maj. Gen. Walter K. Wilson (22 December 1941–15 April 1942), Maj. Gen. John P. Lucas (16 April 1942–25 May 1943), Maj. Gen. Harold It. Bull (12 June 1943–5 October 1943), Maj. Gen. John Millikin (6 October 1943–16 March 1945), Maj. Gen. James A. Van Fleet (17 March 1945–February 1946), Maj. Gen. Ira T. Wyche (February 1946–May 1946), Maj. Gen. Leland S. Hobbs (May 1946 to inactivation). Returned to U.S.: 30 June 1945, Inactivated: 10 October 1946.

III ARMORED CORPS

Activated: 20 August 1942. Redesignated the XIX Corps, 10 October 1943. Commander: Maj. Gen. Willis D. Crittenberger (September 1942–October 1943).

IV CORPS

Activated: 20 October 1939. Overseas: 7 March 1944. Campaigns: Rome-Arno, North Apennines. Commanders: Maj. Gen. J. L. Benedict, Maj. Gen. Oscar W. Griswold (October 1941–April1943), Maj. Gen. A. M. Patch (April 1943–March 1944), Lt. Gen. Willis D. Crittenberger (March 1944–September 1945). Returned to U. S.: 11 October 1945. Inactivated: 13 October 1945.

IV ARMORED CORPS

Activated: 5 September 1942. Redesignated the XX Corps, 10 October 1943. Commander: Maj. Gen. Walton H. Walker (September 1942–October 1943).

V CORPS

Activated: 20 October 1941. Overseas: 23 January 1942. Campaigns: Normandy, Northern France, Ardennes-Alsace, Rhineland, Central Europe. Commanders: Maj. Gen. Edmund L. Daley (April 1941–May 1942), Maj. Gen. Russell P. Hartle (18 May 1942), Maj. Gen. Leonard T. Gerow (15 July 1943), Maj. Gen. Clarence Huebner (15 January 1945),

VI CORPS

Activated: 3 August 1940. Overseas: 8 February 1943. Campaigns: Naples-Foggia, Anzio, Rome-Arno, Southern France, Rhine-land, Central Europe. Commanders: Maj. Gen. George Grunert (December 1941–March 1942), Maj. Gen. Ernest J. Dawley (April 1942–September 1943), Maj. Gen. John P. Lucas (September 1943–February 1944), Lt. Gen. Lucian K. Truscott, Jr. (February 1944–October 1944), Maj. Gen, Edward H. Brooks (October 1944–May 1945), Maj. Gen. William II. H. Morris, Jr. (June 1945–September 1945), Maj. Gen. Withers A. Burress (September 1945–February 1946), Maj. Gen. Ernest N. Harmon (February 1946–May 1946). Redesignated: 1 May 1946, the US Constabulary.

VII CORPS

Activated: 25 November 1940. Overseas: 9 October 1943. Campaigns: Normandy, Northern France, Rhineland, Ardennes-Alsace, Central Europe. Commanders: Maj. Gen. Robert C. Richardson, Jr. (August 1941–May 1943), Maj. Gen. Roscoe B. Woodruff (May 1943–March 1944), Lt. Gen. J. Lawton Collins (March 1944–August 1945

VIII CORPS

Activated: 14 October 1940. Overseas: 13 December 1943. Campaigns: Normandy, Northern France, Rhineland, Ardennes-Alsace, Central Europe. Commanders: Maj. Gen. George V. Strong (May 1941–April 1942), Maj. Gen. Emil F. Reinhardt (December 1943–March 1944), Maj. Gen. Troy H. Middleton (15 March 1944–19 May 1945), Maj. Gen. Ira T. Wyche (August 1945 to inactivation).

IX CORPS

Activated: 1 June 1940. Overseas: 25 September 1944. Campaigns: The IX Corps did not participate in combat in World War II. Commanders: Maj. Gen. Kenyon A. Joyce (24 October 1940), Maj. Gen. Charles H. White (9 April 1942), Maj. Gen. Emil F. Reinhardt (25 March 1944), Maj. Gen. Charles W. Ryder (2 September 1944 to 20 December 1948),

X CORPS

Activated: 15 May 1942. Overseas: 14 July 1944. Campaigns: New Guinea, Leyte. Commanders: Maj. Gen. Courtney H. Hodges (May 1942–February 1943), Maj. Gen. Jonathan W. Anderson (March 1943–July 1944), Maj. Gen. Franklin L. Sibert (August 1944–November 1945)

XI CORPS

Activated: 15 June 1942. Overseas: 16 March 1944. Campaigns: Luzon, New Guinea, Leyte. Commanders: Maj. Gen. Lloyd R. Fredendall (June 1942–October 1942), Lt. Gen. Charles P. Hall, (October 1942–March 1946).

XII CORPS

Activated: 29 August 1942. Overseas: 10 April 1944. Campaigns: Northern France, Rhineland, Ardennes-Alsace, Central Europe, Commanders: Maj. Gen. William H. Simpson (September 1942–September 1943), Maj. Gen. Gilbert R. Cook (October 1943–August 1944), Maj. Gen. Manton S. Eddy (August 1944–April 1945), Maj. Gen. Stafford LeR. Irwin (April 1945–September 1945).

XIII CORPS

Activated: 7 December 1942. Overseas 15 July 1944. Campaigns: Rhineland, Central Europe. Commanders: Maj. Gen. Emil F. Reinhardt (7 December 1942–November 1943), Maj. Gen. Alvan C. Gillem, Jr. (2 December 1943–August 1945), Brig. Gen. R. P. Shugg (29 August 1945). Returned to U. S.: 9 July 1945. Inactivated: 25 Sept.1945.

XIV CORPS

Activated: 19 December 1942. Overseas: 25 January 1943. Campaigns: Northern Solomons. Commanders: Maj. Gen. Alexander M. Patch (January 1943–April 1943), Maj. Gen. Oscar W. Griswold (April 1943–October 1945), Maj. Gen. Joseph M. Swing (October 1945–December 1945

XV CORPS

Activated: 15 February 1943. Overseas: 14 December 1943. Campaigns: Normandy, Northern France, Rhineland, Central Europe. Commanders: Lt. Gen. Wade II. Haislip (23 February 1943–June 1945), Maj. Gen. Walter M. Robertson (2 June 1945–February 1946).

XVI CORPS

Activated: 23 Nov. 1943. Overseas: 20 September 1944. Campaigns: Rhineland, Central Europe. Commanders: Maj. Gen. John B. Anderson (4 January 1944 to inactivation). Inactivated: 7 December 1945.

XVIII CORPS (AIRBORNE)

Activated: 10 October 1943, by the redesignation of the II Armored Corps. Overseas: 17 August 1944. Campaigns: Rhineland, Ardennes-Alsace, Central Europe. Commanders: Maj. Gen. William H. H. Morris, Jr. (October 1943–July 1944), Maj. Gen. Matthew B. Ridgway (September 1944–August 1945). Returned to U. S.: 11 July 1945. Inactivated: 15 October 1945.

XIX CORPS

Activated: 10 October 1943, by the redesignation of the III Armored Corps. Overseas: 18 January 1944. Campaigns: Rhineland, Normandy, Northern France, Central Europe. Commanders: Maj. Gen. Willis D. Crittenberger (10 October 1943–January 1944), Maj. Gen. Charles H. Corlett (15 March 1944–October 1944), Maj. Gen. Raymond S. McLain (5 October 1944–July 1945). Inactivated: 5 September 1945 in Europe.

XX CORPS

Activated: 10 October 1943, by the redesignation of the IV Armored Corps. Overseas: 11 February 1944. Campaigns: Normandy, Northern France, Rhineland, Central Europe. Commanders: Maj. Gen. Walton H. Walker (October 1943–May 1945), Maj. Gen. Louis A. Craig (21 May 1945–September 1945), Maj. Gen. Horace L. McBride (November 1945 to inactivation). Inactivated: 1 April 1946 in Europe.

XXI CORPS

Activated: 6 December 1943. Overseas: 11 September 1944. Campaigns: Rhineland, Central Europe. Commander: Maj. Gen. Frank W. Milburn (28 December 1943–August 1945). Inactivated: 30 September 1945 in Europe.

XXII CORPS

Activated: 15 January 1944. Overseas: 30 November 1944. Campaigns: Rhineland, Central Europe. Commanders: Maj. Gen. Henry Terrel, Jr. (15 January 1944–November 1944), Maj. Gen. Ernest N. Harmon (29 January 1945 to inactivation).

XXIII CORPS

Activated: 15 January 1944. Overseas: 12 October 1944. Campaigns: The XXIII Corps did not participate in combat in World War II. Commanders: Maj. Gen. Louis A. Craig (January 1944–July 1944), Maj. Gen. James I. Muir (5 September 1944–November 1944), Maj. Gen. James A. Van Fleet (6 February 1945–March 1945), Maj. Gen. Hugh J. Gaffey (23 March 1945–August 1945), Maj. Gen. Frank W. Milburn (August 1945–September 1945), Maj. Gen. Edwin P. Parker, Jr. (September 1945 to inactivation).

XXIV CORPS

Activated: 9 April 1944 in Hawaii. Campaigns: Ryukyus, Southern Philippines, Western Pacific, Leyte. Commander: Lt. Gen. John R. Hodge (9 April 1944–24 August 1948).

XXXVI CORPS

Activated: 10 July 1944. Campaigns: The XXXVI Corps did not participate in combat in World War II. Commanders: Maj. Gen. Jonathan W. Anderson (July 1944–January 1945), Maj. Gen. Charles H. Corlett (January 1945- September 1945).

A tank commander talks to his crew on the intercom while manning his .30 caliber machine gun.

The distinctive leather crash helmet of the armored troops was designed to protect the head, not from shrapnel like the standard steel helmet, but from being banged on the metal hull.

APPENDIX D
MAJOR ARMY COMMANDS
OF WORLD WAR II[1]

Not all the organizations that follow were authorized shoulder sleeve insignia.

EASTERN THEATER OF OPERATIONS

Primary mission: Defense against internal as well as external threats to the territory and installations within the theater. Activated 24 December 1941. Redesignated Eastern Defense Command and placed under control of the War Plans Division, War Department General Staff on 18 March 1942. Continued as Eastern Defense Command.

EASTERN DEFENSE COMMAND

Primary mission: The defense of the eastern United States. Responsible in peacetime for planning all measures against invasion of the area of the command. Should such invasion occur, it was to take charge of operations until otherwise commanded.

Chronology of events: Eastern Theater of Operations became the Eastern Defense Command, 18 March 1942. Separation of two headquarters announced 9 September 1943.

SOUTHERN DEFENSE COMMAND

Primary mission: Responsible in peacetime for planning all measures against invasion of the area of command, and in case of invasion, responsible for operations until otherwise directed by the War Department. Activated 17 March 1941. Command placed under direct jurisdiction of the War Department, 18 March 1942. The Headquarters of the Southern Defense Command and of Third Army operated as a combined headquarters until 25 January 1944, when they were separated. Headquarters activated at San Antonio, Texas. Transferred to Fort Sam Houston, 1 December 1942. Southern Defense Command was abolished 1 January 1945 when Eastern Defense Command assumed command of Southern Defense Command.

CENTRAL DEFENSE COMMAND

Primary mission: Responsible in peacetime for planning all measures against invasion of the area of his command. Should such invasion occur, it was to take charge of operations until otherwise commanded. Activated 17 July 1941. The

Central Defense Command was abolished 15 January 1944, Eastern Defense Command assumed its functions.

WESTERN DEFENSE COMMAND

Primary mission: Responsible in peacetime for planning all measures against invasion of area under command, and in case of invasion of area, responsible for all offensive and defensive operations until otherwise directed by War Department. Established 17 March 1941. Headquarters was combined with Headquarters, Fourth Army, with station at San Francisco, California. Each became a separate headquarters on 12 September 1943. Status of Western Defense Command as a theater of operations authorized 11 December 1941, and was terminated 27 October 1943. Western Defense Command discontinued 1 March 1946.

NORTHWEST SERVICE COMMAND

Primary mission: Operate and maintain the new Alcan Highway, starting from Fort St. John, British Colombia, some 1,600 miles in length. Activated 2 September 1942 at White Horse, Yukon Territory. Headquarters transferred to Edmonton, 18 February 1944.

ALASKA DEFENSE COMMAND

Primary mission: Command all troops in Alaska, cooperate with territorial authorities in organization and training of the National Guard in Alaska, and command the Alaskan Coastal Frontier, prepare defense plans and exercises. Designation of the United States troops stationed in Alaska was announced as Alaska Defense Command 4 February 1941. Assigned to Western Defense Command 12 December 1942. Alaska established as separate theater of operations effective 1 November 1943. Alaska Defense Command separated from Western Defense Command, renamed the Alaskan Department and placed under direct control of War Department 27 October 1943. Prior to establishment of Alaska Defense Command, troops stationed in Alaska were under jurisdiction of the Ninth Corps Area, and called Alaskan Defense Force, Headquarters, Fort Richardson.

ALASKAN DEPARTMENT

Primary mission: Supervision and training of Ground Force Tactical units not assigned to the Alaskan Air Command or the Alaskan Service Base, supervision of ROTC, ORC, and National Guard activities within department, administration of certain administrative activities of personnel, and supervision of administration of all ground and service elements and the air Command, and coordination of projects and special operational requirements. Alaska Defense

Command separated from Western Defense Command, renamed the Alaskan Department and placed under direct control of War Department on 27 October 1943. Alaskan Department redesignated United States Army Alaska, 15 November 1947.

US FORCES IN CENTRAL CANADA

Primary mission: The function of command and the general supervision of administration and supply of all the United States Army Forces activities as well as such security defense functions as are assigned by joint Canadian and United States agreement in Central Canada unless otherwise directed. United States Forces in Central Canada established 10 July 1943 with headquarters at Winnipeg, Manitoba, Canada,. Organized by CO, Western Sector, Crimson Project. Personnel of Headquarters and Headquarters Company, Western Sector, Crimson Project, used in its organization. Redesignated Headquarters, USAF in Central Canada, Winnipeg, Manitoba, dated 13 October 1943. Discontinued 1 October 1945.

UNITED STATES ARMY FORCES, SOUTH ATLANTIC

Primary mission: Secured cooperation with Brazilian Armed Forces and supported logistically the Air Transport Command. United States Army Forces operating in north and northeast Brazil and the islands of Fernando de Noronha and Ascension were designated as USAF, South Atlantic, with headquarters at Recife, Brazil 20 November 1942. Headquarters USAF, South Atlantic, activated 24 November 1942 at Ibura Field, Recife

GENERAL HEADQUARTERS, U. S. ARMY (GHQ)

Primary mission: To "facilitate and speed up the process of mobilization by taking over the direct supervision of the . . . task of organizing and training the field forces within the continental United States." On 3 July 1941, mission was expanded to include the planning and command of military operations. General Headquarters, United States Army, was activated on 26 July 1940. On 9 March 1942, General Headquarters, United States Army was superseded by the Army Ground Forces, which inherited its training functions; planning and operational responsibilities were transferred to other agencies of the War Department.

Remarks: Although the commanding general of GHQ was the Army Chief of Staff, Gen. George C. Marshall, the actual work of directing GHQ fell to the Deputy Chief of Staff, Maj. Gen. (later Lt. Gen.) Lesley J. McNair.

ARMY GROUND FORCES

Primary mission: As stated by the War Department, "to provide ground force units properly organized, trained and equipped for combat operations." The Army Ground Forces was established on 9 March 1942 as the successor to General Headquarters, United States Army.

AIRBORNE COMMAND

Primary mission: To provide properly trained airborne forces for offensive. Activated 23 March 1942 after having been activated as Headquarters, Provisional Parachute Group, at Fort Benning 10 March 1941. Redesignated Airborne Center on 1 March 1944

ANTIAIRCRAFT COMMAND

Primary mission: To instruct and train officers and enlisted men for duty with antiaircraft artillery and barrage balloon units, and to activate, organize, equip, and train efficiently such units for combat service.

Activated 9 March 1942 with Headquarters at Washington, DC. Headquarters moved to Richmond, Va. 23 March 1942 and to Fort Bliss, Tex. 13 October 1944.

AMPHIBIOUS TRAINING COMMAND (CENTER)

Primary mission: To train divisions for combat in a shore-to-shore operation. Activated 20 May 1942 as Amphibious Training Command. Headquarters Fort Edwards, Mass. Moved to Carrabelle, Fla., October 1942. Redesignated Amphibious Training Center on 1 November 1942. Disbanded 10 June 1943.

ARMORED FORCE

Primary mission: Formulation of tactical doctrine for, and the training, organizing, and directing of armored units as high as divisions and corps. Headquarters, Armored Force constituted at Fort Knox, Ky., on 15 July 1940. Assigned to Army Ground Forces 1 June 1942. Armored Force is redesignated Armored Command and is assigned to Army Ground Forces 2 July 1943. Armored Command is redesignated Armored Center 20 February 1944.

DESERT TRAINING CENTER (California-Arizona Maneuver Area)

Primary mission: Training mechanized units to live and fight in the desert, to test and develop suitable equipment, and to develop tactical doctrines, technique, and training methods. Activated 7 April 1942. Headquarters Indio, Calif. Redesignated California-Arizona Maneuver area 20 October 1943. Closed 1 July 1944.

REPLACEMENT AND SCHOOL COMMAND

Primary mission: Supervising the operation of the schools and replacement training centers of the traditional arms. In practice the Replacement and School Command controlled the conduct of training in the schools of these arms, while Army Ground Forces retained direct control of the methods and techniques employed in training and of the preparation of training literature embodying new principles of branch doctrine and special branch techniques. Activated 27 March 1942,

US ARMY FORCES IN THE NORTH AFRICAN THEATER OF OPERATIONS (NATOUSA)

Primary mission: To prepare for, and carry on, military operations in the North African Theater against the Axis Powers, including their allies, under the strategic directives of the combined U. S.-British Chiefs of Staff. Later stated as follows: To prepare, organize, and provide United States Army Forces for military operations in the North African Theater of Operations against the Axis Powers, including their allies, under the direction of the Commander in Chief, Allied Forces, Mediterranean. Established 4 February 1943. Redesignated MTOUSA 1 November 1944. Remarks: NATOUSA lost operational control of subordinate units when Gen. Sir Henry M. Wilson succeeded General Eisenhower as Commander in Chief, Mediterranean Theater, and Lieutenant General Devers replaced General Eisenhower as CG NATOUSA (8 January 1944).

U. S. ARMY FORCES IN THE MEDITERRANEAN THEATER OF OPERATIONS (MTOUSA)

Primary mission: The same as that of NATOUSA until the close of hostilities, at which time MTOUSA's mission became military government and, later, the liquidation and redeployment of United States Army Forces, installations, and activities in accord with the provisions of the Italian Peace Treaty. NATOUSA was redesignated MTOUSA effective 1 November 1944.

NORTH AFRICAN SERVICE COMMAND (NASC)

Primary mission: The supply of United States Army Forces in the Northwest African Area, including support of the activities of the ATC; the processing and redeployment of area troops. NASC was organized effective 1 March 1945 with headquarters at Casablanca. All units and activities assigned or attached to Mediterranean Base Section, hitherto a subordinate command of MTOUSA, were assigned or attached to NASC. Its geographical area included French Morocco, Algeria, Tunisia, and that part of French West Africa north of 20° north latitude. On 1 June 1945 this area was extended to include all of French West Africa, and with the disbandment of the West African Service Command on 1 July 1945, NASC assumed control of all territory formerly within the jurisdiction of NASC.

IRAN-IRAQ SERVICE COMMAND

Primary mission: To expedite the flow of war materials to the USSR. The United States Military Iranian Mission Headquarters, Basra, Iran, was redesignated the Iran-Iraq Service Command effective 24 June 1942. Effective 13 August 1942, the Iran-Iraq Service Command was redesignated the Persian Gulf Service Command.

PERSIAN GULF SERVICE COMMAND (PGSC)

Primary mission: To insure the uninterrupted flow of an expanding volume of supplies to Russia. Effective 13 August 1942 the Iran-Iraq Service Command was redesignated the Persian Gulf Service Command. Headquarters PGSC moved from Basra to Teheran on 3 January 1943.PGSC was relieved of its attachment to USAFIME on 10 December 1943 and became a separate theater directly under the War Department. At the same time it was redesignated the Persian Gulf Command. Another PGSC was activated 1 October 1945 with Headquarters at Khorramshahr, Iran, for the purpose of liquidating United States Army installations and activities in the Persian Gulf area. This command was deactivated 31 December 1945.

PERSIAN GULF COMMAND (PGC)

Primary mission: Same as that of the Persian Gulf Service Command. Effective 10 December 1943 the Persian Gulf Service Command was relieved from assignment to USAFIME, redesignated the Persian Gulf Command, and placed directly under the War Department. On 1 October 1945 the PGC was deactivated and replaced by the Persian Gulf Service Command, an organization directly under the control of Headquarters AMET. Headquarters, PGC was at Tehran, that of the succeeding PGSC at Khorramshahr

U. S. ARMY FORCES IN THE MIDDLE EAST (USAFME)

Primary mission: The support of the Ninth Air Force from the time of its activation under its original designation as the United States Middle East Army Air Force on 28 June 1942 through the time of its departure for the United Kingdom in September and October of the same year. Thereafter, the primary mission of USAFIME became that of support of ATC activities within the Middle East area. The United States North African Military Mission was discontinued 17 June 1942 and USAFIME established in its place. On 15 September 1943, Headquarters USAFIME and Headquarters USAFICA (USAF in Central Africa) were consolidated. Effective 1 March 1945, USAFIME was expanded to include Northwest Africa, and at the same time it was redesignated Africa-Middle East Theater (AMET).

U. S. ARMY FORCES, AFRICA-MIDDLE EAST THEATER (AMET)

Primary mission: Support of the ATC and liquidation and redeployment of United States Army forces and activities in the theater. USAFIME took control of Northwest Africa from MTO USA and was redesignated AMET 1 March 1945.

U. S. ARMY FORCES IN CENTRAL AFRICA (USAFICA)

Primary mission: The construction, operation, and defense of Ferry Command and Air Transport Command installations and activities in Central Africa. Activated 5 July 1942 with Headquarters at Accra. SOS USAFICA activated 14 July 1942. Headquarters USAFICA consolidated with Headquarters USAFIME; SOS USA FICA redesignated West African Service Command and made a subordinate command of USAFIME 15 September 1943.

USAF IN LIBERIA (USAFIL)

Primary mission: To defend all United States facilities and installations in Liberia ; to facilitate air transport and ferrying operations; to execute such missions as may be assigned by the War Department in connection with relations between the United States and Liberian governments, which includes the organization and training of a Liberian Military Force of two or three thousand, and the construction of an access road between Roberts Field and Fisherman Lake; to represent the War Department in all dealings with British or other friendly forces. Task Force 5889 4 March 1942. The Forward Echelon of Force 5889 arrived in Liberia 16 June 1942 and set up headquarters at Roberts Field. The main force arrived 10 days later. USAFIL assigned to USAFIME.

EUROPEAN THEATER OF OPERATIONS, U. S. ARMY (ETOUSA)

Primary mission: To prepare for and carry on military operations in the European Theater against the Axis Powers and their allies, under strategic directives of the combined United States-British Chiefs of Staff which the United States Army Chief of Staff will communicate to the Commanding General. After the establishment of SHAEF in February 1944, ETOUSA relinquished its planning and tactical operational functions to the Supreme Allied Headquarters and became primarily responsible for the administration and supply of United States troops and the mounting of Operation OVERLORD.Established as successor command to USAF in the British Isles (USAFBI) 8 June 1943. Redesignated United States Forces, European Theater (USFET) 1 July 1945. HQ, ETOUSA and HQ. COM Z ETOUSA consolidated 17 January 1944. After the establishment of SHAEF, the United States Component at the Supreme Headquarters tended more and more to assume the functions of a theater headquarters, while ETOUSA at the same time became increasingly a COM Z organization only. ETOUSA's mission after VE-day became primarily one of redeployment. An early version of the insignia had no star at the top.

ICELAND BASE COMMAND (IBC)

Primary mission: In March 1943 the commanding general, IBC was charged with the defense of the territory under his control and the training of units under his command in accord with directives issued by the commanding general, ETOUSA. In addition, he was to comply with whatever special and specific instructions the CG ETOUSA might from time to time direct. Defense and training remained the primary mission of the command after its removal from ETOUSA control. Iceland occupied by United States Forces under General Bonesteel 7 July 1941. This Force remained directly under General Headquarters, Washington until 16 June 1942 when, as the Iceland Base Command, it was placed under the jurisdiction of the CG, ETOUSA for training and operations. IBC was removed from ETOUSA and transferred to the jurisdiction of the Eastern Defense Command on 30 July 1944.

SUPREME HEADQUARTERS, ALLIED EXPEDITIONARY FORCE (SHAEF)

Primary mission: Enter the continent of Europe and, in conjunction with the other United Nations, undertake operations aimed at the heart of Germany and the destruction of her armed forces. Chief of Staff, Supreme Allied Commander (COSSAC), the Allied planning agency was established in April 1943 and formally changed its name to SHAEF on 15 January 1944. General Eisenhower was officially designated Supreme Commander 12 February 1944. SHAEF was officially activated 13 February 1944.

UNITED STATES FORCES, EUROPEAN THEATER (USFET)

Primary mission: Liquidation of United States Army activities and installations and the redeployment of troops; the implementation of an occupation policy in accord with directives from the Joint Chiefs of Staff and the Allied Control Council. ETOUSA was redesignated USFET effective 1 July 1945 with headquarters at Frankfurt. USFET was redesignated European Command (EUCOM) effective 15 March 1947 The commanding general acted in a dual capacity as CG, USFET and military governor of the United States zone of occupation. His deputy in Berlin served as Chief of the Office of Military Government for Germany

HAWAIIAN DEPARTMENT

Primary mission: The mission of the Hawaiian Department was to hold Oahu at all costs against attacks by sea, land, and air forces, and against all hostile sympathizers. The Hawaiian Department was established in 1913. In 1941 the islands of Canton and Christmas were added to its jurisdiction. It was reorganized and expanded several times after Pearl Harbor, in January, July, October, and November, 1942. An Office of Military Governor and a Hawaiian Services of Supply were established. On 14 August 1943, the Department was superseded by the newly activated United States Army Forces, Central Pacific Area, its commanding general becoming the commanding general of the new organizations.

U. S. ARMY FORCES, CENTRAL PACIFIC AREA

Primary mission: The Commanding General, USAF, Central Pacific Area, was responsible for the administration and training of all United States Army ground and air troops within the area, and subject to the direction of the Commander in Chief, Pacific Ocean Areas, in the preparation and execution of plans for the employment of Army forces in the area. On 14 August 1943, the Commanding General of the Hawaiian Department was designated Commanding General of United States Army Forces, Central Pacific Area, and placed in command of all United States Army air and ground troops within the area, subject to the direction of Commander in Chief, Pacific Ocean Areas (Admiral Nimitz) in the preparation and execution of plans for the employment of Army forces in the area. On 1 August 1944, Headquarters United States Army Forces, Central Pacific Area was superseded by Headquarters, United States Army Forces, Pacific Ocean Areas 1 August 1944.

U. S. ARMY FORCES, PACIFIC OCEAN AREAS

Primary mission: The administration, training, and supply of all Army ground and air troops in area. Preparation and execution of plans for employment of Army forces in area was subject to Commander in Chief, Pacific Ocean Areas (Admiral Nimitz). United States Army Forces, Pacific Ocean Areas was established 1 August 1944, superseding United States Army Forces in the Central Pacific Area and incorporating in addition all Army forces assigned to the South Pacific Area. On 6 April 1945, Gen. Douglas MacArthur was designated the Commander in Chief of United States Army Forces in the Pacific and incorporated in his command all Army forces in the Pacific Ocean Areas; United States Army Forces, Pacific Ocean Areas thereupon became a subordinate command. On 1 July 1945 it was redesignated United States Army Forces, Middle Pacific, the commanding general retaining command of the Hawaiian Department and the Headquarters, United States Army Forces, Pacific Ocean Areas.

U. S. ARMY FORCES IN THE PACIFIC (AFPAC)

Primary mission: The Commander in Chief of AFPAC was responsible for the provision of Army resources required for such operations in the Pacific as the Joint Chiefs of Staff might direct and was responsible for the conduct of land campaigns in the area. Operations included the conclusion of the campaign in the Philippine Islands and preparations for the invasion of Japan. United States Army Forces in the Pacific was established 6 April 1945, under command of General of the Army Douglas MacArthur, and absorbed forces assigned to United States Army Forces in the Far East and United States Army Forces in the Pacific Ocean Areas. General Headquarters was established in Manila, remaining there until 25 March 1946, when it was transferred to Tokyo.

U. S. ARMY FORCES, MIDDLE PACIFIC

Primary mission: The training, administration, and supply of Army ground and air forces within area, with administrative responsibility to the commanding general of the United States Army Forces, Pacific (General MacArthur), and with logistic responsibility to United States Army Forces, Middle Pacific, was established 1 July 1945 and included all United States Army Forces and establishments assigned to or under the control of the United States Army Forces, Pacific Ocean Areas and the Hawaiian Department, those forces being transferred to the newly established United States Army Forces, Middle Pacific.

SOUTHWEST PACIFIC AREA

Primary mission: Defense of certain strategic bases in Australia; support of friendly operations in the Pacific Ocean area and Indian theater; and preparation for taking the offensive, with the objective of recapturing the Philippines, and other objectives. General Headquarters, Southwest Pacific Area, with Gen. Douglas MacArthur commanding was established 18 April 1942 at Melbourne, Australia. It was a result of an "agreement among the Governments of Australia, the United Kingdom, the Netherlands, and the United States." Simultaneously, the following subordinate units were placed directly under GHQ, SWPA: Allied Land Forces, Southwest Pacific Area (under Gen. Sir Thomas Blamey, Australian Army); Allied Air Forces, Southwest Pacific Area (Under Lt. Gen. George H. Brett, USA); Allied Naval Forces, Southwest Pacific Area (under Vice Adm. Herbert F. Leary, USN); United States Forces in the Philippines (under Lt. Gen. Jonathan M. Wainwright, USA); and United States Army Forces in Australia (under Maj. Gen. Julian F. Barnes, USA). On 4 June 1945, all officers and enlisted men attached to GHQ, SWPA were assigned or attached to GHQ, United States Army Forces, Pacific. On 2 September 1945 the Southwest Pacific Area was abolished, territory south of the Philippines being transferred to British Empire control. At the same time, the Allied Land Forces, Allied Air Forces, and Allied Naval Forces were also abolished, all British troops reverting to control of the British Empire.

U. S. ARMY FORCES IN THE FAR EAST (USAFFE)

Primary mission: United States Army Forces in the Far East was charged with the command of United States troops in the Philippine Department, the mobilization of the Philippine Army, and the defense of the Philippine Islands. United States Army Forces in the Far East was activated 26 July 1941, and included United States troops in the Philippine Department as well as the Philippine Army which was at the same time called into service. Units of the Philippine Army were mobilized and the following defense forces organized: North Luzon Force, South Luzon Force, Visayan-Mindanao Force, Philippine Coast Artillery Command, and USAFFE Reserve.

These defense forces were defeated by the Japanese, in their attack on the Philippines. United States Army Forces in the Far East was "deconstituted" 21 March 1942, and superseded by United States Forces in the Philippines (USFIP). United States Army Forces in the Philippines ceased to exist on 9 June 1942, when the Japanese told General Wainwright that "your high command ceases and you are now a prisoner of war."

USF, INDIA-BURMA THEATER

Primary mission: To support the China Theater in carrying out its mission. This includes the establishment, maintenance, operation, and security of the land line of communication to China, and the security of the air route to China. Responsibility "for the logistic and administrative support of all United States Army Forces in the India-Burma Theater."

The United States Forces, India-Burma Theater, was established 24 October 1944. Created by dividing the USAF, CBI into two separate theaters—the China Theater and the India-Burma Theater. Headquarters located at New Delhi.

USAF, CHINA-BURMA-INDIA

Primary mission: Increase the effectiveness of United States assistance to the Chinese Government for the prosecution of the war and to assist in improving the combat efficiency of the Chinese Army. On 27 May 1944 the mission became "the conduct of such military operations in China as would most effectively support an effort directed against enemy forces in the Pacific" and the exploitation of the development of overland communications to China.

Activated as American Army Forces in China-Burma-India with headquarters at Chungking, China, 4 March 1942. All American troops on Asiatic mainland designated USAF, CBI 15 March 1942. Headquarters at New Delhi named Headquarters USAF, CBI and echelon at Chungking became Forward Echelon, USAF, CBI 1 April 1944. CBI Theater divided into India-Burma Theater and China Theater, 24 October 1944.

U. S. FORCES, CHINA THEATER

Primary mission: With respect to Chinese troops, to "advise and assist the Generalissimo in the conduct of military operations against the Japanese." With respect to American troops, to "carry out air operations from China" and to "continue to assist the Chinese air and ground forces in operations, training and logistical support." Established on 24 October 1944. Headquarters at Chungking, China. Headquarters, USF, CT moved to Shanghai 14 October 1945.

FOOTNOTE

1) This appendix is adapted from the Army Almanac, 1947

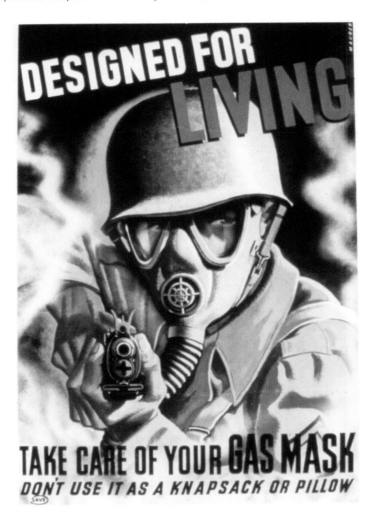

APPENDIX E

THE ARMY AIR FORCE
IN WORLD WAR II

The widespread appeal of military aircraft means that there is a staggering array of books available on aircraft and various aviation units from World War II. This section is only designed to provide a brief overview of the Army Air Forces (AAF) to get you started.

American Military Aviation began as a section in the Signal Corps. The only use for aircraft was seen in delivering messages. In 1918 the small group of aviators became the "Air Service." In 1926 it was enlarged to become the Air Corps, similar to the Corps of Engineers or the Quartermaster Corps. In 1941 it was renamed the Army Air Forces and was finally made a major component of the Army, alongside the Army Ground Forces and the Army Service Forces.

Although technically still a part of the Army, the AAF was unique in a number of ways. Most of the non-aviation units assigned to the AAF (Military Police, Engineer, Quartermaster, etc.) were nearly identical to similar units in the ground forces. Pay, rank, and insignia were almost identical to the rest of the Army, with the exception of the actual aviation units.

In the AAF, men who flew in the aircraft were known as air crew. Pilots, co-pilots, navigators and bombardiers were considered jobs for commissioned officers, whereas all other air crew positions (gunners, radiomen, aerial engineers) were held by enlisted men.

Every aircraft had its own ground crew to maintain it. Each ground crew was supervised by a Crew Chief. The Crew Chiefs were in turn supervised by a Line Chief. Once in the air any mechanical problems that arose were handled by the flight (or aerial) engineer. These men had to be able to perform repairs not only while in flight, but also perform any needed repairs if the aircraft had to make an emergency landing not on its own airbase.

Flying was considered very hazardous duty so men who were regularly assigned to fly qualified for flight pay. This was a 50% increase in their pay over the base amount.

Organizations of the AAF

The combat elements of the AAF are broken up into the numbered Air Forces (1st through 15th and 20th). Unlike an Army division, which had a fairly rigid organization, Air Force units were flexible in nature and elements could be changed as needed. In Europe, for example, the 8th Air Force was heavier in bombers, while the 9th Air Force contained more fighter units.

Other major organizations of the AAF were known as commands. These were:

- Training Command – trained all pilots and flight crew

- Troop Carrier Command – transported paratroopers and glider troops

- Air Transport Command – transported aircraft, personnel, mail, and supplies

- Material Command – developed and purchased aircraft

- Air Service Command – oversaw maintenance and supply of aircraft

- Proving Ground Command – tested and studied aircraft capabilities

Each aircraft had its own crew. This could range from one man (in a fighter) to 10 men in B-17 bomber. Two or more aircraft were known as a flight. A flight is generally two to four aircraft and this changed as needed. The smallest standard unit is a squadron. Squadrons have an administrative as well as aviation component. They vary in size and organization depending upon the type of unit (fighter, bomber, troop carrier, night fighter, etc.). Tables of organization were published for each different type of squadron.

As examples, a heavy bomber squadron (B-17 or B-24) would have 12 aircraft, a medium bomber squadron (B-25 or B-26) 16 aircraft, and a single engine fighter squadron (P-47 or P-51) 25 aircraft. Squadrons are a soldier's home in the Air Force. They usually had their own insignia, and unit histories are frequently written about a specific squadron.

Two to four squadrons were formed into a group. A group was simply a headquarters unit with no aircraft that coordinated the actions of its squadrons, much like a brigade in the ground forces. When all squadrons of a group are based at the same location, the maintenance and support personnel could be pooled to support all aircraft of the group, not just their own squadron.

Two or more groups constituted a wing. The wing was another headquarters unit but concerned primarily with planning and executing operations. It does not handle administrative tasks. Two or more wings constituted a command. Commands generally had additional support units assigned to them such as Military Police, Signal, Engineer, or Ordnance.

In the event that the wings were very large, due to a larger number of squadrons in each group, they could be placed under an intermediate command group called an Air Division. The largest self contained unit was composed of three or more wings and called a numbered Air Force.

The AAF structure was always considered flexible, and any size unit, such as a squadron, could be attached directly to any larger sized command unit. A squadron could report directly to an Air Force instead of having a chain of command reaching down through wing to group to squadron.

Aviation Cadets

The Air Force wanted only the best men for its pilots, and used the Aviation Cadet program to select them. Anyone (civilian or military) wanting to be a pilot, bombardier, or navigator had to pass a number of tests to become an Aviation Cadet. Those who failed the program served as enlisted men wherever needed in the Army. Those who passed were commissioned and put on flight status. The supply of trained pilots grew large enough so that this program was closed down in March 1944 and anyone in it sent back to the Army.

Air Cadet uniforms changed a few times during the war. The most common was an enlisted man's uniform with officer's lapel insignia, and a round 3" blue (or black) shoulder patch with yellow winged propeller. They also wore the officer's service cap with a blue band around it, and a large metal winged propeller in place of the standard eagle cap insignia.

AAF Insignia

The most important insignia to the Air Force are those that indicate the man had been trained in a flight specialty. Commonly called "flight wings" these are silver or gold badges worn on the left breast. Many of the different categories have three grades: regular (indicated by the basic wing), Senior (an advanced classification indicated by a star above the wing), and Command (a more advanced classification indicated by a star with a wreath around it above the wing).

Standard pilot's wings were authorized for every man who graduated from pilot school. No distinction was made for the type of aircraft he was to fly (fighter,

Pilot

Senior Pilot

Command Pilot

bomber, transport, etc.). The addition of a star at the top of the wing made it a Senior Pilot Wing, which was authorized after the man had five years of service and had logged 1500 hours of flight time.

After a man had ten years service and had logged 2000 hours he qualified for a Command Pilot Wing (with a wreath around the star). The AAF was quite small before the war, so very few senior and Command Pilot's Wings would have been authorized during wartime.

Service Pilot

A service pilot was a man who had enough civilian flight experience that he could be used for non-combat flight jobs. Generally these were men too old to pass through the standard AAf training program, but were able to handle tasks such as ferrying planes from the factory to air bases, flying cargo, or acting as a flight instructor.

After five years of service and 1500 flying hours, service pilots qualified for senior Service Pilot wings which added a star to the top of their wings.

Liaison Pilot

Liaison pilots flew the small, lightweight aircraft used for artillery spotting or transportation near the front lines. Training was shorter and less rigorous than for a standard pilot, and many sergeants qualified for this wing.

Aircraft Observer

Sometimes referred to as a combat observer, these were men trained as a pilot or navigator, had served on a combat crew, and who were used to observe and comment upon how operations were handled so as to develop better methods.

Navigator

Navigators were highly trained in finding the location of a plane in flight and directing its course. This took a great deal of math skills, and was always an officer.

Navigator wings were awarded upon completion of the aerial navigation school.

Bombardier Wings

There was a great deal of training and skill involved in plotting the exact location to drop bombs from a high altitude and have them strike a particular target. For this reason bombardiers were officers, and were awarded these wings upon completion of the bombardier school.

Technical Observer

Technical Observers were trained pilots who were used to observe various aspects of aircraft used by the AAF and to suggest ways to improve performance.. Their observations were passed on to improve technical specifications of the aircraft, tactics of the units, or equipment used in flight.

Flight Engineer

The flight engineer wing was not authorized until June 1945. Flight engineers were the chief mechanic for the aircraft once it left the runway. They had to be able to fix problems in mid-air, or get it fixed after an emergency landing. These men wore air crew wings before this insignia was authorized.

Flight Surgeon

The AAF had its own medical specialists trained in aviation medicine. These were M.D.s with training on how flight affected the human body. These wings were awarded after a year of military service and 50 hours of flight time. In September 1944 the color of these wings was changed form gold to silver.

Aerial Gunner

These are similar to bombardier wings, but with the addition of a small set of wing on the central bullet to differentiate them. Aerial gunners had to pass a six-week course. These wings were first authorized in April 1943, and discontinued in 1949.

Aircrew Member Wings

This was for all regularly assigned members of an aircrew (including gunners) not otherwise authorized flight wings. This meant generally gunners and radiomen. Men were permitted to wear the insignia when not on flight status if they had 150 hours flying time as flight crew, had participated on 10 combat missions as flight crew, or were physically incapacitated during a flight before meeting the above requirements.

Army Air Forces Technicians Badge

Enlisted technicians and mechanics were authorized to wear this badge, indicating graduation from a course and at least six months service in the AAF. There were 24 specialties which were indicated by a hanging bar. These ranged from radio operator to bombsight mechanic.

Glider pilots

The men who flew unpowered gliders in airborne landings were normally given six months of training. The first two months were commando-like training to help them survive on the battlefield. Then they had a month of glider maintenance work, a month of flying powered aircraft, and two final months of unpowered glider training. The best candidates were then commissioned as 2d lieutenants, and the rest made flight officers. They were frequently in short supply and men could also qualify if they had three hours flight time and ten landings. Thus it is not uncommon to find Staff Sergeants qualified as glider pilots.

In the ETO some, but not all, aircraft crewmen started to wear a blue-colored rectangular backing behind their wing. This was to show that they were, in fact, permanently assigned to aircrew status and had not just pinned on the wing for a night on the town.

There were five yellow-on-blue specialist sleeve patches worn by AAF enlisted men who were considered technical specialists. These insignia are blue triangles with yellow designs that indicate Armament, Photography, Engineering, Communications, and Weather.

Women in the AAF

There were a number of jobs for women in the AAF. The Woman's Army Corps provided a large number of women to serve as mechanics, technicians, draftsmen and all types of non-flying tasks. Roughly 1,200 women who knew how to fly were used in the WASP program (Woman's Air Service Pilot).They flew all types of non-combat missions, but were primarily used to shuttle aircraft around the country.

WASP wings

One of the most effective ways of saving wounded men was by quickly transporting them by air to a hospital. To take care of casualties being moved via air, a special category of nurse was developed. Flight Nurses were specially trained to keep patients stable while being flown to hospital. Nurses from the Army Nurse Corps were selected for special training, and once qualified were eligible to wear Flight Nurse Wings on their uniform.

Flight Nurse Wings

Nurses that had served 6 months in an AAF hospital and taken an eight week course in aviation medicine qualified as flight nurses. They staffed aircraft that transported casualties from the front back to hospitals in rear areas. The color of this wing was changed from gold to silver in September 1944.

Records

AAF records are similar to that of the ground forces. The majority can be found at the National Archives. Pilots kept a logbook of their flights, but those were normally retained by the men when they left the service. Although there are no records of what specific vehicles were assigned to which unit, the AAF did keep track of which aircraft went to what squadron. When dealing with aircraft questions it is important to get in touch with any association or enthusiast group that deals with the specific type of aircraft or unit. In many cases they have scoured records to produce some amazing databases of information.

Unit histories, report orders and all manner of wartime documents are held by the Air Force Historical Research Agency at Maxwell Air Force Base in Alabama. They will generally provide summaries of information at no cost, but will copy items like the entries of a squadron diary for a specific month for a fee. They also sell copies of group and unit histories on microfilm for $30 per roll. Their address is AFHRA/RSA, 600 Chennault Circle, Maxwell AFB, Alabama 36112-6424.

BOOKS

A good overview on the AAF is *Winged Victory*, by Geoffrey Perret.

An excellent wartime book on the AAF, although hard to find, is *The Official Guide to the Army Air Forces*, by the AAF Aid Society.

For information on AAF uniforms and insignia: *Silver Wings, Pinks and Greens*, by Jon Maquire.

Websites

Air Force Historical Research Agency
www.au.af.mil/au/afhra/

www.armyairforces.com has lots of information on AAF units, airbases, aircraft, AAF reunions, etc.

www.pro5.com/mia/ Is a must for anyone related to an Air Force MIA.

AIR FORCE HISTORIES

FIRST AIR FORCE

Activated at Mitchell Field, New York, 18 December 1940 as the Northeast Air District. Redesignated the 1st Air Force, 9 April 1941. Redesignated the First Air Force, 18 September 1942

With the outbreak of World War II, the primary mission of the First Air Force became the defense of the Atlantic Seaboard, an area including many of the most populous and highly industrialized centers of the country, as well as an important ocean zone. From December 1941 until organization of the AAF Antisubmarine Command in October 1942, it also engaged in extensive anti-submarine operations. Although active in dispatching combat units to overseas theaters, the First Air Force was not free to devote its chief efforts to training until September 1943, when it was relieved from assignment to the Eastern Defense Command. Nevertheless, in the period 1942–44, 350 combat units were activated, trained, or staged at First Air Force installations.

SECOND AIR FORCE

Activated at McChord Field, Washington, 18 December 1940, as the Northwest Air District. Redesignated the 2d Air Force, 9 April 1941. Redesignated the Second Air Force, 18 September 1942. Inactivated 31 March 1946

At the outset of World War II, the Second Air Force, functioning as a part of the Western Defense Command, was engaged in west coast defense. Within a few weeks, however, its primary responsibility was redefined as the carrying out of a training mission. In the three and a half years preceding VE-day, this air force sent 14,000 heavy-bomber crews to Europe, principally to the Eighth and Fifteenth Air Forces. At the same time, it not only trained numerous fighter units and bomber and fighter replacements for other overseas assignments but also was engaged in development of the B-29 program. With the defeat of Germany, its major effort was directed to the training of Superfortress crews for service in the Pacific.

THIRD AIR FORCE

Activated at MacDill Field. Tampa. Florida, 18 December 1940 as the Southeast Air District. Redesignated the 3d Air Force, 9 April 1941. Redesignated the Third Air Force, 18 September 1942.

Between late December 1941 and mid-August 1942, the Third Air Force flew more than 1,000 antisubmarine-patrol sorties over the Atlantic Ocean and the Gulf of Mexico. In addition, it bore responsibility for defense of the Gulf coast and stood ready to lend support to the First Air Force as long as the Eastern United States was in danger of attack. These duties, however, were secondary to its mission as a training unit. In the course of World War II, the operations of this air force, spreading far beyond the original boundaries of its territory, were conducted from bases in more than a dozen states. By early 1945, it had trained a total of 85,377 officers and enlisted men, including 29,021 pilots, 3,987 bombardiers, 9,057 navigators, 774 flight engineers, 407 bombardier-navigators, 4,532 radar observers, 7,247 flexible gunners, 99 photo gunners, 10,000 armorer gunners, 9,844 mechanic gunners, 8,342 radio operator-mechanic gunners, 774 radio operator-mechanics, 774 remote control gunners, and 519 electrical mechanic gunners.

FOURTH AIR FORCE

Activated at March Field, California, 18 December 1940 as the Southwest Air District. Redesignated the 4th Air Force, 9 April 1941. Redesignated the Fourth Air Force, 18 September 1942.

During the early years of World War II, the Fourth Air Force, as an air component of the Western Defense Command, was responsible for coastal defense of the western United States. In this connection, it flew patrols and directed antiaircraft and aircraft warning services. Decreasing emphasis on its defense mission after relief from assignment to this command in September 1943 enabled the Fourth Air Force to concentrate upon training. Soon, at more than 20 bases scattered over five states, it was preparing heavy-bomber crews, twin-engine fighter-pilot replacements, Engineer Aviation Battalions, and Signal Warning units for overseas combat, and in addition, was furnishing instruction in night-fighter aircraft and the use of radar. Toward the end of the war, the Fourth Air Force also participated in the B-29 program by cooperating with Twentieth Air Force organizations in the training of lead crews.

FIFTH AIR FORCE

Activated at Nichols Field, Philippine Islands, 20 September 1941 as the Philippine Department Air Force. Redesignated the Far East Air Force, 16 November 1941. Units absorbed into the 5th Air Force, activated 3 September 1942. Redesignated the Fifth Air Force, 18 September 1942.

Operating against the Japanese in the Southwest Pacific, the Fifth Air Force made a total of 415,979 sorties, dropped 232,496 tons of bombs, claimed 6,298 enemy planes destroyed, and lost 2,494 aircraft due to enemy action. Its combat experiences included: delaying operations in the Philippines and Netherlands East Indies; defensive action in Australia; battle of the Coral Sea; Papuan offensive, with transport of 15,000 troops across the Owen Stanley Mountains and subsequent supply by air; attack upon Bismarck Sea convoy and targets in the Bismarck Archipelago; New Guinea campaign; supporting action in the Palau Islands operation and the invasion of the Halmaheras; bombing of Celebes and Ceram areas and the Balikpapan oil center in Borneo; reduction of the Philippines; neutralization of Formosa; strikes against the China coast; and finally attacks upon Kyushu, flown from bases in Okinawa. Present station: Nagoya, Honshu, Japan.

SIXTH AIR FORCE (Caribbean Air Command)

Activated at Albrook Field, Canal Zone, 20 November 1940, as the Panama Canal Air Force. Redesignated the Caribbean Air Force, 5 August 1941. Redesignated the 6th Air Force, 5 February 1942. Re-designated the Sixth Air Force, 18 September 1942.

Defense of the Panama Canal against attack from the air was the primary responsibility of the Sixth Air Force in World War II. Continuing patrols begun by its predecessors months before the time of Pearl Harbor, the Sixth flew thousands of operational hours in keeping watch over the Isthmus of Panama and the vast expanses of water and jungle that constitute approaches to the canal. In operations coordinated with those of the AAF Antisubmarine Command and the Antilles Air Command, it participated in antisubmarine search and attack missions during the critical period of the U-boat menace in the Caribbean. Its units engaged in numerous reconnaissance and photographic sorties in connection with establishment of new bases in Central and South America, and gave protection to the southern air transport route. Before the end of 1942, the Sixth Air Force also undertook a program of training, designed originally to meet its own needs only. As danger to the Canal became less acute, this work was gradually expanded to include operational training for crews destined to serve in other theaters.

SEVENTH AIR FORCE (Pacific Air Command)

Activated at Fort Shafter, Hawaii, 1 November 1940 as the Hawaiian Air Force. Redesignated the 7th Air Force, 5 February 1942. Redesignated the Seventh Air Force, 18 September 1942. Redesignated the Pacific Air Command, 15 December 1947.

Operating against the Japanese in the Central Pacific, the Seventh Air Force made a total of 59,101 sorties, dropped 32,733 tons of bombs, claimed the destruction of 794 enemy airplanes, and lost 378 aircraft due to enemy action. Its combat experience included participation in the Battle of Midway, Guadalcanal campaign, offensive against the Gilbert and Marshall Islands, attacks upon Truk, Woleai, and other objectives in the Caroline Group, and neutralization of Wake Island. Although having little part in preliminary operations against the Marianas, Seventh Air Force fighters and bombers moved to Saipan soon after capture of the island, providing air defense, support for ground operations, and cover for the invasion of Guam and Tinian. Seventh Air Force units also mined anchorages in the Bonins, operated from the Palau Islands against targets in the Philippines, and from Iwo Jima, after its capitulation, escorted B-29's on missions to the Japanese homeland. Shortly after the invasion of Okinawa, Seventh Air Force units moved in to assist ground forces in overcoming Japanese resistance and they participated in tactical isolation of the island of Kyushu.

EIGHTH AIR FORCE

Activated at Savannah, Georgia, 28 January 1942.

The Eighth Air Force was the daylight precision-bombing force in a combined Anglo-American air assault against Germany. In successive phases of the offensive begun in 1942, its objectives were submarine yards and pens, aircraft industries, transportation, oil plants, and other critical war industries. Although predominantly strategic in character, the Eighth Air Force repeatedly employed its striking power to attack tactical targets in operations coordinated with ground armies, such as advances in Normandy after D-day and the Battle of the Bulge. In addition, it engaged in a large number of special missions—leaflet-dropping, supply of partisan groups, and repatriation of displaced persons and prisoners of war. At peak strength, the Eighth Air Force included 40-1/2 heavy bombardment, 15 fighter, and 2 photo reconnaissance groups—an organization capable of dispatching in a single mission (Christmas Eve 1944) more than 2,000 heavy bombers and almost 1,000 fighters, carrying 21,000 men. It claimed the destruction of 20,419 enemy aircraft and, on its 1,034,052 flights (332,904 by heavy bombers), consumed a total of 1,155,412,000 gallons of gasoline. Transferred to the Pacific in the summer of 1945, the Eighth Air Force established headquarters on Okinawa but had little opportunity to engage in combat before VJ-day.

NINTH AIR FORCE

Activated at Bowman Field, Kentucky, 2 September 1941, as the 5th Air Support Command Redesignated the 9th Air Force, 8 April 1942 Redesignated the Ninth Air Force, 18 September 1942. Established in the Middle East, 12 November 1942. (From 28 June to 12 November 1942 the U. S. Army Middle East Air Force operated in the area as a kind of advance echelon.) Inactivated, 2 December 1945, in the ETO.

Arriving in the Middle East when Rommel's armies stood at El Alamein, the Ninth Air Force and its predecessor, the United States Army Middle East Air Force, concentrated on disruption of enemy supply lines in the eastern Mediterranean and cooperated with the British Eighth Army in driving Axis forces across North Africa. As the campaign moved westward, its heavy bomber attack was extended to targets in Tunisia, Italy, and Sicily.

Reorganized in the United Kingdom on 16 October 1943 as the tactical arm of the United States Army Air Forces in the ETO, the Ninth Air Force engaged in the pre-invasion air offensive, took part in D-day, and crossed to France soon thereafter. Following close on the heels of the enemy, it operated from five different countries in less than a year. In addition to its primary mission of furnishing tactical support for United States armies in the theater, the Ninth participated with the Eighth Air Force in the strategic bombing program, providing escort and bombing when suitable targets were available.

By VE-day, the Ninth Air Force had made 659,513 sorties, dropped 582,701 tons of bombs, claimed destruction of 9,497 enemy aircraft, and lost 6,731 planes to enemy action.

TENTH AIR FORCE

Activated as 10th Air Force at Patterson Field, Ohio, 12 February 1942. Redesignated the Tenth Air Force, 18 September 1942.

In the China-Burma-India Theater, the Tenth Air Force had, as its primary function, defense of the ferry route over the Hump. From the Kunming terminal, its China Air Task Force struck at enemy installations, port facilities, and shipping in the China Sea, while its India Air Task Force guarded the Indian end and insured neutralization of airfields at Myitkyina and other places in northern Burma. Although duties of the China Air Task Force were assumed by. the Fourteenth Air Force in March 1943, the Tenth continued to operate from bases in Assam, disrupting enemy lines of communications, flying sweeps over the Bay of Bengal, and mining harbors at Rangoon, Bangkok, and Moulmein.

Later, as components of the Eastern Air Command (15 December 1943–1 June 1945), Tenth Air Force units participated in all important phases of the Burma campaign, furnishing airborne support to General Wingate's forces, dropping supplies to Merrill's Marauders, and facilitating General Stilwell's reconquest of North Burma. By April 1945, some 350.000 men were wholly dependent upon air supply by these units. In August 1945, the Tenth moved to China, anticipating an offensive against Japan proper.

ELEVENTH AIR FORCE (Alaskan Air Command)

Activated at Elmendorf Field, Alaska, 15 January 1942, as the Alaskan Air Force. Re-designated the 11th Air Force, 5 February 1942. Redesignated the Eleventh Air Force, 18 September 1942.

When carrier-based planes of a Japanese task force struck at Dutch Harbor on 3 June 1942, aircraft of the Eleventh Air Force, from well-concealed bases in an advanced area, participated in operations that resulted in the enemy's withdrawal to Kiska and Attu. During the next 14 months, whenever weather permitted, units of the Eleventh bombed Japanese installations in the outer Aleutians first from Umnak then from Adak, and finally from Amchitka. In addition, they ran search missions, struck at shipping, engaged in photographic reconnaissance, and kept patrols in the air. Before the close of the Aleutian campaign (24 August 1943), elements of the Eleventh Air Force began to fly offensive sweeps against the Kuriles. These missions later gave way to more direct attacks, in which airfields, canneries, staging areas, the Kataoka Naval Base, and shipping in Paramushiru Strait were the principal targets. On occasion, the Eleventh provided cover for naval vessels shelling the Kuriles and, through its aircraft concentrating on high-altitude photographic reconnaissance, obtained the first pictures of Japan's northern defenses. The Eleventh Air Force made 7,318 sorties, dropped 4,331 tons of bombs, claimed destruction of 113 enemy aircraft, and lost 88 planes to enemy action.

TWELFTH AIR FORCE

Activated at Bolling Field, Washington, DC, 20 August 1942. Inactivated in the MTO, 31 August 1945.

On 8 November 1942, when Allied landings were made in French Morocco and Algeria, elements of the Twelfth Air Force participated in the initial operations and secured bases newly won. Operating, after February 1943, within the framework of the Northwest African Air Forces, and later under direction of the Mediterranean Allied Air Forces, the Twelfth took an active part in the Tunisian campaign, bore the brunt of the attack upon Pantelleria, and flew hundreds of missions contributing to the capitulation of Sicily. Its units assisted in securing the beachheads at Salerno, Anzio, and Nettuno, and gave tactical assistance to the Fifth Army in its advance through Italy. In connection with the Allied landing in Southern France, aircraft of the Twelfth Air Force carried out preliminary bombings, provided cover on D-day, and facilitated the northward progress of Allied forces. In the final assault upon northern Italy, its units played a substantial part in immobilizing German lines of communications. Also, out of the XII Bomber Command came the Fifteenth Air Force. The Twelfth Air Force made 430,681 sorties, dropped 217,156 tons of bombs, claimed destruction of 3,565 enemy aircraft, and lost 2.843 planes to enemy action.

THIRTEENTH AIR FORCE

Activated at Noumea, New Caledonia, 13 January 1943. The Thirteenth Air Force provided air defense for Guadalcanal, struck at enemy shipping, and bombed airfields in the Middle Solomons. After capture of Munda, New Georgia, its attacks swung northward, culminating in the landing on Bougainville in Empress Augusta Bay.

With the Fifth Air Force, it participated in the air offensive against New

Ireland and Rabaul, New Britain. In support of landings at Hollandia and Aitape, New Guinea, it neutralized Woleai by a series of bombings and struck at the Caro-lines again in connection with the Central Pacific push against the Marianas. Its aircraft attacked defenses on Biak and Noemfoor prior to invasion, hammered at enemy airfields in western New Guinea and the Halmaheras in support of Morotai operations, and bombed the oil refining center at Balikpapan, Borneo.

After participation in the Philippine campaign, the Thirteenth extended its striking power to distant targets in Java, Malaya, Indo-China, and the China coast. By VJ-day, some units had begun movement to Okinawa in preparation for an assault upon Japan. In all, the Thirteenth Air Force made 93,726 sorties, dropped 65,318 tons of bombs, claimed destruction of 1,395 enemy aircraft, and lost 645 planes to enemy action.

FOURTEENTH AIR FORCE

Activated at Kunming, China, 10 March 1943.

In March 1943, the Fourteenth Air Force replaced the China Air Task Force, which had continued the work of the Flying Tigers after disbandment of the American Volunteer Group in July 1942.

Pursuing against the Japanese a policy of attrition similar to that of its predecessors, the Fourteenth whittled away at the enemy's air force, interdicted lines of communications, and ferreted out troop concentrations. From Hengyang, its units struck at Hankow, Canton, and traffic on inland waterways; from Kweilin, they swept the coast of the South China Sea and mined shipping lanes; from Yunnanyl, they protected the eastern end of the Hump route and bombed military targets near the Burmese towns of Myitkyina, Bhamo, Lashio, and Katha.

To Chinese armies, the Fourteenth gave tactical support and furnished air supply—especially during the Japanese drive toward Hsian, Ankang, and Chihkiang in the spring of 1945. In the Chengtu area, it gave protection to forward bases of B-29's then stationed in India; it also engaged in night reconnaissance, and flew diversionary missions coordinated with the invasion of Luzon and the landings on Okinawa.

FIFTEENTH AIR FORCE

Activated at Tunis, Tunisia, 1 November 1943. Inactivated 15 September 1945 in the MTO.

Composed initially of heavy-bombardment groups of the XII Bomber Command, the Fifteenth Air Force was established in the Mediterranean Theater of Operations to complete the strategic encirclement of Germany and her satellites. In attacks coordinated with Eighth Air Force missions, its units, operating from Foggia and bases farther south, attacked enemy airfields, hammered at aircraft factories in the Wiener-Neustadt and Regensburg areas, bombed oil refineries at Ploesti, Blechhammer, distant Ruhland, and Vienna, and struck tank, armament, and munition plants at Linz, Pilsen, Budapest, Prague, and Munich.

Overshadowed but never obscured by this effort was the Fifteenth's campaign against enemy lines of communications. Not only were marshalling yards, bridges, and tunnels hit, but whenever the Italian ground situation demanded, more direct tactical support was given, as in the Rome-Arno operation and the stalemate at Cassino.

In connection with the Allied landing in Southern France, the Fifteenth participated in pre-invasion bombings and provided cover on D-day. Its units carried supplies to partisans in the Balkans and rescued large numbers of air crews shot down in enemy territory.

The Fifteenth Air Force flew 242,377 sorties, dropped 309,278 tons of bombs, destroyed 6,258 enemy aircraft, and lost 3,410 planes to enemy action.

TWENTIETH AIR FORCE

Activated 4 April 1944, at Washington, DC.

The Twentieth Air Force, equipped with Superfortresses, had as its principal function the carrying of war to the Japanese homeland. This program was inaugurated on 15 June 1944, when India-based B-29's of the XX Bomber Command, staged through forward areas in China, bombed steel works at Yawata.

Attacks upon aircraft factories, oil refineries, ordnance plants, and other critical industries followed until late March 1945, when these groups were transferred to the Marianas. Here units of the XXI Bomber Command, stationed on Saipan, Tinian, and Guam, had hammered at Japanese targets since 24 November 1944, when they made the first B-29 attack upon Tokyo. During the last five months of the war, the Twentieth Air Force mined Japanese home waters, initiated incendiary raids, and on 6 and 9 August dropped two atomic bombs, on Hiroshima and Nagasaki.

In addition, the Twentieth Air Force lent support in the Burma campaign, facilitated invasion of Okinawa by bombing airfields on Kyushu, and, after VJ-day, dropped food and medical supplies to Allied prisoners of war in Japan.

In all, it flew 38,808 sorties, dropped 171,060 tons of bombs, claimed destruction of 1,225 enemy aircraft, and lost 494 planes to enemy action.

It took a lot of manpower to keep aircraft in top condition.

Here an Army Air Force ground crew works on the engine of a C-47, the backbone of air transportation in World War II.

They were used for dropping paratroops, transporting wounded men, as well as for hauling supplies.

Author's Collection

APPENDIX F

VEHICLE MARKINGS IN WORLD WAR II

One of the best ways of identifying someone's unit is by the bumper markings found in a photograph of a vehicle. These were, by regulation, to appear on every official vehicle according to a standard set of rules. If you have a photo that shows the front or back of an Army vehicle you may be able to determine what unit—down to company level—that vehicle was in. This does not necessarily mean it was the unit of your soldier, since he may have been taking a photo of a friend from a different unit, or been using trucks from another group.

Every vehicle used by the US Army was to be marked with white stars identifying it as American. Early experience in the Mediterranean showed that the white star could, from a distance, be mistaken for the white outlines of the black cross used on all German vehicles. To prevent further misidentifications a white circle was added to the national star.

Every Army vehicle had a registration number painted on both sides of the hood (or similar front area) that identified the specific vehicle. In the early days of the war this was done in a light blue colored paint, but was soon changed to white paint. There are no records to allow these numbers to be traced to a unit. The numbers were applied by the manufacturer upon delivery to the Army and no records exist for which vehicle went where. An "S" suffix to this number indicates the vehicle had been equipped with electrical noise suppression equipment to allow a radio to be operated from it.

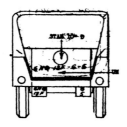

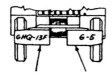

The unit bumper markings were applied by the unit itself in gasoline based paint so that, when necessary for security reasons, they could be wiped off with a gasoline soaked rag.

These numbers appear in a series of four groups that indicate (from right to left) the number of the vehicle in the company, the company, the unit the company is part of (generally a regiment or battalion), and the parent organization.

The official unit designations for the first group of numbers (see caption to illustration on previous page):

Infantry Division—Arabic numeral of the division
Armored Division—Arabic numeral followed by a triangle
Cavalry Division—Arabic numeral followed by the letter C
Corps—The Corps Roman numeral
Army—Arabic numeral followed by the letter A
Air Force—Arabic numeral followed by a star
Zone of Communications—ZC
Army Ground Forces—AGF
Zone of Communications—COMZ
Services of Supply—SOS
General Headquarters—GHQ
Zone of the interior—ZI
Reception Center—RC
Replacement Training Center—RTC preceded by arm or service (i.e. IRTC means Infantry Replacement Training Center).
Training Center—TC
Firing Center—FC
All others—abbreviations in letters that do not conflict with the others.

The second group to the left hand side designates the parent organization: brigade, regiment, battalion, etc. If the second group is the letter "X" it means the vehicle belongs to the headquarters company of the 1st number group. Thus VII-X would indicate a vehicle from the headquarters of the VIIth Corps. The second group is generally a Regiment or Battalion.

Official unit types for the second letter group:

Airborne—AB
AAF units—star 3 inches high
Antiaircraft—AA
Amphibious—AB
Armored Regiment—A half-inch-long dash followed by a triangle 3 inches high
Cavalry—C
Chemical Warfare Service—G
Coast Artillery Corps—CA
Corps of Engineers—E
Field Artillery—F
Infantry—A half inch long dash followed by the letter I
Medical Department—M
Military Police—P
Ordnance Department—A half inch long dash followed by the Letter O
Quartermaster Corps—Q
Signal Corps—S
Tank Destroyer—TD
Tank Group—TG

The third group designates the company the vehicle belongs to. If it was a traditional lettered company (such as company A, or company L) that letter is used. HQ is used for a headquarters or headquarters company of the unit in the

2d group. In the rare occasion the unit is small enough that the company was described in the 2d group then the third group uses the letter "X."

Official unit types for the third letter group:

Company letter
Antitank—AT
Cannon—CN
Maintenance—MT

Reconnaissance—R
Service Company—SV
Train—TN
Weapons—W

The fourth group is the number of the vehicle in the company's normal order of march. There is nothing important about this number. Some units had no vehicles; others had quite a few. It all depended upon the table of organization for that type of company.

Examples are shown in the following chart:

MARKING	1ST GROUP	2d GROUP	3d GROUP	4th GROUP
1 X HQ 10	1st Infantry Division	(part of 1st group HQ)	Headquarters Company	10th vehicle
1 33F D 2	1st Infantry Division	33d field artillery.	Battery D	2d vehicle
29 116-I B 1	29th Infantry Division	116th Infantry Regiment	Company B	1st vehicle
IV X 44P 4	IVth Corps	(part of 1st group HQ)	44th Military Police Company	4th vehicle
3A 61Q A 5	Third Army	61st Quartermaster Bn.	Company A	5th vehicle
1Δ 1Δ A 1	1st Armored Division	1st Armored Regiment	Company A	1st vehicle
2Δ 67Δ C 3	2d Armored Division	67th Armored Reg.	Company C	3d vehicle
☆ 862Q MT 10	AAF	862d Quartermaster	Maintenance Company	10th vehicle
☆ 850E A 2	AAF	850th Engineer BN.	Company A	2d vehicle
COMZ 523Q C 4	Zone of Comm.	523d Quartermaster Bn	Company C	4th Vehicle

The first two groups (the left hand side of the bumper markings) were frequently removed so that the enemy could not easily identify the unit. The company and vehicle number were left visible as there were so many companies with similar letters or codes that no useful information could be extracted from it.

Some, but not all, vehicles had a white star painted in the center of the bumper. This should not be confused with the star used as part of the markings indicating an air force unit.

The right hand soldier in this photo has on a shoulder patch, but it is not clear enough to see what unit it is.

The left hand jeep has bumper markings for the 24th Infantry Division, 34th Infantry Regiment. Checking the information on the 24th Division, the 34th Infantry was part of it during World War II. The 24th served in the Pacific, which matches the men wearing the warm weather cotton khaki uniforms.

The right hand jeep is marked as vehicle number 13 in Company M. Just enough of the letter M can be seen on the other jeep to determine that these men are from Company M, the heavy weapons company, of the 3d Battalion, 34th Infantry Regiment. Author's Collection.

At some point in the war a curious method of encoding the left hand unit information was developed so that the soldiers could easily identify the vehicles of their company, but no one could identify unit information higher than the company. This seems to have been mainly used during invasions, and primarily in Normandy.

These are today known as bar codes because they used color bars to make each company easily identifiable. A 5-digit unit serial number was assigned to every company. No master list of these serial numbers has ever been found. The last three digits of the number indicated the company, and these were painted on the bumper in bars, or stripes, that corresponded to specific numbers. Thus a soldier would know that "blue/red/blue" was his company and everything painted with that marking may belong to his unit. A closer look at the 5-digit number would confirm if it was his company or another. These colored bar codes appear not just on vehicle bumpers but on all manner of equipment and cases.

The system is still not well understood, although it appears it was also used to identify equipment or personal baggage being sent home after VE day, possibly by units preparing to redeploy to the Pacific.

According to Army regulations, units could also adopt a tactical marking to identify their unit in a combat area. Not every unit had a tactical marking, and some changed over time. Most are only simple white designs. The 70th Tank Bn. however had an elaborate colored version of the turtle (known as "Joe Peckerwood") that was their unit mascot. Few records of tactical markings were

This photo of a truck in Europe has the unit marking cut out by a censor (the white area).

The left hand side of the bumper has a three-stripe bar code which is not helpful in identifying the unit.

The right hand side reads "S55." As vehicle number 55 it should be with a unit with a number of vehicles. Since "SV" stands for Service Company, S must mean a signal company.

Another photo from the same batch showed the man with an 83d Infantry Division patch, which makes it likely he was in the 83d Infantry Division Signal Company (which according to the T/O had more than 55 vehicles). It's a slightly odd vehicle, and checking the truck type it appears to be what was known as a small arms repair truck, which the signal corps used as a repair truck. The T/O lists two of these trucks in each infantry division signal company.

Not proof of his unit, but a good start for more research.

Author's Collection

This lieutenant (note the rank insignia on his helmet) proudly points to the jeep's name, *Angele.*

Normally a name starting with the letter "A" is a good clue the vehicle was assigned to Company A; however in this case the photo gives the impression he has named it after a wife or girlfriend and is sending her a photo to show his devotion.

Author's collection

made and no one has done a good study of them. Unless you are able to locate a document identifying them, they can only be used to identify which vehicles were part of the same unit

A form of unofficial naming was done to vehicles by giving them a nickname. These were most often tough sounding military names (like Kraut Killer) or women's names. The only pattern to these nicknames is that some, but not all, units relied on a system of choosing vehicle names that started with the letter of their company. Company C vehicles could then be called Cindy, Colleen, or Candy Wagon. Possibly more common was that drivers named their vehicles after a girlfriend of wife.

The unit markings on this jeep are obscured in the left hand photo. The white number 2036832-S is the vehicle registration number and does not provide any information on location or unit (other than the "S" means the vehicle has the radio noise suppressors in place). The metal strut at the front of the jeep is designed to cut wires stretched across the road, and is normally only seen in the ETO. The soldier wears a CIB indicating he is an infantryman. It is rare to see photos of men with decorations in the field until after the war had ended.

In the second photo the bumper is clear, but the left hand unit designation has been obscured by what appears to be a tactical marking (circle in a rectangle). These markings were done on a unit basis and almost no records exist of them. The photo does tell us that he was in Company F, and he is probably the driver of this jeep (vehicle number one).

Author's collection

This jeep is clearly marked 102 406-I HQ-23, making it vehicle 23 of Headquarters Company, 406th Infantry Regiment, of the 102d Infantry Division.

The upright metal bar on the bumper is a wire cutter almost exclusively found on vehicles overseas, and rarely in the USA.

Author's collection

Above: Some of the vehicles found in an armored division are shown: (L-R) motorcycles, the amphibious jeep (the "seep"), 1/4 ton truck (the "jeep," or "peep"), M3 halftrack, and the M5 light tank ("Stuart"). The bumper markings indicate these are from various elements of the 13th Armored Division

Below: From (L-R) the M4 Medium Tank ("Sherman"), the M8 assault gun, the M3 halftrack, and a 3/4 ton truck with 37mm antitank gun facing to the rear.

The 1/4 ton truck, commonly known as the jeep had many different uses. Here, in Italy, it serves as a radio vehicle.

The left hand unit bumper markings were blacked out by the censor. The chains on the tires are for traction in the slippery mud.

National Archives.

APPENDIX G

CAMPAIGNS OF WORLD WAR II

In earlier wars it was easy to divide the fighting up into specific battles. Both sides maneuvered for position, then came together for a fight which had a specific beginning and end. Combat in World War II, however, was a constant day to day effort, with one major clash slowly becoming another and so the Army decided to credit men and units not for specific battles but for campaigns.

Each campaign covered a specific geographic area and time frame, and the pages which follow give details of each of the officially accredited campaigns of the war.

AMERICAN THEATER: 7 December 1941 to 2 March 1946.

Antisubmarine, American Theater: 7 December 1941 to 2 September 1945. To protect Allied shipping from enemy submarines, The AAF flew many antisubmarine patrols in the American Theater during World War II. Perhaps the most important of these operations were conducted from bases in Newfoundland and along the east coast of the United States.

By the fall of 1942 these patrols, in conjunction with naval operations, had succeeded in driving off the German U-boat packs that had been taking such a heavy toll on shipping in the western Atlantic. In addition, AAF flew patrols in the Gulf of Mexico, in the Caribbean Sea, and along the west coast of the United States. In the latter part of 1943 the Navy assumed the antisubmarine responsibilities.

EUROPEAN–AFRICAN–MIDDLE EASTERN THEATER: 7 December 1941 to 8 November 1945.

Egypt-Libya: 11 June 1942 to 12 February 1943. Answering a British appeal for assistance against Axis forces that were on the offensive in Libya, additional men and equipment were sent into the area. In the Middle East, some American air units helped to stop Rommel's drive toward the Suez Canal, took part in the Battle of El Alamein (25 October–5 November 1942), and worked with Montgomery's Eighth Army in driving Axis forces westward into Tunisia.

Algeria-French Morocco: 8 to 11 November 1942. Three days after their victory at El Alamein, the Allies opened a new front with an assault on Algeria and French Morocco. Some units came ashore from the invasion fleet, and some paratroops arrived from England. The campaign was brief, for the French in Algeria and French Morocco offered little resistance to the Allies.

Tunisia: 12 November 1942 to 13 May 1943. Having gained Algeria, the Allies quickly turned eastward, hoping to take Tunis and Bizerte before the Germans could send reinforcements into Tunisia. But the drive broke down short of the goal. In February 1943, after Rommel had been driven into Tunisia, the Axis took the offensive and pushed through the Kasserine Pass before being stopped. The Allies drove the enemy back into a pocket around Bizerte and Tunis, where Axis forces surrendered in May. Thus Tunisia became available for launching an attack on Sicily as a preliminary to an assault on Italy.

Sicily: 14 May to 17 August 1943. The invasion of Sicily got underway on the night of 9/10 July with airborne landings that were followed the next day by an amphibious assault. The enemy offered strong resistance, but Montgomery's Eighth Army and Patton's Seventh Army pushed them back. By 17 August 1943 the Allies were in possession of the island, but they had not been able to prevent a German evacuation across the Strait of Messina.

Naples-Foggia: 18 August 1943 to 21 January 1944. Montgomery crossed the Strait of Messina on 3 September 1943 and started northward. Five days later Eisenhower announced that the Italian government had surrendered. Fifth Army, under Clark, landed at Salerno on 9 September and managed to stay despite furious counterattacks. By 18 September the Germans were withdrawing northward. On 27 October Fifth Army took Naples. As the Allies pushed up the Italian peninsula, the enemy slowed the advance and brought it to a halt at the Gustav Line.

Anzio: 22 January to 24 May 1944. On 22 January, in conjunction with a frontal assault, the Allies attempted to turn the Gustav Line by landing troops behind it on the beach at Anzio. But the frontal attack failed, and the Allies were unable to break out of the beachhead at Anzio until the Gustav Line was breached in May 1944.

Rome-Arno: 22 January to 9 September 1944. The unsuccessful attempt to break the Gustav Line on 22 January was followed by another unsuccessful effort in March when the infantry failed to push through the line at Monte Cassino. The Germans could not repulse a new drive launched by the Allies in May and resistance crumbled. By 4 June 1944 the Allies had taken Rome. But the advance ground to a halt against a new defensive line the enemy established along the Arno River.

Southern France: 15 August to 14 September 1944. While the Germans were retreating in Italy in the summer of 1944, the Allies diverted some of their strength in the theater to the invasion of Southern France. After preliminary bombardment, a combined seaborne-airborne force landed on the French Riviera on 15 August. Marseilles having been taken, Seventh Army advanced up the Rhone Valley and by mid-September was in touch with Allied forces that had entered France from the north.

North Apennines: 10 September 1944 to 4 April 1945. In Italy during the fall and winter of 1944–1945 the Allied ground forces beat against the Gothic Line north of the Arno. Although little progress was made on the ground, the action in the Apennines tied down a large German army at a time when those troops could have been used in decisive campaigns being directed against Germany by the Allies in the west and the Russians in the east.

Po Valley: 5 April to 8 May 1945. After an Allied attack the Germans were unable to make a stand and were driven from their defensive positions south of the Po River. Allied forces crossed the river on 25 April, and on 4 May, at the Italian end of the Brenner Pass, Fifth Army met the Seventh, which had driven into Germany and turned southward into Austria. With the joining of these forces the war in Italy was over.

Air Offensive, Europe: 4 July 1942 to 5 June 1944. At the time the AAF entered combat in the Middle East in June 1942, the Eighth Air Force was moving to England for operations against Germany. Operations with heavy bombers began on 17 August 1942. In 1943 the Eighth gradually increased the intensity of its operations, attacking factories, shipyards, transportation, airfields, and other targets on the continent. Bomber formations frequently sustained heavy losses, but they were reduced after long-range escort became available. In the aerial offensive Eighth Air Force was joined by the Ninth, which was transferred from the Mediterranean to England in October 1943 to provide tactical air power, and by the Fifteenth, which operated heavy bombers from Italy.

Normandy: 6 June to 24 July 1944. Early on D-Day, airborne troops landed in France to gain control of strategic areas. Then the invasion fleet landed Eisenhower's assault forces. Soon the beachhead was secure, but its expansion was a slow and difficult process in the face of strong opposition. It was not until late in July that the Allies were able to break out of Normandy.

Northern France: 25 July to 14 September 1944. Bombardment along a five-mile stretch of the German line enabled the Allies to break through on 25 July. While some armored forces drove southward into Brittany, others fanned out to the east and, overcoming a desperate counterattack at Mortain, executed a pincers movement that trapped many Germans in a pocket at Falaise. The enemy fell back on the Siegfried Line, and by mid-September 1944 nearly all of France had been liberated.

Rhineland: 15 September 1944 to 21 March 1945. Attempting to outflank the Siegfried Line, the Allies tried an airborne attack on Holland on 17 September 1944. But the operation failed, and the enemy was able to strengthen his defensive line from Holland to Switzerland. Little progress was made on the ground. Then, having regained the initiative after defeating a German offensive in the Ardennes in December 1944, the Allies drove through to the Rhine, establishing a bridgehead across the river at Remagen.

Ardennes-Alsace: 16 December 1944 to 25 January 1945. During their offensive in the Ardennes the Germans drove into Belgium and Luxembourg, creating a great bulge in the line. The fighting was fierce and the weather bad, but by the end of January 1945 the lost ground had been regained and the Battle of the Bulge, the last great German offensive, was over.

Central Europe: 22 March to 11 May 1945. Following the Battle of the Bulge the Allies had pushed through to the Rhine. On 22 March 1945 they began their assault across the river, and by 1 April the Ruhr was encircled. Armored columns raced across Germany and into Austria and Czechoslovakia. On 25 April, American and Russian forces met on the Elbe. Germany surrendered on 7 May 1945 and operations officially came to an end the following day, although sporadic actions continued until 11 May.

Air Combat, EAME Theater: 7 December 1941 to 11 May 1945. Some of the AAF's aerial operations in the EAME Theater—such as those in the Balkans (including the raids on Ploesti), over the Mediterranean Sea, and in Iceland—were outside the areas of the campaigns listed above. A special campaign, Air Combat, EAME Theater, was established to provide campaign credits for these operations. (Provision was made for similar campaigns for the other theaters, but no aerial combat occurred in the American Theater, and no credits were awarded by the War Department for Air Combat, Asiatic-Pacific Theater.

Antisubmarine, EAME Theater: 7 December 1941 to 2 September 1945. AAF antisubmarine operations began from England in November 1942 and from North Africa in March 1943. The most successful of these operations were carried out in the Bay of Biscay in the summer of 1943, and in the Mediterranean during the campaigns in Sicily and southern Italy. AAF units received credit for this campaign if they were engaged in antisubmarine warfare outside of the regularly designated campaign areas of the EAME Theater.

ASIATIC-PACIFIC THEATER: 7 December 1941 to 2 March 1946.

Philippine Islands: 7 December 1941 to 10 May 1942. A few hours after the raid on Pearl Harbor on 7 December 1941, Japanese aircraft attacked the Philippines. Three days later, Japanese troops landed on Luzon. Unable to obtain reinforcements and supplies, MacArthur could do nothing more than fight a delaying action. The fighting ended, at Bataan and Corregidor, with the loss of the Philippines in May 1942.

East Indies: 1 January to 22 July 1942. While engaged in the conquest of the Philippines, the Japanese thrust southward, landing troops in Sumatra, Borneo, Celebes, and elsewhere in the East Indies. Defeated in the Battle of the Java Sea at the end of February 1942, the Allies lost Java. Then the Japanese put forces into New Guinea and the Solomons, on the road to Australia. But their attempt to take Port Moresby early in May was thwarted when the Japanese were checked by American naval forces in the Battle of the Coral Sea.

Papua: 23 July 1942 to 23 January 1943. In another effort to take Port Moresby the Japanese landed troops at Buna, Gona, and Sanananda in July 1942. At first the Allies could offer only feeble resistance to the enemy forces that pushed southward through Papua, but the Allies were building up their strength in Australia. By mid-September the Japanese drive had been stopped. The Allies then began to push the enemy back, with Buna taken on 2 January 1943, and enemy resistance at Sanananda ended three weeks later.

Guadalcanal: 7 August 1942 to 21 February 1943. The seizure of Guadalcanal in June 1942 marked the high tide of the Japanese advance in the Southwest Pacific. U.S. Marines landed on the island on 7 August and quickly took Henderson Field, which was needed in order to gain control of the air. The Japanese made several attempts to retake the field, and they repeatedly bombed the base to curtail Allied aerial activity. The contest, which became one of reinforcement and supply, was decided when Japanese troop transports that were heading for the island were destroyed by American ships and planes in November, but the Japanese held out on Guadalcanal until the following February.

Northern Solomons: 22 February 1943 to 21 November 1944. After the conquest of Guadalcanal, Halsey's forces began a campaign to capture Japanese strongholds in the Northern Solomons. In February 1943 American forces landed in the Russell Islands to obtain an air strip. American troops landed on Rendova and on New Georgia at the end of June. Munda was taken in August. Landings were made in the Treasury Islands in October. Allied air power struck the great Japanese naval and air bases at Rabaul on New Britain to support the assault on Bougainville, which began on 1 November 1943. Enemy garrisons on Bougainville were contained, and other Japanese forces in the Northern Solomons were isolated.

Bismarck Archipelago: 15 December 1943 to 27 November 1944. To isolate and neutralize Rabaul on New Britain and the Japanese base at Kavieng on New Ireland, American forces landed at Arawe and Cape Gloucester in December 1943, on Green and Los Negros Islands in February 1944, and at Talasea on New Britain and on Manus Island in March. Some other enemy forces in the Bismarck Archipelago were bypassed.

New Guinea: 24 January 1943 to 31 December 1944. After the loss of Buna and Gona in New Guinea, the Japanese fell back on their stronghold at Lae. Their attempt to reinforce Lae by sea in March 1943 met with disaster when Allied aircraft sank most of the convoy in the Battle of the Bismarck Sea. Salamaua and Lae then became the objectives for an Allied advance along the northern coast of New Guinea. The Allies dropped paratroops at Nadzab, just beyond Lae. Enemy resistance at Salamaua broke on 14 September 1943; Lae fell two days later. After taking Hollandia in April 1944, the Allies attacked islands off the northern coast of New Guinea, taking Wakde and Biak in May, Owi in June, and Noemfoor in July. Sansapor on New Guinea also was gained in July. Morotai was seized in October to provide air bases for the invasion of the Philippines.

Leyte: 17 October 1944 to 1 July 1945. On 17 October 1944 the invasion of the Philippines got under way with the seizure of islands guarding Leyte Gulf. The landing on Leyte itself on 20 October was strongly contested by Japanese forces on land and at sea. Organized resistance on the island did not end until after Christmas, and mopping up operations continued for a long time. Meanwhile, at the end of October, the neighboring island of Samar was occupied with little difficulty.

Luzon: 15 December 1944 to 4 July 1945. After Leyte came Mindoro, which was invaded on 15 December 1944. American troops landed on the shores of Lingayen Gulf on 9 January 1945 and pushed to Manila, which the Japanese defended vigorously until 24 February. Rather than meet the Americans in a decisive battle, the Japanese decided to fight delaying actions in numerous places. Organized resistance ended in southern Luzon in April and in central and northern Luzon in June.

Southern Philippines: 27 February to 4 July 1945. After Luzon had been invaded and Manila taken, a series of landings were made in the southern Philippines, on Palawan, Mindanao, Panay, Cebu, Negros, and other islands. In some places the Japanese offered little resistance; in others they held out for considerable time. The liberation of the Philippines was announced by MacArthur on 5 July 1945.

Central Pacific: 7 December 1941 to 6 December 1943. The war in the Central Pacific began with the Japanese attack on Pearl Harbor on 7 December 1941. Not until 20 November 1943 were landings made in the Gilberts and on Makin. The Marine landing at Tarawa was one of the bloodiest battles of the war.

Eastern Mandates: 7 December 1943 to 16 April 1944. After the operations in the Gilberts, American air and naval forces bombed and shelled Japanese bases in the Marshall Islands. In February 1944 American troops went ashore on Kwajalein, Roi, Namur, and Eniwetok. Other islands, including Jaluit and Wotje in the Marshalls and Truk in the Carolines, were bombed and shelled but were bypassed.

Western Pacific: 17 April 1944 to 2 September 1945. The American troops that landed on Saipan on 15 June 1944 met bitter opposition; but after a desperate Japanese counterattack on 7 July, organized resistance soon terminated. Tinian, invaded on 25 July, was won by 1 August. Guam, which had been seized by the

Japanese on 10 December 1941, was invaded on 20 July and regained after 20 days of fighting. With the conquest of the Marianas, the United States gained valuable bases for an aerial offensive against Japan itself. To provide bases for operations against the Philippines, the Palaus were invaded in mid-September.

Ryukyus: 26 March to 2 July 1945. Some small islands close to the southern tip of Okinawa were seized on 26–27 March 1945, and the invasion of Okinawa itself began on 1 April. Only light resistance was encountered in the northwestern part of the island, where the American troops landed. Japanese pilots, however, made suicidal (kamikaze) attacks on the invasion fleet. Savage opposition was met ashore as the troops moved southwest to clear the island. The campaign was costly, but it gave the United States a position from which it could use medium bombers and fighter aircraft to attack the Japanese home islands.

Air Offensive, Japan: 17 April 1942 to 2 September 1945. The aerial offensive against the Japanese home islands began in April 1942 with the Doolittle raid, in which the B-25's of a special task force were launched from a carrier. The strength of the offensive increased rapidly after B-29's of the Twentieth Air Force began operating from the Marianas late in 1944. To destroy Japanese shipping, the very heavy bombers sowed mines in the waters around Japan. The offensive, increasing in intensity and effectiveness, reached its climax with the dropping of atomic bombs on Hiroshima (6 August 1945) and Nagasaki (9 August 1945).

Burma, 1942: 7 December 1941 to 26 May 1942. While some Japanese forces were conquering the Philippines, the East Indies, and islands of the South Pacific, others were penetrating Burma from Thailand. Moving rapidly, they controlled southern Burma by the end of January 1942, took Rangoon in March, and cut the Burma Road in April. Pushing on, the enemy forced the British westward into India and drove Stillwell's Chinese forces back into China. By the end of May the Japanese had taken all of Burma.

India-Burma: 2 April 1942 to 28 January 1945. By 2 April 1942, Singapore, the Malay Peninsula, Sumatra, and Thailand, as well as most of Burma, were under Japanese domination. For a long time afterward the only counterblows were provided by the small air forces the Allies had in the area, and by Wingate's Raiders operating behind the enemy's lines. In the spring of 1944, while Anglo-Indian troops were resisting a Japanese invasion of the Imphal plain, Chinese troops and Merrill's Marauders in northern Burma started an offensive that captured the key town of Myitkyina in August and opened the Burma Road the following January.

Central Burma: 29 January to 15 July 1945. Having repulsed the Japanese invasion of India, Anglo-Indian troops took the offensive. They crossed the Irrawaddy River in February 1945, took Mandalay in March, and recaptured Rangoon on 4 May, by which time the Japanese were virtually beaten in Burma.

China Defensive: 4 July 1942 to 4 May 1945. The American Volunteer Group (Flying Tigers) under General Chennault helped to defend China until 4 July 1942, when regular AAF units (formed into the Fourteenth Air Force in March 1943) took over the task. Support for Chiang Kai-shek's armies was limited because of the lack of supplies, which had to be transported by air over the Hump route from India. A strong Japanese offensive along the Hankow railway in 1944 resulted in the loss of important air bases in southeastern China. By December 1944 the Japanese columns driving southward had met others that were moving up from Indochina.

China Offensive: 5 May to 2 September 1945. In the spring of 1945 the Chinese began an offensive in southern China. Some of the bases lost the previous year were retaken, and the Allies were in a better position to support the Chinese as they recovered the territory lost to the Japanese during 1944.

Aleutian Islands: 3 June 1942 to 24 August 1943. On 3–4 June 1942, at the time of the Battle of Midway, a Japanese force attacked Dutch Harbor and inflicted considerable damage before it was driven off. The Japanese then occupied Attu and Kiska. The United States troops that landed on Attu on 11 May 1943 had possession of the island by the end of the month. The troops that invaded Kiska on 15 August 1943 discovered that the Japanese, under the cover of fog, had secretly evacuated their garrison.

Note: In the Asiatic-Pacific Theater the theater commander had authority to award campaign credits to units that were engaged in combat in the Northern Solomons, Bismarck Archipelago, New Guinea, Luzon, Southern Philippines, Eastern Mandates, Western Pacific, and Ryukyus after the closing dates shown above for those campaigns.[1]

FOOTNOTE

1) Campaign descriptions adapted from *Air Force Combat Units of World War II*

APPENDIX H

OFFICIAL ABBREVIATIONS USED IN WORLD WAR II

absent without leave	AWOL	automatic	auto
acting	actg	aviation	avn
active duty	AD		
additional	add	Bakery	bkry
adjutant	adj	balloon	bln
adjutant general	AG	barracks	bks
administrative	adm	battalion	bn
air base.	AB	battery	btry
Airborne Command	A/B Com	bombardier	bmbdr
Air Corps	AC	bombardment	bomb
aircraft warning (company)	AW (Co)	bugler	bglr
Aircraft Warning Service	AWS	by direction of the President	DP
air intelligence section	A Int Sec		
airplane	ap	caliber	cal
airship	ash	camouflage	cam
Air Transport Command	ATC	captain	capt
allotment	almt	casual	cas
allotted	alot	Cavalry	Cav
allowances	alws	certificate	cert
American Expeditionary Forces	AEF	certificate of disability for discharge	CDD
American Red Cross	ARC	chaplain	Ch
ammunition	am	character	char
Amphibious Command	Amph Comd	chauffeur	cfr
antiaircraft	AA	chemical	cml
antiaircraft artillery	AAA	Chemical Warfare Service	CWS
appointed	aptd	chief warrant officer	CWO
appointment	apmt	circular	Cir
apprehended or apprehension	app	civil authorities	C Auth
Armored Force	Armd F	class	cl
armorer	armr	clerk	clk
Army	A	Coast Artillery Corps	CAC
Army Air Forces	AAF	coast defense	CD
Army Ground Forces	AGF	command	comd
Army Nurse Corps	ANC	commander	comdr
Army of the United States '	AUS	commanding	comdg
Army post office	APO	commanding general	CG
Army Regulations	AR	commanding officer	CO
arrest	ar	communication	com
article of war	AW	company	co
artificer	artif	confined	conf
artillery	arty	confinement	conft
assigned	asgd	cook	ck
assignment	asgmt	corporal	cpl
assistant	asst	Corps of Engineers	CE
attached	atchd	Corps of Military Police	CMP
authorized	auth	court martial	CM

current	cur	Infantry	inf
current series	cs	insurance	Ins
		intelligence	Int
Dental Corps	DC	inventory and. inspection report	I&I R
deserted or desertion	des		
detached service	DS	join	jn
detachment	det	joined	jd
discharge or discharged	disch	junior	jr
dishonorable or dishonorably	dishon		
Distinguished Flying Cross	DFC	killed	kd
Distinguished Service Cross	DSC	killed in action	kia
Distinguished Service Medal	DSM		
division	div	laundry	ldry
division headquarters	DH	leave	lv
		letter	lr
Enlisted	enl	lieutenant	lt
enlisted man or men	EM	lieutenant colonel	lt col
Enlisted Reserve Corps	ERC	light machine gun	LMG
enlistment	enlmt	limited service	ltd serv
excellent	ex	line of duty	LD
expert gunner	EG	line of duty status	LDS
expert rifleman	ER		
expiration	exp	machine gun	MG
expiration term of service	EMS	machine records unit	MRU
		major	Maj
Field Artillery	FA	Manual for Courts Martial	MCM
final statement	F/S	marksman	mkm
Finance Department	FD	master sergeant	m sgt
first	1st	mechanic	mech
first class	1cl	Medal of Honor	MOH
flight	flt	medical	med
forfeit	forf	Medical Administrative. Corps	Med Adm C
fraudulent	fraud	Medical Corps	MC
from	fr	Medical Department	MD
furlough	fur	memorandum	memo
		memorandum receipt	M/R
general court martial	GCM	message	msg
general hospital	Gen Hosp	military aviator	mil av
general orders	GO	military occupational specialty,	
Government	Govt	specification, serial number	MOS
grade	gr	military police	MP
group	gp	miscellaneous	misc
gunner	gnr	missing in action	mia
		Mobilization Regulations	MR
harbor defense	HD	Model	mdl
harbor defense command	HDC	morning report	M/R
headquarters	Hq	motorcycle	mtrcl
heavy	hy	musician	mus
honor or honorable	hon		
hospital	hosp	noncommissioned officer	NCO
howitzer	how		
		observer	obsr
inclosure	incl	office, officer,. order or orders	O
include	incld	officer candidate	OC
indorsement	ind	officer candidate school	OCS
inducted	indctd	officer of the day	OD

officer of the guard	OG	sentenced	sentd
olive drab	od	separate	sep
on or about	o/a	sergeant	sgt
opinions	ops	service	serv
Ordnance Department	Ord Dept	service command	Serv C
organization	orgn	service record	S/R
over, short, and damaged report	OS&D R	service unit	SU
		sharpshooter,	s
paid	pd	sick	sk
parachute	prcht	Signal Corps	Sig C
paragraph	par	Soldier's Medal	SM
partial	part	special	SP
payment	pmt	special court martial	SCM
pay roll	P/R	special duty	SD
personnel	pers	specialist	specl
pioneer	pion	special orders	so
port of embarkation	P/E	special troops	sp trs
post hospital	PHosp	squadron	sq
post laundry	PL	staff sergeant	s sgt
prisoner	pris	statementof charges	S/C
Prisoner of War	PW	station complement	sta com
private	pvt	submachine gun	SMG
private, first class	pfc	subsistence	subs
provost marshal	PM	summary court	SC
Purple Heart	PH	summary court martial	SCM
pursuit	pur	supplemental	Suppl
		surrender or surrendered	surr
qualified	qual	suspended	susp
Quartermaster Corps	QMC		
Quarters	qrs	Tables of Allowances	T/A
		Tables of Basic Allowances	T/BA
rations	rat	Tables of Organization	T/O
reappointed	reaptd	tank	tk
received	recd	Tank Destroyer	TD
reception center	recp cen	technical	tech
recruit	rct	technical. sergeant	t sgt
reduce or reduced	rd	technician	techn
regiment	regt	temporary duty	T/D
regimental orders	RO	The Adjutant General	TAG
Regular Army	RA	transferred	trfd
Regular Army Reserve	RAR	transportation request	T/R
rejoined	rejd	troop	tr
relieved	reld		
replacement	repl	unassigned	unasgd
replacement training center	RTC	unsatisfactory	unsat
report	rpt		
report of survey	R/S	verbal orders	VO
requalified	requal	volunteer officer candidate	VOC
resigned	resgd	voucher	you
same date	sd	warrant	wrnt
school	sch	warrant officer	W O
searchlight battery	SL Btry	warrant officer, junior grade	WOJG
section	sec	Women's Army Corps	WAC
Selective Service	SS	Women's Army Auxiliary Corps	WAAC
sentence	sent	wounded in action	wia

Radio was still a new technology so the majority of communications in World War II were done with telephone lines.

These soldiers are using a field switchboard to tie together a number of telephone lines. The large bags they wear contain gasmasks in case of a chemical attack.

Author's Collection

APPENDIX I

THE GREEN BOOKS AND
SELECT BIBLIOGRAPHY

United States Army in World War II Series

The Official US Army Histories of WWII, also known as "the Green Books," should be one of the first sources you turn to for historical information on the US Army. These are available from most major libraries. Most are still in print and can be purchased directly from the US Government Printing Office online (http://bookstore.gpo.gov). They are also available in electronic format on three CD-ROMs.

The Government Printing Office sells a large number of military history books from all periods. It's worth looking at their catalog to see what is available.

All of these titles have been published as a green-colored hardcover, but recently some have been reprinted as inexpensive softcovers. The following descriptions (with ISBN numbers) are taken from the Center for Military History's own listing. Some of these books are available for free on line at the CMH website http:// www.army.mil/cmh/.

The European Theater of Operations

THE SUPREME COMMAND, by Forrest C. Pogue. 008-029-00076-8. A description of General Eisenhower's wartime command, focusing on the general, his staff, and his superiors in London and Washington. Also contrasts Allied and enemy command organizations.

LOGISTICAL SUPPORT OF THE ARMIES, VOLUME I: MAY 1941–SEPTEMBER 1944, by Roland G. Ruppenthal. The buildup of American armies under General Eisenhower in the United Kingdom in preparation for the Normandy invasion, and an account of how they were supplied during the first three months of operations on the Continent.

LOGISTICAL SUPPORT OF THE ARMIES, VOLUME II: SEPTEMBER 1944–MAY 1945, by Roland G. Ruppenthal. 008-029-00024-5. A continuation of the story of supply on the European continent to the end of hostilities. Both volumes emphasize the influence of logistical support on the planning and conduct of combat operations by field armies.

CROSS-CHANNEL ATTACK, by Gordon A. Harrison. 008-029-00020-2. This first European Theater of Operations tactical volume covers the prelude to the assault on 6 June 1944 and combat operations of the First US Army in Normandy to 1 July 1944.

BREAKOUT AND PURSUIT, by Martin Blumenson. 008-029-00021-1. Operations of the First US Army from 1 July through 10 September 1944 and of the Third US Army from 1 August through 31 August 1944, including the "battle of the hedgerows," the Mortain counterattack, the reduction of Brest, and the liberation of Paris.

THE LORRAINE CAMPAIGN, by Hugh M. Cole. 008-029-00019-9. This account focuses on the tactical operations of the Third Army and its subordinate units between 1 September and 18 December 1944.

THE SIEGFRIED LINE CAMPAIGN, by Charles B. MacDonald. 008-029-00068-7. The story of the First and Ninth US Armies from the first crossings of the German border in September 1944 to the enemy's counteroffensive in the Ardennes in December, including the reduction of Aachen, Huertgen Forest, and Operation MARKET-GARDEN in Holland.

THE ARDENNES: BATTLE OF THE BULGE, by Hugh M. Cole. 008-029-00069-5. The German winter counteroffensive of December 1944–January 1945 with a detailed description of German plans and Allied efforts to eliminate the bulge in their lines.

RIVIERA TO THE RHINE, by Jeffrey J. Clarke and Robert Ross Smith. 008-029-00213-2. A history of combat operations by Sixth Army Group from its landing in southern France to its crossing of the Rhine.

THE LAST OFFENSIVE, by Charles B. MacDonald. 008-029-00297-3. Focusing on the role of five American armies and their tactical air support, with some account of Allied forces, this book brings to an end the war in Europe.

The Mediterranean Theater of Operations

NORTHWEST AFRICA: SEIZING THE INITIATIVE IN THE WEST, by George F. Howe. 008-029-00070-9. The assault on North Africa on 8 November 1942 led to a bitter conflict that finally culminated in the defeat of the Axis forces in Tunisia seven months later. The campaign was, for the US Army, a school in coalition warfare and an introduction to enemy tactics.

SICILY AND THE SURRENDER OF ITALY, by Albert N. Garland and Howard McGaw Smyth. 008-029-00078-4. Operations during the invasion and conquest of Sicily and the military diplomacy that led to Italy's surrender.

SALERNO TO CASSINO, by Martin Blumenson. 008-029-00026-1. Operations from the invasion of the Italian mainland near Salerno through the winter fighting up to the battles for Monte Cassino (including the Rapido River crossing) and the Anzio beachhead.

CASSINO TO THE ALPS, by Ernest F. Fisher, Jr. 008-029-00095-4. Continues the account of operations in Italy from Operation DIADEM and the capture of Rome to the negotiations for the surrender of German armies in Italy.

The War in the Pacific

STRATEGY AND COMMAND: THE FIRST TWO YEARS, by Louis Morton. 008-029-00032-6. An analysis of organization and logistics as well as strategy and command, covering the coming of the war, Japanese policy and American strategy before Pearl Harbor, Japanese victories in the first six months of the war, first efforts in New Guinea and the Solomons to stem the Japanese tide, and the limited offensive in the summer of 1943.

THE FALL OF THE PHILIPPINES, by Louis Morton. 008-029-00035-1. A detailed description of the three-month defense of Bataan, the siege of Corregidor, the soldiers' life in the crowded intimacy of Malinta Tunnel, MacArthur's evacuation, and the surrender of 78,000 American and Allied troops.

GUADALCANAL: THE FIRST OFFENSIVE, by John Miller, jr. 008-029-00067-9. This account of the first victory over Japanese ground forces, told at the level of companies, platoons, and even individuals, demonstrates the relationship between air, ground, and surface forces in modern warfare.

VICTORY IN PAPUA, by Samuel Milner. For the 32d Division, the Papua Campaign was "a military nightmare," its men living under intolerable conditions, plagued by disease, short of equipment, ill-prepared for jungle fighting, and pitted against a skilled and resolute foe.

CARTWHEEL: THE REDUCTION OF RABAUL, by John Miller, Jr. 008-029-00039-3. An analysis of techniques by which the Allies employed their strength to bypass fortified positions and to seize weakly defended but strategically important areas.

SEIZURE OF THE GILBERTS AND MARSHALLS, by Philip A. Crowl and Edmund G. Love. 008-029-00037-7. A study in amphibious warfare that describes how the imperfections of American amphibious doctrine, first revealed at Tarawa and Makin, were corrected in the highly successful landings on Kwajalein and Roi-Namur.

CAMPAIGN IN THE MARIANAS, by Philip A. Crowl. 008-029-00040-7. The fight for Saipan, Tinian, and Guam, including an account of Marine and Navy participation.

THE APPROACH TO THE PHILIPPINES, by Robert Ross Smith. 008-029-00034-2. Operations of Allied forces in the Southwest Pacific from April through October 1944 told generally at the level of the regimental combat team—the infantry regiment with its supporting artillery, engineer, tank, medical, and other units.

LEYTE: THE RETURN TO THE PHILIPPINES, by M. Hamlin Cannon. 008-029-00036-9. The landing of American forces on Leyte and the successful conclusion of a campaign which led to the severance of the Japanese mainland from its southern empire.

TRIUMPH IN THE PHILIPPINES, by Robert Ross Smith. 008-029-00033-4. The reconquest of the Philippine archipelago (exclusive of Leyte), with detailed accounts of Sixth Army and Eighth Army operations on Luzon, as well as of the Eighth Army's reoccupation of the southern Philippines.

OKINAWA: THE LAST BATTLE, by Roy E. Appleman, James M. Burns, Russell A. Gugeler, and John Stevens. 008-029-00066-1. The story of the last and most costly battle of the war in the Pacific, told by US Army historians who had accompanied American forces to the Ryukyus.

The War Department

CHIEF OF STAFF: PREWAR PLANS AND PREPARATIONS, by Mark Skinner Watson. 008-029-00053-9. An account of the nation's unpreparedness for war and the efforts of General Marshall and his staff to correct it with maximum dispatch. The powers of the Chief of Staff and their origins are described.

WASHINGTON COMMAND POST: THE OPERATIONS DIVISION, by Ray S. Cline. 008-029-00054-7. An account of the War Department's principal staff agency that describes the way the members of the Operations Division worked together, defined their responsibilities, and carried out their common aims.

STRATEGIC PLANNING FOR COALITION WARFARE: 1941–1942, by Maurice Matloff and Edwin M. Snell. A description of wartime national planning and military strategy as they affected the missions and dispositions of the US Army in the defensive phase of coalition warfare.

STRATEGIC PLANNING FOR COALITION WARFARE: 1943–1944, by Maurice Matloff. 008-029-00058-0. A continuation of the strategic planning story that describes how the Army came to grips with the problems of the offensive phase of coalition warfare. The midwar international conferences are covered in detail.

GLOBAL LOGISTICS AND STRATEGY: 1940–1943, by Richard M. Leighton and Robert W. Coakley. 008-029-00056-3. US Army logistics, primarily of ground forces, in its relation to global strategy; the treatment is from the viewpoint of the central administration in Washington—Joint and Combined Chiefs of Staff, the War Department General Staff, and the Services of Supply.

GLOBAL LOGISTICS AND STRATEGY: 1943–1945, by Robert W. Coakley and Richard M. Leighton. The changing character of the strategic-logistical problems faced by the Washington high command in the last two years of the war when US and Allied forces achieved material superiority over their enemies in both the Atlantic and Pacific theaters of war.

THE ARMY AND ECONOMIC MOBILIZATION, by R. Elberton Smith. 008-029-00057-1. An analysis of the complex tasks associated with Army procurement and economic mobilization, featuring the War Department's business relationships from prewar planning and the determination of military requirements to the settlement and liquidation of the wartime procurement effort.

THE ARMY AND INDUSTRIAL MANPOWER, by Byron Fairchild and Jonathan Grossman. 008-029-00059-8. The ways in which the Army dealt with organized labor told principally from the vantage point of the Office of the Under Secretary of War and the Industrial Personnel Division, Army Service Forces.

The Army Ground Forces

THE ORGANIZATION OF GROUND COMBAT TROOPS, by Kent Roberts Greenfield, Robert R. Palmer, and Bell I. Wiley. Six studies dealing with basic organizational problems. They examine the antecedents of the Army Ground Forces; problems and decisions regarding their size, internal organization, and armament; and the part played by the Army Ground Forces in the redeployment and reorganizations for the final assault on Japan.

THE PROCUREMENT AND TRAINING OF GROUND COMBAT TROOPS, by Robert R. Palmer, Bell I. Wiley, and William R. Keast. 008-029-00065-2. A series of studies on training, the principal mission of the Army Ground Forces, including procurement of soldiers and officers and the policies and problems involved in training individuals and units for their special functions in ground combat.

The Army Service Forces

THE ORGANIZATION AND ROLE OF THE ARMY SERVICE FORCES, by John D. Millett. Told from the point of view of the commanding general of the Army Service Forces (ASF), this study focuses on the organizational experience of the ASF, detailing the controversies surrounding this administrative experiment.

The Western Hemisphere

THE FRAMEWORK OF HEMISPHERE DEFENSE, by Stetson Conn and Byron Fairchild. 008-029-00061-0. The development of plans to protect the United States and the rest of the Western Hemisphere that concentrates on policy in the three years before Pearl Harbor, the gradual merger of hemisphere defense into a broader national defense policy, the transition to offensive plans after Pearl Harbor, and the military relationships of the United States with other American nations.

GUARDING THE UNITED STATES AND ITS OUTPOSTS, by Stetson Conn, Rose C. Engelman, and Byron Fairchild. 008-029-00062-8. The deployment and operations of Army forces in defense of the continental United States and its outposts, from the Aleutians through Hawaii to the Galapagos in the Pacific, and from Iceland through Bermuda to Trinidad in the Atlantic.

The Middle East Theater

THE PERSIAN CORRIDOR AND AID TO RUSSIA, by T. H. Vail Motter. U.S. Army activities in the Near East in support of the aid-to-Russia supply program, with a discussion of the problems faced by Allies who met in strange lands without tested and well-coordinated policies to govern their diplomatic and military relations.

The China-Burma-India Theater

STILWELL'S MISSION TO CHINA, by Charles F. Romanus and Riley Sunderland. 008-029-00013-X. An account of General Stilwell's work with the Nationalist Government in the execution of his orders to "support China" and to assist in "improving the combat efficiency of the Chinese Army." The famous march from Burma, relations with Chiang Kai-Shek and the Stilwell-Chennault controversy are also described.

STILWELL'S COMMAND PROBLEMS, by Charles F. Romanus and Riley Sunderland. 008-029-00074-1. Continuing the story of General Stilwell's experiences in the CBI between October 1943 and his recall in October 1944, this volume chronicles the seizure of Myitkyina in Burma and the Salween River fighting in China.

TIME RUNS OUT IN CBI, by Charles F. Romanus and Riley Sunderland. 008-029-00014-8. Carrying the narrative from General Wedemeyer's assumption of command to the end of the war, this volume concludes with Americans still working to improve the Chinese Army while attempting to fly in sufficient supplies from India and Burma.

The Technical Services

THE CHEMICAL WARFARE SERVICE: ORGANIZING FOR WAR, by Leo P. Brophy and George J.B. Fisher. Organization and administration of the service from its origins in World War I, with an emphasis on the training of military personnel for offensive and defensive chemical warfare.

THE CHEMICAL WARFARE SERVICE: FROM LABORATORY TO FIELD, by Leo P. Brophy, Wyndham D. Miles, and Rexmond C. Cochrane. 008-029-00011-3. An account of the research and development phase and the procurement and supply of both offensive and defensive materiel.

THE CHEMICAL WARFARE SERVICE: CHEMICALS IN COMBAT, by Brooks E. Kleber and Dale Birdsell 008-029-00012-1. The use of chemical weapons in combat and an analysis of administrative and supply problems overseas.

THE CORPS OF ENGINEERS: TROOPS AND EQUIPMENT, by Blanche D. Coll, Jean E. Keith, and Herbert H. Rosenthal. 008-029-00017-2. An account of how the traditional tasks of American military engineers changed in response to wartime tactical and logistical demands, and how the corps organized, equipped, and trained its troops to carry out these tasks.

THE CORPS OF ENGINEERS: CONSTRUCTION IN THE UNITED STATES, by Lenore Fine and Jesse A. Remington. 008-029-00081-4. Military construction as performed first by the Quartermaster Corps and then, during the war, by the Corps of Engineers, including such varied projects as munitions factories, training camps, the Pentagon, and construction for the Manhattan Project.

THE CORPS OF ENGINEERS: THE WAR AGAINST GERMANY, by Alfred M. Beck, Abe Bortz, Charles W. Lynch, Lida Mayo, and Ralph F. Weld. 008-029-00131-4. Engineer operations during the campaigns in North Africa, Sicily, Italy, and northwest Europe.

THE CORPS OF ENGINEERS: THE WAR AGAINST JAPAN, by Karl C. Dod. 008-029-00018-1. Engineer activities in the Pacific war, with particular emphasis on those in General MacArthur's Southwest Pacific Area.

THE MEDICAL DEPARTMENT: HOSPITALIZATION AND EVACUATION, ZONE OF INTERIOR, by Clarence McKittrick Smith 008-029-00080-6. The logistics of hospitalization and evacuation, the care of wounded and their transport.

THE MEDICAL DEPARTMENT: MEDICAL SERVICE IN THE MEDITER-RANEAN AND MINOR THEATERS, by Charles M. Wiltse. 008-029-00025-3. Emphasizing the evolution of organizations and the use of personnel, this volume analyzes methods of evacuating the wounded or sick soldier and the effort to control disease in those areas under the control of the Army. An appendix looks at German medical service in these African and European areas.

THE MEDICAL DEPARTMENT: MEDICAL SERVICE IN THE EUROPEAN THEATER OF OPERATIONS, by Graham A. Cosmas and Albert E. Cowdrey. 008-029-00227-2. A comprehensive history of medical combat support in the ETO, beginning with the buildup for the invasion and ending with a brief account of medical conditions in conquered Germany.

THE MEDICAL DEPARTMENT: MEDICAL SERVICE IN THE WAR AGAINST JAPAN, by Mary Ellen Condon-Rall and Albert E. Cowdrey. 008-029-00335-0. A comprehensive history of medical support in the Asian-Pacific theaters of operations during World War II. The narrative begins with a discussion of medical prewar planning and, in the context of fierce combat operations waged in remote and disease-ridden environments, describes how the Army Medical Department coped with great distances, diverse climates, and rapidly changing circumstances to maintain the fighting strength of American troops.

THE ORDNANCE DEPARTMENT: PLANNING MUNITIONS FOR WAR, by Constance McLaughlin Green, Harry C. Thomson, and Peter C. Roots. 008-029-00031-8. A discussion of planning and of the problems encountered in prewar and wartime research and development programs. The search for greater mobility and increased firepower is described, as well as the development of guns, rockets, and bombs.

THE ORDNANCE DEPARTMENT: PROCUREMENT AND SUPPLY, by Harry C. Thomson and Lida Mayo. 008-029-00029-6. A description of how the War Department and private industry manufactured huge quantities of munitions and how the Field Service stored, catalogued, maintained, and distributed those munitions to the ports of embarkation.

THE ORDNANCE DEPARTMENT: ON BEACHHEAD AND BATTLEFRONT, by Lida Mayo. 008-029-00030-0. A description of how America's munitions reached US and Allied troops and how Ordnance soldiers stored, maintained, supplied, and salvaged materiel in the major theaters of operations.

THE QUARTERMASTER CORPS: ORGANIZATION, SUPPLY, AND SERVICES, Volume I, by Erna Risch. A two-volume account of the activities of the Corps in the zone of interior and efforts to maximize stockage through conservation, reclamation, and salvage.

THE QUARTERMASTER CORPS: ORGANIZATION, SUPPLY, AND SERVICES, Volume II, by Erna Risch and Chester L. Kieffer. 008-029-00045-8.

THE QUARTERMASTER CORPS: OPERATIONS IN THE WAR AGAINST JAPAN, by Alvin P. Stauffer. 008-029-00047-4. This study focuses on logistics as the indispensable companion of strategy and tactics, and includes a description of conditions under which GIs lived in primitive environments.

THE QUARTERMASTER CORPS: OPERATIONS IN THE WAR AGAINST GERMANY, by William F. Ross and Charles F. Romanus. 008-029-00046-6. A history of the Quartermaster establishment in Europe, the largest organization in military history for feeding and clothing people and providing other services to American and Allied forces, impoverished civilians, and prisoners of war.

THE SIGNAL CORPS: THE EMERGENCY (TO DECEMBER 1941), by Dulany Terrett. 008-029-00048-2. A description of the Corps' responsibility for developing, procuring, and furnishing signal equipment. The development of radar is featured, as well as the development of frequency modulation and its impact on the use of tanks.

THE SIGNAL CORPS: THE TEST (DECEMBER 1941 TO JULY 1943), by George Raynor Thompson, Dixie R. Harris, Pauline M. Oakes, and Dulany Terrett. 008-029-00075-0. A description of the rapid expansion of the communications industry in close partnership with the Signal Corps and the race with the enemy to produce electronic weapons and counterweapons.

THE SIGNAL CORPS: THE OUTCOME (MID-1943 THROUGH 1945), by George Raynor Thompson and Dixie R. Harris. 008-029-00049-1. The activities of the Corps as a service and combat arm in the various theaters of operations.

THE TRANSPORTATION CORPS: RESPONSIBILITIES, ORGANIZATION, AND OPERATIONS, by Chester Wardlow. 008-029-00050-4. A discussion of the transportation task, the functions and organization of the Corps, and its operating problems in the zone of interior.

THE TRANSPORTATION CORPS: MOVEMENTS, TRAINING, AND SUPPLY, by Chester Wardlow. 008-029-00051-2. Troop and supply movements within the zone of interior and to overseas commands, the organization and training of personnel, and the development, procurement, and distribution of Corps materiel.

THE TRANSPORTATION CORPS: OPERATIONS OVERSEAS, by Joseph Bykofsky and Harold Larson. 008-029-00052-1. An account of the successes and failures in the massive deployment of men and materiel from the zone of interior to the theaters.

Special Studies

CHRONOLOGY: 1941–1945, compiled by Mary H. Williams. 008-029-00015-6. This chronology focuses on tactical events from the attack on Pearl Harbor on 7 December 1941 to the signing of the instrument of surrender on the USS *Missouri* on 2 September 1945. The work includes a comprehensive index.

BUYING AIRCRAFT: MATERIEL PROCUREMENT FOR THE ARMY AIR FORCES, by Irving Brinton Holley, jr. 008-029-00008-3. A description of the expansion of and problems associated with the aircraft industry to meet the military requirements of the Army before and during the war.

CIVIL AFFAIRS: SOLDIERS BECOME GOVERNORS, by Harry L. Coles and Albert K. Weinberg. A documentary history with brief narrative introductions illustrating the evolution of civil affairs policy and practice in the Medi-ter-ranean and European theaters.

THE EMPLOYMENT OF NEGRO TROOPS, by Ulysses Lee. 008-029-00028-8. A description of the black soldier's experience during World War II, including a detailed account of the effect of segregated service on the morale and perform-ance of black units. The study concludes with an analysis of the partially inte-grated service of black infantry platoons on the European front in the last months of the war.

MANHATTAN: THE ARMY AND THE ATOMIC BOMB, by Vincent C. Jones. 008-029-00132-2. The role of the War Department, Manhattan District, and other Army agencies and individuals from 1939 through World War II in developing and employing the atomic bomb.

MILITARY RELATIONS BETWEEN THE UNITED STATES AND CANADA: 1939– 1945, by Stanley W. Dziuban. An account of Allied cooperation in hemispheric defense and in the fight against Germany and Japan. The common effort ranged from growing wheat to the climactic development of the atomic bomb. Includes a section on the First Special Service Force.

REARMING THE FRENCH, by Marcel Vigneras. The reemergence of French national forces in the war against the Axis Powers, and the role of large-scale American aid.

THREE BATTLES: ARNAVILLE, ALTUZZO, AND SCHMIDT, by Charles B. MacDonald and Sidney T. Mathews. 008-029-00009-1. "River Crossing at Arnaville" is the story of a battle that started badly and ended in victory; "Objective: Schmidt," of a battle that began with an unexpectedly easy success and turned into tragic defeat. "Breakthrough at Monte Altuzzo" is the account of how, after a succession of misguided efforts, a comparatively small number of men penetrated the formidable Gothic Line in Italy.

THE WOMEN'S ARMY CORPS, by Mattie E. Treadwell. 008-029-00084-9. The experience of female soldiers both at home and overseas as their new Corps struggled against tradition and administrative hurdles.

UNITED STATES ARMY IN WORLD WAR II: READER'S GUIDE, comp. and ed. by Richard D. Adamczyk and Morris J. MacGregor, Jr. 008-029-00251-5. This volume provides a brief analytical description of each of the volumes in the United States Army in World War II series.

Pictorial Record

THE WAR AGAINST JAPAN. 008-029-00043-1. An account in photographs of the Pacific war from pre-Pearl Harbor training in Hawaii to Allied landings on the Japanese home islands, including a section on the China-Burma-India theater.

THE WAR AGAINST GERMANY AND ITALY: MEDITERRANEAN AND ADJACENT AREAS. 008-029-00041-5. A major collection of photographs with explanatory text that graphically portrays various aspects of the war in North Africa and the Middle East; Sicily, Corsica, and Sardinia; and Italy and southern France.

THE WAR AGAINST GERMANY: EUROPE AND ADJACENT AREAS. 008-029-00042-3. The buildup of forces in the United Kingdom and the campaigns in Normandy, northern France, Rhineland, Ardennes-Alsace, and central Europe recorded in photographs.

Medical Corps: The Clinical Series.

The Medical Corps also published a series of books dealing with the history of, and advances in, specific fields of medicine in WWII. These are not considered Green Books per se (actually they have dark red bindings) as they deal with subjects such as Dental Service, Vascular Surgery, Opthalmology, and Communicable Diseases. They will probably not be of interest as they were written for doctors and are very specialized.

U.S. Navy Histories

The US Navy did not publish a similar official set of histories, but allowed author Samuel Eliot Morison to write a 15-volume History of United States Naval Operations in World War II. These are readily available at most libraries and in recent years have been reprinted at a low price. Many contain valuable information regarding combined Army/Navy combined operations.

Vol. I: *The Battle of the Atlantic*

Vol. II: *Operations in North African Waters*

Vol. III: *The Rising Sun in the Pacific*

Vol. IV: *Coral Sea, Midway and Submarine Actions*

Vol. V: *The Struggle for Guadalcanal*

Vol. VI: *Breaching the Bismarks Barrier*

Vol. VII: *Aleutians, Gilberts, and Marshalls*

Vol VIII: *New Guinea and the Marianas*

Vol. IX: *Sicily–Salerno–Anzio*

Vol X: *The Atlantic Battle Won*

Vol. XI: *The Invasion of France and Germany*

Vol. XII: *Leyte*

Vol. XIII: *The Liberation of the Philippines, Luzon, Mindinao*

Vol XIV: *Victory in the Pacific*

Vol XV: *Supplement and General Index*

If you are looking for information on a specific ship: *Dictionary of American Naval Fighting Ships* is an official series of books that presents brief histories, arranged alphabetically by ship name, of all United States Navy warships, auxiliaries, and service craft from 1775 to the present. Appendices include tabulated data on specific ship types, as well as other related subjects of interest. Recently the US Navy has brought much of this material on line at http://www.history.navy.mil/danfs/

Other Official Publications

TM 12-250, *The Army Clerk*, 1943.

TM 12-247, *Military Occupational Classification of Enlisted Personnel*. 12 July 1944.

TM 20-205, *Dictionary of United States Army Terms*. 18 January 1944.

The US Army GHQ Maneuvers of 1941, by Christopher Gabel, US Army (1992).

The Ordnance Soldier's Guide, 1944.

TM-20-205, *Dictionary of Army Terms*. 1942.

Commercially Published Books

Army Air Force Aid Society. AAF: *The Official Guide to the Army Air Forces*. Pocket Books, NY, 1944.

Beebe, Gilbert. *Battle Casualties*. Thomas Publishers, Springfield, Il. 1952.

Bennett, Donald V. *Honor Untarnished: A West Point Graduate's Memoir of World War II*. Forge Books, NY, 2003.

Bergerud, Eric. *Touched by Fire: the Land War in the South Pacific*. Viking Press, NY, 1996.

Black, Robert. *Rangers in World War II*. Ivy Books, NY, 1992.

Blunt, Roscoe. *Footsoldier: A Combat Infantryman's War in Europe*. Da Capo Press, 2001.

Brown, Christopher. *U.S. Military Patches of World War II*. Turner Publishing, Padukah, KY, 2002.

Coffman, Edward. *The Regulars*. Belnap Press, Cambridge, MA. 2004.

Colley, David. *Blood for Dignity*. St. Martin's Press, NY, 2003.

Colley, David. *The Road to Victory*. Warner Books, NY, 2001.

Colley, David. *Safely Rest*. Berkley Books, NY, 2004.

Controvich, James T. *United States Army Unit and Organizational Histories, Vol. 2: WW1 to the Present*. Scarecrow Press, Lanham, Maryland, 2003.

Cowdry, Albert. *Fighting for Life*. Free Press, NY, 1994.

Devin, Gerald. *Silent Wings*. St. Martins Press, NY, 1985.

Gantter, Raymond. *Roll Me Over*. Ivy Books, NY, 1997.

Maquire, Jon. *Silver Wings, Pinks and Greens*. Schiffer Publishing, Atglen PA., 1994.

Air Force Combat Units of Word War II: The Concise Official Military Record. Chartwell Books, Edison NJ, 1994.

The Officer's Guide, 1940–1945 editions. Military Service Publishing Company, Harrisburg, PA.

Monahan, Evelyn. *And If I Perish: Frontline U.S. Army Nurses in WWII*. Knopf Books, NY, 2003.

Nichol, John. *The Last Escape*. Viking, New York, 2002.

Sinelli, Angelo. *Life Behind Barbed Wire*. Fordham University Press, NY. 2004.

Stanton, Shelby. WWII *Order of Battle*. Gallahad Books, NY, 1984.

Strandberg, John, & Roger Bender. *The Call of Duty*. Bender Publishing, San Jose, CA 1994.

Yenne, Bill. *Black '41*. John Wiley and Sons, NY, 1991.

In northern Europe the most desirable place to be was Paris, and many soldiers were able to visit there.

The white stripe on the back of the helmet indicates the man in the center is an NCO (a vertical stripe means an officer). This marking was unique to the ETO.

The American uniform is very drab and plain compared to that of the French Marine on the left.

National Archives

FINDING YOUR FATHER'S WAR

Typeset in ITC Novarese Book, Gill Sans, Goudy and Univers

Book layout and design by Casemate.

Particular thanks are due to Philippe Charbonnier,
Frank Orville Gray,
The US Institute of Heraldry,
all those who graciously allowed us to use their photographs
and the usual gang of suspects.

For more information see

www.fatherswar.com

First Printed by Estudios Graficos ZURE, Spain, European Union, July MMVI.
Reprinted with minor corrections, October MMVI.